Dividing Lines Between the European Union and Its Member States

The Impact of the Treaty of Lisbon

DIVIDING LINES BETWEEN THE EUROPEAN UNION AND ITS MEMBER STATES

THE IMPACT OF THE TREATY OF LISBON

by

Stephen C. Sieberson

T.M.C. ASSER PRESS
The Hague

Published by T.M.C. ASSER PRESS
P.O. Box 16163, 2500 BD The Hague, The Netherlands
<www.asserpress.nl>

T.M.C. ASSER PRESS' English language books are distributed exclusively by

Cambridge University Press, The Edinburgh Building, Shaftesbury Road,
Cambridge CB2 2RU, UK,
or,
for customers in the USA, Canada and Mexico:
Cambridge University Press, 100 Brook Hill Drive, West Nyack, NY 10994-2133, USA
<www.cambridge.org>

© cover photographs Carmelicia Sieberson, 2008

ISBN 978-90-6704-284-0

FOREWORD

Stephen Sieberson has written a book about a sensitive and politically relevant subject matter: the delimitation of competences between Member States and the European Union. Indeed, the more the process of European integration develops, the more responsibilities and competences are handed over to – or at least shared with – the layer of government at the European level, the European Union.

The Treaty of Lisbon is a document as significant as the Single European Act (entry into force in 1987), the Treaty of Maastricht (1993), the Treaty of Amsterdam (1999) and the Treaty of Nice (2003). It is the successor to the so-called European Constitution, the treaty that was signed in October 2004, but which failed to enter into force because of the negative outcomes of referenda in France and the Netherlands in 2005. After new negotiations, the Heads of State and Government in June 2007 agreed on an alternative treaty text which later on – the signature was on 13 December 2007 – became the Lisbon Treaty. Careful analysis demonstrates that the new document incorporates the main contents of the European Constitution.

More particularly, the Treaty of Lisbon simplifies the institutional structures of the EU cooperation, while providing for more democracy and more efficiency at the European level. Obviously, when referring to more 'democracy' in Europe, the role of the European Parliament and the rights of individual European citizens are significant. On the other hand, when addressing 'efficiency', one should think first of (qualified) majority voting in the Council of Ministers. Indeed, in a framework of intensive cooperation like that of the European Union, with at present 27 Member States, progress can be achieved only if decision making through (majority) voting at least is made available as a possibility.

The study reflected in this book is a complete and detailed one. It covers all the relevant innovations and reforms brought by the Lisbon Treaty. The study is original as well, because the author has used his own specificities as the framework of his research: the EU's values and objectives; the EU's state-like attributes; democracy; a number of key principles of the EU cooperation, such as subsidiarity and primacy; and the Union as a 'flexible' entity. In so doing he has applied his research techniques horizontally to the characteristics of EU cooperation, the EU institutions and organs, as well as to all the policy domains of the Union.

In substantive matters addressed in the Lisbon Treaty, the author has paid particular attention to the policy reforms in the area of freedom, security and justice (the former justice and home affairs cooperation) and to the external action of the Union, including the common foreign and security policy, the common commercial policy, development cooperation and the like.

This book is well-researched and very readable. Also, for those who lack a thorough knowledge of the essentials of EU cooperation, the substance of the book is easily accessible.

During the period of his work, Steve and I had many discussions. It was always a pleasure to hear his comments, offered from the point of view of an American living in the United States and a relative outsider to the European integration debate. Nonetheless, I was always surprised to notice how deeply interested he was in European integration, well informed about latest developments, and motivated to write this study.

The book provides an interesting review of the most recent developments in European cooperation. Will the Lisbon Treaty be the last treaty, as certain politicians tell us or at least seem to believe? In my personal conviction, certainly not. European integration is a gradual process, and as new circumstances develop, further steps will be necessary. At the appropriate moment, when sufficient political will has been created, future actions will be taken to secure the fundamental values of peace, stability and prosperity on the European continent, in the interest of the Member States and the well being of their citizens.

The Hague, March 2008   Jaap W. de Zwaan
Director of the Netherlands Institute of International
Relations, 'Clingendael', The Hague
Professor of the Law of the EU at the Law School of
Erasmus University Rotterdam, Rotterdam, the Netherlands

PREFACE

In my professional activities relating to Europe during the past 30 years, including teaching, law practice and government service, I have often discussed with European friends what it means to be a European, and how that compares to being Dutch, Czech, Italian, etc. Invariably these conversations turn to deeper levels of identity, loyalty and political expectations. The EU and European integration are always swirling around these conversations, and it is clear that none of my acquaintances ever expects to lose his or her nationality, even in a highly integrated Europe. There are some lines, such as loss of one's language or culture, that nobody – even today's students who are possessed of a strong sense of European-ness – wants to cross. But what about significant loss of political power at the national level? Before the EU Constitution was proposed, such a prospect surfaced occasionally, especially at key moments of integration such as institution of the euro. However, most Europeans continued (and still continue) to view the Union as an undertaking of sovereign nations.

The Constitution and its successor, the Lisbon Treaty, have renewed public interest in the overall course of European integration. It is widely felt that the Constitution represented a major change in the landscape – change was ultimately unacceptable in the form proposed. The discussions raised first by the Constitution and now by the Lisbon Treaty have inspired the theme of this treatise: What are the existing dividing lines between the European Union and its Member States, and how will they be impacted by amending the existing Treaties? Because the Lisbon Treaty retains most of the Constitution's substantive changes, and because of the great amount of scholarly commentary on the Constitution, the analysis in this treatise will approach the Lisbon Treaty through its own text, but also through the lens of the Constitution.

In the process of preparing this treatise, I have drawn upon three articles that I have written on the Constitution during the past several years. The first, titled "The Proposed European Union Constitution: Will it Eliminate the EU's Democratic Deficit?" was published at 10 Columbia Journal of European Law 173 (2004). Portions of this article are the basis for Chapters 1 and 9 of this treatise. The second is entitled "How the New European Union Constitution Will Allocate Power between the EU and its Member States – a Textual Analysis," and it was published at 37 Vanderbilt Journal of Transnational Law 993 (2004). This work provided a conceptual framework and outline for parts Two and Three of the text. The third piece, "Worth Doing Well – The Improvable European Union Constitution," appeared at 26 Michigan Journal of International Law 587 (2005), and it is reflected in Chapters 2 and 3. Each journal has kindly consented to my re-use of the relevant material

Work on this project has taken place at the University of Oregon School of Law, in Slovakia at the Comenius University Institute of International Relations and Approximation of Law, at the University of Tennessee College of Law and at my current professional home, the Creighton University School of Law. I would like to thank the administrators of those institutions for their support in this work, which came in the form of research grants, administrative assistance and unquestioning encouragement. Particular gratitude is extended to Dean Margaret L. Paris at Oregon, who urged me to start down this path, and Deans Patrick J. Borchers and Marianne Culhane at Creighton, who supported the final stages of the research and writing. I would also like to acknowledge and thank those law students who have provided research assistance at various times.

My deepest appreciation goes to Prof. Dr. Jaap W. de Zwaan of the Faculty of Law at Erasmus University of Rotterdam, also currently Director of the Clingendael Institute in The Hague. He has served as mentor, colleague, editor and friend during the past four years, and without his patient support and persistent attention to detail, this treatise would not have come into being. I have learned so much from Jaap and he has contributed so much to this effort, that merely saying thanks seems like very little consideration in return. But thanks nevertheless.

Finally, I would like to dedicate this treatise to my parents, Steve and Lois, and to my wife, Carmelicia.

Omaha, Nebraska, March 2008   Stephen C. Sieberson, J.D., Ph.D.
                                                                               Member of the faculty
                                                                   Creighton University School of Law

Summary of Contents

TABLE OF CONTENTS

LIST OF ABBREVIATIONS

AFSJ	Area of freedom, security and justice
CAP	Common Agricultural Policy of the Community
CFSP	Common foreign and security policy
COREPER	Committee of Permanent Representatives
CSDP	Common security and defence policy
EC Treaty	Treaty Establishing the European Economic Community
ECB	European Central Bank
ECHR	European Convention for the Protection of Human Rights and Fundamental Freedoms
ECJ	European Court of Justice
ECSC	European Coal and Steel Community
ECU (ecu)	European Currency Unit
EDA	European Defence Agency
EU	European Union
EURATOM	European Atomic Energy Community
IGC	Intergovernmental conference
IGO	Intergovernmental organisation
MEP	Member of the European Parliament
NAFTA	North American Free Trade Agreement
NATO	North Atlantic Treaty Organisation
OMC	Open method of co-ordination
QMV	Qualified majority vote
TEU	Treaty on European Union (Maastricht Treaty)
TFEU	Treaty on the Functioning of the European Union
U.N.T.S.	United Nations Treaty Series
WEU	Western European Union
WTO	World Trade Organisation

List of Abbreviated Journal Titles

Am. Atheist Mag.	American Atheist Magazine
Am. J. Int'l L.	American Journal of International Law
Berkeley J. Int'l L.	Berkeley Journal of International Law
Cardozo L. Rev.	Cardozo Law Review
Chi. J. Int'l L.	Chicago Journal of International Law
C.M.L.R.	Common Market Law Review
Colum. J. Eur. L.	Columbia Journal of European Law
Colum. L. Rev.	Columbia Law Review
Common Mkt. Stud.	Journal of Common Market Studies
ECR	European Court Reports

Eur. Hum. Rts. L. Rev.	European Human Rights Law Review
Eur. L. Rev.	European Law Review
Eur. L.J.	European Law Journal
Fin. Times	Financial Times
Fordham Int'l L.J.	Fordham International Law Journal
Harv. Int'l L.J.	Harvard International Law Journal
Ind. J. Global Legal Stud.	Indiana Journal of Global Legal Studies
Int'l & Comp. L.Q.	International and Comparative Law Quarterly
Int'l Herald Trib.	International Herald Tribune
J. Common Mkt. Stud.	Journal of Common Market Studies
J. Democracy	Journal of Democracy
Law & Phil.	Law and Philosophy
New Left Rev.	New Left Review
O.J.	Official Journal of the European Communities
The Fed. Tr. Eur. Newsl.	The Federal Trust European Newsletter
U. Chi. L. Rev.	University of Chicago Law Review
U.C. Davis J. of Int'l Law & Policy	University of California at Davis Journal of International Law and Policy

Introduction
THE TREATY OF LISBON

On December 13, 2007, European leaders gathered in Lisbon to sign the Treaty of Lisbon,[1] a new treaty amendment that has now been sent to all of the EU's Member States for ratification. It is nothing new for the Union to amend its Treaties, but the Lisbon Treaty came about after the EU's noteworthy failure to ratify the "Treaty establishing a Constitution for Europe."[2] From 2004 to 2007 the Constitution had dominated the European agenda, and its ultimate rejection was a painful episode – even a crisis. The Lisbon Treaty will now amend the EU's two principal treaties, the EC Treaty and Treaty on European Union (TEU),[3] but it will do so without fully replacing them as the Constitution would have done.

Among the more important issues raised by the Lisbon Treaty is how it may affect the delicate relationship between the European Union and its Member States. This is a significant issue, because the EU has always had a dual focus. On the one hand, the development of the Union has necessitated a collective orientation, with significant resources being invested in a group of supranational institutions whose mandate is to manage specified tasks. On the other hand, there has always been a concern that these Union programmes might interfere with national competences. Stated in different terms, it has been understood that the benefits offered by the EU must always be measured against the threat that it poses to the essential sovereignty of the Member States. Collective success and separate identity are often contradictory, and they are frequently the subject of intense political and academic debate.

One way to illustrate the tension that is always lurking in Europe is to speak of *dividing lines* between the Union and its Member States. The most obvious of these lines relate to the concrete allocation of governmental competences. To some critics, every increase in EU competence seems to cause a corresponding diminishment of

---

[1] Treaty of Lisbon amending the Treaty on European Union and the Treaty establishing the European Community, December 3, 2007, CIG 14/07, 1 (hereafter Lisbon Treaty).

[2] Treaty establishing a Constitution for Europe, officially published at December 16, 2004, O.J. (C 310) 1 [hereafter Constitution]. The final Constitution was a revised version of the draft produced by the Convention on the Future of Europe on July 18, 2003. Draft Treaty Establishing a Constitution for Europe, July 18, 2003, O.J. (C 169) 1.

[3] Treaty establishing the European Economic Community (hereafter EC Treaty) and the Treaty on European Union [hereafter TEU]. Collectively, these are referred to in this treatise as the "Treaties." Both of these have been most recently amended by the 2001 Treaty of Nice. The official citations to the Treaties are: Treaty Establishing the European Economic Community, March 25, 1957, O.J. (C 340) 173, and Treaty on European Union (Maastricht), February 7, 1992, O.J. (C 191) 1. The Treaty of Nice is officially cited as the Treaty of Nice amending the Treaty on European Union, the Treaties Establishing the European Communities and Certain Related Acts, February 26, 2001, O.J. (C 80) 1. The most recent consolidated version of the Treaties is found at December 29, 2006, O.J. (C 321) 1. The third foundational treaty is the Treaty establishing the European Atomic Energy Community (EURATOM), March 25, 1957, 298 U.N.T.S. 259, but this treaty will remain in effect even if the Lisbon Treaty is adopted.

the powers of the Member States. But the lines may be more subtle than that. Some of them relate to the influence the Member States have on the make-up of the EU institutions or on how the institutions make their decisions. Some arise from the Union's guiding principles, such as conferral, primacy and subsidiarity. Others may simply be points of rhetorical emphasis in the treaty texts.

The most important dividing lines may be described in terms of the balance of power *within* the EU system, where both EU institutions and the Member States are active. Relevant questions relating to these dividing lines include the following:

–   What institutions are necessary to ensure that the EU reaches its potential, and what authority should they be granted? What is the influence of the Member States on those institutions?
–   What instruments and decision-making procedures should be employed, and which institutions (including those of the Member States) should participate in particular actions?
–   In an expanding Union, how should the internal market be managed, and should there be a role for the Member State governments in its management?
–   At what level should social policy be determined? Should key concepts be uniform throughout the EU, or should the Member States maintain local control?
–   How should foreign affairs and defence be conducted? Should they be the central responsibility of the Union or the separate responsibility of each Member State?

But it is more than just substantive competence and institutional control that are of interest. The dividing lines relate to the very character of the EU and of the Europe it encompasses. The Member States in many ways define the EU as much as the Union's institutions do. The Member States represent the origins of the Union, its diversity of cultures and its multi-faceted political outlook, and their continuing vitality and integrity are at the core of the EU. Questions at this deeper level might include:

–   Should the Member States continue to enjoy their status as sovereign nations within the world community?
–   Where is the loyalty and attachment of the individual European citizen to be focused?
–   Where are the manifestations of democracy to be found – at the national level only, the Union level, or both?
–   How much integration is necessary, and where should it stop?

All of the above questions form the backdrop for the analysis in this treatise, and we will revisit the questions in the Conclusion.

OUTLINE OF THIS TREATISE

The analysis does not follow the order of provisions in the Lisbon Treaty. It would have been possible to do so, but such an approach would not prove very useful in the pursuit of a particular theme such as the EU's dividing lines. Rather, it has been more suitable to arrange the material as the subject itself suggests. Proceeding from the foregoing questions, we examine the EU in a series of logical steps:

Part One: The nature of the beast – an overview
Chapter 1 examines the debate over whether the EU is an intergovernmental organisation, a federation, or a bit of both. Chapters 2 and 3 describe the foundational documents of the Union, particularly the origins and contents of the new Lisbon Treaty. Chapters 4, 5 and 6 build on that background and offer a preview of the material presented in the heart of the treatise. Chapter 4 describes what is new overall in the Lisbon Treaty, without reference to the EU's dividing lines. Chapter 5 then identifies the dividing lines that may be found in the Treaties. Finally, Chapter 6 summarises which of those lines are affected by the Lisbon Treaty.

Part Two: The character of the EU
The initial focus, in Chapter 7, is on the expressed values on which the Union is founded, and on the concrete objectives for Union activity. Chapter 8 examines the attributes of the Union that permit it to function as a quasi-state. These include its legal status, its grant of citizenship, its budgetary autonomy and its external action, as well as the institutions that carry out its activities. In Chapter 9 we explore whether the EU is or should be democratic in its institutions and procedures. Chapter 10 examines how the Union will be able to facilitate "widening and deepening" – the accession of more Member States and the expansion of EU activity into new fields. Flexibility is the key, and mechanisms for change are explored. At the same time, it is inevitable that the constituent documents of the Union will need periodic amending to permit new forms or levels of action to be taken. Chapter 11 explores the amendment requirements and Lisbon Treaty's modest proposals to simplify the process. The final topic in Part Two is the examination in Chapter 12 of a series of legal concepts that guide the Union. These concepts include conferral, subsidiarity, primacy, exclusivity and others, and they represent a series of carefully crafted political decisions that have a profound impact on how the Union functions.

Part Three: Institutions and decision-making
In Part Three the analysis proceeds to the actual structure and operation of the EU – its institutions and how they create Union law. Chapter 13 examines the primary EU institutions, while Chapter 14 describes the processes of EU lawmaking. Chapter 15 explores the critically significant role of decisional requirements for the Council, whether unanimity is mandated or whether a qualified majority is sufficient.

Part Four: The subjects of EU activity
Chapter 16 examines the area of freedom, security and justice, in which the Lisbon Treaty's most dramatic changes are presented. Chapter 17 then reviews a variety of other developments relating to the EU's internal activities and external action.

Part Five: Conclusion

A recap of all of the findings is presented in Part Five. By following this outline
we are able to understand the attributes and competences of the EU, but we are
also able to discern the role of the Member States within the Union. We will
see where the lines between them are drawn. Other changes not relevant to these
dividing lines are beyond the scope of the present analysis, but one can predict that
the EU's "constitutional development" will be the subject of much writing in the
coming years.[4]

A PREVIEW OF THE CONCLUSIONS

Two somewhat contradictory conclusions emerge from this analysis. The first is
that the drafters of the Lisbon Treaty have been for the most part faithful to the
Treaties in carefully preserving the existing dividing lines between the Union and
the Member States. We are struck by the fact that in many instances in which the
amended Treaties describe the EU, they counterbalance those descriptions with
explicit reminders of the powers reserved to the Member States. Under the Lisbon
Treaty the Member States will continue to enjoy a substantial measure of sovereignty
despite having previously delegated certain competences to the Union. To those
who may be concerned that the Lisbon Treaty represents a great shift of power to
Brussels, this treatise argues that their fears are not well-founded.

The second conclusion is that notwithstanding the preservation of most of the
dividing lines, the Lisbon Treaty does signal something of a new legal order for
the Union. It reduces the Three Pillars to two. It creates an improved European
Union with legal personality, and this entity will be the successor to the European
Community. It adopts the Charter of Fundamental Rights as a document with the
same legal value as the Treaties. It offers new coherency and efficiency to the EU's
institutions. It extends the jurisdiction of the Court of Justice into the Second Pillar
and what was formerly the Third. The importance of all of these developments is
debatable, and one might argue that they represent more style than substance. The

---

[4] Overviews on the developing constitutionalism in Europe have long populated the bookshelves of
EU scholars. Even before the Constitution, this was a popular topic. See, e.g., Constitution-Building in
the European Union (Brigid Laffan, ed., 1996); Joseph H.H. Weiler, The Constitution of Europe: "Do the
New Clothes Have an Emperor?" and Other Essays on European Integration (1999). As the Constitution
was being debated, much additional commentary was being produced. See, e.g., The Post-Nice Process:
Towards a European Constitution (Peter A. Zervakis & Peter J. Cullen, eds., 2002); Brendan P.G. Smith,
Constitution Building in the European Union (2002); Stefan Collignon, The European Republic: Reflections
on the Political Economy of a Future Constitution (2003); Jo Shaw, et al., The Convention on the Future of
Europe: Working Towards an EU Constitution (2003); A Constitution for the European Union (Charles B.
Blankart & Dennis C. Mueller, eds., 2004); Political Theory and the European Constitution (Lynn Dobson
& Andreas Føllesdal, eds., 2004); Developing a Constitution for Europe (Erik Oddvar Eriksen, et al., eds.,
2004); The Constitution for Europe and an Enlarging Union: Unity in Diversity? (Kirstyn Inglis & Andrea
Ott, eds., 2005); The EU Constitution: The Best Way Forward? (Deirdre Curtin, Alfred E. Kellermann &
Steven Blockmans, eds., 2005).

better position is that there is substance to the proposed changes. However, even those who would call them stylistic must acknowledge that in politics and diplomacy new terminology may signal a change in attitude and may portend a shift in direction. Style may yield substance in the long run.

Detailed analysis of a document as lengthy as the proposed Lisbon Treaty requires discipline and patience. To overcome some of the logistical challenges inherent in this endeavor, this treatise employs chapter and section arrangements that are clear enough to facilitate easy location of particular subjects. It is hoped that this treatise – either as a whole or in its parts – will prove to be of value to others who may be studying the ongoing course of European integration.

AUTHOR'S NOTES

Note on Scholarly Resources

This treatise is being published in the first few months after the signing of the Lisbon Treaty. As a consequence, very little scholarly analysis has yet been published on the document. However, abundant commentary is available on the Constitution. Since most of the Constitution's innovations have been carried over into the Lisbon Treaty, much of the scholarship on the Constitution remains relevant to the new amendment. This treatise contains many references to such scholarship.

Note on Citations

At the time this treatise was published, a consolidated version of the EC Treaty and TEU, as amended by the Lisbon Treaty, had not been released. A table of equivalences had been published, showing the numbers of the current treaty provisions, an interim renumbering stated in the text of the Lisbon Treaty, and a final renumbering after ratification of the Lisbon Treaty. However, it is predictable that EU officials will further adjust the final numbering (for example, provisions of the Lisbon Treaty were renumbered in each of its versions in July, October and December of 2007). The temptation for tinkering will likely prove to be irresistible. The only thing certain as of the date of this treatise is that the Lisbon Treaty contains its own sequential numbering, and this is presented in final form in the signed version of the treaty. Article 1, which amends the TEU, is comprised of 61 articles or "points," numbered from 1(1) to 1(61). Article 2 amends the EC Treaty in 295 articles, numbered from 2(1) to 2(295). The author has chosen to refer to these numbers wherever a provision of the Lisbon Treaty is cited in this treatise.

Part One
Another Treaty Amendment

Chapter 1
THE DEBATE OVER FORM – WHAT IS THE EU?

From its inception the European Union has had its own structures and institutions, but both the Union and its institutions have always been subject to certain levels of control by the Member State governments. As integration has progressed from the Union's modest beginnings as the European Coal and Steel Community (ECSC), academic and political observers have struggled to define just what the organization is, and, moreover, what it should be. The following analysis will describe the two opposing camps in a debate that regularly resurfaces in Europe. This debate underlies the movement to the Lisbon Treaty,[5] and the two schools of thought have radically different ideas as to the proper dividing lines between the EU and its members.

1.   TWO SCHOOLS OF THOUGHT

Some commentators and politicians favor an intergovernmental form for the EU, a structure in which all critical decisions must be agreed to by each Member State. Others urge a federal arrangement in which the Union serves as an independent and powerful central government that stands above the national governments. These two approaches will be described, and they will be followed by a description of the middle ground, the "blended entity" theory that better defines the realities of the EU today.

1.1   The EU as an intergovernmental organisation

The European Union was created by means of treaties among its founding members, it exists today by virtue of successor treaties, and there are those who believe it should remain as a treaty-based intergovernmental entity.
    According to the intergovernmental theory, the EU has in fact continued to operate in large part like an intergovernmental organisation (IGO). Peter Lindseth comments that one strand of social science literature "points to the considerable evidence of the Community's continuing intergovernmental nature, notably at the levels of Treaty amendment and of major harmonisation legislation."[6] Andrew Moravcsik observes that the EU's ability to act in areas such as "budget, defence, police, cultural, educational and social policies" is sufficiently limited that its actions in these fields, if any take place at all, "are hardly different from those of a classic international

    [5] For a description of the events leading to the creation of the Constitution and the Lisbon Treaty, see Chapter 2.
    [6] Peter Lindseth, Democratic Legitimacy and the Administrative Character of Supranationalism: The Example of the European Community, 99 Colum. L. Rev. 628, 655 (1999).

organisation."[7] G.F. Mancini describes the EU structure as one in which "not only its foreign and security policies, which are openly carried out on an intergovernmental basis, but the very management of its supranational core, the single market, are entrusted, with or without a circumscribed control by the European Parliament, to diplomatic round tables."[8]

Despite the Union's treaty origins and its retention of IGO-like features, it is clear that the EU contains elements that are not strictly intergovernmental in nature.[9] These elements are described below in the descriptions of the federalist and blended entity theories. Lindseth has acknowledged that the EU's range of delegated powers and its "relative independence from unilateral Member State control" distinguish it from other international organisations.[10] However, he argues that its "legal character" remains similar to that of "other less ambitious experiments with supranational delegation, such as the dispute settlement panels of the WTO."[11] All such IGOs, he asserts, are "essentially of an administrative character" and provide efficient problem-solving mechanisms in place of more cumbersome diplomatic procedures.[12]

The essence of the intergovernmentalist position is that the Member States of the EU must retain their essential sovereignty.[13] The British are strongly identified with this position and are said to champion a "club of sovereign nation-states,"[14] preferring, for example, a greater involvement of national parliaments in EU policy-making over an enhanced role for the European Parliament.[15] Joseph Weiler has called this approach "Thatcherism" and sees its vision of the European Union as "an arrangement, elaborate and sophisticated, of achieving long-term maximisation of the national interest in an interdependent world."[16] This school of thought, according to Weiler,

---

[7] Andrew Moravcsik, Conservative Idealism and International Institutions, 1 Chi. J. Int'l L. 291, 309 (2000) [hereafter Moravcsik 2000].

[8] G.F. Mancini, Democracy and Constitutionalism in the European Union: Collected Essays 65 (2000).

[9] Jan Muller has stated: "Clearly, the Union started as an intergovernmental enterprise, and only over time acquired supranational and infranational characteristics." Jan Muller, Constitutionalism and the Founding of Constitutions: Carl Schmitt and the Constitution of Europe, 21 Cardozo L. Rev. 1777, 1790 (2000).

[10] Lindseth, *supra* note 6, at 656, 734.

[11] Id. at 656, 734.

[12] Id.

[13] Michael Newman identifies the insistence on Member State sovereignty with the "realist theory" of international relations. Proponents of this theory, he writes, "have viewed states as the irreducible element in international politics." The EU is "regarded as a means of managing potential conflict and competition so as to enhance security. But it could never transcend the Member States in the sense suggested by Federalists, for those states are basically using it to promote their own interests. Thus while federalists might condemn governments for opposing the construction of a full political union, realists will argue that this is to be expected: states remain the 'real' actors which operate the international institutions that they establish."

Michael Newman, Democracy, Sovereignty and the European Union 17 (1996). Newman groups the realist theory, which many analysts recognize to be "over-simplified," with other schools of thought into a broader category he calls "international relations theories." Id. at 20-21.

[14] Christopher Dickey & Michael Meyer, Is Europe Broken?, Newsweek, August 12, 2002, at 14.

[15] Europe's Convention: The Tortoise is Thinking of Moving, Economist, July 20, 2002, at 41, 42.

[16] Weiler, *supra* note 4, at 93-94.

measures the EU's value "ultimately and exclusively with the coin of national utility and not community solidarity."[17]

The difficulty with the intergovernmental position is that the EU has evolved significantly from its IGO roots. George Bermann asserts that the Union has:

> "traveled further along the road from 'pure' intergovernmentalism than virtually any other international governance regime, and than one might realistically ever have imagined at the outset. No other international governance regime can even plausibly present itself as governing a 'polity', especially a polity in the most day-to-day, operational, 'business as usual' sense of the term."[18]

A vigorous counterpoint to the intergovernmentalist theory is offered by the federal camp.

1.2   The EU as a federation

There have always been federalists in Europe, politicians and others who see the European Union evolving into a centralised federal system that must eventually become a United States of Europe. According to Michael Newman, their school of thought traces back to Altiero Spinelli and his 1941 Ventotene Manifesto, which sets forth the theory that divesting the European nation states of their individual sovereignty would prevent future wars on the continent and solve a host of other vexing problems that would withstand an intergovernmental approach.[19] Joseph Weiler comments that this "*unity* vision of the promised land sees then as its 'ideal type' a European polity, finally and decisively replacing its hitherto warring Member States with a political union of federal governance."[20] These ideas were clearly reflected in the original Treaty of Rome,[21] and Newman asserts that today's federalist perspective "generally holds that the EU is in *the process of becoming a Federation . . .* [and] that the old state-centered world has passed."[22]

---

[17] Id.

[18] George Bermann, The European Union as a Constitutional Experiment, 10 Eur. L.J. 363 (2004).

[19] Newman, *supra* note 13, at 16.

[20] Weiler, *supra* note 4, at 93.

[21] "Anxious to strengthen the unity of their economies and to ensure their harmonious development by reducing the differences existing between the various regions and backwardness of the less favoured regions...". Preamble to the Treaty Establishing the European Economic Community (consolidated text), March 25, 1957, O.J. (C 325) 41 (2002).

[22] Newman, *supra* note 13, at 16. Weiler has described the current state of the EU as a "confederation." He writes: "It is not an accident that some of the most successful federations which emerged from separate polities – the United States, Switzerland, Germany – enjoyed a period as a confederation prior to unification. This does not mean that confederation is a prerequisite to federation. It simply suggests that in a federation created by integration, rather than by devolution, there must be an adjustment period in which the political boundaries of the new polity become socially accepted as appropriate for the larger democratic rules by which the minority will accept a new majority." Weiler, *supra* note 4, at 83.

The European Commission, in its White Paper on European Governance that preceded the Constitutional Convention, agrees that the EU is evolving.[23] While careful to avoid using the word "federal," the document asserts: "It is time to recognise that the Union has moved from a diplomatic to a democratic process, with policies that reach deep into national societies and daily life."[24] Weiler concurs that "the Community's 'operating system' is no longer governed by general principles of public international law."[25] He contends that "constitutionalisation" and a new system of remedies within the EU have eliminated "the most central legal artifact of international law: the notion (and doctrinal apparatus) of exclusive state responsibility and its concomitant principles of reciprocity and counter-measures."[26] Like the Commission, he stops short of saying that these changes have made the EU into a federal state, but he believes that "the Community truly becomes something 'new.'"[27] By way of example, Weiler notes that in establishing the doctrine of "direct effect" of Community law on citizens of the EU, the ECJ set aside the traditional right of a state to determine to what extent the state's treaty obligations will impact its individual citizens.[28]

The seminal decision on direct effect was *Van Gend en Loos* v. *Nederlandse Administratie Der Belastingen.*[29] In that case the Court ruled that that it had the competence to determine whether a Dutch company had standing under Community law to directly challenge a Dutch government tariff on certain imported products from Germany. The Dutch government had argued that its national courts should have the exclusive jurisdiction to interpret the scope of the EC Treaty in this instance. The Court declared:

> "The objective of the EEC Treaty, which is to establish a Common Market, the functioning of which is of direct concern to interested parties in the Community, implies that this Treaty is more than an agreement which merely creates mutual obligations between the contracting states. This view is confirmed by the preamble to the Treaty which refers not only to governments but to peoples. It is also confirmed more specifically by the establishment of institutions endowed with sovereign rights, the exercise of which affects Member States and their citizens. . . .

> The conclusion to be drawn from this is that the Community constitutes a new legal order of international law for the benefit of which the states have limited their sovereign rights, albeit within limited fields, and the subject of which comprise not only Member States but also their nationals."[30]

---

[23] European Governance: White Paper from the Commission to the European Council, COM (2001) 428 final at 11 [hereafter White Paper].

[24] Id. at 30.

[25] Weiler, *supra* note 4, at 12.

[26] Id. at 29.

[27] Id.

[28] Id. at 19-20, 107-109.

[29] Case 26/62, *Van Gend en Loos* v. *Nederlandse Administratie Der Belastingen*, 1963 ECR 1.

[30] Id.

Armin von Bogdandy is less reticent about labeling EU development as federalism. He contends that "the Union has become an organisation of comprehensive regulation and coordination."[31] To illustrate, he cites the EU's economic policy, its "power over certain mechanisms of macroeconomic policy coordination, which can culminate in restrictions on national budgetary policy and the possible imposition of severe sanctions on Member States" and its increasing activities in "classical state functions" such as "justice, security and (indirect) regulation of citizenship."[32] He argues that in these spheres the Union "can hardly be distinguished from the central level of a federal state."[33] Furthermore, Von Bogdandy notes that the Maastricht and Amsterdam Treaties "promulgate objectives and competencies for the creation and preservation of a unitary territory" and that the concept of EU citizenship is becoming more clearly defined and significant.[34] He asserts that in analysing these developments "one finds clear federal dynamics in the sense that a government for a defined territory and a defined citizenship exists and the sovereign authority defines itself in these terms."[35]

Although the European Union may already possess federal elements, its ardent federalists believe that more is needed. German Foreign Minister Joschka Fischer, in his noteworthy speech of May 12, 2000, at Humboldt University in Berlin, expressed his concerns that a "tension has emerged between the communitarisation of economy and currency on the one hand and the lack of political and democratic structures on the other."[36] He urged that "productive steps" be taken to avoid crises in the EU and to complete "the process of integration."[37] In even bolder terms he proposed "the transition from a union of states to full parliamentarisation as a European Federation."[38] In similar tones G.F. Mancini has asserted that "the confederal set-up has given rise to contradictions which grow in direct proportion to the growth of the Union's powers and which only a leap towards federalism can hope to overcome."[39] Luís Lobo-Fernandes argues that a "neo-federal modality" for the EU would "make possible a qualitative institutional leap," and he asserts that "a federal type of arrangement has a decisive advantage over the traditional diplomatic mechanism: it does not allow the

---

[31] Armin von Bogdandy, The European Union as a Supranational Federation: A Conceptual Attempt in the Light of the Amsterdam Treaty, 6 Colum. J. Eur. L. 27, 33 (2000).

[32] Id.

[33] Id.

[34] Id. at 34-36.

[35] Id. at 36.

[36] Joschka Fischer, From Confederacy to Federation: Thoughts on the Finality of European Integration, Speech at the Humboldt University in Berlin, 4 (May 12, 2000), transcript available at www.auswaertiges-amt.de/www/de/infoservice/download/pdf/reden/redene/r000512b-r1008e.pdf.

[37] Id.

[38] Id. at 7.

[39] Mancini, *supra* note 8, at 66. Youri Devuyst similarly argues for a "reinvigoration of the European integration process through the creation of a Federation of Nation States based on a coherent Constitutional system among those European countries willing to leave behind ancient notions of sovereignty." Youri Devuyst, The European Union's Constitutional Order? Between Community Method and Ad Hoc Compromise, 18 Berkeley J. Int'l L. 1, 7, 51-52 (2000). Further federal development, according to Devuyst, would "pursue the institutional logic behind the Rome Treaty." Id. at 51.

system to be taken over by any group or coalition, because it guarantees the expression of various interests in an environment of reinforced democratic legitimacy."[40]

But Europe is Europe after all, and even the federalists stop short of calling for an EU resembling the American model. The deeply entrenched national identities of the European people and their rich cultural (and often national) histories suggest that even a federal system must look "European." G.F. Mancini speaks of "a European political entity organised along the lines of a state – a state, of course, without a nation – respectful of the identity of the peoples of which it is composed."[41] Joschka Fisher likewise acknowledges that the idea of a new federal state that would replace the Member States as the new sovereign power "shows itself to be an artificial construct which ignores the established realities in Europe."[42] He adds that further integration of the EU will be workable only if it "takes the nation-states along with it into such a Federation, only if their institutions are not devalued or even made to disappear."[43] In short, he admits that the successful completion of European integration must be based on "a division of sovereignty between Europe and the nation-state."[44]

Critics of the federal approach would agree. Joseph Weiler contends that it would be "more than ironic if a polity with its political process set up to counter the excesses of statism ended up coming round full circle and transforming itself into a (super) state."[45] He adds that it would be "equally ironic that an ethos that rejected the nationalism of the Member States gave birth to a new European nation and European nationalism."[46] He concludes that "we are not about to see the demise of the Member States, at least for a long time."[47] In view of all of the practical and political challenges to creation of a true federal state, Giandomenico Majone maintains that "[f]ully fledged federalism . . . does not enjoy widespread political support at present."[48] Andrew Moravcsik expresses it even more strongly: "Save perhaps in the minds of a few remaining true federalist believers and their conservative idealist critics, the dream of a European state supplanting the nation-state is finished, if indeed it ever existed."[49] Michael Newman examines the federalist and intergovernmentalist schools of thought and comments: "Federalism and realism constitute the two extremes in academic analysis of the EU and most contemporary theorists fall somewhere between them."[50] It is now appropriate to survey that middle ground.

---

[40] Luís Lobo-Fernandes, *Por um sistema bicamarário na UE*, Expresso (Lisbon), June 7, 2003, at 30 (Luís Lobo-Fernandes trans.).

[41] Mancini, *supra* note 8, at xxvi.

[42] Fischer, *supra* note 36, at 7.

[43] Id.

[44] Id.

[45] Weiler, *supra* note 4, at 94.

[46] Id.

[47] Id.

[48] Giandomenico Majone, *Europe's 'Democratic Deficit': The Question of Standards*, 4 Eur. L.J. 5, 27 (1998).

[49] Moravcsik 2000, *supra* note 7, at 308.

[50] Newman, *supra* note 13, at 18.

2.   THE EU AS A BLENDED ENTITY

Despite their differences of opinion, intergovernmentalists and federalists must agree that the European Union is today a system that contains features of both models. As such, it might be described as a blended entity, a political cocktail whose bartenders are constantly experimenting to get the mix of ingredients just right.

Many similar labels have been applied to describe the EU. Murray Forsyth has compared the European Community of the early 1980's to several confederal entities.[51] Lothar Funk has called the Union a "hybrid."[52] Ian Ward has described it as a "post-modern polity,"[53] to which Jeremy Rabkin adds that it "twists and bends traditional attributes of statehood or national sovereignty."[54] Kalypso Nicolaidis describes the EU as "neither simply a *Union of democracies* [described in this treatise as the IGO model] nor a *Union as democracy* [described in this treatise as the federal model]," but a "third way," manifested as a "demoi-cracy" comprised of many peoples and their various states.[55] Pavlos Eleftheriadis has asserted that the EU is comprised of a "complex set of institutions that follow both statist and federalist paths," and he adds that its institutions "are not defined by the rights of a single 'European people' but by a cosmopolitan project of republican states."[56] He also refers to the Union's *sui generis* nature that "manages to go beyond the model of national democracy without creating a Federal Europe."[57] Armin von Bogdandy describes the EU as a "functionally-oriented form of political and legal organisation" rather than a "territorially-oriented one"[58] and sees its organisational structure as "characterised by polycentrism and fragmentation."[59] Michael Newman cites a variety of "integration theories" such as "neo-functionalism . . . co-operative federalism, neo-federalism and also a non-specif-

---

[51] Murray Forsyth, Unions of States, at 10-16, 160-87 (1981).

[52] Lothar Funk, A Legally Binding EU Charter of Fundamental Rights?, 37 Intereconomics 253, 262 (2002). Another commentator has called the EU a hybrid, an entity "exceeding the territory of international law, yet without the coherence of a federal state." Jiři Priban, European Union Constitution-Making, Political Identity and Central European Reflections, 11 Eur. L.J. 135, 149 (2005).

[53] Ian Ward, Identity and Difference: The European Union and Postmodernism, in New Legal Dynamics of European Union, 15, 21-26 (Jo Shaw & Gillian More, eds., 1995).

[54] Jeremy Rabkin, Is EU Policy Eroding the Sovereignty of Non-Member States?, 1 Chi. J. Int'l L. 273, 275 (2000).

[55] Kalypso Nicolaidis, The New Constitution as European Demoi-cracy? The Federal Trust Online Paper 38/03, at 5, available at www.fedtrust.co.uk/uploads/constitution/38_03.pdf.

[56] Pavlos Eleftheriadis, The European Constitution and Cosmopolitan Ideals, 7 Colum. J. Eur. L. 21, 39 (2001).

[57] Id. at 28. Giandomenico Majone also refers to the "sui generis institutional architecture of the Community." Majone, *supra* note 48, at 8.

[58] Von Bogdandy, *supra* note 31, at 32.

[59] Id. at 28. Von Bogdandy also comments that "the Treaty of Amsterdam has a substantial unifying potential. However, even if this potential is fully realized, the Union will remain an organisation that does not represent a societal and political unity in the sense of a nation. Similarly, its political system is constitutively far more fragmented than political systems of a state." Id. at 38.

ic form of economic determinism."[60] Joseph Weiler refers to a "community vision" in which the Member States and the EU "continue their uneasy co-existence, although in an ever-increasing embrace."[61]

The "uneasy co-existence" is due to the prominent role of the Member States within the EU. Pavlos Eleftheriadis asserts that "the debate concerning European integration and its institutions is not about degrees of democracy. That would be too simple. The debate is also about the role of states in a cosmopolitan framework."[62] Jan Muller views the Union as a "dual system," one in which "the member states are both inside and outside the constitutional system. Sovereignty is then shared in 'normal times' of European governance...but it reverts to the plural constituent power [i.e. that of the Member States] in moments of constitutional remodeling."[63] Within the EU there is also a division of power that at times heavily favors the influence of the Member States. The Maastricht Treaty (TEU) established three "pillars" of government,[64] and Giandomenico Majone has described the EU's arrangement as containing "two distinct elements: an intergovernmental component, where international features dominate (European Council, Council of ministers, and the second and third 'pillars' of the TEU), and a communitarian component where supranational features are most evident (European Parliament and Courts, Commission, and the policies and activities included in the first 'pillar' of the TEU)."[65]

The unusual structure of the EU is not the only feature that distinguishes it from a typical nation-state. Andrew Moravcsik illustrates a number of substantive differences by describing the many competencies of a state that have *not* been granted to the Union, including "taxation and the setting of fiscal priorities, social welfare provision, defence and police powers, education policy, cultural policy, non-economic civil litigation, direct cultural promotion and regulation, the funding of civilian infrastructure, and most other regulatory policies unrelated to cross-border economic activity." He notes that "the EU has made modest inroads into many of these areas, but only in limited areas directly related to cross-border flows."[66] He has also asserted: "Institutionally, [the EU's] actions in these areas, if there are any at all, are hardly different from

---

[60] Newman, *supra* note 13, at 18-19.

[61] Weiler, *supra* note 4, at 93.

[62] Eleftheriadis, *supra* note 56, at 39.

[63] Muller, *supra* note 9, at 1792.

[64] Art. 1 of the TEU states: "The Union shall be founded on the European Communities, supplemented by the policies and forms of cooperation established by this Treaty." TEU Art. 1. The First Pillar covers the entirety of the European Community's traditional common market activity, while the Second and Third Pillars cover cooperation among the Member States in the areas of common foreign and security policy (Second Pillar) and police and judicial cooperation in criminal matters (Third Pillar). See Neill Nugent, The Government and Politics of the European Union 69 (2003).

[65] Majone, *supra* note 48, at 12.

[66] Andrew Moravcsik, In Defence of the "Democratic Deficit": Reassessing Legitimacy in the European Union, 40 J. Common Mkt. Stud. 603, 607 (2002) [hereafter Moravcsik 2002]. Moravcsik further argues that "by limiting the EU's fiscal, administrative or coercive resources, the member states have imposed permanent limits on nearly all the policies most politically salient to European voters." Andrew Moravcsik, The EU Ain't Broke, Prospect, March 2003, at 40-41, available at www.prospect-magazine.co.uk. [hereafter Moravcsik 2003].

those of a classic international organisation."[67] Moravcsik contends that "the spectre of a European superstate is an illusion."[68] Eleftheriadis concurs: "The European Union is not a state and does not resemble one closely. It does not have the 'monopoly of force' or other features of statehood: an army, courts or a comprehensive central government."[69] Giandomenico Majone notes that the EU has no general taxing and spending powers and that "with a budget of less than 1.3 percent of Union gross national product . . . which, moreover, must always be balanced, it can only undertake a limited range of policies."[70] Armin von Bogdandy also emphasises that the EU lacks the ability to redistribute wealth to any appreciable extent and that it "lacks the power for coercing Member State compliance . . . with the Union's law."[71] He adds: "A close analysis of the developing lines of the European Union from a dynamic perspective reveals more differences than analogies to a state-building process. These differences underline the Union's qualification as a new form of government."[72]

The state-like elements that do exist within the European Union, such as delegation of certain competencies to the central government, separation of powers into legislative, executive and judicial functions, and a popularly elected parliament, are not necessarily a sign that the EU is becoming a federal state. Larry Cata Backer reminds us that in the early United States the "nature and structure of the union" and "the relative powers of state and general government within the federal scheme" were "hotly debated," and that the current form of American government was not an inevitable result.[73] Thus, he argues, even though a "form of federal union" may have appeared in Europe, it need not presage an American-style superstate.[74] He asserts: "Federations ought not to frighten states' rights advocates in Europe. The nature of federalism is not set in stone, nor has the world yet witnessed all of the multiple forms of governance which can be constructed within the spirit of this principle."[75] Armin von Bogdandy likewise observes that "federal thought is not restricted to state polities. The notion of federation has always been used for non-state organisations. It is not necessarily connected with a vision of nation-building."[76] Majone predicts that even if aspects of federalism increase within the EU, "there is no reason at all to think that the political and constitutional arrangements of the future will mirror the institutional architecture of the nation-state."[77]

---

[67] Moravcsik 2000, *supra* note 7, at 309.

[68] Moravcsik 2003, *supra* note 66, at 39.

[69] Eleftheriadis, *supra* note 56, at 26.

[70] Majone, *supra* note 48, at 10.

[71] Von Bogdandy, *supra* note 31, at 36-37.

[72] Id. at 41.

[73] Larry Cata Backer, The Extra-National State: American Confederate Federalism and the European Union, 7 Colum. J. Eur. L. 173, 176-77 (2001).

[74] Id. at 195.

[75] Id. at 238.

[76] Von Bogdandy, *supra* note 31, at 51.

[77] Majone, *supra* note 48, at 27.

Predictions on the future of the EU as a blended entity range from cautious to enthusiastic. Muller, while lauding the Union's "high degree of flexibility,"[78] believes that there will be "further muddling through well-intentioned proposals for amendments, which then fail at intergovernmental conferences, (ICGs) and, above all, constitutional clashes at the EU's core. As a result of the latter, there will be actual gradual reform."[79] Majone warns that the Union's "historically unique approach to integration can succeed only if the economic and the political tracks are carefully kept separate,"[80] and he predicts a system with "[o]verlapping jurisdictions, legal pluralism, extensive delegation of powers to transnational organisation – in short, a new 'medievalism.'"[81] Newman maintains that most integrationists "now accept that integration will proceed in 'fits and starts' rather than 'ever upward' . . . and that the features which have made [the EU] so distinct will become more pronounced as time goes on."[82] Udo Di Fabio sees hope in "an emerging new model of multi-level democracy, characterised by contemporaneous hierarchies and cooperative relationships."[83] The doxology is provided by Andrew Moravcsik, who, on the eve of the EU's Constitutional Convention, wrote:

> "Let us appreciate how much Europe has achieved. We should not be trapped by rhetoric or fears about what it aspires to be. The EU is not a United States of Europe in the making. Instead, it should be seen for what it is – the most successful international organisation in history. The secret of that success lies not only in the Europeans' willingness to centralise certain types of political power, but also in knowing how to mold and limit that power."[84]

It is clear that the blended entity theory is the realistic point of view, that it offers an attractive – and correct – alternative to the extremes of the intergovernmental and federal schools of thought.[85] The ECJ recognized the "in-between" status of the Community in the *Van Gend en Loos* decision, when it declared that "the Community constitutes a new legal order of international law" in which the Member States "have

---

[78] Muller, *supra* note 9, at 1791.

[79] Id. at 1795. The abandonment of the Constitution in 2007 and its replacement with the Lisbon Treaty is precisely the type of dynamic predicted by Muller. A previous example was the failure of the December 2003 Intergovernmental Conference to approve an earlier draft of the Constitution. See Thomas Fuller, Split on voting rights sinks the EU constitution, Int'l Herald Trib., December 15, 2003, at 1. The disagreements in 2003 were resolved on October 29, 2004, when a revised version of the Constitution was signed by representatives of all of the Member States.

[80] Majone, *supra* note 48, at 14.

[81] Id. at 27.

[82] Newman, *supra* note 13, at 19-20

[83] Udo Di Fabio, A European Charter: Towards a Constitution for the Union, 7 Colum. J. Eur. L. 159, 167 (2001).

[84] Moravcsik 2003, *supra* note 66.

[85] David Miliband, a Member of the UK Parliament, asserts that there is a need for "a realistic and hard-headed alternative to the false choice between inter-governmentalism and supra-nationalism." David Miliband, Perspectives on European Integration: A British View (Max Planck Inst. for the Study of Societies, Working Paper No. 02/02, 2002), available at www.mpi-fg-koeln.mpg.de/pu/workpap/wp02-2/wp02-2.html.

limited their sovereign rights, albeit within limited fields."[86] An excellent description of the limits of the EU's power and the retained sovereignty of the Member States is the following statement by Juliane Kokott, an Advocate General of the Court, and Alexandra Rüth:

> "[T]he Constitution is not the product of an autonomous *pouvoir constituant europeén.* Instead, it is established by an international treaty as the expression of a *volonté constituante* of the Member States, which is, however, itself based on the sovereignty of their people."[87]

The ensuing analysis of the Lisbon Treaty will illustrate whether and how the Union's existing blend will be preserved.

---

[86] Case 26/62, Van Gend en Loos, *supra* note 29.

[87] Juliane Kokott & Alexandra Rüth, The European Convention and its Draft Treaty Establishing a Constitution for Europe: Appropriate Answers to the Laeken Questions?, 40 C.M.L.R. 1315, 1320 (2003). For a useful recent analysis of sovereignty within the EU system, see Anneli Albi & Peter Van Elsuwege, The EU Constitution, National Constitutions and Sovereignty: An Assessment of a "European Constitutional Order," 29 Eur. L. Rev. 741 (2004).

Chapter 2
THE GENESIS OF THE LISBON TREATY

The birth of the new treaty was in two stages. First, the Constitution came and went. Then the Lisbon Treaty was devised to replace it. Without the highly public five-year effort to draft and approve the Constitution, the creation of the Lisbon Treaty may have received little attention. The new amendment may well have been seen as little more than Nice II or Amsterdam III. The reality is that the history of the Lisbon Treaty is primarily the story of the Constitution. This chapter will review that story and its aftermath.

1.   CREATING THE CONSTITUTION

The Constitution was intended to replace the EU's primary constituent documents, the Treaty Establishing the European Economic Community (EC Treaty) and the Treaty on European Union (TEU).[88] The Treaties have been a work in progress, the subject of regular amendment,[89] but in their evolution, they have grown to be increasingly complex.

The EC Treaty establishes the European Community, and it contains most of the provisions that define the body's institutions and regulate the internal market.[90] The TEU creates the European Union, which essentially retains and shares the EC Treaty's institutional provisions. It also leaves in place the EC Treaty's economic provisions as the "First Pillar" of a broader system.[91] However, the TEU expands the scope of activity by establishing a Second Pillar relating to a common foreign and security policy (CFSP) and a Third Pillar governing police and judicial cooperation in criminal matters.[92] Awkwardly, the operative entity for the First Pillar is still the European Community, while the European Union acts under the Second and Third Pillars. At the same time the Union forms an umbrella organisation over all three of the Pillars. And if that isn't complicated enough, notwithstanding the continuing separate exis-

---

[88] Constitution Art. IV-437. References to the EC Treaty and TEU are found in note 3 *supra*. The EURATOM treaty, *supra* note 2, would remain in effect.

[89] The major amendments have included: Treaty Establishing a Single Council and a Single Commission of the European Communities (Merger Treaty), April 8, 1965, O.J. (L 152) 2; Single European Act, February 7, 1986, O.J. (L 169) 1; Treaty of Amsterdam Amending the Treaty on European Union, The Treaties Establishing the European Communities and Certain Related Acts, October 2, 1997, O.J. (C 340) 1; Treaty of Nice, *supra* note 3.

[90] EC Treaty pt. III.

[91] The Treaties do not actually refer to "pillars." Art. 1 of the TEU states: "The Union shall be founded on the European Communities, supplemented by the policies and forms of cooperation established by this Treaty." TEU Art. 1. See Nugent, *supra* note 64. See also Deirdre Curtin, The Constitutional Structure of the Union: A Europe of Bits and Pieces, 30 C.M.L.R. 17, 22-30 (1993).

[92] TEU Arts. 11-28 (Second Pillar), 29-42 (Third Pillar).

tence of the Union and Community it has become common to refer to the Union when describing any activity relating to any Pillar.

Criticisms of the EU treaty structure are not new, but one of the more apt comments has come from British Foreign Secretary Jack Straw:

> "While the practical achievements of the EU have been profound, the Union's treaties fail almost every test of clarity and brevity. . . For a start, there is not one constitution, but two. One "on European union," the other "establishing the European community". . . both have overlapping preambles with "objectives," "tasks," and "principles." As for the institutional arrangements, they are shared between the two treaties. These complex texts make the case for a single, coherent constitution for the EU. . . real reform is urgently needed."[93]

Other commentators have referred to the Treaties as a "hodgepodge"[94] and an "ad hoc and often incoherent set of documents."[95]

The drive for a new constitution was born of such frustrations. German Foreign Minister Joschka Fischer, in a seminal address on May 12, 2000, at Humboldt University in Berlin,[96] expressed his concerns that the Union was in danger of becoming "utterly intransparent."[97] He asserted that "productive steps" should be taken to complete the process of integration,[98] and he proposed "the transition from a union of states to full parliamentarization as a European Federation."[99] He added: "This Federation will have to be based on a constituent treaty," and he urged moving beyond the "fears and formulae of the 19th and 20th centuries"[100] to a Europe "established anew with a constitution . . . centred around basic, human and civil rights, an equal division of powers between the European institutions and a precise delineation between European and nation-state level."[101]

Fischer's call received a response in early 2001 from the IGC that approved the Treaty of Nice, a document that provided the latest amendments to the EC Treaty and TEU.[102] The IGC appended to the Treaty a declaration that called for a "deeper and wider debate about the future of the European Union."[103] Among the basic issues to be addressed in this debate were the following:

- how to establish and monitor a more precise delimitation of powers between the European Union and the Member States, reflecting the principle of subsidiarity;

---

[93] Jack Straw, Special Report: A Constitution for Europe, The Economist, October 12, 2002, at 55.

[94] Simon Heffer & Edward Heathcoat Amory, Blueprint for Tyranny, Daily Mail (London), May 8, 2003, at 12.

[95] Unconventional Wisdom, Times London, May 14, 2003, at 23.

[96] Fischer, *supra* note 36.

[97] Id. at 6-7.

[98] Id. at 4.

[99] Id. at 7.

[100] Id.

[101] Id. at 9.

[102] Treaty of Nice, *supra* note 3.

[103] European Council, Declaration on the future of the Union, March 10, 2001, O.J. (C 80) 85 (2001) [hereafter Nice Declaration].

- the status of the Charter of Fundamental Rights of the European Union . . .;
- a simplification of the Treaties with a view to making them clearer and better understood without changing their meaning;
- the role of national parliaments in the European architecture.[104]

The Nice Declaration indicated that a further pronouncement from the European Council would be forthcoming at its December 2001 meeting in Laeken, Belgium.[105]

In July of 2001, the European Commission entered the discussion by publishing its White Paper on European Governance,[106] which asserted: "Many people are losing confidence in a poorly understood and complex system to deliver the policies that they want."[107] Among the "principles of good governance" to which the EU should aspire, openness and coherence were listed as critical to making EU policy "accessible" and "easily understood."[108] The Commission, however, observed that these principles were not being followed: "The European Union's policies and legislation are getting increasingly complex."[109] The White Paper also noted that the EU "needs clear principles identifying how competence is shared between the Union and the Member States."[110] Therefore, a call was issued for "a comprehensive programme of simplification of existing rules . . . regrouping legal texts, removing redundant or obsolete provisions, and shifting non-essential obligations to executive measures."[111] The Commission committed that it would "simplify further existing EU law"[112] and propose appropriate "Treaty changes" or "constitutional reform" to the European Council at the upcoming IGC in Laeken.[113]

As anticipated, on December 14-15, 2001, the European Council issued its Declaration on the Future of the European Union (the Laeken Declaration).[114] The document observed that EU citizens "are calling for a clear, open, effective, democratically controlled Community approach,"[115] and it described the need for clearer division of competence between the Union and the Member States, simplification of EU legislation and more democracy, transparency and efficiency in Union institutions.[116] The crux of the problem, according to the Declaration, was a need for simplification of the

---

[104] Id. at 85-86.
[105] Id. at 85.
[106] White Paper, *supra* note 23.
[107] Id. at 3.
[108] Id. at 10.
[109] Id. at 18.
[110] Id. At 34.
[111] Id. at 23.
[112] Id. at 5.
[113] Id. at 34–35.
[114] European Council, Laeken Declaration on the Future of the European Union, in Presidency Conclusions: European Council Meeting in Laeken, December 14-15, 2001, Annex I, SN 300/1/01 REV 1, at 19, 20, available at http://europa.eu.int/futurum/documents/offtext/doc151201_en.htm [hereafter Laeken Declaration].
[115] Id. at 21.
[116] Id. at 21-23.

Union's Treaties. In a series of statements under the heading "Towards a Constitution for European Citizens" the European Council presented the following challenges:

> "The European Union currently has four Treaties.[117] The objectives, powers and policy instruments of the Union are currently spread across those Treaties. If we are to have greater transparency, simplification is essential.
>
> Four sets of questions arise in this connection. The first concerns simplifying the existing Treaties without changing their content. Should the distinction between the Union and the Communities be reviewed? What of the division into three pillars?
>
> Questions then arise as to the possible reorganisation of the Treaties. Should a distinction be made between a basic treaty and the other treaty provisions? Should this distinction involve separating the texts? Could this lead to a distinction between the amendment and ratification procedures for the basic treaty and for the other treaty provisions?
>
> Thought would also have to be given to whether the Charter of Fundamental Rights should be included in the basic treaty and to whether the European Community should accede to the European Convention on Human Rights.
>
> The question ultimately arises as to whether this simplification and reorganisation might not lead in the long run to the adoption of a constitutional text in the Union. What might the basic features of such a constitution be? The values which the Union cherishes, the fundamental rights and obligations of its citizens, the relationship between Member States in the Union?"[118]

The Laeken Declaration called for a Convention on the Future of Europe to be convened in 2002. This unprecedented conference was expected to produce a document that would provide a "starting point" for discussions at the next IGC.[119]

In the inaugural session of the Convention, on February 26, 2002, Chairman Valery Giscard d'Estaing warned that "[t]he process of European union is showing signs of flagging. . . . The decision-making machinery has become more complex, to the point of being unintelligible to the general public."[120] He referred to a "tangled skein of powers [and] the complexity of procedures,"[121] and commented: "We shall have to respond to the request for simplification of the Treaties, with the aim of achieving a single Treaty, readable by all, understandable by all."[122]

---

[117] In addition to the EC Treaty and TEU, the other treaties in effect in 2001 were the Treaty establishing the European Atomic Energy Community (EURATOM), *supra* note 3, as amended, and the Treaty establishing the European Coal and Steel Community (ECSC), April 18, 1951, 261 U.N.T.S. 140, as amended. The ECSC lapsed as a separate treaty in 2002, and its assets, liabilities and programmes were transferred to the European Community. Under the Lisbon Treaty, EURATOM will remain in effect, amended by the Lisbon Treaty. Lisbon Treaty Art. 4.

[118] Laeken Declaration, *supra* note 114, at 23-24.

[119] Id. at 24-25.

[120] Valery Giscard d'Estaing, Introductory Speech to the Convention on the Future of Europe 5 (February 26, 2002), available at http://european-convention.eu.int/docs/speeches/1.pdf [hereafter Giscard d'Estaing].

[121] Id. at 7. During the Convention Giscard d'Estaing observed that his study of the Mandarin language was easier than mastering the EU Treaties and agreements. Dickey & Meyer, *supra* note 14, at 14.

[122] Giscard d'Estaing, *supra* note 120, at 11. As the Convention proceeded, Jean-Luc Dehaene echoed

On July 18, 2003, seventeen months after Giscard d'Estaing's opening address, he and his fellow Convention representatives produced the Constitution under the title of "Draft Treaty Establishing a Constitution for Europe."[123] Although the assembly's procedures were criticized,[124] and although some commentators questioned whether there had been true accord among the delegates,[125] the Convention's Praesidium felt at liberty to claim that it had accomplished what the Laeken Declaration had mandated, and it referred the document to the European Council as the product of "broad consensus."[126]

A nearly-completed draft of the Constitution was submitted to the European Council at its meeting in June of 2003. Some final work was permitted after the session, and the final Draft was released by the Convention on July 18th. This Draft was the subject of discussion at the ICG that convened on October 4, 2003, and some amendment to the constitutional text ensued. The 2003 IGC met again in December of 2003 and in June of 2004, and on June 18, 2004, it approved what became the final version of the Constitution. It was this version that was signed in Rome on October 29th of

---

Giscard d'Estaing's sentiments as follows: "If, in the Convention, we succeed to make the EU, its Treaty and its texts, its procedures and its processes, more 'understandable,' we will have helped to remove a major obstacle that stand[s] in the way of achieving informed interest and involvement of citizens with EU affairs." Jean-Luc Dehaene, Vice President of the European Convention, Understanding Europe: The EU Citizen's Right to Know, Speech Before the Conference Organized by the Friends of Europe in Brussels 6 (April 3, 2003), available at http://european-convention.eu.int/docs/speeches/8285.pdf.

[123] Peter Norman has written an invaluable on-the-scene account of the Convention from inception to adjournment. His book supplies great detail about the activities of Giscard d'Estaing's Praesidium, the various working groups, and the plenary sessions, including the mechanics of drafting the Constitution and the politics of negotiating its more controversial provisions. Norman also provides valuable information about the personalities who affected the Convention and thus the Constitution itself. See Peter Norman, The Accidental Constitution – The Story of the European Convention (2003).

[124] The Convention's plenary sessions were held only once or twice per month, and generally for no more than two days per session. See the official website for the European Convention, at http://european-convention.eu.int/sessplan.asp?lang=EN. Larry Siedentop has commented that the meetings were not "frequent enough for members to come up with new ideas. Intimacy is needed for such a group to develop a mind of its own." Larry Siedentop, We the People Do Not Understand, Fin. Times, June 5, 2003, at 21. Another commentator has referred to a "serious truncation and imbalance in the Convention's debates." Kirsty Hughes, A Dynamic and Democratic EU or Muddling Through Again?, The Federal Trust Online Paper 3 (August 2003), available at www.fedtrust.co.uk/uploads/constitution/25_03.pdf.

[125] No votes were taken at the Convention's plenary meetings. Daniel Dombey & George Parker, Dual Ambitions, Fin. Times, May 24, 2002, at 13. Giscard d'Estaing was accused of inventing consensus where it hardly existed and brushing aside dissenting voices. Id. See also George Parker, Political Leaders Are Starting to Take Seriously Discussions on a New Constitution for an Enlarged Union, Fin. Times, December 31, 2002, at 13. Three Benelux delegates wrote that they "deplored the procedure followed." Letter from the Benelux countries to Valery Giscard d'Estaing, Chairman of the European Convention (April 25, 2003) (on file with the Netherlands Ministry of Foreign Affairs), available at www.minbuza.nl/default.asp?CMS_ITEM=64E 844AE637C4B2E89B3957CE2028F89X88X67360X33. A Finnish government representative described the workings of the Convention as "extremely ugly to watch." Teija Tiilikainen, Finnish Delegates Reject Draft EU Constitution, Helsingin Sanomat (Helsinki), July 10, 2003, available at www.helsinki-hs.net/.

[126] 2003 Draft Constitution, *supra* note 2.

that year.[127] The next step was to be a two-year period of ratification, but that was never achieved.

The foregoing description of the Constitution's birth should not be taken as the complete story. In the pre-Convention period many activities and many proposals contributed to a process that eventually led to the writing of the Constitution. Some might well argue that the entire history of the European Union served as run-up to the Convention, and that the Constitution was the inevitable result of continuing integration. However, such a *post hoc ergo propter hoc* approach would not do justice to what is the unique and remarkable heart of this story – there had never before been a convention for the purpose of amending the Treaties. Past practice would more logically have suggested that an IGC be convened to consider a post-Nice treaty amendment.

Looking back, the issuance of the Laeken Declaration stands out as the seminal event among all those that contributed to the drafting of the Constitution. At that moment in December of 2001 the European Council made a deliberate decision to propel EU development into a new direction. The demise of the Constitution has called that decision into question, but as the Lisbon Treaty takes center stage the ultimate success or failure of Laeken's bold mandate remains to be seen.

2.   WHAT HAPPENED TO THE CONSTITUTION?

From the moment the Constitution was signed in October of 2004, the ratification process commenced and was well underway in the late spring of 2005. Then, on May 29 of that year nearly 55% of French voters rejected the document in a public referendum.[128] Three days later, on June 1st, the Constitution received a 61.6% negative vote in an advisory Dutch referendum.[129] The EU's official response to the problem was reflected in the following statement by the European Council just a few weeks after these two plebiscites:

> "To date, 10 Member States have successfully concluded ratification procedures, thereby expressing their commitment to the Constitutional Treaty. We have noted the outcome of the referendums in France and the Netherlands. We consider that these results do not call into question citizens' attachment to the construction of Europe. Citizens have nevertheless expressed concerns and worries which need to be taken into account. Hence the need for us to reflect together on this situation. . . .
>
> The recent developments do not call into question the validity of continuing with the ratification process. We agree that the timetable for the ratification in different Member States

---

[127] For a description of the final negotiations on the text of the Constitution and the discussions at various meetings of the 2003 IGC, see "Work of the IGC 2003/2004," available at http://europa.eu.int/scadplus/cig2004/index_en.htm.

[128] The European Constitution: post-referendum survey in France, Flash Eurobarometer 171, June 2005, at 13, http://ec.europa.eu/public_opinion/flash/fl171_en.pdf.

[129] The European Constitution: post-referendum survey in The Netherlands, Flash Eurobarometer 172, June 2005, at 11, http://ec.europa.eu/public_opinion/flash/fl172_en.pdf.

will be altered if necessary in response to these developments and according to the circumstances in these Member States.

We have agreed to come back to this matter in the first half of 2006 to make an overall assessment of the national debates and agree on how to proceed."[130]

During the "period of reflection" – and consistent with the apparent expectations of the European Council – six additional Member States ratified the Constitution. Latvia, Cyprus, Malta, Estonia and Finland gave their approval through parliamentary action, and Luxembourg produced a positive result in its own referendum. Prior to the June, 2007 meeting of the European Council, which abandoned the Constitution, 16 Member States had given their full approval, while ratifications by Germany and Slovakia were being challenged in the courts of those nations. On the other hand, Poland, the United Kingdom and Ireland had indefinitely postponed their own planned referenda, and other nations likewise decided to bide their time.[131]

When the European Council met in June of 2006, it looked back on the previous twelve months and noted in its Presidency Conclusions that a broad debate on the Constitution was ongoing. It commented: "While worries and concerns have been voiced during all public debates, citizens remain committed to the European Project."[132] The body then offered a "two-track approach" to the situation. First, after referring to the five latest ratifications, it opted to give the reflection process more time:

"It considers that, in parallel with the ongoing ratification process, further work, building on what has been achieved since last June, is needed before decisions on the future of the Constitutional Treaty can be taken. . . .

[T]he Presidency will present a report to the European Council during the first semester of 2007, based on extensive consultations with the Member States. This report should contain an assessment of the state of discussion with regard to the Constitutional Treaty and explore possible future developments.

The report will subsequently be examined by the European Council. The outcome of this examination will serve as the basis for further decisions on how to continue the reform process, it being understood that the necessary steps to that effect will have been taken during the second semester of 2008 at the latest. Each Presidency in office since the start of the reflection period has a particular responsibility to ensure the continuity of this process.

---

[130] European Council, Declaration by the heads of state or government of the Member States of the European Union on the ratification of the Treaty Establishing a Constitution for Europe, June 18; 2005, SN 117/05.

[131] Graham Bowley, Luxembourg approves EU charter, Int'l Herald Trib., July 11, 2005. The current status of Member State ratification is recorded the EU's official Europa website: http://europa.eu.int/constitution/ratification_en.htm. For a prescient discussion (prior to the French and Dutch referenda) on the possible responses to a negative referendum result, see Bruno de Witte, The Process of Ratification and the Crisis Options: A Legal Perspective, in The EU Constitution: The Best Way Forward? (Deirdre Curtin, Alfred E. Kellermann & Steven Blockmans, eds., 2005).

[132] European Council, Presidency Conclusions, June 16, 2006, CONCL 2, 10633/06 1.

The European Council calls for the adoption, on 25 March 2007 in Berlin, of a political declaration by EU leaders, setting out Europe's values and ambitions and confirming their shared commitment to deliver them, commemorating 50 years of the Treaties of Rome."[133]

The second statement in the Presidency Conclusions was more assertive. Declaring that "the Union's commitment to becoming more democratic, transparent and effective goes beyond the reflection period,"[134] the European Council expressed its intention to immediately begin the implementation of a number of the reforms suggested in the Constitution notwithstanding the current uncertainty about the document's ultimate ratification. It declared that "best use should be made of the possibilities offered by the existing treaties in order to deliver the concrete results that citizens expect."[135] A detailed agenda for a "Europe at work" was presented, with areas of activity to include "promoting freedom, security and justice," "promoting the European way of life in a globalised world," "improving the efficiency, coherence and visibility of the Union's external policies," and "improving the functioning of the Union."[136] The programme most obviously reflective of the Constitution is the adoption of an "overall policy on transparency," the primary feature of which will be the opening of many Council of Ministers meetings to the public.[137]

On the heels of the June 2006 European Council summit, the incoming Finnish Presidency commented on how it would address the challenge of the Constitution, but its message was mixed. On one hand, Prime Minister Matti Vanhanen stated: "I am convinced that an enlarging Union needs the Constitutional Treaty that was negotiated by its Member States. . . Thus, Finland has come out in favor of the Treaty as negotiated." Vanhanen also indicated that Finland would ratify the Constitution during the Finnish Presidency in the second half of 2006,[138] and this did happen. On the other hand, Foreign Minister Erkki Tuomioja commented: "We now have almost 100 percent certainty that the constitution in its present form will not be preserved." He suggested that a future treaty revision should retain "as much as possible" of the Constitution's text, but that the name Constitution should be avoided.[139]

Ultimately, pessimism prevailed. German Chancellor Angela Merkel pledged to use Germany's first semester 2007 EU Presidency to revive the Constitution, putting pressure on countries that had not yet ratified at that point. However, a legal action in the German Federal Constitutional Court, challenging Germany's own ratification of the document, resulted in a court statement that it would not make a definitive ruling

---

[133] Id. at 16-17.

[134] Id. at 2.

[135] Id. at 16.

[136] Id. at 2-15.

[137] Id. at 23 (Annex 1).

[138] Prime Minister Matti Vanhanen, Speech at the plenary session of the European Parliament, (July 5, 2006), available at www.eu2006.fi/news_and_documents/speeches/ko27/en_GB/1152081630727.

[139] Lucia Kubusova, Finland seeks better climate for revised EU constitution, Euobserver.com, June 30, 2006, http://euobserver.com/9/21995.

in the foreseeable future.[140] With Germany's position in doubt, Chancellor Merkel was left in a most awkward position. Meanwhile, Commission President José Manuel Barroso was described as delivering "last rites" to the Constitution by soundly criticizing the decision to call it by that name,[141] while at the same time he publicly pledged his support for the document's institutional reforms.[142] Not to be deterred by the delicate politics of the moment, others such as MEP Andrew Duff boldly called for a wholesale reconsideration of the Constitution at the IGC level, with the expectation that all of the proposed reforms – and others – would be fair game for negotiation.[143] Finally, hopes that the Netherlands and France would reverse themselves were effectively dashed when national elections in those countries offered no realistic expectations of national reconsideration.[144]

3.   THE REFORM TREATY IS BORN

By the time the European Council met on June 21 to 23, 2007, Chancellor Merkel and new French President Nicolas Sarkozy had joined together to vigorously press for an end to two years of stalemate between the pro- and anti-Constitution camps. After a protracted session described as rancourous and bitter,[145] the body emerged with a compromise calling for a new IGC to be convened in July, 2007.[146] The IGC's mandate would be to draw up a treaty amendment that would supplant the Constitution. The European Council's highly ambitious agenda called for the "Reform Treaty" to be drafted in a matter of months, with the expectation that the IGC would approve it before the end of 2007 and then refer it to the Member States for ratification before June, 2009.

---

[140] Merkel's Constitution hopes on ice, Euractiv.com, www.euractiv.com/en/constitution/merkel-constitution-hopes-ice/article-159355.

[141] For an interesting discussion of the impact of the word "Constitution," see Joseph H.H. Weiler, On the Power of the Word: Europe's Constitutional Iconography, in The EU Constitution: The Best Way Forward? (Deirdre Curtin, Alfred E. Kellermann & Steven Blockmans, eds., 2005).

[142] Barroso calls for EU to move beyond constitution debacle, Guardian Online, http://www.guardian.co.uk/print/0,329602512-106710,00.html.

[143] Duff, Andrew, Plan B: How to Rescue the European Constitution, Notre Europe, available at www.unizar.es/euroconstitucion/library/working%20papers/Duff% 202006.pdf.

[144] The results of national elections in the Netherlands in November, 2006, offered no mandate whatsoever that the new government would endorse a second attempt at ratification of the Constitution. The same may be said for the French election in May, 2007. New President Nicolas Sarkozy expressed a preference for a modest document (such as the Treaty of Nice) that would amend the existing Treaties, rather than a wholesale re-formulation of the Treaties as in the proposed Constitution. Nicolas Sarkozy's European Plans, Economist, May 10, 2007 at www.economist.com/world/europe/displaystory.cfm?story_id=9149133.

[145] Charlemagne, Treaty Blues, Economist, June 30, 2007, at 61.

[146] European Council, Presidency Conclusions, June 23, 2007, CONCL 2, 11177/07.

Exactly one month after the conclusion of the June meeting, the first draft of the Reform Treaty was released.[147] A revised draft was produced in October, 2007,[148] and the final version was released on December 3, 2007.[149] The final version was signed in Lisbon on December 13 and forwarded to the Member States for ratification. It is this version that is analysed in this treatise.

The speed with which the Lisbon Treaty was written is matched by the ambitions for its ratification. The treaty is expected to take effect on January 1, 2009,[150] meaning that all 27 Member States must ratify the document during 2008.

4.   WHAT WAS WRONG WITH THE CONSTITUTION?

It appears that the Constitution's chief flaws were its name and – notwithstanding the urging of the Laeken Declaration – the fact that it would have replaced the EU's two renowned treaties. The title "Treaty Establishing a Constitution for Europe," and the shorthand reference throughout the document to the "Constitution" seem to have touched more than a few raw nerves in Europe. As noted above, a number of officials loudly criticised the label, which sounds so nation-like. Likewise, a single constituent document in place of familiar "treaties" seems to have signaled a dramatically new regime in Brussels.

Oddly, the French and Dutch referenda that crippled the ratification process had little to do with the name Constitution, the consolidation of the Treaties or even the contents of the document. In France, the "no" voters were primarily concerned with the country's economic and employment situation, and the referendum gave them an opportunity to vent their broader frustrations.[151] In the Netherlands, many of those voting in the negative expressed concern over national sovereignty and the pace of EU integration, but most cited other factors for their votes.[152]

---

[147] Draft Treaty Amending the Treaty on European Union and the Treaty Establishing the European Community, July 23, 2007, CIG 1/07.

[148] Draft Treaty Amending the Treaty on European Union and the Treaty Establishing the European Community, October 5, 2007, CIG 1/1/07 REV1.

[149] Lisbon Treaty, *supra* note 1.

[150] Lisbon Treaty Art. 6(2).

[151] In surveys taken immediately after the 2005 referenda, EU officials found that fifty-seven percent of French who voted no stated that they voted out of concern over the economic and employment situation in France. Only ten percent based their negative vote on "loss of national sovereignty," "the draft goes too far/ advances too quickly," or "I do not want a European political union/a European federal State/the 'United States' of Europe." The European Constitution: Post-referendum Survey in France, Eurobarometer, June 2005, at 18, http://ec.europa.eu/public_opinion/flash/ 1171_en. pdf.

[152] In the Netherlands nineteen percent cited "loss of national sovereignty," with an additional twenty-four percent basing their votes on "I am against Europe/European construction/European integration," "the draft goes too far/advances too quickly," "I do not want a European political union/a European federal State/the 'United States' of Europe," or "Europe is evolving too fast." The largest single group of Dutch "no" voters was a thirty-two percent bloc who cited "lack of information." The European Constitution: Post-referendum Survey in The Netherlands, Eurobarometer, June 2005, at 15, http://ec.europa.eu/public_ opinion/flash/fl172_en. pdf.

Beyond the voter surveys, one commentator speculated that the results of the referenda might have been a reaction to a number of things, including the Union's 2004 enlargement or economic competition from the new low-wage Member States.[153] It could also have represented anxiety over the prospect that Muslim Turkey might soon become a member. Other analyses focused on difficulties with large immigrant populations and the attendant loss of national identity.[154] Commission President Barroso echoed these thoughts when he spoke of a "federation of fear" arising in Europe.[155] Another possibility is that the average voter was simply unable to understand the lengthy and highly technical Constitution.[156] The political leaders in France and the Netherlands may have dropped the ball and failed to effectively sell the Constitution to their constituents.[157]

Regardless of the political realities in France and the Netherlands in mid-2005, the following two years were filled with hand-wringing and a developing sense that the British, Czechs, Poles and others would likely have rejected the Constitution as well. The running theme that emerged throughout much of the EU, whether logical or not, was that a constitution was not necessary or appreciated. To be sure, its substantive and institutional innovations were welcome, but its format was too controversial.[158] The European Council in June 2007 reflected these concerns as it proposed a new way forward through a more familiar type of treaty amendment. The amended EC Treaty and TEU, they declared, "will not have a constitutional character."[159] More pointedly, they stated that "the constitutional concept, which consisted of repealing all existing Treaties and replacing them by a single text called 'Constitution' [was] abandoned."[160]

---

[153] Graham Bowley, EU's Coming Agenda: Addressing its Divisions, Int'l Herald Trib., September 6, 2005, available at www.iht.com/articles/2005/09/05/news/union.php?page=1. See also Graham Bowley, *supra* note 131.

[154] Marlise Simons, Discontented Dutch Follow French on EU Treaty, Int'l Herald Trib., June 2, 2005, available at www.iht.com/articles/2005/06/01/news/dutch.php. See also Richard Bernstein, Europeans in Revolt Against EU's Elites, Int'l Herald Trib., June 3, 2005, available at www.iht.com/articles/2005/06/02/news/eu.php.

[155] France Votes 'non,' Int'l Herald Trib., June 1, 2005, available at www.iht.com/articles/2005/05/31/opinion/edvote.php.

[156] Giles Merritt, EU Constitution II: What's in a Document's Name? A Lot, Int'l Herald Trib., April 23, 2005, available at www.iht.com/articles/2005/ 04/22/opinion/edmerritt.php.

[157] Simons, *supra* note 154.

[158] One commentator has argued that when the IGC of 2004 approved the Constitution and sent it to the Member States for ratification, the European Council "underestimated the importance of the change of paradigm which the constitutional treaty brings with it." Jacob Hoeksma, Beyond the Constitution, The Fed. Tr. Eur. Newsl., January, 2006, at 3, 6.

[159] 2007 Presidency Conclusions, *supra* note 146, at 3.

[160] Id. at 15. The European Council also agreed to abandon the Constitution's revised names for EU legislation, its designation of a "Union Minister for Foreign Affairs," and its textual recognition of the EU flag, motto and other symbols. Furthermore, the Constitution's textual statement of the primacy of EU law was set aside in favor of a declaration stating the IGC's acknowledgment of case law on primacy as developed in the ECJ. Id. at 3. The author has recently published an analysis of the Constitution's symbolic aspects. See Stephen C. Sieberson, Did Symbolism Sink the Constitution? Reflections on the European Union's State-Like Attributes, 14 U.C. Davis J. of Int'l Law & Policy 1 (2008).

Even before the ink was dry on the final version of the Constitution, in 2004 Joseph Weiler had commented: "It is not the content of the [Constitution] which gives it epochal significance but the (mere) fact that an altogether run-of-the-mill Treaty amendment has been given a grand name: Constitution." [161] He added that had it not been so named it would have been seen as a "sensible adaptation of the Treaties. . . . No one would have used any superlatives to describe its content, it would have attracted very limited public attention or debate in most Member States . . . ." [162] The Lisbon Treaty now presents a more familiar form of treaty amendment, and it contains most of the innovations proposed in the Constitution. Whether the new treaty is seen as a "sensible adaptation," and whether it will attract limited publication and debate, remains to be seen.

---

[161] Weiler, *supra* note 141, at 3.

[162] Id. at 6.

Chapter 3
FROM TREATIES TO CONSTITUTION AND BACK –
A CONTRAST IN DESIGN

In Chapters 1 and 2 we examined the context of the Lisbon Treaty, its historical underpinnings and its creation. The remainder of this treatise focuses on how the Lisbon Treaty will amend the TEU and EC Treaty and how those changes will affect the EU's dividing lines. Such analysis may be enhanced by a brief overview of the structure of the current Treaties, the Constitution and the Lisbon Treaty. This review demonstrates how significantly the Constitution would have differed from the existing Treaties and how the Lisbon Treaty returns to the existing treaty format. To the reader who is new to these documents, this chapter can serve as a reference guide to the analysis in Chapters 4 and following.

1.   THE ORGANISATION OF THE EC TREATY

In its original form the Treaty establishing the European Community was signed in Rome on March 25, 1957, and took effect on January 1, 1958. Its original focus was the Common Market, but the document has evolved in 50 years to include many other subjects. As most recently amended by the Treaty of Nice, the document opens with a preamble that sets broad aspirations and goals, including the "ever closer union among the peoples of Europe." The body of the document is divided into six numbered parts and two final provisions. A number of annexes and protocols are appended.

1.1   Part One: Principles[163]

These seventeen introductory articles create the European Community and describe its activities. Article 5 limits the Community to its assigned competences and subjects it to the principle of subsidiarity. Articles 7, 8 and 9 identify the Community's institutions, and Article 10 requires Member States to "ensure fulfillment" of their treaty obligations. Articles 11 and 11a provide for programmes of enhanced cooperation among groups of Member States. Articles 12 and 13 prohibit discrimination on the grounds of nationality, sex, race and other classifications.

---

[163] EC Treaty Arts. 1-16.

1.2   Part Two: Citizenship of the Union[164]

Six articles create EU citizenship and describe its attendant rights. These include the right to move freely and to vote in municipal and EU Parliament elections in one's country of residence.[165]

1.3   Part Three: Community policies[166]

This part comprises approximately half of the EC Treaty in length, and it governs the wide range of activities that make up the EU's internal market. It is divided into 160 articles divided among 21 titles. Although the term "pillars" is not used in the Treaties, Part Three of the EC Treaty constitutes the Union's First Pillar (with the Second and Third Pillars being presented in the TEU). Because of the large number of subjects covered in Part Three, the following descriptions will be brief:

- Title I – Free movement of goods.[167] These provisions create a free trade area within the Community and a customs union governing trade with third countries. With limited exceptions for public policy, all restrictions on trade among the Member States are prohibited. The free movement of goods is one of the Community's "four freedoms."
- Title II – Agriculture.[168] This section defines the Common Agricultural Policy of the Community (CAP).
- Title III – Free movement of persons, services and capital.[169] These are the remaining aspects of the "four freedoms." Workers may move freely throughout the Community. Services providers may do so as well, and there is a related right to establish companies and branches in other Member States. The free flow of capital and payments may not be restricted.
- Title IV – Visas, asylum, immigration and related policies.[170] Common policies and Community oversight on these matters are part of the creation of an "area of freedom, security and justice." These matters are closely connected to the TEU's Third Pillar. Among the more significant developments proposed in the Lisbon Treaty, the Third Pillar would transfer into this section of the First Pillar.[171]
- Title V – Transport.[172] These articles define a common transport policy for the Community.

---

[164] EC Treaty Arts. 17-22.
[165] See discussion in Part 2.1 of Chapter 8.
[166] EC Treaty Arts. 23-181a.
[167] Id. Arts. 23-31.
[168] Id. Arts. 32-38.
[169] Id. Arts. 39-60.
[170] Id. Arts. 61-69.
[171] See discussion in Chapter 16.
[172] EC Treaty Arts. 70-80.

- Title VI – Competition, taxation and approximation of laws.[173] Pursuant to these provisions the Community has aggressively developed a sweeping set of laws prohibiting anti-competitive behaviour.
- Title VII – Economic and Monetary Policy.[174] The fruits of TEU, these articles provide for coordination of Member States economic policies, along with creation of a common currency and monetary policy under the supervision of the European Central Bank.
- Titles VIII – XXI.[175] These titles deal with a variety of matters that are of lesser scope than those covered in the first seven. Subjects include employment, a common commercial policy, social policy, consumer protection, environmental matters and others.

1.4   Part Four: Association of the overseas countries and territories[176]

This brief section of seven articles contains special provisions governing the relationship between the Community and the overseas countries and territories of several Member States.

1.5   Part Five: Institutions of the Community[177]

This part provides most of the institutional detail for both the EC Treaty and the TEU.[178] Its 94 articles are divided into two titles.

- Title I – Provisions governing the institutions.[179] There are 81 articles in this title, divided into five chapters. Chapter 1 contains extensive descriptions of the European Parliament, the Council, the Commission, the Court of Justice and the Court of Auditors.[180] Chapter 2 addresses common institutional provisions. Chapters 3 and 4 govern, respectively, the Economic and Social Committee and the Committee of the Regions, the EU's advisory committees. Chapter 5 describes the European Investment Bank.
- Title II – Financial provisions.[181] These thirteen articles do not address the financial dealings of the institutions. Rather, they govern the revenues and expenditures of the EU overall. There are detailed procedures for adopting an EU budget,

---

[173] EC Treaty Arts. 81-97.
[174] Id. Arts. 98-124.
[175] Id. Arts. 125-181a.
[176] Id. Arts. 182-188.
[177] Id. Arts. 189-280.
[178] Art. 3 of the TEU refers to a "single institutional framework," while TEU Art. 5 names the institutions that are defined in the EC Treaty.
[179] EC Treaty Arts. 189-267.
[180] The institutions are analysed in detail in Chapter 13 of this treatise.
[181] EC Treaty Arts. 268-280.

which must be in balance and financed by the Union's "own resources."[182] The Union is required to operate within its budget.

1.6   Part Six: General and final provisions[183]

There are 32 articles in this part, addressing certain structural and procedural necessities for the Community. There is a grant of legal personality and legal capacity. Operating rules govern the treatment of Community employees, the gathering of statistics, Community liabilities, the use of languages in official activities and certain rights of citizens. The treaty sets forth procedures for the Community to enter into international agreements and to affiliate with international organisations. Article 308 is the flexibility clause that permits the Community to take actions beyond the mandate of the treaty. Article 309 permits the suspension of a Member State's rights under the EC Treaty if its rights have been suspended under the TEU.[184]

2.   THE STRUCTURE OF THE TEU

The Treaty on European Union was signed in Maastricht, the Netherlands, on February 7, 1992, and it became effective on November 1, 1993. The TEU constituted a great leap forward by creating the European Union, setting in motion the EU's economic and monetary union, and instituting the Second and Third Pillars. Much shorter than the EC Treaty, the TEU consists of a preamble plus 63 articles divided into eight titles.[185] The TEU's protocols are the same as those appended to the EC Treaty.

–   Title I – Common provisions.[186] Article 1 creates the new European Union, "founded on the European Communities." Article 2 sets the EU's objectives, and Articles 3 and 5 establish that the Union will be served by the existing Community institutions. Article 4 fills a gap in the EC Treaty by defining the European Council and its mandate. Article 6 states the EU's fundamental principles, while Article 7 provides for suspension of certain rights of a Member State that violates those principles.
–   Title II – IV.[187] These are Maastricht provisions that amended the EC Treaty, the Coal and Steel Treaty and the EURATOM Treaty. Those provisions relevant to this treatise are addressed in the discussion of the EC Treaty as consolidated after the Treaty of Nice.

---

[182] See Part 3 of Chapter 8 of this treatise.

[183] EC Treaty Arts. 281-312.

[184] See TEU Arts. 6 and 7. Also see discussion in Part 3 of Chapter 9 of this treatise.

[185] The first and last numbered articles in the TEU titles may not accurately indicate the total number of articles in the title. This discrepancy arises due to the fact that some article numbers refer to several different articles. For example, TEU Art. 27 is followed by Arts. 27a through 27e.

[186] TEU Arts. 1-7.

[187] Id. Arts. 8-10.

- Title V – The CFSP.[188] These 23 articles establish the EU's Second Pillar, define its objectives and identify the means of pursuing those objectives. Forms of action unique to the Second Pillar include common strategies, joint actions and common positions. Article 17 anticipates the eventual creation of a common defence policy. Article 23 establishes the important principle that most decisions under the Second Pillar must be taken unanimously by the Council. Articles 27a through 27e permit programmes of enhanced cooperation in this title. Significantly, the ECJ is given no jurisdiction in the Second Pillar.[189]
- Title VI – Police and judicial cooperation in criminal matters.[190] The EU's Third Pillar is created in these 16 articles. Along with Title IV of Part Three of the EC Treaty these provisions contribute toward the creation of an "area of freedom, security and justice." The primary goal of the Third Pillar is crime prevention through police and judicial cooperation in criminal matters. Various types of cooperation are described in Articles 30 and 31. Under Article 35 the Court of Justice is assigned limited jurisdiction over Third Pillar matters. Enhanced cooperation within this title is expressly permitted. Under Article 34(2) most Third Pillar action depends on a unanimous vote of the Council.
- Title VII – Enhanced cooperation.[191] These six articles set the requirements for all programmes of enhanced cooperation under the Treaties.
- Title VIII – Final provisions.[192] Eight articles provide technical guidelines for jurisdiction of the Court of Justice under the TEU, as well as for ratifying and amending the treaty.

3.   THE INNOVATIVE DESIGN OF THE CONSTITUTION

The Constitution offered a major stylistic departure from the treaties of Amsterdam and Nice, which merely fine-tuned the EC Treaty and TEU. The Constitution would have completely replaced the Treaties with a single document. Starting from scratch, the Convention proposed a text whose organisation was novel.

The Constitution begins with a Preamble that describes the Union's heritage and objectives. The body of the document is divided into four parts: Part I, which is untitled, broadly defines the Union, its competences and its institutions. Part II is captioned "The Charter of Fundamental Rights of the Union." Part III is entitled "The Policies and Functioning of the Union." Part IV contains "General and Final Provisions." Various protocols and declarations follow the Constitution's text. The individual articles of the Constitution are numbered consecutively from 1 to 448, although it is standard practice to refer to each article by its Part number and its article number, i.e., I-60 or IV-448.

---

[188] TEU Arts. 11-28.
[189] See discussion in Part 5.1 of Chapter 13 of this treatise.
[190] TEU Arts. 29-42.
[191] Id. Arts. 43-45.
[192] Id. Arts. 46-53.

3.1   Constitution Part I: Untitled[193]

Part I presents an overview of the European Union. Such a feature was absent in the Treaties, and this introduction may reflect the desire for a "basic treaty" as referred to in the Laeken Declaration. Part I consists of 60 articles in nine titles:
–   Title I – Definition and Objectives of the Union.[194] These eight provisions create the Union, grant it legal personality, affirm the primacy of EU law over Member State law, and identify the Union's values and objectives, while acknowledging respect for the integrity of the Member States.
–   Title II – Fundamental Rights and Citizenship of the Union.[195] This brief section of two articles describes the EU's commitment to human rights and presages the subject matter of the Charter of Fundamental Rights in Part II of the Constitution. It also creates and defines EU citizenship.
–   Title III – Union Competences.[196] Clearly responding to a demand in the Laeken Declaration, these eight articles define what the EU may do, both in terms of its exclusive competences and with regard to competences shared with or left to the Member States. These are critical concepts, on the one hand confirming Union authority and on the other hand underscoring that powers not specifically conferred to the EU are reserved to the Member States.
–   Title IV – The Union's Institutions.[197] In straightforward terms, these 14 provisions describe the institutions, their composition and their responsibilities. The new positions of a permanent European Council President and Union Minister for Foreign Affairs are established.[198] Groups of three Member States will share presidencies of the Council for eighteen months, rather than rotating to a single state every six months,[199] and the Commission will be reduced in size to less than one commissioner per Member State.[200] This title also includes the controversial new formula for qualified majority voting on the European Council and Council.[201]
–   Title V – Exercise of Union Competence.[202] Significantly simplifying the Treaties, these 12 articles reduce the number of EU legal instruments to six – European laws, European framework laws, European regulations, European decisions, recommendations and opinions.[203] This title describes which institution may adopt these measures, and it describes the procedures for such activity. An important procedural development is that legislative co-decision by the European Par-

---

[193] Constitution Arts. I-1 to I-60.
[194] Id. Arts. I-1 to I-8.
[195] Id. Arts. I-9 to I-10.
[196] Id. Arts. I-11 to I-18.
[197] Id. Arts. I-19 to I-32.
[198] Id. Arts. I-22, I-28.
[199] Id. Art. I-24(7).
[200] Id. Art. I-26(6).
[201] Id. Art. I-25(1), (2).
[202] Id. Arts. I-33 to I-44.
[203] Id. Art. I-33.

liament becomes the norm.[204] Furthermore, several provisions provide specific guidelines for Union action in the CFSP, common defence and cooperation in freedom, security and justice.[205] A final article in this section contains procedures for enhanced cooperation among groups of Member States in circumstances in which the entire Union is unable to act.[206]

– Title VI – The Democratic Life of the Union.[207] These eight provisions respond to demands for more trappings of democracy within the EU. They demand equality for all EU citizens and guarantee openness and transparency in the workings of the Union's institutions. The varied articles include a right of citizen initiative, the work of a European Ombudsman, protection of personal data, and Union respect for the status of churches and other organizations under national law.

– Title VII – The Union's Finances.[208] A concise summary of the EU's budgetary system and processes is presented in four articles.

– Title VIII – The Union and its Immediate Environment.[209] This is a single provision that calls for the EU to establish close relationships with neighboring states.

– Title IX – Union Membership.[210] These three provisions deal with accession to the EU, suspension of the rights of a Member State that violates the Union's core values, and voluntary withdrawal of a State from the Union. The articles on accession and suspension have antecedents in the Treaties,[211] while the provision on withdrawal is unprecedented.

3.2   Constitution Part II: The Charter of Fundamental Rights[212]

This part of the Constitution incorporates the Charter that had previously been adopted as a "solemn proclamation" of the EU, but was not included in the Treaties.[213] Part II consists of its own Preamble and 54 concise articles that are divided into titles designated as Dignity, Freedoms, Equality, Solidarity, Citizens' Rights, and Justice.

---

[204] Constitution Art. I-34(1).

[205] Id. Arts. I-40 to I-43.

[206] Id. Art. I-44.

[207] Id. Arts. I-45 to I-52.

[208] Id. Arts. I-53 to I-56.

[209] Id. Art. I-57.

[210] Id. Arts. I-58 to I-60.

[211] TEU Art. 49 (regarding accession); TEU Art. 7, EC Treaty Art. 309 (regarding suspension of rights).

[212] Constitution Arts. II-61 to II-114.

[213] Charter of Fundamental Rights of the European Union, December 18, 2000, O.J. (C 364) 1, 5 [hereafter Charter of Fundamental Rights]. For an analysis of the Charter and its background, see Giorgio Sacerdoti, The European Charter of Fundamental Rights: From a Nation-State Europe to a Citizens' Europe, 8 Colum. J. Eur. L. 37 (2002).

3.3   Constitution Part III: Policies and Functioning of the Union[214]

The longest part of the Constitution, the 322 articles of Part III incorporate much of the text of the EC Treaty and TEU. This section contains great detail on the internal market, social, economic and monetary policy, external action and the competences of the EU institutions. The following is a summary of its seven titles:

–   Title I – Clauses of General Application.[215] These eight provisions express general operating principles and objectives for the Union.
–   Title II – Non-Discrimination and Citizenship.[216] This brief section of seven articles restates certain civil rights of EU citizens, such as the rights to move and reside freely within the Union. Concepts of equality and non-discrimination are also reiterated.
–   Title III – Internal Policies and Action.[217] One of the most substantial sections in the Constitution, this title consists of 156 articles, divided as follows: Chapter I on the internal market, including competition law; Chapter II on economic and monetary policy; Chapter III on certain specific areas such as employment, social policy, agriculture, environment, consumer protection, transport and energy; Chapter IV on border policies, immigration, asylum and police and judicial cooperation; and Chapter V on areas in which the EU may take action supplementary to that of the Member States, including public health, industry, culture, education and civil protection.
–   Title IV – Association of the Overseas Countries and Territories.[218] This title mirrors the provisions in Part Four of the EC Treaty.
–   Title V – The Union's External Action.[219] Various external matters have been consolidated into this section, whose 38 articles are divided into eight chapters. Most notably, the chapters cover the TEU's Second Pillar (the common foreign security policy, including defense) and Third Pillar (judicial cooperation in criminal matters, and police cooperation). Other subjects include a common trade policy, restrictive trade measures, humanitarian aid, the EU's conclusion of international agreements and joint responses to terrorist attacks or disasters.
–   Title VI – The Functioning of the Union.[220] Another lengthy section, the 94 articles of this title are divided into three chapters. Chapter I contains detail on the EU institutions and advisory bodies, most of which was imported from the EC Treaty. Chapter II governs the Union's budget and multiannual financial framework. Chapter III offers details about enhanced cooperation among groups of Member States.

---

[214] Constitution Arts. III-115 to III-436.
[215] Id. Arts. III-115 to III-122.
[216] Id. Arts. III-123 to III-129.
[217] Id. Arts. III-130 to III-285.
[218] Id. Arts. III-286 to III-291.
[219] Id. Arts. III-292 to III-329.
[220] Id. Arts. III-330 to III-423.

–   Title VII – Common Provisions.[221] A final section of 13 articles deals with cer-
    tain capacities of the Union and rights of the Member States, as well as several
    miscellaneous provisions.

3.4   Constitution Part IV: General and Final Provisions[222]

The final part of the Constitution's text consists of 12 varied articles that deal with
subjects such as the repeal of the EC Treaty and TEU, the continuity of the EU and its
succession to the rights and obligations of the European Community. Procedures are
described for the Constitution's ratification and entry into force, and there are provisions governing future amendments to the document, including several streamlined
amendment procedures.[223]

4.   DÉJÀ VU – THE LISBON TREATY

One of the more visible consequences of the Constitution's demise is the Lisbon
Treaty's return to the approach of Amsterdam and Nice. Where the Constitution
would have completely supplanted the EC Treaty and TEU, the Lisbon Treaty simply
offers another set of amendments to them. The reasons for this retreat from the bold
stroke of the Constitution are discussed in Part 5 of this chapter. This section will describe the structure and contents of the Lisbon Treaty.

4.1   The structure of the Lisbon Treaty

The formal name of the Lisbon Treaty is "Treaty amending the Treaty on European
Union and the Treaty establishing the European Community." It consists of seven
articles. Article 1 offers 61 numbered points or provisions that describe amendments
to the TEU. Article 2 contains 295 provisions amending the EC Treaty, which is
renamed the Treaty on the Functioning of the European Union (TFEU). Articles 3
through 7 are brief provisions addressing the treaty's ratification and other technical
matters. A number of protocols and declarations are appended to the treaty. As noted,
under the Lisbon Treaty the EC Treaty and TEU would retain their separate existence
as foundational instruments of the European Union.

   The following sections will describe the major structural changes the Lisbon Treaty brings to the TEU and EC Treaty. This is not an overview of the Lisbon Treaty's
substantive innovations – that is presented in Chapter 4. Rather, the focus here is on
the major shifts of textual material and the primary additions to the texts.

---

[221] Constitution Arts. III-424 to III-436.
[222] Id. Arts. IV-437 to IV-448.
[223] See discussion in Chapter 11 of this treatise.

4.2. How the Lisbon Treaty amends the TEU

- Existing TEU Title I – Common provisions.[224] The Lisbon Treaty provides several changes to Title I. Notably, the European Union replaces and succeeds the European Community. In addition, new provisions are added from the Constitution, expanding on the EU's goals, emphasising the limits of EU competence and confirming the equality of Member States. The Charter of Fundamental Rights is adopted and granted "the same legal value as the Treaties," but its text is not included (as it was in the Constitution).
- Existing TEU Titles II, III and IV. The Lisbon Treaty drops these titles in favor of three new or renumbered titles.
- New TEU Title II – Provisions on democratic principles.[225] The Lisbon Treaty draws this new TEU title from the Part I of the Constitution. It offers four articles that emphasise democratic rights, transparency of EU activities, a citizen initiative process and expanded participation by national parliaments in EU decision-making.
- New TEU Title III – Institutions.[226] The Lisbon Treaty also adopts these provisions from Part I of the Constitution. The European Council is identified as an institution, and its permanent President is described. New formulas are specified for qualified majority voting on the Council. The new High Representative of the Union for Foreign Affairs and Security Policy is defined.
- New TEU Title IV – Enhanced cooperation.[227] This title replaces existing Title VII of the TEU[228] with a single article referring to new provisions in the EC Treaty that will consolidate all procedures relating to enhanced cooperation within the EU.[229]
- Existing TEU Title V – Common foreign and security policy (CFSP).[230] The Lisbon Treaty expands this title to cover external action and the CFSP. Chapter 1 adds general principles on external action, which are taken from the Constitution. Chapter 2 consists of a section on common CFSP provisions and a section on the common security and defence policy (CSDP). Extensive line-by-line amendments are offered to the TEU articles.[231]
- Existing TEU Title VI – The Third Pillar.[232] A single provision in the Lisbon Treaty transfers the Third Pillar to the EC Treaty, thus merging it into the First Pillar. The Lisbon Treaty renumbers existing TEU Title VIII as TEU Title VI.
- Existing TEU Title VII – Enhanced cooperation. See new TEU Title IV above.

---

[224] TEU Arts. 1-7; Lisbon Treaty Arts. 1(2)-1(10).
[225] Lisbon Treaty Art. 1(12).
[226] Id. Arts. 1(13)-1(20).
[227] Id. Art. 1(22).
[228] TEU Arts. 43-45.
[229] See Lisbon Treaty Art. 2(277)-2(278).
[230] TEU Arts. 11-28; Lisbon Treaty Arts. 1(23)-1(50).
[231] Substantive changes in this title are addressed in Part 2 of Chapter 17 of this treatise.
[232] TEU Arts. 29-42; Lisbon Treaty Art. 1(51).

– Existing TEU Title VIII – Final provisions.[233] The Lisbon Treaty renumbers this
   title as TEU Title VI. Major additions include a grant of legal personality to
   the Union, simplified treaty amendment procedures and a provision permitting a
   Member State to withdraw from the Union.

4.3   Major amendments to the EC Treaty

– Treaty to be renamed – The Lisbon Treaty renames the EC Treaty the "Treaty on
   the Functioning of the European Union."[234] NOTE: For consistency and simplic-
   ity, this treatise will continue to use the current name, EC Treaty.
– Horizontal Amendments[235] – These technical changes affect terminology and
   cross-references to treaty articles. Notably, all references to the Community are
   changed to the Union, and references to the ecu are changed to the euro.
– Existing EC Treaty Part One – Principles.[236] The Constitution's novel delineation
   of EU and Member State competences is inserted into Part One, as are new constitutional articles on personal data privacy and on the national status of churches.
   Other provisions of Part One are extensively rearranged and amended.
– Existing EC Treaty Part Two – Citizenship.[237] The title of Part Two is changed
   to "Non-Discrimination and Citizenship." Two existing provisions on discrimination are transferred to this section. In addition, the rights granted to EU citizens
   are refined.
– Existing EC Treaty Part Three – Community policies.[238] This lengthy Part is
   subject to many technical amendments. The most significant substantive changes
   include expansion of Title IV of this Part to include all of the Third Pillar provisions transferred from the TEU.[239] In addition, new subject areas are added,
   including the creation of European intellectual property rights, certain aspects
   of public health, space, climate control, energy, tourism, civil protection and administrative cooperation. Furthermore, the Lisbon Treaty transfers the following
   Part Three titles to a new Part Five on external action: Title IX on the common
   commercial policy; Title X on customs cooperation; Title XX on development
   cooperation; and Title XXI on economic, financial and technical cooperation with
   third countries.
– Existing EC Treaty Part Four – Overseas countries and territories.[240] Only minor
   changes are proposed in the Lisbon Treaty.

---

[233] TEU Arts. 46-53; Lisbon Treaty Arts. 1(54)-1(61).
[234] Lisbon Treaty Art. 2(1).
[235] Id. Arts. 2(2)-2(8).
[236] EC Treaty Arts. 1-16; Lisbon Treaty Arts. 2(11)-2(30).
[237] EC Treaty Arts. 17-22; Lisbon Treaty Arts. 2(31)-2(38).
[238] EC Treaty Arts. 23-181a; Lisbon Treaty Arts. 2(39)-2(150).
[239] Lisbon Treaty Arts. 2(63)-2(68).
[240] EC Treaty Arts. 182-188; Lisbon Treaty Arts. 2(151)-2(153).

–   New EC Treaty Part Five – External action.[241] The Lisbon Treaty gathers provisions from throughout the EC Treaty into this new Part, which is divided into seven titles. These do not address the Union's CFSP, which remains in the TEU. Subjects of Part Five include the common commercial policy, cooperation with third countries, humanitarian aid (new), development cooperation, restrictive measures, international agreements, EU relations with international organisations and third countries, and a solidarity clause (new).

–   New EC Treaty Part Six – Institutions and financial provisions.[242] The Lisbon Treaty renumbers existing EC Treaty Part Five as new Part Six, and it offers extensive technical amendments to the EC Treaty provisions. In addition, new material describes the European Council and refines qualified majority voting on the Council. The treaty updates legislative procedures and institutes budgeting guidelines called the multiannual financial framework. The European Parliament is given full participation in approving the budget. The procedural details on all programmes of enhanced cooperation are defined in a new Title III.

–   New EC Treaty Part Seven – General and final provisions.[243] The Lisbon Treaty renumbers existing EC Treaty Part Six as new Part Seven. Substantively, the Lisbon Treaty refines the EC Treaty's flexibility clause, Article 308. It also revises EC Treaty Article 309 relating to suspension of a Member State's rights.

5.   WHY THIS BOOMERANG?

Interrupted development is nothing new for the European Union. Integration during the EU's first half-century has progressed despite the tensions caused by ambitious proposals, harsh rhetoric, and occasional setbacks. One might well recall the French "empty chair" in the 1960's and the British blocking of budgetary matters in the 1980's. These were political crises of the first magnitude, threatening the very viability of the EU, but they were overcome. Denmark's initial rejection of TEU and Ireland's negative referendum on the Treaty of Nice were likewise seen as major setbacks. In both of those instances the necessary public support was generated to reverse the rejections and permit final ratification of the treaties. The demise of the Constitution may be considered as yet another obstacle that will be surmounted, this time through the adoption of a substitute treaty amendment. Nevertheless, it is appropriate to ask why the authors of the Constitution attempted to redesign the Treaties and why there has been a retreat from its approach.

Chapter 2 describes the birth of the Constitution, from its original mandates to its final IGC approval at the end of 2004. An overriding theme behind its drafting was that the EU under the current Treaties is simply too complex: several treaties, a Union and a Community, Three Pillars and many different forms of action. This multiplicity

---

[241]   Lisbon Treaty Arts. 2(154)-2(176).
[242]   EC Treaty Arts. 189-280; Lisbon Treaty Arts. 2(177)-2(278).
[243]   EC Treaty Arts. 281-312; Lisbon Treaty Arts. 2(279)-2(295).

of documents and structures was accused of making the EU "utterly intransparent."[244]
The 2001 Nice and Laeken Declarations called for a simplification of the Treaties,
and Laeken mandated full consideration of the Union/Community duality as well as
the Three Pillars.[245] Laeken even challenged the Convention on the Future of Europe
to consider the adoption of a "constitutional text."[246] Under the ambitious leadership of
Chairman Valery Giscard d'Estaing, the Convention thus proposed a bold departure
from the current form and concept of the Treaties.

The negative results in the French and Dutch referenda in 2005 ultimately led to
the death of the Constitution, a process also described in Chapter 2. As it developed,
the 2005 referenda were viewed as manifestations of a deep distrust of the Constitution and its supranational character. After two years of an unsuccessful salvage operation, the European Council set the Constitution aside in favor of a treaty amendment
(now the Lisbon Treaty) that would retain the EC Treaty and TEU as separate documents, additionally dropping the Constitution's textual recognition of the EU's flag,
anthem and other symbols. Most significantly, the name "Constitution" was scrapped.
The European Council pointedly noted that "the constitutional concept, which consisted in repealing all existing Treaties and replacing them by a single text called
'Constitution', [was] abandoned."[247] The advance into Constitution Land was one step
too far, and the Union pulled back to familiar ground.

---

[244] Fischer, *supra* note 36.
[245] Nice Declaration, *supra* note 103, at 85; Laeken Declaration, *supra* note 114, at 23-24.
[246] Id.
[247] 2007 Presidency Conclusions, *supra* note 146.

Chapter 4
AN OVERVIEW OF THE LISBON TREATY'S SIGNIFICANT INNOVATIONS

Before we proceed with our detailed examination in Parts Two, Three and Four of this treatise, it is appropriate to offer an additional overview of the Lisbon Treaty. This chapter will provide a brief summary of the major points in which the Lisbon Treaty will change the Treaties, and it will attempt to answer the question: In a nut-shell, what will the Lisbon Treaty do? This capsule description will be followed in Chapter 5 by another summary, one that illustrates how the Treaties define the role of the Member States within the Union. In the course of these descriptions we iden-tify the principal dividing lines between the EU and its Member States. Chapter 6 continues our introduction to the dividing lines, offering a brief summary of how and where the Lisbon Treaty will cause those lines to shift from their positions under the current Treaties. As we continue beyond Part One and into the heart of this treatise, these three chapters will contribute a "big picture" perspective to help us maintain our bearings in the sea of details that lies ahead. Also, since these chapters serve as intro-duction to the remainder of the treatise, the discussion will include references to the corresponding treatments in later chapters.

The significant changes relating to the essential character of the EU have already been described at the end of the Introduction to this treatise. Unlike the Constitution, the Lisbon Treaty will maintain the EC Treaty and TEU as separate documents, but it will merge the Community into the European Union. Furthermore, it will endow the entire EU with legal personality, and it will merge the Third Pillar into the First. It also affirms, through a declaration, the primacy of EU law over national law. These developments will create a new legal order for Europe, although not as sweeping in its scope as the Constitution had proposed.

1.   CHANGES TO THE TREATY ON EUROPEAN UNION

a.   *Title I, Common Provisions.* In an expanded Title I,[248] the Lisbon Treaty states that the European Union will "replace and succeed the European Community." This merger represents a welcome simplifying of the EU structure. The Lisbon Treaty then updates the EU's goals and basic principles, at the same time emphasising that the Member States confer the Union with its competences. Member State identity and equality are confirmed. The foundational principles of conferral, subsidiarity and proportionality are defined.[249] The Charter of Fundamental Rights, while not included in the treaty text as it was in the Constitution, is declared to have the same legal value

---

[248]   Lisbon Treaty Arts. 1(2)-1(11).
[249]   A discussion of these principles and others may be found in Chapter 12 of this treatise.

as the Treaties.[250] In addition, the EU is required to accede to the European Convention on Human Rights, which it has not been able to do under the current Treaties. Fundamental rights arising from the constitutional traditions of the Member States are also affirmed as EU principles. Finally, special mention is made of the EU's relationships with neighbouring countries.

b. *Title II, Principles on Democratic Principles.* An entirely new Title II is added to the TEU.[251] Many of its precepts are stated or implied in the current Treaties, but the new title adds both an overview and new emphasis. The equality of citizens is expressed, and a new article describes principles of "representative democracy." These include direct representation in the European Parliament, indirect representation on the Council and European Council, openness in Union activity and EU-level political parties. The Union is mandated to maintain dialogue with citizen groups and civil society. An entirely unprecedented right of citizen initiative is created. Finally, emphasis is given to the role of national parliaments in monitoring EU activity.

c. *Title III, Provisions on the Institutions.* Also new, Title III offers an overview of the EU institutions.[252] In the current TEU, little is said of the institutions, but this new section provides a general overview of all of the primary EU bodies. Some important detail is presented. For example, the size of the Parliament, including maximum and minimum Member State allocations, is stated. The Parliament's full participatory role in legislating and creating the budget is also expressed. The European Council, which receives scant mention in the current Treaties, is described. Notably, the Lisbon Treaty creates the new "permanent" President for the European Council. With regard to the Council, a new qualified majority formula (effective in 2014) is defined. There is also an adjustment to the system of rotating presidencies on the Council. A provision on the Commission offers details on the eventual reduction in size of the body, effective in 2014. In addition to the new European Council President, the Lisbon Treaty creates a new post of High Representative of the Union for Foreign Affairs and Security Policy. This person will both chair the Foreign Affairs formation of the Council and sit as external action Vice-President of the Commission. Title III is an overview only. Most detail regarding the institutions remains in the EC Treaty, as amended.[253]

d. *Title IV, Enhanced Cooperation.* Under the current Treaties, provisions on enhanced cooperation are scattered in several different titles. Enhanced cooperation is the process by which groups of Member States may undertake joint action where the entire EU cannot. The Lisbon Treaty eliminates much of the overlap in the current treatment of this subject. First, the amended TEU offers an overview in a single

---

[250] See discussion in Part 3 of Chapter 7 of this treatise.

[251] Lisbon Treaty Art. 1(12). See the discussion of the EU's democracy in Chapter 9 of this treatise.

[252] Lisbon Treaty Arts. 1(13)-1(21).

[253] Id. Arts. 2(177)-2(256). A detailed analysis of the institutions is presented in Chapter 13 of this treatise.

provision set aside as a new Title IV.[254] Thereafter, the details of the procedure are consolidated in a series of provisions in the amended EC Treaty.[255]

e.   *Title V, External Action and the CFSP.* The primary substantive material in the amended TEU is its retention of the Union's Second Pillar in Title V.[256] This title is introduced by two articles expressing general principles for external action, as well as the role of the European Council in identifying the EU's strategic interests and objectives.[257] As presented, these articles have no antecedent in the current TEU, and they assist in defining the Second Pillar. The remaining material in this title is divided into two sections, one on the broader CFSP and the other on the CSDP of the Union.[258] Notable developments in CFSP are the role of the new High Representative as the Union's face to the world, the possibility of changing unanimous voting on the Council to qualified majority vote (QMV) without a treaty amendment (but subject to a unanimous European Council decision), and some extension of the jurisdiction of the ECJ into the Second Pillar.[259] In the CSDP the Lisbon Treaty offers the prospect of an EU military operational capacity, a European Defense Agency to conduct research and development, and "permanent structured cooperation" among groups of Member States with higher military capabilities. However, all significant matters of defence remain subject to unanimous approval of the Council or European Council.[260] One final development in the Second Pillar is the Lisbon Treaty's movement away from special forms of action toward the ordinary types of legislation that governing the other fields of EU activity.[261]

f.   *Title VI, Final Provisions.* The final section of the amended TEU covers several functional necessities.[262] Among its innovations it grants legal personality to the entire European Union; under the current Treaties only the Community holds such status. In addition, the title contains the provisions governing treaty amendments. These articles include the "ordinary" procedure and two "simplified" procedures. The simplified forms of amendment are entirely new. However, each of them requires unanimous Member State approval at some stage, in the form of a vote of the entire European Council, acquiescence by all national parliaments, or ratification by all of the Member

---

[254] Lisbon Treaty Art. 1(22).

[255] Id. Arts. 2(277), 2(278). A discussion of enhanced cooperation and other aspects of EU flexibility may be found in Part 5 of Chapter 12 of this treatise.

[256] Lisbon Treaty Arts. 1(23)-1(50).

[257] Id. Art. 1(24).

[258] Id. Arts. 1(24)-1(47), 1(48)-1(50).

[259] The CFSP is addressed in Part 2.1 of Chapter 17 of this treatise. Expansion of the Court's jurisdiction is analysed in Part 5.1 of Chapter 13.

[260] The CSDP is discussed in Part 2.2 of Chapter 17 of this treatise.

[261] See discussion in Part 1.1 of Chapter 14 of this treatise.

[262] Lisbon Treaty Arts. 1(54)-1(61).

States.[263] Finally, accession and withdrawal provisions are presented, with the latter being entirely unprecedented.[264]

An additional significant change to the TEU is the Lisbon Treaty's transfer of the Third Pillar (judicial cooperation in criminal matters and police cooperation) from the TEU to the EC Treaty.[265] This effectively eliminates the Third Pillar, making it part of the First Pillar and subjecting it to the ordinary forms of legislation provided in the amended EC Treaty.

As presented, the amended TEU serves three primary purposes. First, it offers an overview of the Union, its democratic trappings and its institutions. In this respect, the treaty resembles Part I of the Constitution. Second, it maintains the Second Pillar as a discrete field of EU action, deliberately kept separate from most of the Union's activity under the EC Treaty (which now contains the combined First and Third Pillars). In the Constitution all aspects of external action were presented in its Part III, which covered all substantive matters except the Charter of Fundamental Rights (which was Part II of the document). Finally, the amended TEU contains a grant of legal personality to the Union, amendment provisions that apply to both Treaties, and accession and withdrawal provisions.

2.   AMENDMENTS TO THE EC TREATY

As revised, the text of the EC Treaty is expanded from six parts to seven. However, in its first amendment the Lisbon Treaty changes the name of the EC Treaty to "Treaty on the Functioning of the European Union."[266] Its acronym will be TFEU. However, for consistency of approach and avoidance of confusion, this treatise will continue to use the current label "EC Treaty," referring to it either in its current form or as amended by the Lisbon Treaty. The second significant name change in the Lisbon Treaty is a sweeping statement that all EC Treaty references to "Community" will be changed to "Union."[267]

a.   *Part One, Principles.* Part One, as amended, contains a novel and highly useful title on "Categories and Areas of Union Competence."[268] For the first time in any

---

[263] See discussion on legal personality in Part 1 of Chapter 8 of this treatise. See Chapter 11 of this treatise for an analysis of the amendment procedures. Note that the three formal amendment procedures are supplemented by several novel provisions in which voting or legislative procedures in the Treaties may be changed without a formal treaty amendment. These *passerelle* or "bridging" provisions are discussed in Part 2 of Chapter 11.

[264] Accessions and withdrawal are analysed in Parts 1 and 2 of Chapter 10.

[265] Lisbon Treaty Art. 1(51).

[266] Id. Art. 2(1).

[267] Id. Art. 2(2). Various other name changes are included in the "horizontal amendments" to the EC Treaty. See Lisbon Treaty Arts. 2(2)-2(8).

[268] Lisbon Treaty Art. 2(12).

of the Treaties these new articles define which subjects fall into the EU's exclusive competence, which are areas in which the Union and Member States will share competence, and which are fields in which the EU may only support, coordinate or supplement Member State actions without encroaching on national competences. These provisions substantially clarify issues that are dealt with rather clumsily in the current Treaties.[269] Also significant is a beefed-up mandate for the EU institutions to conduct their work openly. The Lisbon Treaty requires the European Parliament to meet in public and for the Council to do so when legislating. Furthermore, all EU institutions are subject to having their documents made public.[270] Two other noteworthy articles in Part One are an enhanced guaranty of the protection of personal data and an unprecedented statement that the EU will respect the status of churches and other organisations under national law.[271]

b.   *Part Two, Non-Discrimination and Citizenship of the Union.*[272] Part Two of the revised treaty refines existing provisions that define the rights of EU citizens, and it adds from current Part One two provisions prohibiting discrimination within the Union. There are no significant substantive changes in this section.[273]

c.   *Part Three, Union Policies and Internal Action.* Part Three, as amended, describes most of the EU's substantive activity.[274] The Lisbon Treaty rearranges the text of a number of provisions, and it presents many technical amendments. However, its substantive changes are not sweeping. Most significantly, the area of freedom, security and justice (AFSJ) is consolidated from provisions taken from the TEU (Third Pillar) and the EC Treaty.[275] Its scope is expanded somewhat, and it will be subject to the ordinary forms of legislative instrument. Furthermore, there is a pronounced move to more qualified majority voting on the Council in this field, and the jurisdiction of the ECJ will be extended. The Lisbon Treaty offers no significant changes in the economic and monetary union, one of the EU's most visible programs. On the other hand, a number of new subjects are added to the Union's competences. These include the creation of EU intellectual property rights, certain aspects of public health, space, climate change, energy, tourism, culture, sport, civil protection and administrative cooperation. Certain existing fields, such as multi-state social security calculations and professional licensing will move from unanimous voting on the Council to QMV.[276]

---

[269] The different categories of EU competence are analysed in Part 4 of Chapter 12 of this treatise.
[270] Lisbon Treaty Art. 2(28). See the discussion of transparency in Part 3.1 of Chapter 9 of this treatise.
[271] Lisbon Treaty Arts. 2(29), 2(30).
[272] Id. Arts. 2(31)-2(38).
[273] EU citizenship is analysed in Part 2 of Chapter 8 of this treatise.
[274] Lisbon Treaty Arts. 2(39)-1(150).
[275] Id. Arts. 2(63)-2(68).
[276] Union policies and internal action are the subject of analysis in Part 1 of Chapter 17 of this treatise.

d.   *Part Four, Association of the Overseas Countries and Territories.* There is little change in these provisions.[277]

e.   *Part Five, External Action by the Union.* The EC Treaty's provisions on external action (which are different from the CFSP in the TEU) are consolidated into a new Part Five of the treaty.[278] The most noteworthy innovations in this section include a provision relating to EU humanitarian aid, greater detail on how the Union may enter into international agreements, refinements on how the EU may institute restrictive measures against non-EU parties, and a solidarity clause requiring the Union and all Member States to assist any Member State that becomes the victim of a terrorist attack or natural disaster.

f.   *Part Six, Institutional and Financial Provisions.* Part Six preserves most of the institutional details currently found in the EC Treaty.[279] The most significant changes are identified in Part 1(c), above, in the description of the TEU's institutional overview. Part Six contains a significantly enhanced chapter describing the EU's legislative procedures.[280] This includes the statement that the "ordinary legislative procedure" includes co-decision by the European Parliament. The movement toward co-decision has been steady, but the Lisbon Treaty represents the final step toward full participation by the Parliament. In addition, the Lisbon Treaty adds an unprecedented chapter on a multiannual financial framework, an enhancement to the current budgeting process.[281] Finally, Part Six contains a newly consolidated set of provisions governing the process of enhanced cooperation.[282]

g.   *Part Seven, General and Final Provisions.*[283] The primary innovation in this section is that the Lisbon Treaty expands the scope of the EC Treaty's flexibility clause, Article 308. The provision in the current treaty allows action to be taken outside stated EU competences only if such action relates to the internal market. The Lisbon Treaty permits expanded action on any subject relating to the Treaties.[284]

---

[277]   Lisbon Treaty Arts. 2(151)-2(153). See brief discussion in Part 1.5 of Chapter 17 of this treatise.

[278]   Lisbon Treaty Arts. 2(154)-2(176). External action under the amended EC Treaty is analysed in Part 1.5 of Chapter 17 of this treatise.

[279]   Lisbon Treaty Arts. 2(177)-2(278). The EU's institutions are the subject of Chapter 13 of this treatise.

[280]   Lisbon Treaty Arts. 2(233)-2(245). Legislative instruments and procedures are the subject of Chapter 14 of this treatise.

[281]   The multiannual financial framework and other matters of the budget are addressed in Lisbon Treaty Arts. 2(257)-2(276).

[282]   Lisbon Treaty Arts. 2(277)-2(278). See discussion of enhanced cooperation in Part 4.1 of Chapter 10 of this treatise.

[283]   Lisbon Treaty Arts. 2(279)-2(295).

[284]   Action under Art. 308 is analysed in Part 5.1 of Chapter 12 of this treatise.

3.   COMMENT ON THE LISBON TREATY'S STRUCTURE

At the time of publication of this treatise, a consolidated version of the amended Treaties had not been released by the EU. As a result, comparison of the Lisbon Treaty
and the existing Treaties is at best a tedious business. Nevertheless, it is evident that
the new amendments will make the TEU and the renamed EC Treaty much more approachable than their current versions. The new groupings of provisions described in
this chapter are logical and welcome.

Chapter 5
WHAT ARE THE DIVIDING LINES?

This chapter will offer an overview of how the EC Treaty and TEU, *as amended by the Lisbon Treaty,* will articulate the dividing lines between the EU and its Member States. This analysis serves as a further preview of Parts Two, Three and Four of this treatise, and the format here is to address the subjects of Chapters 7 through 17 in sequence. For the sake of brevity, we will briefly describe attributes of the Union as expressed in the amended Treaties, and each of these descriptions will be followed by examples of how the Member States relate to each of the attributes. When these same subjects are addressed in detail in the chapters, the analysis will also describe precisely where the Lisbon Treaty will amend the current Treaties. Citations are omitted in this overview, but they are abundant in the ensuing chapters.

1.   THE CHARACTER OF THE EU (Treatise Part Two)

1.1   **EU values and objectives; Member State values and traditions** (Chapter 7)

The amended Treaties identify a number of values underlying the European Union and its activities, such as equality, democracy and the rule of law. The Union's institutions are mandated to adhere to these values. At the same time, the Treaties note that the EU's values are common to and derive from the Member States. Recognition is also paid to the "peoples" of Europe and the diversity of cultures and traditions in the states. The EU is required to respect the status of churches and other such organisations under national law.

Springing from the Union's values are an extensive set of objectives for the EU. These include the fostering of prosperity, progress and peace, as well as promotion of human rights. In fact, nearly all EU activities, including those relating to the internal market and to external relations, are mentioned as Union objectives. Both the EU institutions and the Member States are mandated to promote the Union's values and pursue its objectives. Particular emphasis is placed on the fact that the Union's authority to pursue its objectives derives from the competences conferred on it by the Member States.

Much emphasis is placed on human rights as a Union value, with the protection of such rights as a significant objective for the EU. The Lisbon Treaty contains a reference to the Charter of Fundamental rights, incorporating the Charter into EU law as a document of "the same legal value as the Treaties." There are numerous other textual references to individual rights. Nevertheless, this is not a field reserved for the EU. Rather, there are references to rights as recognized by Member State laws and traditions. For example, the Charter mentions respect for national laws in regard to education, conduct of business, workers' rights, social security and social assistance, health care, and access to services of general economic interest. In general terms, the EU must respect the Member States' human rights traditions, and the Lisbon Treaty even notes, somewhat curiously, that the elevation of the Charter to treaty status is not intended to extend the scope of Union law.

1.2   The EU's state-like attributes; respect for the Member States (Chapter 8)

a.   *The legal character of the EU; the identity of the Member States*

As a functioning organisation with powerful institutions and wide-ranging activities, the European Union in many ways resembles a nation state. The Lisbon Treaty reaffirms the Union's state-like attributes, granting it legal personality, privileges and immunities and legal capacity. The EU possesses national characteristics such as a currency and a system of its own resources. Under the Lisbon Treaty the Union is a permanent entity, the successor to the European Community.

Under the Lisbon Treaty the European Union is required to respect the equality of the Member States, their national identities and their essential state functions. The EU must also treat the Member States with full mutual respect and deal with them in sincere cooperation. It must respect the cultural and linguistic diversity within Europe. The EU must promote solidarity among the Member States, and its institutions must serve the interests not only of the Union, but those of the Member States as well. In its capacity as a legal entity, the EU can acquire property under Member State law and be a party to legal proceedings under Member State law. Tort claims against the Union are to be made in accordance with principles common to the laws of the Member States.

b.   *Citizenship of the Union; national citizenship*

As under the current Treaties, citizens of the Member States are granted EU citizenship, pursuant to which they possess certain rights to reside, work and even vote in other Member States. However, EU citizenship is specifically supplemental to Member State citizenship and does not replace it. National law retains the primary responsibility for citizens' rights, and for example, when a citizen of one Member State votes in another Member State, he or she is bound by the conditions of local election laws.

c.   *The Union budget; Member State input*

The EU is granted budgetary independence, manifested in its own revenue stream and its authority over its own expenditures. However, this is tempered considerably by the fact that many critical decisions relating to the budget require unanimous Council approval, and in some instances approval by the parliaments of the Member States, thus affording each state the opportunity to strongly assert itself in the budgeting process. A unanimous vote of the Council is also required to approve a law setting the newly instituted multiannual financial framework of the Union.

d.   *The EU's external action; limitations*

The Union is empowered to carry out a wide array of activities in external affairs, but, as elaborated below and in Chapter 17, its authority is carefully contained. Furthermore, each Member State retains a significant measure of competence to manage its own foreign affairs.

e.   *The institutions of the Union; respecting the Member States*

The EU is manifested with a variety of institutions that carry out the Union's work and pursue its objectives. These institutions to a great extent mirror the institutional framework of a nation. However, beyond the mandate for the institutions to manage the Union, the Lisbon Treaty requires them to respect the Member States and serve their interests. The institutions are reminded to always adhere to the principles of subsidiarity and proportionality, thus protecting local interests where appropriate. The individual institutions are discussed in detail in Chapter 13.

1.3   **The EU as a democracy; democracy in the Member States** (Chapter 9)

The Lisbon Treaty requires the Union to adhere to democratic principles in its procedures and activities. EU citizens are to be treated equally, but they are also granted participatory rights through the European Parliament and through a new initiative process. EU decisions are to be taken openly, and the public right of access to Union documents is expanded. The Lisbon Treaty's provisions on democracy within the EU are emphasised more strongly than their counterparts in the Treaties, but despite this emphasis the democratic legitimacy of the Member States is in no way diminished. Members of the European Council and Council of Ministers are democratically elected representatives of their separate national constituencies, and the Lisbon Treaty assumes that each of the Member States will fully maintain its own democratic traditions.

1.4   **The EU as a malleable entity; Member State autonomy** (Chapter 10)

One of the more pronounced characteristics of the European Union is the fact that it has steadily expanded and is likely to continue in its growth. But its structural flexibility has other manifestations. Under the Lisbon Treaty a Member State may withdraw from the Union if it so chooses. In addition, there is the possibility for groups of Member States to engage in enhanced cooperation by themselves, and for individual states to opt out of Union activities such as the common currency. All of the foregoing may be seen as positive flexibility on the part of the EU, but they also underscore the fact that the Member States retain a substantial amount of autonomy despite their Union membership.

1.5 Amending the Treaties; the impact of the unanimity requirement
(Chapter 11)

The current Treaties can be amended only upon ratification by all of the EU's Member States. An innovation in the Lisbon Treaty is that it provides for certain simplified amendment procedures, one of which avoids the ratification process. However, even if ratification is not necessary, there is the right of a national parliament to object and a veto right by any member of the European Council. Regardless of the procedure followed, full consensus must be reached among the Member States, and this fact emphasises the continuing sovereignty of the states as full treaty partners.

1.6 Principles underlying EU action; emphasis on the Member States
(Chapter 12)

The critical principles that guide all EU activity are tied in various ways to the separate identity and competence of the Member States. Union competences arise by *conferral* from the Member States, and competences not conferred in the Treaties remain with the states. The *exclusivity* of EU competence in certain areas is balanced by the fact that its competence in other areas may be shared with the Member States or limited to supporting, coordinating or supplementing national activity. The principles of *subsidiarity* and *proportionality* are specifically intended to limit the scope of Union activity, leaving for the Member States those activities that can be more effectively dealt with at the national level. The *flexibility* given to the EU to act in areas not specifically provided for in the Treaties is tempered by the fact that any such action must be unanimously approved by the Council and may not entail harmonisation of national law if the Treaties otherwise restrict harmonisation. The *primacy* of EU law over Member State law is tempered by the implied principle that such law must be authorised under the Treaties to be legally effective, and by the practical effect that the details of implementation and administration of Union law are often left to the Member States.

2. INSTITUTIONS AND DECISION-MAKING IN THE EU
(Treatise Part Three)

2.1 The EU institutions; the involvement of the Member States (Chapter 13)

European Union institutions do not exist in a vacuum. Rather, they are in many ways representative of or reflective of the Member States, and decisions as to their make-up and authority may be subject to agreement by all of the Member States.

The seat of all institutions is subject to the common accord of the Member State governments. Their operating languages are subject to unanimous decisions by the Council. The composition of the European Parliament is to be decided by a unanimous vote of the European Council. The system for electing Parliament and rules governing the activities of parliamentarians are to receive unanimous approval by the

Council. Members of the European Council represent their respective Member States, and this body must normally act by consensus, thus giving each state a veto on decisions. Members of the Council also represent their respective Member States. A Council member is empowered to commit his or her government and cast its vote. The presidency of most Council formations is to be assigned on the basis of equal rotation among the Member States.

Under the Lisbon Treaty, until 2014 the Commission will continue to be composed of one commissioner per Member State. Thereafter, the size of the Commission will reflect two-thirds of the Member States, and unanimous votes of the European Council or Council will be necessary to change the body's size and set its rotation. In any event, after appointment the commissioners will be required to act without instruction or influence from their national governments.

The ECJ and Court of Auditors are comprised of one judge per Member State, each being proposed by a Member State. The Court's jurisdiction is exclusive only to the extent the Treaties so state; in other cases the courts of the Member States will have concurrent jurisdiction. The Governing Council of the European Central Bank includes the governors of the national central banks of the euro-zone Member States, although such governors and the Governing Council are to be independent of influence from the Member States. The members of the European Investment Bank are the Member States themselves. Members of the Union's two advisory committees, the Economic and Social Committee and the Committee of the Regions, are proposed by the Member States and unanimously agreed by the Council.

2.2   Unanimous voting on the Council; the veto power (Chapter 15)

As previously noted, the unanimity requirement for certain Council decisions affords each Member State the possibility to exercise a veto over the matter. Chapter 15 and the Addendum examine in detail the subjects for which unanimity, consensus or common accord may or may not be required.

3.   SUBSTANTIVE AREAS OF EU ACTIVITY (Treatise Part Four)

In specific matters of EU activity, numerous protections for the positions of the Member States may be found in the Treaties. First and foremost, such protections are set forth in Lisbon Treaty provisions that assign the EU's competences to three primary categories: (i) exclusive; (ii) shared; and (iii) supporting, coordinating or supplementary. In matters of exclusive competence, only the Union may act unless it specifically empowers the Member States to do so. In areas of shared competence, the Member States are free to act on their own if the EU decides not to. In areas of supporting, coordinating or supplementary action the Union's role is limited, and its activities may not supersede the competences of the Member States. Additional safeguards in specific areas are discussed below.

It is important to note that the following descriptions do not include the many instances in which a unanimous vote of the Council or European Council (or consensus or another form of unity) may be required to approve a particular law or adopt a particular decision.

3.1 The area of freedom, security and justice; expanded EU activities, but a role for the Member States (Chapter 16)

With the Lisbon Treaty's transfer of the Third Pillar into the First, all AFSJ activity will take place under the ordinary procedures of the Union and with the use of the EU's normal legislative instruments. The dramatic result is that most AFSJ decisions will be subject to a QMV decision of the Council, whereas the TEU requires unanimity in the Third Pillar.

Despite this significant development, certain EU action in the area AFSJ is marked for particular attention by the national parliaments of the Member States. Also, notwithstanding the need for EU policies on border controls, asylum and immigration, the Lisbon Treaty emphasises that the Member States retain competence to define their own borders under international law, special consideration is to be given to a state that experiences a sudden influx of third country nationals, and each Member State retains control over the number of third country nationals permitted to enter and take up employment. In the field of police cooperation among the Member States a role is created for Europol, but any coercive measures are strictly reserved to national authorities. In broad terms the Lisbon Treaty requires that legislation in the AFSJ must also respect the different legal systems and traditions of the Member States.

3.2 The Union's internal activities and external action (Chapter 17)

a. *Internal market; limits on EU competence*
While the EU possesses a general mandate to manage the Union's internal market, the Treaties contemplate derogations by Member States in time of economic need, wars or other disturbances. States may derogate from the free movement of persons and services by favoring nationals in public service positions and by restricting services related to a state's exercise of official authority. Furthermore, restrictions may be imposed on foreign nationals on grounds of public policy, public security or public health. The free movement of goods within the Union may be restricted on similar grounds, and the Member States may operate their own monopolies of a commercial character. The free flow of capital may be restricted in case of an external threat or on other grounds of public policy. The EU's exclusive authority in competition law is limited to rules that are necessary for the functioning of the internal market, and Member States are permitted to grant aids to their business sectors for social, cultural and development reasons. In general, Member State law relating to the internal market may vary from EU harmonisation requirements for reasons of public policy, morality, health, culture and even protection of a state's working environment.

b.   *Economic and monetary union; the non-participants*
Despite the fact that the EU is to provide economic policy coordination and guidelines, the Treaties emphasise that the Member States will have their own economic
policies. And although monetary union is a signature programme of the Union, certain Member States have been permitted to opt out of the euro-zone and maintain
substantial control over their own monetary policies.

c.   *Retention of national competence in other areas*
The amended Treaties address a wide range of subjects, many of which give particular consideration to the Member States. The Union's coordination of employment
policies recognises that these policies are essentially national in character, and harmonisation of Member State employment laws is prohibited. EU social policy harmonisation is to take account of diverse forms of national practice. In the field of environmental protection, the EU and the Member States are recognised as having their
own spheres of competence, and Member States as well as the Union are permitted to
enter into international agreements. Trans-European networks relating to transport,
tele-communications and energy supply are considered an area of shared competence,
but any network that touches upon the territory of a Member State must be approved
by the affected state. In the areas of research, technological development and space,
the Union may complement Member State activity, but national competence is retained, and in some cases an EU programme may involve certain states only.

d.   *Areas of supporting, coordinating or supplementary action; a limited EU role*
In the areas in which the EU is permitted to offer supporting, coordinating or supplementary action, harmonisation of Member State laws is specifically prohibited with
respect to industrial policy, cultural development, tourism support, education, sport,
civil protection and administrative cooperation. The Treaties also recognise that each
Member State is responsible for the content of its own education and vocational training, as well as for the cultural and linguistic diversity in its education system. While
the EU will offer administrative support to the Member States with regard to their
implementation of Union law, any state may decline to accept this assistance.

e.   *External action; national sovereignty*
The EU is charged with a variety of responsibilities in external action, including development of a CFSP and the framing of a CSDP. Nevertheless, these are fields in
which the Member States retain substantial autonomy, and significant protections for
the states are built into EU competences.
    All policy decisions on the CFSP are subject to a unanimous vote of the European
Council. In the CFSP the Treaties emphasise containment of EU competences, mutual
solidarity among the Member States and use of national as well as EU resources,
while the Union is encouraged to strengthen systematic cooperation among the states.
Normal EU legislation is not permitted in the CFSP; rather, action is to take the form
of decisions. A Member State that objects to a decision may, as an alternative to exercising its veto power, opt out of the matter and permit the other states to proceed. Enhanced cooperation in foreign policy is permitted for groups of Member States.

In matters of defence, the EU is charged with the progressive framing of a common policy, but all decisions are to be unanimously made by the Council or European Council. Furthermore, the separate policies of the Member States and the obligations of certain states in North Atlantic Treaty Organisation (NATO) are to be respected. Member States are required to assist each other in case of attack, and the Lisbon Treaty recognises the needs for a state's own defence secrecy and trade in arms. Military resources are to stay in the hands of the Member States, and groups of states may be enlisted to carry out EU policy, while certain states may engage in permanent structured cooperation.

The common EU commercial policy includes Member State protections such as unanimous Council voting on certain matters, a declaration that such policy may not affect EU and Member State competences, and a prohibition of harmonisation of state laws in certain cases. In matters of development cooperation, EU policy must complement Member State policies, and the Lisbon Treaty recognises the right of the states to conclude their own international agreements. Similar recognition of Member State competence is expressed with regard to economic, financial and technical cooperation with third countries and with regard to humanitarian aid. The general authority of the EU to enter into international agreements is expressly qualified by a statement that the Member States' competence to enter into such agreements is not to be prejudiced by Union action. Furthermore, in its activities in third countries and with international organisations, the EU is required to cooperate with Member State diplomatic and consular missions.

4.   SUMMARISING THE DIVIDING LINES

As broadly described in the foregoing preview, the European Union's dividing lines may be characterised in several ways. Many of them are obvious; these would include specified limitations on EU competences and the right of a Member State to block a decision that requires unanimity. The procedures available to amend the Treaties represent the ultimate expression of intergovernmentalism, with each Member State separately permitted to determine whether to approve or reject a proposed amendment.

Other dividing lines prove to be more subtle. For example, where values and objectives are stated for the Union, this does not imply that national values and objectives are thus diminished. Objectives relating to centralised activities may well be shared by the Member States. Another such subtlety is found in the highly detailed descriptions of the EU institutions, their competences and their operating procedures. Beneath the surface of these descriptions one may find many instances in which the Member States exert their individual influences on the EU institutions or on the activities being carried out by those institutions.

Lastly, we must recognize that the dividing lines may be complex, and richly so. The principles underlying EU action – for example, primacy and subsidiarity – may be rather simply defined, but history has proven them to be full of nuance and the subject of vigorous academic and political debate. A great deal of the intensity of such discourse stems from the push and pull of national interests within the Union.

Similarly, a review of the wide range of the subjects of EU activity reveals many points of debate as to how Union activity should or should not impact Member State competence in the same field.

In broad terms, the dividing lines serve as metaphor for the entire course of European integration. Individual sovereign nations have decided to band together for the greater good, but they do not wish to lose their nationhood in the process. No matter how successful the EU has proven to be, one may never lose sight that it is not yet a United States of Europe. Many Europeans have viewed each stage of Union development with a critical eye and an earnest intention that the EU will never become integrated to that extent.

Chapter 6
NOTABLE CHANGES THAT MAY AFFECT THE EU'S DIVIDING LINES

We conclude this introductory section by previewing the innovations in the Lisbon Treaty that will arguably affect the existing dividing lines within the EU. Certain of the changes may offer a shift toward the Union and more central authority, at the same time diminishing the sovereignty or autonomy of the individual Member States. Other changes may flow in the opposite direction. It is worth emphasising that, unlike previous treaty amendments, it is not a primary purpose of the Lisbon Treaty to expand EU competences or increase the pace of integration. Nor is it intended to "give back" any significant power to the Member States. Rather, the thrust of the new amendment is to clarify and improve the existing EU institutions and procedures. That being said, some shifting of the lines is the inevitable result of any treaty amendment.

1.   SHIFTING AWAY FROM THE MEMBER STATES

Let us begin with a reminder that the new "legal order" under the Lisbon Treaty may reflect movement toward a more supranational Union that may pose further challenges to Member State sovereignty. The elements of this new order are identified in Part 1.1 below. They, along with other provisions discussed in Part 1, arguably will shift the EU's dividing lines toward more Union competence.

1.1   Structural and procedural matters

a.   *A single Union.* The Lisbon Treaty reconstitutes the European Union as the successor to the European Community.[285] The new EU is a single, more cohesive entity than its predecessors, theoretically better positioned to assert itself.

b.   *Legal instruments.* Along with the new Union is a single set of legal instruments for most EU law-making.[286] This is brought about through (a) the merger of the Third Pillar into the First, and (b) replacement of the Second Pillar's own processes with the general use of the "decision," which is one of the standard forms of legal act. These developments create greater uniformity in Union action and perhaps greater effectiveness.

---

[285] Lisbon Treaty Art. 1(2)(b).
[286] Id. Art. 2(235). See discussion in Part 1.1 of Chapter 14 of this treatise.

c.   *Legal status.* The grant of legal personality to the Union[287] and the acknowledgement of its legal capacity[288] may be seen as affirming and strengthening its existence.

d.   *Primacy.* The IGC's affirmation of the primacy of EU law over Member State law, even if not expressed in the treaty text as it was in the Constitution,[289] affirms and may even boost the standing of the EU. This principle had developed in the case law of the ECJ, but it has always been the subject of debate.

e.   *Categories of competence.* The new delineation of the Union's competences as "exclusive," "shared" or "supporting, coordinating or supplementary"[290] arguably cements the authority of the EU, but it could also be posited that the clarification equally protects the competences of the Member States.

f.   *Flexibility clause.* The Lisbon Treaty's flexibility clause is broader than its EC Treaty counterpart,[291] potentially opening the door to expanded EU activity. However, unanimous Council approval is required for any action taken under the flexibility clause, and the Lisbon Treaty includes a new requirement of advance notification to the Member State parliaments.

g.   *More QMV.* The most notable procedural changes are those instances in which unanimous voting on the Council or European Council is replaced with qualified majority voting. These provisions are described in detail in Chapter 15 of this treatise. As the analysis indicates, although these provisions do remove the veto power of each Member State in those subjects, the changes are in areas that are not matters of vital national concern. In instances where sensitivities were strong, proposals for change (such as a suggested QMV for company tax harmonisation) were rebuffed at the Convention or the ensuing sessions of the IGC.[292] Proposals to permit amendment of the Constitution by a super-majority were also rejected,[293] with the result that the ordinary amendment procedure requires Member State ratification. In fact, even the simplified amendment procedures added by the Lisbon Treaty – as well as a number of *passerelle* provisions permitting a streamlined approach to more QMV – require some form of consent by each of the Member States or their representatives.[294]

---

[287]   Lisbon Treaty Art. 1(55).

[288]   EC Treaty Art. 282. The substance of this provision is preserved, and the Community's legal capacity is transferred to the Union by the general wording change of "Community" to "Union." Lisbon Treaty Art. 2(2).

[289]   2007 Presidency Conclusions, *supra* note 146, Annex I at 16, n. 1. Also see Constitution Art. I-6 and the discussion in Part 3 of Chapter 12 of this treatise.

[290]   Lisbon Treaty Art. 2(12).

[291]   Id. Art. 2(289), amending EC Treaty Art. 308.

[292]   See discussion in Part 1.1(e) of Chapter 17 of this treatise.

[293]   See Norman, *supra* note 123, at 81, 293, 332.

[294]   See discussion in Part 2 of Chapter 11.

1.2   Institutional changes

a.   *Permanent President.* The permanent President for the European Council[295] has the potential to give greater attention to the EU, both within Europe and without. A more prominent face to the Union might draw attention away from Member State officials.

b.   *High Representative.* The new High Representative for Foreign Affairs[296] – as a Commission Vice-President and as permanent chair of the Foreign Affairs formation of the Council – might create greater EU visibility in a manner similar to that of the new European Council President. This new position poses a challenge to the prominence, if not actual power, of the national foreign ministers.

c.   *Smaller Commission.* The reduction in composition of the Commission to less than one commissioner from each Member State[297] was anticipated in the Treaties, and the Lisbon Treaty will fix the body's eventual size and the date of its restructuring. The eventual end to permanent participation of each Member State in this institution will to some extent diminish the individual voices of the Member States in Brussels.

1.3   Substantive developments

a.   *Charter.* The new prominence of the Charter of Fundamental Rights, as a document with the "same legal value as the Treaties," will extend the Union's reach into individual rights.[298] This is true despite the Lisbon Treaty's disclaimer that the Charter will not extend Union competences. Furthermore, as a result of the Charter's new status, there will be an inevitable extension of the jurisdiction of the ECJ into these matters.

b.   *IP rights.* The Lisbon Treaty authorises the Union to create EU intellectual property rights,[299] a field previously left to the Member States. In addition, EU action will for the first time be permitted in the areas of space, energy policy, tourism, sport, civil protection, administrative cooperation and certain aspects of public health.[300] To the extent the Union actually enters these fields, the previous autonomy of the Member States on such matters will be lost. Additionally, the EC Treaty's requirement of unanimous Council decisions in matters of culture is changed to qualified majority voting – a minor but potentially interesting loss of the national veto power.[301]

---

[295] Lisbon Treaty Art. 1(16)(5).
[296] Id. Art. 1(19).
[297] Id. Art. 1(18)(5).
[298] Id. Art. 1(8).
[299] Id. Art. 2(84).
[300] See discussion in Parts 1.3 and 1.4 of Chapter 17 of this treatise.
[301] See discussion in Part 1.4 of Chapter 17 of this treatise.

c.   *New fields of competence*. The Lisbon Treaty identifies as areas of "shared competence" the following: the internal market, social policy, policies relating to economic, social and territorial cohesion, agricultural and fisheries policy, the environment, consumer protection, transport, trans-European networks, energy, the AFSJ,
and common safety concerns in public health.[302] The concept of shared competence
had not been articulated in the Treaties, and it is possible that in some instances the
Union's newly articulated right to pre-empt action in these fields might diminish current Member State activity.

d.   *Expanded jurisdiction*. The Constitution extends the jurisdiction of the ECJ
into several aspects of the CFSP and into the area of freedom, security of justice.[303]
These extensions have the potential of undercutting the authority of the Member State
courts.

e.   *AFSJ*. In the AFSJ, there are several additional developments that arguably diminish the authority of the Member States. First, there is a shift from unanimous
Council voting in the Third Pillar to qualified majority voting in many instances.
Second, the right of Member States to initiate legislation in the field is changed from
the right of a single state to do so to the requirement that one-fourth of the states must
participate.[304] Third, new EU action is permitted with respect to developing uniform
standards for cross-border crime, support for crime prevention programmes, and the
establishment of an EU Public Prosecutor.[305]

f.   *QMV in the CFSP*. In the field of the CFSP the Lisbon Treaty creates new areas
in which qualified majority decisions are permitted on the Council. It also allows the
European Council to unanimously decide to extend qualified majority voting into new
areas, without amending the TEU.[306]

g.   *Defence*. With respect to the Union's CSDP, the Lisbon Treaty speaks for the
first time of the EU developing its own operational capacity, and it provides for establishment of a European Defence Agency.[307] Although this strongly suggests expansion
of EU activity at the expense of the Member States, it is important to note that the
establishment of a common defence requires a unanimous decision of the European
Council,[308] and further decisions must be taken unanimously by the Council.[309]

---

[302] Lisbon Treaty Art. 2(12)(2C). See discussion in Chapters 16 and 17 of this treatise.
[303] See discussion in Part 5 of Chapter 13 of this treatise.
[304] See discussion in Part 1(j) of Chapter 16 of this treatise. The increased difficulty of creating a Member State initiative arguably strengthens the residual right of initiative held by the Commission.
[305] Lisbon Treaty Arts. 2(67)(69B), (69C), (69E).
[306] See discussion in Part 2.1(b) of Chapter 17 of this treatise.
[307] See discussion in Part 2.2 of Chapter 17 of this treatise.
[308] Lisbon Treaty Art. 1(49)(b).
[309] TEU Art. 23(1); Lisbon Treaty Art. 1(49)(c)(4).

h. *Military cooperation.* Where the TEU anticipates bilateral cooperation between Member States within the framework of the Western European Union (WEU) and NATO,[310] the Lisbon Treaty provides that such activities may also take the form of structured cooperation "within the Union framework."[311] A greater presence for the EU may entail encroachment upon Member State autonomy in matters of defence.

2. NEW EMPHASIS ON THE MEMBER STATES

More remarkable perhaps than the new emphases on the Union are the numerous examples of how the Lisbon Treaty underscores the importance of the Member States within the EU system. All of the items included in the following descriptions are novel, that is, they are not found in the Treaties at all or are given significant new emphasis in the Lisbon Treaty.

2.1 Reminders of the Member States and their citizens

a. *Textual emphasis on the Member States.* In its statements about the Union's objectives, the Lisbon Treaty makes frequent references to the role of the Member States in pursuing those objectives.[312] More substantively, the Lisbon Treaty requires the EU to respect the equality of the Member States, their national identities and their essential state functions,[313] all in terms more forceful than those found in the current Treaties. The Union is to treat the states with "full mutual respect" and deal with them in "sincere cooperation,"[314] phrases not found in the current Treaties. The EU must respect the cultural and linguistic diversity within Europe,[315] and it must respect the status of churches and other such organisations under national law.[316] It must also respect the Member States' human rights traditions.[317] The EU is recognized as a legal entity, and in that capacity it may have responsibilities under Member State law.[318] EU citizenship is specifically supplemental to Member State citizenship and does not replace it.[319]

---

[310] TEU Art. 17(4).

[311] Lisbon Treaty Art. 1(49)(c)(6).

[312] See discussion in Part 2 of Chapter 7 of this treatise.

[313] Lisbon Treaty Art. 1(5)(2).

[314] Id. Art. 1(5)(3).

[315] Id. Art. 1(4)(3).

[316] Id. Art. 2(30)(1).

[317] Id. Art. 1(8)(3).

[318] Id. Art. 1(55). Also see EC Treaty Arts. 282, 288. These Community provisions are made applicable to the Union as a whole by the Lisbon Treaty's changing the word "Community" to "Union." Lisbon Treaty Art. 2(2)(a).

[319] Lisbon Treaty Art. 2(34)(a).

b.   *Citizen rights.* The Union must offer more open meetings of its institutions,[320] greater access to its documents[321] and more availability for consultation with citizens and civil society.[322]

2.2   EU structural, institutional and procedural concepts

a.   *Competences.* The Lisbon Treaty goes well beyond the current Treaties by carefully defining the exclusive, shared and other competences of the EU.[323] Arguably this new clarity may benefit the Member States as well as the EU, as it may curb Union encroachment into areas reserved to the states.

b.   *Conferral.* The Lisbon Treaty also expands on a vaguely-worded concept in the EC Treaty, emphasising that the Union's powers are conferred by the Member States, and that all competences not conferred are reserved to the states.[324]

c.   *Flexibility clause.* If the Union acts under its flexibility clause,[325] the Lisbon Treaty adds a requirement that the EU must give advance notification to the Member State parliaments.[326]

d.   *Supporting action.* In areas of EU supporting, coordinating or supplementary action, the Lisbon Treaty clearly states that EU action may not supersede Member State competence in the same fields and may not require harmonisation of Member State law.[327]

e.   *National parliaments.* The Lisbon Treaty's revised protocols on national parliaments and subsidiarity provide new clarity and an expanded involvement on the part of the Member States.[328]

f.   *Consensus.* The Lisbon Treaty clarifies that the European Council must normally act by consensus.[329]

---

[320] Lisbon Treaty Art. 2(28)(a).
[321] Id. Art. 2(28)(b).
[322] Id. Art. 1(12)(8B).
[323] Id. Art. 2(12).
[324] Id. Art. 1(6)(2). See the discussion of conferral in Part 1 of Chapter 12 of this treatise.
[325] The flexibility clause is currently EC Treaty Art. 308.
[326] Lisbon Treaty Art. 2(289).
[327] Id. Art. 2(12)(2A)(5).
[328] Protocol on the role of national Parliaments in the European Union, Lisbon Treaty, December 3, 2007, CIG 14/07, TL/P/en 2 [hereafter Protocol on National Parliaments]; Protocol on the application of the principles of subsidiarity and proportionality, Lisbon Treaty, December 3, 2007, CIG 14/07, TL/P/en 6 [hereafter Protocol on Subsidiarity]. See discussion of these protocols in Part 2 of Chapter 12 of this treatise.
[329] Lisbon Treaty Art. 1(16)(4).

g.   *Representing the Member States*. The Lisbon Treaty emphasises that the members of the European Council and Council of Ministers are to actively represent the interests of their respective Member States.[330]

h.   *Unanimous voting*. The Council must act unanimously to set the newly created multiannual financial framework.[331] Likewise, laws passed under the Lisbon Treaty's flexibility clause must receive unanimous Council approval.[332]

i.   *Citizen initiative*. The new citizen initiative process offers greater participation directly to European citizens, rather than to their national governments, but a significant number of Member States must be represented in the signature lists for an initiative proposal to be legitimate.[333]

j.   *Withdrawal from the Union*. The ultimate procedural development in favor of the Member States is the new withdrawal provision, which permits any state to declare its intention to exit the Union and then do so without being punished.[334]

2.3   EU internal policies

Various matters of new EU activity within the Union provide emphasis on the Member States.

a.   *IP language*. The selection of language arrangements for new EU intellectual property rights requires a unanimous Council vote.[335]

b.   *Space*. EU activities in space may not interfere with Member State competence in such endeavors.[336]

c.   *No harmonisation*. In the new fields of tourism, sport, civil protection and administrative cooperation, EU activity may not entail harmonisation of Member State laws.[337]

d.   *AFSJ*. In the AFSJ a new provision requires the European Council, acting unanimously, to set strategic guidelines for legislative and operational planning within the field.[338] In addition, the EU is called upon to respect the different legal systems

---

[330] Lisbon Treaty Art. 1(12)(8A)(2).
[331] Id. Art. 2(261)(2).
[332] Id. Art. 2(289).
[333] Id. Art. 1(12)(8B)(4).
[334] Id. Art. 1(58).
[335] Id. Art. 2(84).
[336] Id. Art. 2(12)(2C)(3).
[337] See discussion in Part 1.4 of Chapter 17 of this treatise.
[338] Lisbon Treaty Art. 2(64)(61A). See discussion of the AFSJ in Chapter 16 of this treatise.

and traditions of the Member States.[339] National parliaments are to ensure that certain activities in the AFSJ field must comply with the principle of subsidiarity.[340] In the matter of border checks, asylum and immigration, new emphasis is placed on the right of each Member State to determine the geographical demarcation of its borders under international law[341] and to determine the volumes of third-country nationals to be granted work permits.[342] In addition, the principles of solidarity and fair sharing of responsibility are highlighted.[343] In the area of police cooperation, any coercive measures are to be carried out by national authorities, rather than by Europol.[344]

2.4   EU external action

a.   *Objectives*. The European Council must act unanimously to set the strategic interests and objectives of the EU in the CFSP.[345]

b.   *National resources*. Use of Member State resources in the CFSP is contemplated.[346]

c.   *Competences*. Special note is made of the fact that Union activity in the CFSP may not affect the other competences specifically granted to the EU in the Treaties, and by implication CFSP activity may not affect Member State competences either.[347]

d.   *Mutual assistance*. In the CFSP the Member States are called upon to assist each other, and related obligations of certain EU members under NATO are respected.[348]

e.   *Military cooperation*. Groups of states with higher military capabilities must establish their own permanent structured cooperation within the EU framework.[349]

f.   *Humanitarian aid*. In matters of humanitarian aid, EU action is to complement Member State action.[350]

g.   *Solidarity*. The Member States must assist each other under a new solidarity clause.[351]

---

[339] Lisbon Treaty Art. 2(64)(61)(1).
[340] Id. Art. 2(64)(61B).
[341] Id. Art. 2(65)(62).
[342] Id. Art. 2(65)(63a).
[343] Id. Art. 2(65)(63b).
[344] Id. Art. 2(68)(69G).
[345] Id. Art 1(29)(a).
[346] Id. Art. 1(29)(c).
[347] Id. Art. 1(45)(25b).
[348] Id. Art. 1(49)(c)(7).
[349] Id. Art. 1(49)(c)(6).
[350] Id. Art. 2(168)(1).
[351] Id. Art. 2(176).

3.   SUMMARISING THE CHANGES

There is a risk of over-simplification in offering a capsule summary of the changes that are already presented in summary fashion. Nevertheless a few broad comments are possible. First, the structural and procedural changes proposed in the Lisbon Treaty may indeed suggest a new legal order for the European Union, but this will not be accompanied by an overt shift of competences to the EU institutions. Second, the major institutional changes may well serve to increase the Union's efficiency and visibility, but again there are few proposals for increases in institutional competences. Finally, selected areas of substantive change, such as elevation of Charter of Fundamental Rights to treaty status, do potentially increase the EU's area of competence. Also, the increase of QMV decision-making in the AFSJ and elsewhere will eliminate some opportunities for individual Member States to block EU action. Overall, however, it is difficult to see these developments as anything other than incremental. In short, although certain dividing lines will shift under the Lisbon Treaty, the potential movement is not nearly as dramatic as many critics have claimed.

Part Two
The Character of the EU

We now move into the detailed analysis of the Lisbon Treaty and how it will change the existing Treaties. This part will examine the essential character of the European Union as endowed by the amended Treaties, because the very nature of the EU and its institutions reflects the dividing lines between the Union and its Member States.

The outline of this part was previewed in Chapter 5, and the analysis begins with Chapter 7 addressing the values on which the EU is founded and the objectives it must pursue. Chapter 8 then explores the various ways in which the Union resembles a nation state – it offers a type of citizenship, it manages its own budget and it is manifested in a set of institutions. As an organisation with citizens, the EU is perceived as having responsibilities to deal openly and transparently with them, and Chapter 9 analyses the extent to which the Union offers democratic rights. Certain of the complexities in managing the EU are dealt with in Chapters 10, 11 and 12. Because of the tension between the need for effective central action and the insistence that the Member States retain their own national sovereignty, a built-in fluidity has evolved to permit the Union to move forward even where full consensus may be lacking. Chapter 10 analyses that flexibility. In contrast, Chapter 11 deals with the historical fact that the EU is a treaty organisation, and thus the Lisbon Treaty retains the requirement that the amended Treaties cannot be amended without the complete agreement of all Member States. Finally, Chapter 12 discusses a series of legal principles that guide and limit EU action.

These six chapters are intended to provide a meaningful portrait of the European Union, as well as an explanation of how its character is reflected in part by an identifiable set of dividing lines. With this portrait in mind, Part Three will address more fully the EU's institutions and the processes by which they make and carry out its laws.

Chapter 7
VALUES AND OBJECTIVES

The underpinnings of any organisation are the guiding principles on which it is based and the goals it will pursue. Both the EC Treaty and the Treaty on European Union contain broad statements of values and objectives,[352] and the drafters of the Lisbon Treaty have amplified on these expressions. However, in all of the documents the authors have chosen to include affirmations of the Member States and their separate traditions as an integral part of the expressed intentions for the Union.

1.   VALUES UNDERLYING THE EU

1.1   Shared values

The TEU contains several clear expressions of the EU's values. Its Preamble confirms the principles of "liberty, democracy and respect for human rights and fundamental freedoms and of the rule of law." It also affirms the importance of "fundamental social rights" and "solidarity" between the "peoples" of the Member States. TEU Article 6(1) contains the broadest and most significant statement: "The Union is founded on the principles of liberty, democracy, respect for human rights and fundamental freedoms, and the rule of law."

According to Article 49 of the TEU, any European state that respects the principles of Article 6(1) may apply for Union membership, and indeed, the accession process should include careful scrutiny of a candidate country's human rights record. Once membership is achieved, a Member State must adhere to these values, and TEU Article 7 provides that any Member State which is in "serious and persistent breach" of these values may have its treaty rights suspended, including its voting rights on the Council.

The EC Treaty tends to speak of goals and objectives, but values are implicit when its Preamble refers to "solidarity," "prosperity" and "peace and liberty." Likewise, Article 2 mentions "social protection," "equality between men and women," and "economic and social cohesion and solidarity among Member States." However, the primary thrust of the first 6 articles of the EC Treaty is values relating to the economic sphere. For example, Article 2 mentions "a harmonious, balanced and sustainable development of economic activities," while Article 4(1) emphasises "the principle of an open market economy with free competition." Article 6 ties in the concept of environmental protection.

---

[352] See EC Treaty Preamble; EC Treaty Arts. 2-6; TEU Preamble; TEU Arts. 1-3, 6.

The Lisbon Treaty adds a new recital to the TEU, emphasising the "cultural, religious and humanist inheritance of Europe" and the "universal values of the inviolable and inalienable rights of the human person, democracy, equality, freedom and the rule of law."[353] The treaty also inserts a new TEU provision to replace existing Article 6(1) as the basic expression of EU values.[354] The new article identifies the core values as "respect for human dignity, liberty, democracy, equality, the rule of law and respect for human rights, including the rights of persons belonging to minorities." In addition, the provision states: "These values are common to the Member States in a society in which pluralism, non-discrimination, tolerance, justice, solidarity, and equality between women and men prevail."

The Union and its institutions are called upon in the Lisbon Treaty to promote EU values.[355] These principles are to be the foundation for the EU's international actions[356] and for its relationships with its neighboring countries.[357] In addition, Member States may be requested to take action to "protect the Union's values and serve its interests."[358]

Certain of the values and concepts mentioned in the Lisbon Treaty are unprecedented. These include the new TEU Preamble reference to the "cultural, religious and humanist inheritance of Europe" and the statement regarding "the rights of persons belonging to minorities." Overall, the Lisbon Treaty expands somewhat the tone and content of the description of EU values. The additional emphasis may be seen as stylistic, but in an age in which substantial immigrant populations have developed throughout the Union, the reference to the rights of minorities is particularly appropriate.

Among the more interesting European values are two references that were not included in the Constitution or the Lisbon Treaty. These documents contain no reference to God and no mention of the Christian heritage of Europe. Such concepts were proposed and vigorously debated at the constitutional Convention,[359] but to no avail. Under the Lisbon Treaty the TEU Preamble will contain the bland but more inclusive opening line acknowledging that the Member States are "drawing inspiration from the cultural, religious and humanist inheritance of Europe." These references may constitute an acknowledgment that Christianity is no longer the force that it has been in the past, or they may be tailored to make the millions of Muslim immigrants or a nation such as Turkey feel more at home in the Union. In any event, the agreed statements reflect a secular approach at the EU level, akin to the official stance and status of the French government.[360]

---

[353] Lisbon Treaty Art. 1(1).

[354] Id. Art. 1(3).

[355] Id. Arts. 1(4)(1), 1(14)(1).

[356] Id. Arts. 1(4)(5), 1(24)(1), 1(24)(2), 1(26)(1).

[357] Id. Art. 1(10)(1).

[358] Id. Art. 1(49)(c)(5).

[359] Jean-Claude Piris, The Constitution for Europe – A Legal Analysis, 131 (2006).

[360] The editorial committee of the Common Market Law Review has commented on the sought-after reference to the Christian heritage of Europe: "At a strictly legal level, the debate is of little interest and the

1.2   National traditions

The TEU Preamble mentions the "peoples" (not "people") of Europe in three separate statements: first, the Member States share a desire "to deepen the solidarity between their peoples while respecting their history, their culture and their traditions;" second, they have a goal of "economic and social progress for their peoples;" and third, they strive for "an ever closer union among the peoples of Europe." TEU Article 1 again mentions the ever closer union of the "peoples," as well as consistency and solidarity in relations "between the Member States and their peoples." The Member States and their values are particularly emphasised in TEU Article 6(1), which recites the Union's core values and notes that they are "common to the Member States." Article 6(2) also speaks of human rights "as they result from the constitutional traditions common to the Member States."

The Preamble to the EC Treaty also refers to the "peoples" of Europe and states the goal of economic and social progress "of their countries." Article 2 looks for "solidarity among Member States" and "the flowering of the cultures of the Member States."

In its re-working of the Union's statement of values, the Lisbon Treaty preserves the TEU's statement that core EU values are "common to the Member States."[361] It also adds to the EC Treaty a novel provision declaring Union respects for churches, religious associations or communities in the Member States." The same provision respects the position that non-religious organisations may enjoy under national law. Further, the EU is required to maintain dialogue with nationally recognized churches and organisations.[362]

The provisions mentioned in this section illustrate how the treaty drafters have sought to define the Union while at the same time offering reminders of the importance of the Member States and their values and traditions. The Treaties are first and foremost the constituent documents of the Community and the Union, and yet there is an apparent need for well-placed reminders that the EU should not be spoken of as an entity on its own – its identity is still tied up with the separate identities and integrity of the Member States. Commenting on use of the word "peoples" rather than the singular form "people," Kalypso Nicolaidis argues that the word choice is appropriate to emphasise that a homogeneous European community is not necessary. "Our European demoi-

---

question of the origins of Europe is a matter for historians. At a political level, it is extremely sensitive. A reference to religious origins can entail reservations from States which are strictly secular as well as the opposition of those who consider that the traditions inherited from the enlightenment are at least equally valuable. A reference to the Christian origin rightly causes indignation among non-Christian religions, whose contribution to the development of Europe has been important." Editorial Comments, A Constitution for Europe, 41 C.M.L.R. 899, 903 (2004).

[361] Lisbon Treaty Art. 1(3).

[362] Id. Art. 2(30). For a scathing criticism of the Constitution's identical provision, see Nicola Giovannini, The Draft European Constitution and its antisecular article 51, 42 Am. Atheist Mag. 39 (March 22, 2004).

cracy is predicated on the mutual recognition, confrontation and ever more demanding sharing of our respective and separate identities – not on their merger."[363]

2.   UNION OBJECTIVES

2.1   A wide-ranging set of internal and external objectives for the EU

a.   *General statements in preambles*
The Preamble to the TEU speaks of "a new stage in the process of European integration" and a deepening of solidarity between the peoples of the Member States. There is a desire to "enhance further the democratic and efficient functioning of the [EU] institutions," to "achieve the strengthening and convergence of their economies" and to accomplish monetary union, economic and social progress, EU citizenship, a common foreign policy and a common defence. The objectives are summarised as a desire to "continue the process of creating an ever closer union among the peoples of Europe." TEU Article 1 repeats the goal of "an ever closer union among the peoples of Europe."

The Preamble to the EC Treaty also mentions an "ever closer union among the peoples of Europe," while affirming as the "essential objective" of the efforts of the Member States "the constant improvements of the living and working conditions of their peoples." Many of the broad statements in this Preamble focus on the goals of the internal market, but there is also recognition of the need for the states to "strengthen peace and liberty" and to "promote the development of the highest possible level of knowledge for their peoples through a wide access to education."

The Treaties both express a goal of achieving "ever closer union" among the Member States. The Constitution would have dropped the phrase. Interestingly, the Lisbon Treaty does not delete these words, even though the treaty amendment is viewed as somewhat of a retreat from the level of integration suggested in the name and concept of a "constitution."[364]

b.   *Specific objectives within the EU*
Article 2 of the TEU lists a number of objectives for the EU, which the Union must promote, achieve, create, strengthen, establish, maintain and develop:
–   economic and social progress,
–   a high level of employment,
–   balanced and sustainable development,
–   an area without internal frontiers,

---

[363] Nicolaidis, *supra* note 55, at 5.

[364] In announcing its decision to replace the Constitution with a new treaty revision, the European Council stated that "the constitutional concept, which consisted in repealing all existing Treaties and replacing them by a single text called 'Constitution', [was] abandoned." 2007 Presidency Conclusions, *supra* note 146.

- strengthening of economic and social cohesion,
- establishment of economic and monetary union, including a single currency,
- implementation of a CFSP,
- framing of a common defence policy,
- protection of the rights and interests of Member State nationals through offering EU citizenship, and
- an AFSJ.

TEU Article 2 also stresses the need to maintain the full *acquis communautaire* of the Community. Article 2 is then supplemented by a number of provisions in the TEU and in the EC Treaty. TEU Article 6 calls upon the Union to respect:
- human rights and fundamental freedoms,
- the rule of law, and
- the national identities of the Member States.[365]

TEU Article 3 notes that the Union, in seeking to meet its objectives, must act "while respecting and building upon the *acquis communautaire.*"
    Article 2 of the EC Treaty calls on the EU to promote all of the following within the Community:
- a harmonious, balanced and sustainable development of economic activities,
- a high level of employment and of social protection,
- equality between men and women,
- sustainable and non-inflationary growth,
- a high degree of competitiveness and convergence of economic performance,
- a high level of protection and improvement of the quality of the environment,
- the raising of the standard of living and quality of life, and
- economic and social cohesion and solidarity among Member States.

EC Treaty Article 3 lists the activities of the Community, and this list includes further emphasis on principles such as strengthening of economic and social cohesion and elimination of inequalities between men and women. It also offers a wide-ranging set of specific objectives:
- elimination of restrictions in trade among the Member States,
- a common commercial policy,
- free movement of goods, persons, services and capital,
- common policies or "measures" in agriculture, fisheries, transport, environment, industry competitiveness, consumer protection, energy, civil protection and tourism,
- regulation of competition,
- approximation of Member State laws to support the internal market,
- coordination of employment policies,

---

[365] TEU Art. 6(1), (2), (3).

- a European Social Fund,
- economic and social cohesion,
- promotion of research, technological development and trans-European networks,
- a high level of health protection,
- contributing to education, training and culture, including a "flowering of the cultures of the Member States,"
- development cooperation, and
- cooperation with overseas countries and territories.

Article 6 of the EC Treaty emphasises environmental protection as a Community
goal, as well as promotion of sustainable development. Many other sections of the EC
Treaty state or imply objectives in relation to particular substantive programmes of
the Community.

Because Union objectives are scattered throughout the substantive provisions of
the Treaties, the above lists are not exhaustive. Rather, they focus on the objectives as
stated in the introductory articles of the documents. Against this backdrop the Lisbon
Treaty engages in a great deal of "clean up" and restructuring. TEU Article 2 is completely re-written, although most of its objectives are preserved.[366] TEU Article 3 is
eliminated, and its Article 6 respect for the national identities of the Member States is
expressed in a new provision that also proclaims the "equality of the Member States
before the Treaties."[367] The lists of EC Treaty objectives identified above (EC Treaty
Articles 2 and 3) are deleted,[368] although Article 6 remains. In addition, new EC Treaty
articles focus on employment, social protection, education and health,[369] as well as
elimination of all forms of discrimination.[370]

The primary approach of the Lisbon Treaty is to consolidate the broad statements
of objectives and eliminate redundancies. However, several items in the Lisbon Treaty are new. Where the current texts emphasise equality between men and women, the
Lisbon Treaty calls for a general end to social exclusion and discrimination, solidarity
between generations, protection of the rights of the child[371] and combating discrimination based on sex, racial or ethnic origin, religion or belief, disability, age or sexual
orientation.[372] However, note that the expanded list of prohibited bases for discrimination is already contained in the Charter of Fundamental Rights endorsed by the EU.[373]
A general objective of animal welfare is another innovation,[374] although protection of

---

[366] Lisbon Treaty Art. 1(4).
[367] Id. Art. 1(5)(2).
[368] Id. Art. 2(11), 2(14).
[369] Id. Art. 2(17).
[370] Id. Art. 2(18).
[371] Id. Art. 1(4).
[372] Id. Art. 2(18).
[373] See the discussion in Part 3 of this chapter.
[374] Lisbon Treaty Art. 2(21).

animals is mentioned in the EC Treaty,[375] and the Lisbon Treaty incorporates language already found in a protocol to the treaty.[376] Additionally, the Lisbon Treaty's statement of respect for the Union's cultural and linguistic diversity[377] is a new and sharper statement compared to the EC Treaty's goal of a flowering of the Member State cultures.

c. *Goals for the EU's external relations*

Article 2 of the Treaty on European Union includes as an EU objective that the Union should "assert its identity on the international scene," and TEU Article 3 calls for "consistency of its external activities as a whole." The goals for this external activity may be found in TEU Article 11, which introduces the provisions on the Union's CFSP.[378] Article 11 states the objectives of the CFSP to be the safeguarding, strengthening, preservation, promotion or development of the following:

– common values, fundamental interests, independence and integrity of the Union in conformity with the principles of the United Nations Charter,
– the security of the Union in all ways,
– peace,
– international security,
– international cooperation,
– democracy and the rule of law, and
– respect for human rights and fundamental freedoms.

The Lisbon Treaty removes the list of objectives from Article 11 of the TEU, which relates only to the CFSP. In its place, the treaty amendment creates three new provisions for the TEU that express goals for all of the Union's external activity, not just the CFSP. In the first of these the goals are stated to be:

– peace,
– security,
– the sustainable development of the Earth,
– solidarity and mutual respect among peoples,
– free and fair trade,
– eradication of poverty,
– protection of human rights, in particular the rights of the child, and
– strict observance and development of international law, including respect for the United Nations Charter.[379]

---

[375] EC Treaty Art. 30.
[376] Protocol on protection and welfare of animals, November 10, 1997, O.J. (C 340/110) (hereafter Protocol on Animals).
[377] Lisbon Treaty Art. 1(4)(3).
[378] See TEU Arts. 11-28 (describing the CFSP).
[379] Lisbon Treaty Art. 1(4)(2)(5).

The second provision requires the Union to develop a "special relationship" with its neighbouring countries to promote "prosperity and good neighbourliness" based on the core EU values and "close and peaceful relations."[380]

The third new article retains the existing Article 11 goals and adds several new objectives, such as:

– sustainable economic, social and environmental development of developing countries,
– integration of all countries into the world economy,
– sustainable development of global natural resources, and protection of the environment, and
– assistance to countries facing disasters.[381]

Overall, the expanded list of external goals seems to be a sensible reflection of the scope of current EU interests and activities on the world scene. The Lisbon Treaty may represent an updated description of the EU's objectives, but its formulation cannot be seen as a meaningful change in EU policy.

d.   *Who is charged with achieving the objectives?*

Article 3 of the TEU requires the institutions of the EU to "ensure the consistency and the continuity of the activities carried out in order to attain [the Union's] objectives." Article 3 then mentions consistency in the Union's external activities, suggesting without explicitly stating that such activities must also meet Union objectives. Where TEU Article 43 permits programmes of enhanced cooperation among groups of Member States, the programmes must be "aimed at furthering the objectives of the Union and of the Community." Article 10 of the EC Treaty requires the Member States to "facilitate the achievement of the Community's tasks" and to "abstain from any measure which could jeopardise the attainment of the objectives of this Treaty."

The Lisbon Treaty replaces TEU Article 3 with a new provision that broadly requires the EU institutions to "promote its values [and] advance its objectives."[382] At the same time, a new TEU provision replaces EC Treaty Article 10 in calling upon the Member States to "facilitate the achievement of the Union's tasks."[383] In another newly formulated provision, the Lisbon Treaty retains the mandate of TEU Article 43 that programmes of enhanced cooperation – which arguably undercut the solidarity of the EU – must further Union objectives.[384] Overall, the Lisbon Treaty's changes are stylistic, and the substance of the Treaties is retained with respect to which parties must pursue Union objectives.

---

[380] Lisbon Treaty Art. 1(10)(1).
[381] Id. Art. 1(24)(10A)(1).
[382] Id. Art. 1(14)(1).
[383] Id. Art. 1(5)(3). EC Treaty Art. 10 is repealed by Art. 2(22) of the Lisbon Treaty.
[384] Id. Art. 1(22)(1).

2.2   EU objectives and the Member States

The Union's objectives, as described in the current Treaties, are logically focused on what the EU should accomplish. However, the Treaties also contain reminders that EU activities are to be influenced by the separate identities of the Member States. For example, the preambles of both Treaties mention the welfare and progress of the "peoples" of Europe, rather than a single European citizenry. TEU Article 6 emphasises respect for national identities as a Union objective, while EC Treaty Article 2 looks for solidarity among the Member States, and its Article 3 seeks the flowering of the cultures of the states. Article 10 of the EC Treaty anticipates an active role by the Member States, requiring them to "facilitate the achievement of the Community's tasks." At the same time, TEU Article 11(2) speaks of the Member States supporting the Union's CFSP and working together to "enhance and develop their mutual political solidarity" while refraining from any action that might impair the Union's effectiveness internationally.

The Lisbon Treaty adds some new emphasis to the role of the Member States *vis-à-vis* the Union's objectives. Article 1 of the TEU is supplemented by a statement that the Member States confer competences on the Union "to attain objectives they [the Member States] have in common."[385] The pursuit of Union objectives is expressly limited by this principle of conferral.[386] Another new TEU provision requires the EU to promote "solidarity among Member States," while respecting Europe's "cultural and linguistic diversity."[387] The new language of the Lisbon Treaty is not dramatically different from the existing treaty language, but it offers a somewhat greater level of recognition to the Member States as separate parties who have a relationship to Union objectives. Despite the Lisbon Treaty's new wording, a similar approach in the Constitution was criticised. Andreas Føllesdal warned that the Constitution paid "insufficient attention to the relationship between the objectives of the Union institutions and those of Member States, and their relative importance."[388] His comments would apply equally to the Lisbon Treaty, which also lacks a definitive, well-crafted exposition of EU objectives or a careful delineation as to how exactly the Member States are to promote such objectives. However, when compared with the many specific programmes and procedures addressed in Lisbon Treaty, concerns over broad statements of objectives should be viewed as relatively insignificant.

The discussion of EU objectives would not be complete without mentioning the debate over whether the word "federal" is appropriate to describe the Union's aspirations. An early draft of the Constitution stated that the EU would "administer certain

---

[385] Lisbon Treaty Art. 1(2)(a).

[386] Id. Arts. 1(4)(6), (1)(6)(2).

[387] Id. Art. 1(4)(3).

[388] Andreas Føllesdal, Achieving Stability? Forms and Areas of Institutional and National Balances in the Draft Constitutional Treaty, The Federal Trust Online Paper 06/04, at 5, available at www.fedtrust.co.uk/uploads/constitution/06_04.pdf (hereafter Føllesdal TFT).

competences on a federal basis."[389] No doubt due to the anti-federalist sensitivities of many European leaders, who fear that federation means a stronger supranational (and correspondingly weaker intergovernmental) system, there was vigorous opposition at the Convention to the term "federal."[390] Instead, the Constitution mandated the EU to exercise its conferred competences to achieve the Union objectives "on a Community basis."[391] The "infamous F-word"[392] was never used in the Constitution in relation to Union objectives or activities. The Lisbon Treaty similarly avoids the term "federal," and happily it also discards the Euro-speak formulation "Community basis."[393]

The semantic tussle over "federal" versus "Community" is reminiscent of the delicate and somewhat confusing use of words in the opening provisions of the Treaty on European Union. Article 1 of the TEU creates the new Union, which is "founded" on the existing European Communities, but "supplemented by the policies and forms of cooperation established by this Treaty." Thus, both a supranational "community" approach and an intergovernmental "union" approach are contemplated. Article 2 reiterates this duality by calling on the new Union to "maintain in full the [Communities'] *acquis communautaire*" (essentially perpetuating the supranational First Pillar regime) but also to "build on" the *acquis* by creating the new, more intergovernmental Second and Third Pillars.[394] However, Article 2 notes that this dual task of "maintenance" and "building on" is to be done "with a view to considering to what extent the policies and forms of cooperation introduced by this Treaty may need to be revised with the aim of ensuring the effectiveness of the mechanisms and institutions of the Community." This suggests that the intergovernmental Union may gradually yield to Community approach, and to some extent it has done exactly that, especially in the Third Pillar.[395] The tension between the intergovernmental and supranational

---

[389] The Preliminary Draft of the Constitution described "[a] Union of European States which, while retaining their national identities, closely coordinate their policies at the European level, and administer certain competences on a federal basis." Praesidium of The European Convention, Preliminary Draft Constitutional Treaty, October 28, 2002, CONV 369/02, Part One, Art. 1.

[390] Kokott & Rüth, *supra* note 87, at 1321. Kokott and Rüth note that the term "constitution" was "especially for the British, as much a taboo as the term 'federal' itself. It seems, therefore, all the more remarkable that the Convention, backed by the political momentum of its convocation, quite quickly managed to raise the necessary support for picking up the Laeken reference to a 'constitutional text' and, in the end, by calling the text a 'Treaty establishing a Constitution' even went beyond what was terminologically expected until very recently." Id. at 1320. The Lisbon Treaty abandons the name "constitution."

[391] Constitution Art. I-1(1).

[392] Markus G. Puder, Constitutionalizing the European Union – More Than a Sense of Direction From the Convention on the Future of Europe, 26 Fordham Int'l L.J. 1562, 1583 (2003).

[393] Kalypso Nicolaidis argues that the word "federal" might appropriately be used for the EU in its current form, but in the sense of a "federal union, not as a federal state." He concedes that the phrase "Community way" is "an acceptable second best." Nicolaidis, *supra* note 55, at 6.

[394] Note that TEU Art. 3 also refers to "respecting and building upon the *acquis communautaire.*"

[395] The Treaty of Amsterdam caused matters such as visas, asylum and immigration policies, as well as civil law cooperation, to be transferred from the Third Pillar to the First Pillar. See Jaap W. de Zwaan, The Legal Personality of the European Communities and the European Union, in Vol. XXX Netherlands Yearbook of International Law 75, 94-95 (1999) [hereafter De Zwaan 1999].

theories is evident in these provisions of the TEU, and the Convention's struggle over the word "federal" seems to have reflected the ongoing debate. As a textual matter the Lisbon Treaty sidesteps these issues by deleting the TEU Article 1 and 2 references to the Communities and their *acquis*.[396] Nevertheless, Lisbon does preserve the procedural differentiation between the First and Second Pillars.

3.   PROTECTION OF THE RIGHTS OF INDIVIDUALS

3.1   A complex EU approach to individual rights

The Treaties' approach to individual rights has been multi-faceted and far from cohesive. The Preamble of the TEU affirms the EU's "respect for human rights and fundamental freedoms." TEU Article 6(1) notes that these are founding principles of the Union. Article 11(1) of the TEU states that respect for human rights and fundamental freedoms is to be an objective of the Union's CFSP. EC Treaty Article 177(2) states that respect for such rights is an objective of the Community's activities in the field of development cooperation, and Article 181a(1) of the EC Treaty states a similar goal for Community action in the field of economic, financial and technical cooperation with third countries.

Beyond these general affirmations, TEU Article 6(2) states that the EU must respect the rights granted by the European Convention for the Protection of Human Rights and Fundamental Freedoms (ECHR).[397] However, in 1996 the Court of Justice ruled that the Community lacked competence to become a signatory to the Convention.[398] In response to this limitation, the Union in 2000 took steps to adopting its own bill of rights, the Charter of Fundamental Rights of the European Union.[399] However, the Charter was not incorporated into the Treaties, but was adopted as a "solemn proclamation."[400] The result has been an uneasy co-existence between the ECHR and the Charter, with neither one being fully incorporated into EU law. As a further tension, the ECHR is to be enforced by the European Court of Human Rights in Stras-

---

[396] See Lisbon Treaty Arts. 1(2), 1(4).

[397] "The Union shall respect fundamental rights, as guaranteed by the European Convention for the Protection of Human Rights and Fundamental Freedoms . . . as general principles of Community law." TEU Art. 6(2). See ECHR, November 4, 1950, 213 U.N.T.S. 221, 221 (entered into force September 3, 1953).

[398] The Court declared: "As Community law now stands, the Community has no competence to accede to the European Convention for the Protection of Human Rights and Fundamental Freedoms because no provision of the Treaty confers on the Community institutions in a general way the power to enact rules concerning human rights or to conclude international agreements in this field . . .''. Case 2/94, Accession by the Community to the ECHR, Advisory Opinion, 1996 ECR I-1759. For commentary on the EU's accession to the ECHR, see Jacqueline Dutheil de la Rochère, The EU and the Individual: Fundamental Rights in the Draft Constitutional Treaty, 41 C.M.L.R. 345, 352-53 (2004).

[399] Charter of Fundamental Rights, *supra* note 213.

[400] Id. at 3. For a background perspective on the Charter, along with a review of the EU's experience to date with the Charter and with human rights in general, see Dutheil de la Rochère, *supra* note 398.

bourg (an independent, non-EU institution), while respect for the Charter is a matter of interpretation by the Union's Court of Justice.[401] To add to the complications of this situation, the Charter requires the Court of Justice to follow the interpretations issued by the European Court of Human Rights in cases which the Charter's provisions correspond with provisions of the ECHR.[402]

Various commentators have criticised this state of affairs, noting that the EU should create more clarity and certainty by incorporating a declaration of human rights as part of its treaty framework.[403] As the Charter was being adopted, Youri Devuyst warned that it would be a "mere political declaration" if it were not incorporated into the Treaties.[404] Markus Puder has argued that either having the EU accede to the ECHR or incorporating the Charter into the EU Treaties would "enhance the protection of citizens' rights . . . and forcefully assert ethical and moral values within the integration system."[405] "Bolstering the fundamental rights at the European level has been described by Georgio Sacerdoti as a "crucial" factor in combating recent electoral successes of "racist and xenophobic" parties in countries such as Austria and Belgium.[406]

In response to such criticism, the Laeken Declaration challenged the Convention to consider whether the Charter should be included in the Treaties or whether the EU should accede to the ECHR.[407] The Convention decided to do both. The full text of the Charter was included as Part II of the Constitution,[408] and a constitutional provision required the Union to accede to the ECHR.[409] In addition, the Constitution incorporated

---

[401] For an extensive analysis of the EU's relationship to the ECHR and the Charter, and the complex jurisdictional issues involving the European Court of Human Rights and the Court of Justice, see Sacerdoti, *supra* note 213.

[402] Charter of Fundamental Rights, *supra* note 213, Art. 52(3). For an analysis of the Charter and the ECHR as "complementary instruments," see Ingolf Pernice, Integrating the Charter of Fundamental Rights into the Constitution of the European Union: Practical and Theoretical Propositions, 10 Colum. J. Eur. L. 5, 12-16 (2004).

[403] For an analysis of the Charter "in the context of the much broader, less easily captured, and often slippery notion of European constitutionalism," see Gráinne de Búrca & Jo Beatrix Aschenbrenner, European Constitutionalism and the EU Charter of Fundamental Human Rights, 9 Colum. J. Eur. L. 355 (2003); see also Joseph H. H. Weiler, Human rights, constitutionalism and integration, in Eriksen, *supra* note 4, at 59; Neil Walker, The Charter of Fundamental Rights of the EU: Legal, Symbolic and Constitutional Implications, in Zervakis, *supra* note 4, at 119.

[404] Devuyst, *supra* note 39, at 49.

[405] Puder, *supra* note 392, at 1584. Puder notes that other alternatives would be to simply refer to the Charter in the EU Treaties or to adopt the Charter as sub-constitutional EU legislation. Id.

[406] Sacerdoti, *supra* note 213, at 51.

[407] Laeken Declaration, *supra* note 114, at 24. For an analysis of the suitability of the Charter as a Bill of Rights in the Constitution, see Sionaidh Douglas-Scott, The Charter of Fundamental Rights as a Constitutional Document, 2004 Eur. Hum. Rts. L. Rev. 37, 42-48 (2004).

[408] Ingolf Pernice has commented: "Inserting the Charter into [the Constitution] . . . is not only an important step in the process of constitutionalization of the European Union, but will affirm its very foundation. It will draw the citizens' attention to their fundamental role in this process, and to their responsibilities in an integrated Europe." Pernice, *supra* note 402, at 8.

[409] Constitution Art. I-9(2). For a thoughtful analysis of how the Charter, as Part II of the Constitution, will deal with the status of individuals under the law, see Guido Alpa, The Meaning of 'Natural Person' and

as "general principles of the Union's law" the fundamental rights resulting "from the constitutional traditions common to the Member States."[410] In substance, the Lisbon Treaty follows the Constitution's three-pronged approach of adopting the Charter, requiring accession to the ECHR and recognising Member State traditions.[411] However, the new treaty does not insert the full text of the Charter into the TEU or EC Treaty. Rather, it states that the Charter "shall have the same legal value as the Treaties."[412] Significantly, a protocol to the Lisbon Treaty also limits the application of the Charter in Poland and the United Kingdom.[413]

The current Treaties do recognise respect for human rights as a fundamental principle of the European Union. Nevertheless, the Lisbon Treaty's steps to formalize such rights – accompanied by the prospect that the Court of Justice might take a more active role in their interpretation – are among the new treaty's most significant proposals. In an era of increasing international attention to genocide and other human rights violations, the EU Member States have taken steps to update the Union's commitment to long-accepted core principles.

3.2   Member State law and practice in human rights

The current Treaties offer no more than passing reference to Member State practice in the field of human rights. TEU Article 6(1) states that respect for human rights and fundamentals is a founding principle of the Union, but also a principle "common to the Member States." Article 6(2) mandates the EU to respect "as general principles of Community law" the fundamental rights as guaranteed by the ECHR, but also "as they result from the constitutional traditions common to the Member States." Reflecting concerns over local religious rights and customs, a protocol to the EC Treaty requires the Union to respect the laws and traditions of the Member States with regard to the treatment of animals.[414] The Lisbon Treaty amplifies these acknowledgements of national traditions.

In the Lisbon Treaty's basic statement of EU values, respect for human rights is prominently included, and all of the core values are described as "common to the Member States."[415] The new treaty also retains the TEU statement that fundamental rights arising from Member State constitutional traditions serve as general principles of EU law.[416] Furthermore, the "enacting terms" of the existing EC Treaty protocol

---

the Impact of the Constitution for Europe on the Development of European Private Law, 10 Eur. L.J. 734, 747-749 (2004).

[410] Constitution Art. I-9(3).

[411] Lisbon Treaty Art. 1(8).

[412] Id. Art. 1(8)(1).

[413] Protocol on the application of the Charter of Fundamental Rights of the European Union to Poland and to the United Kingdom, Lisbon Treaty, December 3, 2007, CIG 14/07, TL/P/en 17.

[414] Protocol on Animals, *supra* note 376.

[415] Lisbon Treaty Art. 1(3).

[416] Id. Art. 1(8)(3).

relating to national traditions and the treatment of animals are transposed into the Lisbon text.[417] The most prominent development, however, is the elevation of the Charter to a position of the same legal value as the Treaties. The significance of this step is that the Charter itself contains numerous references to Member State laws and principles.

In the Charter, Article 14(3) states that the right to education is to be respected "in accordance with the national laws governing the exercise of such freedom and right." Under Article 16 the right to conduct business is recognised, but "in accordance with Union law and national laws and practices." The same joint reference to EU law and national norms is found in three provisions relating to certain rights of workers[418] and in Article 34 regarding rights relating to social security and social assistance. Moreover, under Articles 35 and 36, health care rights and rights of "access to services of general economic interest" are tied to "the conditions established by national laws and practices."

In the general provisions at the end of the Charter, Article 51 places emphasis on the principle of subsidiarity and on the limits of Union competence. In forceful terms Article 51(2) states that the Charter "does not establish any new power or task for the Community or the Union, or modify powers or tasks defined by the Treaties."[419] Article 53 also prohibits any interpretation of its provisions in a manner that would adversely affect human rights recognised elsewhere by Union law, by international agreements to which the EU or States may be party, or by Member State constitutions.

The Lisbon Treaty's treatment of human rights is more comprehensive than that of the current Treaties, but its approach may be too complicated.[420] The primary concern is that when the Charter, the ECHR and especially the "constitutional traditions common to the Member States" all become part of EU foundational law, then anyone analysing fundamental rights in the Union will face the daunting task of studying a

---

[417] Lisbon Treaty Art. 2(21). The Protocol requires to respect "the legislative or administrative provisions and customs of the Member States relating in particular to religious rites, cultural traditions and regional heritage." Protocol on Animals, *supra* note 376.

[418] Charter of Fundamental Rights, *supra* note 213, Arts. 27, 28, 30.

[419] Two commentators have noted that "the General Provisions of the Charter [such as Art. 51(2)] are very clear in their intention not to confer additional competences on the EU . . . Whether respect for human rights becomes a more significant normative orientation of the EU legal order or whether these values remain (as some of those involved in drafting the Charter have expressly wished) more as a negative constraint on political action, remains to be seen." De Búrca & Aschenbrenner, *supra* note 403, at 380-81.

[420] Regarding the Constitution's similar approach, one commentator has stated: "A first reading of the Draft Constitution gives an impression of an accumulation of references to rights and values, not contradictory but, in my view, excessively cumulative, and therefore unable to promote a clear idea of the ambition of the Union for the individual." Dutheil de la Rochère, *supra* note 398, at 350. For analysis of the various components of the EU's human rights regime, see id., at 350-54. For further discussion of the complexities of the Charter in relation to other sources of human rights law, see Claudia Attucci, An institutional dialogue on common principles – Reflections on the significance of the EU Charter of Fundamental Rights, in Dobson, *supra* note 4, at 151-63.

myriad of legal texts.[421] In addition, it has been argued that consideration of Member State sources of law could undermine the primacy of EU law.[422] There will likely be a need for a series of decisions by the Court of Justice to sort out any inconsistencies among these sources of law, and the Court may well be required to set rules of priority among them. Overall, the elevation of the Charter to treaty status is a significant development despite its attendant complexities.

4. VALUES, OBJECTIVES AND THE DIVIDING LINES

It is perhaps a bit easy to dismiss statements of values and objectives as mere "window dressing" intended to make the Treaties more attractive to the masses while offering nothing of legal substance. This may be more true for broad values than for specific objectives. Nevertheless, lawyers and politicians could be expected at some point to find useful material in such statements, whether for use in courtroom arguments or in the conference rooms of Brussels. Where substantive legal text is not precise, persuasive arguments can be made on the basis of value expressions. Court decisions or new programmes might be justified by constitutional or treaty provisions that reveal the intentions of those who drafted and ratified the document.

The Lisbon Treaty essentially restates the values and objectives already found in the EC Treaty and TEU. The new treaty does pay somewhat greater attention to the role of the Member States as participants in the pursuit of common objectives, and a few of its phrases – such as references to minorities and to the "cultural, religious and humanist inheritance of Europe" – are novel and even controversial. However, these differences could hardly be said to move any of the EU's dividing lines. The only apparent shift is created by granting treaty status to the Charter of Fundamental Rights, a development that could lead to an expansion of EU competences.

---

[421] For an analysis of the interplay between the various sources of human rights law, see Pernice, *supra* note 402, at 12-17.

[422] Michael Dougan, The Convention's Constitutional Treaty: A "Tidying-Up Exercise" that Needs Some Tidying-up of Its Own, The Federal Trust Online Paper No. 27/03, at 3, available at www.fedtrust. co.uk/uploads/constitution/27_03.pdf. Dougan was commenting on Constitution Art. II-113, which was a direct transposition of Charter Art. 53. Similar concerns have been expressed by Ingolf Pernice. See Pernice, *supra* note 402, at 30-32. Also see the discussion of primacy in Part 3 of Chapter 12.

Chapter 8
THE EU'S STATE-LIKE ATTRIBUTES

If the European Union is to be more than a mere aspiration, its stated values and objectives must be given substance. The entity must exist, and it must have form and identity. In this chapter we will observe that the EU has been endowed with the characteristics of a governmental entity, including many attributes that resemble those of modern nation-states. In addition, the EU is comprised of official bodies that are similar to those found in a typical national government.[423] However, a closer look reveals a variety of carefully crafted limitations on the Union and its institutions.

1.   THE EU'S LEGAL STATUS

A number of core characteristics define the Union's legal status. These include its existence and legal personality, its legal capacity, its privileges and immunities, its permanence as an entity, and even a number of nation-like symbols it possesses. Interestingly, as these are described in the Treaties, the treaty text provides numerous reminders that the EU project does not diminish the residual sovereignty and integrity of the Member States.[424]

1.1   The legal character of the EU

a.   *Existence; legal personality*
Under the current treaties the European Community possesses legal personality, but the European Union does not. Article 281 of the EC Treaty states simply: "The Community shall have legal personality." Article 1 of the TEU states that "the HIGH CONTRACTING PARTIES establish among themselves a EUROPEAN UNION," but neither it nor any other sections of the treaty mention a grant of legal personality.

The lack of legal personality for the EU has been regarded as "one of the more pronounced oddities of the existing European treaty structure."[425] Consider, for exam-

---

[423] George Bermann has noted that the EU enjoys "a complex institutional apparatus enabling it to deliver a variety of state-like functions, among which we may discern functions broadly recognizable as law-making, law-applying, and law-enforcing. The very fact that the EU even has departments that we can liken, however approximately, to legislative, executive and judicial distinguishes it from most other such regimes. Not even the North American Free Trade Association (NAFTA), the World Trade Organization (WTO), or the International Criminal Court – which are among the best-equipped international governance regimes – are nearly as well equipped." Bermann, *supra* note 18, at 365.

[424] Bermann qualifies the statement in the immediately preceding footnote by stressing that "the Member States are far from displaced, not only as norm-givers, but as the administrative apparatus upon which the effectiveness of EU policy still chiefly depends." Id.

[425] Norman, *supra* note 123, at 84. For an extensive analysis of the legal personality of the European Communities and of the Union, see De Zwaan 1999, *supra* note 395.

ple, the question of whether the Union may enter into binding international agreements. Article 24(1) of the TEU empowers the Council to "conclude" international agreements in the Second Pillar, on the following terms:

> "When it is necessary to conclude an agreement with one or more States or international organisations in implementation of this title [Provisions on a Common Foreign and Security Policy], the Council may authorise the Presidency, assisted by the Commission as appropriate, to open negotiations to that effect. Such agreements shall be concluded by the Council on a recommendation from the Presidency."

Article 24(6) further provides: "Agreements concluded under the conditions set out by this Article shall be binding on the institutions of the Union." Historically, the Council has in fact entered into agreements under TEU Article 24,[426] but the lack of full legal personality for the EU has raised questions as to just how far the EU as an entity could proceed to legally bind itself.[427]

The Convention, working under a mandate to simplify the Treaties,[428] authored a constitutional provision that was intended to clear up these doubts.[429] The Constitution granted legal personality to the Union,[430] and its simple statement has been carried over to the Lisbon Treaty: "The Union shall have legal personality."[431] With the merger of the Community into the Union,[432] this statement covers the entire European Union.

---

[426] Two recent examples of Art. 24 agreements include Agreement between the European Union and the Swiss Confederation on the participation of the Swiss Confederation in the European Union Monitoring Mission in Aceh (Indonesia), December 31, 2005, O.J. (L 349) 30 (2005); and Agreement between the European Union and Canada establishing a framework for the participation of Canada in the European Union crisis management operations, December 1, 2005 (L 315) 20 (2005).

[427] The European Community has authority under the EC Treaty to negotiate agreements in a variety of fields. See EC Treaty Arts. 111, 133, 139, 170, 174, 181, 181a, 186, 300 and 310. Because of the clearly expressed legal personality of the Community, the binding nature of these agreements has not been questioned.

[428] Laeken Declaration, *supra* note 114, at 19, 23.

[429] Juliane Kokott and Alexandra Rüth have commented: "It might be briefly pointed out that the [Convention's] Working Group charged with the question rightly took as its starting point the assumption that the Union does indeed already at present possess an implicit international legal personality. While this was not the case under the regime of TEU, and while the situation after the reform of Amsterdam initially remained unclear due to the (deliberately) imprecise wording of the newly introduced article on treaty-making power [TEU Art. 24], the actual practice confirmed the existence of an implicit legal personality of the Union. By deciding not to perpetuate this duality with the attribution of an explicit legal personality to the Union alongside those of the Communities, but instead to merge both into a single personality and to accompany this step by a merger of the Treaties, the Convention adequately put into practice what the Laeken Declaration had implied. This must be warmly welcomed for reasons of effectiveness, legal certainty, transparency and as it heightens the profile of the Union vis-à-vis third States and European citizens." Kokott & Rüth, *supra* note 87, at 1323.

[430] Constitution Art. I-7.

[431] Lisbon Treaty Art. 1(55).

[432] Id. Art. 1(2)(b).

b.   *Legal capacity*

The legal personality described above might be labeled as an "international law personality," in that it most significantly relates to the Union's ability to enter into agreements with third countries or international organisations. A second form of personality might be called "private law personality," a status that permits the EU to be a party to private legal matters. The EC Treaty refers to this as "legal capacity,"[433] and the operative language is found in its Articles 282 and 288. Under Article 282 the Community is granted "the most extensive legal capacity accorded to legal persons" under the laws of the Member States, and in particular, the rights to own property and to be party to legal proceedings. Article 288 subjects the Community, as a legal person, to the contract law of individual Member States and to tort law based on "the general principles common to the laws of the Member States."

Neither the EC Treaty nor the TEU mentions any legal capacity for the European Union, and the Lisbon Treaty clears up this discrepancy by substituting the word "Union" for "Community" throughout the Treaties.[434] With this simple change, the operative language of EC Treaty Articles 282 and 288 will encompass the European Union as a whole.

c.   *Privileges and immunities*

The matter of privileges and immunities may be seen as both an outgrowth of the Union's legal personality and a further strengthening of the personality concept. Article 291 of the EC Treaty provides that within the territory of the Member States the Community is allowed "such privileges and immunities as are necessary for the performance of its tasks," and the treaty refers to a protocol that further delineates these privileges and immunities.[435] However, these characteristics relate to the Community only. Neither the TEU nor the EC Treaty mentions any privileges or immunities with respect to the Union. The Lisbon Treaty extends the concepts to the Union by changing the word "Community" to "Union."[436]

The concepts of legal personality for the Union, legal capacity and privileges and immunities in essence provide the Union with the status and capabilities that are afforded to any nation. In addition, with the merger of the Community into the Union the EU is able to operate as a single entity to carry out all necessary and appropriate activities within its mandate under the Treaties.

---

[433] Jaap W. de Zwaan provides a valuable description of the different forms of legal personality and how they manifest themselves in practice. See De Zwaan 1999, *supra* note 395, at 79-85.

[434] Lisbon Treaty Art. 2(2).

[435] Protocol on the privileges and immunities of the European Communities (1965), December 29, 2006, O.J. (C 321) E/318. This protocol will be amended by the Lisbon Treaty. See Lisbon Treaty, December 3, 2007, CIG 14/07, TL/P/en 53.

[436] Lisbon Treaty Art. 2(2).

d.   *A permanent entity*

Article 312 of the EC Treaty and Article 51 of the TEU state: "This Treaty is con-cluded for an unlimited period." The amendments to be instituted under the Lisbon Treaty do not affect the permanence of the Treaties, and in fact the Lisbon Treaty itself contains the same declaration.[437]

The effectiveness of the Treaties for an "unlimited period" and the continued exis-tence of the Union provide essential stability. Both now and in the future the EU is not to be reinvented, replaced or reconfigured easily. As discussed in Chapter 11 of this treatise, this permanence is arguably reinforced by the unanimity requirement for amending the Treaties. However, permanence and stability do not necessarily mean that the EU will remain forever frozen in its current form. To the contrary, the Union is designed as a flexible entity with the capacity to expand and contract,[438] and despite the unanimity requirement the Treaties can and undoubtedly will be amended.

e.   *Nation-like symbols*

The Constitution would have textually recognised certain EU symbols that are similar to those of a typical nation, including a flag, an anthem, a motto and an annual holiday, as well as the Union's currency, the euro.[439] Except for references to the euro, which is a significant achievement of the Union and a cornerstone of EU integration, the Treaties are silent as to these symbols. Article 4 of the EC Treaty refers to introduction of the single currency (called the "ecu"), and Chapters II, III and IV of Title VII of the EC Treaty[440] describe the programme for achieving the second and third stages of economic and monetary union, including numerous references to the common currency.[441] The TEU mentions the single currency in its Preamble and in the objectives stated in its Article 2.

Although several of the other EU symbols have been used under the Treaties, their formal adoption in the Constitution would have represented a conscious effort by EU leaders to institutionalise the outward manifestations that are associated primarily with nation states. The EU would have the "look and feel" of a state, and its use of the symbols was to be embedded in its Constitution.

In one of the most visible departures from the rejected Constitution, the Lisbon Treaty omits any reference to symbols, except for the euro. The European Council in June, 2007, stated emphatically that "there will be no article in the amended Treaties mentioning the symbols of the EU such as the flag, the anthem or the motto."[442]

---

[437] Lisbon Treaty Art. 3.

[438] For an analysis of the Union's flexibility, see Chapter 10.

[439] Constitution Art. I-8. The Constitution contains numerous other references to the euro. See Constitu-tion Arts. I-13, I-15, I-30, III-177, III-186, III-191, III-194 to III-198, III-326, III-410.

[440] EC Treaty Arts. 105-124.

[441] See EC Treaty Arts. 118, 119, 121, 122, 123.

[442] 2007 Presidency Conclusions, *supra* note 146, Annex I, Art. 3. For an analysis of the impact of the Constitution's symbols, see Sieberson, *supra* note 160.

1.2   The integrity of the Member States within the EU system

a.   *Equality of the Member States*
The current Treaties do not contain any direct statement affirming the equality of
the Member States. However, such equality is surely implied. The Protocol on the
Enlargement of the European Union, attached to the Treaties through the Treaty of
Nice, guarantees that Member States will be treated equally with regard to representation on the Commission when the Commission is comprised of less than one member
per Member State.[443] Furthermore, ratification and amendment of a treaty require the
consent of each Member State on an equal basis. Michael Dougan has written that the
ratification requirement "reflects one of the organising principles of the Union order –
of ultimate equality between the Member States in their capacity as Treaty authors."[444]
    The Lisbon Treaty follows the lead of the Constitution in offering a simple state-
ment of equality: "The Union shall respect the equality of Member States before the
Treaties . . .".[445] Without addressing the stature of the states *vis-à-vis* the EU itself, this
provision recognises the separate identity of each Member State. The smallest states
are entitled to all of the respect that flows toward the largest states. The constitutional
version of this provision, Constitution Article I-5, came about after a request by Por-
tuguese representatives at the Convention to have the Constitution recognize the principle of the "sovereign equality" of the States.[446] A commentary has noted:

> "This request raised drafting difficulties, because, presented in those terms, it could clash
> with the desire to reduce the number of Commissioners and could have made the question
> of voting rights more difficult to resolve. It was for those reasons that it was decided to state
> in Article I-5 the fact that the Union respected the equality of the Member States before the
> Constitution. This wording is merely the expression of the fact that the law and the Consti-
> tution apply in the same way to all. It does not prohibit discrimination provided it is objec-
> tively justified and respects the principle of proportionality. There is no doubt that the Court
> will be required to fine-tune this interpretation."[447]

One of the more sensitive political issues arising from the Convention was the formula for qualified majority voting on the Council. As discussed in Chapter 13 of this
treatise,[448] adjustments were necessary to the Convention's proposed formula in order
to achieve IGC approval first of the Constitution and later of the Lisbon Treaty. The
inescapable fact is that there are substantial variations in the populations of the EU's
Member States, ranging from more than 80 million in Germany to less than half a
million in Luxembourg and Malta. In an expanding Union it will be much more difficult to manage EU affairs on the basis of informal consensus among the Member

---

[443] Protocol on the enlargement of the European Union, December 24, 2002, O.J. (C 325) 163 Arts. 4(2),
4(3) (2002) [hereafter Protocol on Enlargement].
[444] Dougan, *supra* note 422, at 13.
[445] Lisbon Treaty Art. 1(5)(2). See Constitution Art. I-5(1).
[446] Editorial Comments, *supra* note 360, at 903.
[447] Id.
[448] See Part 3 of Chapter 13.

States, and therefore the smaller nations may justifiably be concerned about their ability to avoid being completely dominated by the larger states. The equality clause in Lisbon Treaty confirms the worth of the smaller states, although even they must recognise that in political terms their voices will not be as loud as those of the larger states.

b.   *Respect for national identities*
Article 6(3) of the TEU offers a simple mandate for the Union to "respect the national identities of the Member States." The Lisbon Treaty expands on this, and it demands that the EU shall respect the Member States' "national identities, inherent in their fundamental structures, political and constitutional . . . [and] shall respect their essential State functions, including ensuring the territorial integrity of the State, maintaining law and order and safeguarding national security."[449] This enhancement underscores the continuing importance and vitality of the Member States as sovereign nations whose national identities are manifested in the functions and structures of nationhood. As nations, they do not lose their essential character by participating in the European Union. This concept complements the notion of equality of the Member States, but again it is appropriate to acknowledge that political identity is quite a different matter from political power, whether in the EU or in the world community.

c.   *Cooperation and full mutual respect*
Under the Lisbon Treaty the Union on the one hand and the Member States on the other are required to adhere to "the principle of sincere cooperation." Pursuant to this principle, both the Union and the states must "in full mutual respect, assist each other in carrying out tasks which flow from the Treaties."[450] The phrases "sincere cooperation" and "full mutual respect" are not found in the current Treaties, but the Lisbon Treaty's words have certain antecedents. EC Treaty Article 10 requires the Member States to "take all appropriate measures, whether general or particular, to ensure fulfilment of the obligations arising out of this Treaty or resulting from action taken by the institutions of the Community." Article 10 also requires Member States to "facilitate the achievement of the Community's tasks" and to "abstain from any measure which would jeopardise the attainment of the objectives of this Treaty." Cooperation is often mentioned, but only in relation to specific policies. In the TEU, on the other hand, there is a general mandate for cooperation in Article 1, which refers to "the policies and forms of cooperation established by this Treaty." The same provision calls upon the Union to "organise, in a manner demonstrating consistency and solidarity, relations between the Member States and their peoples."

Despite some similarities with respect to cooperation, there are new emphases in the Lisbon Treaty. EC Treaty Article 10 requires the Member States to "facilitate the achievement of Community tasks," but the obligation as expressed in the treaty's text

---

[449] Lisbon Treaty Art. 1(5)(2).
[450] Id. Art. 1(5)(3).

does not flow in the other direction.[451] In TEU Article 1 the Union is mandated to "organise, in a manner demonstrating consistency and solidarity, relations between the Member States and between their peoples." In neither treaty are the EU and Member States called upon to treat each other with "full mutual respect." Thus, the Lisbon Treaty arguably increases the stature of each Member State in its dealings with the European Union. The words of new treaty appear intended to prohibit a hegemonic relationship with the EU acting in supreme power over the Member States. Rather, the expressions prescribe a partnership in which the central authority will carry out a necessary coordinating function without asserting complete dominance. The concept of full mutual respect is entirely consistent with the principles of equality of the Member States and respect for their separate national identities.

2.   CITIZENSHIP

2.1   Citizenship of the Union

A unique feature of the European Union among IGOs is its grant of EU citizenship to all the citizens of its Member States. The EC Treaty contains most of the provisions relating to this citizenship, beginning with the basic grant under Article 17. Article 18 permits EU citizens to "move and reside freely" anywhere in the EU, a benefit that Jaap W. de Zwaan has described as the "core business" of EU citizenship.[452] Article 19 grants EU citizens the right to vote and stand as a candidate in municipal elections where a person resides. Article 20 offers EU citizens the right to limited diplomatic and consular protection from other Member State governments. Article 21 ensures EU citizens the right to petition the European Parliament, the right to apply to the European Ombudsman, and the right to deal with Union institutions in any of the official EU languages, and Article 22 contemplates additional legislation on several of these matters. Article 154 offers EU citizens the "full benefit from the setting-up of an area without internal frontiers." EU citizens receive further mention in Articles 62, 191, 194, 195 and 255. In addition to these EC Treaty provisions, the Preamble of the TEU mentions the resolve "to establish a citizenship common to nationals of their countries," while TEU Article 2 speaks of "the introduction of a citizenship of the Union."

The Lisbon Treaty drops the reference to introduction of citizenship in Article 2 of the TEU,[453] because this introduction has already taken place. In the Lisbon Treaty's amendments to the EC Treaty, the citizenship provisions are reworded somewhat, but their substance is essentially preserved.[454] The primary enhancement of citizens' rights

---

[451] Note, however, that the ECJ has declared the obligation of support to be mutual. See ECJ, judgment of 6 December 1990, Case C-2/88, *J.J. Zwartveld and others*, [1990], ECR I-3365, Para. 17.

[452] Jaap W. de Zwaan, European Citizenship: Origin, Contents and Perspectives, in The EU Constitution: The Best Way Forward? 245, 247 (Deirdre Curtin, Alfred E. Kellermann & Steven Blockmans,, eds., 2005) (hereafter De Zwaan 2005).

[453] See Lisbon Treaty Art. 1(4).

[454] Lisbon Treaty Arts. 2(31)-2(38).

is found in a new title to the TEU, called "Provisions on Democratic Principles."[455] The new provisions include a statement of equality of citizens, rights to participate in EU processes, rights of representative associations and civil society, and the creation of an initiative process by which citizens may petition the Commission to propose new legislation on a particular subject.

Union citizenship under the Treaties has been interpreted in a number of decisions by the ECJ, described by Jaap W. de Zwaan as follows:

> "In fact it took the Court some time to give European Citizenship, notably the free movement dimension thereof, a proper dimension. This, however not so much with respect to *economically active* EU citizens. Indeed their situation is already governed in clear terms by the rules of the internal market, notably the provisions of the EC Treaty and secondary law concerning the free movement of workers and the right of establishment for independents.
>
> No, the developments initiated by the Court of Justice concern the scope of – what is called – *non-economic* EU citizens who claim a right of residence in another Member State . . . such as
> – persons whose status under Community law is not clear;
> – job seekers;
> – students; or
> – family members."[456]

There is no indication in the Lisbon Treaty that the Court's rulings are to be overturned, or that the scope of citizenship under the EC Treaty should be reduced. To the contrary, De Zwaan contends that under the Constitution (whose proposals are reflected in the Lisbon Treaty) EU citizenship would be "strengthened and promoted as a principle of EU law of major importance."[457] He bases this opinion not so much on the textual content of the Constitution's citizenship provisions – which in substance mirror the EC Treaty – but on the expansion of citizen rights in other parts of the constitutional text. He sees this expansion in the formal recognition of the Charter of Fundamental rights and in the "Citizen's Europe" provisions in the Constitution,"[458] which are restated in the Lisbon Treaty's "Provisions on Democratic Principles."

By definition, the members of a traditional IGO are nations, as represented by their governments. The IGO grants certain rights, privileges and services to its member states, and these benefits – such as free movement of goods and persons – may well flow through the states to their respective citizens. However, the organisation does not create a citizen class that is entitled to involvement at the IGO level. Citizens of the IGO's members do not generally expect to enjoy a direct relationship with the organisation separate and apart from their relationship with their own national government. In contrast, the EU Treaties have created a Union citizenship, and its citizens possess

---

[455] Lisbon Treaty Art. 1(12).

[456] De Zwaan 2005, *supra* note 452, at 247-48. For De Zwaan's full description of the various Court decisions, see id., at 247-52.

[457] Id. at 257.

[458] De Zwaan 2005, *supra* note 452, at 257. See Constitution Arts. I-45 to I-52.

a number of significant rights directly related to the Union and its institutions.[459] In this respect the EU is clearly distinct from a classic IGO. The Lisbon Treaty reaffirms the EU's citizenship provisions and enhances them with greater emphasis on citizen rights.

2.2   National citizenship retains its vitality

Unlike a federal nation, the EU does not offer a full, stand-alone version of citizenship. Article 17(1) of the EC Treaty states that Union citizenship "shall complement and not replace national citizenship." Article 19 limits the right to vote and stand for election in other Member States to their municipal elections and elections for the European Parliament. National and provincial elections are not mentioned, and "municipal" is not defined. Article 19 adds that voting will be subject to "the same conditions" as are applicable for nationals of the host state. In other words, the national government will be fully competent to set its own election rules. Article 19 also declares that "detailed arrangements" to further define these rights are subject to a unanimous vote on the Council. Such arrangements are also subject to "derogations where warranted by problems specific to a Member State." Article 22 anticipates EU legislation "to strengthen or add to" the citizen rights offered by the EC Treaty, but such legislation will require a unanimous vote on the Council and separate ratification by each of the Member States according to their respective constitutional requirements.

Two directives have expanded on the provisions of EC Treaty Article 19. Council Directive 93/109[460] sets forth the conditions for an EU citizen to vote or stand for election as a candidate for the European Parliament. Most of the conditions are technical in nature, but Article 14 of the Directive permits a Member State to impose restrictions (based on length of residency) if more than 20 percent of eligible voters in the state are non-nationals.[461] The second directive is Council Directive 94/80,[462] which elaborates on the rights of EU citizens to vote and stand for office in municipal elections in the Member State in which they reside. There are two interesting restrictions in this Directive. Article 12(1) permits residency-length requirements if more than 20 percent of the voters in a Member State are non-nationals, and Article 5(3) permits a Member State to limit to its own nationals the right to serve as "elected head, deputy or member of the governing college of the executive of a basic local government."[463]

---

[459] In addition to the rights described in Arts. 17-22 of the EC Treaty, EU citizens enjoy, for example, the benefits of the "four freedoms," which include free movement of goods, persons, services (with the related right of establishment) and capital. See analysis in Part 1 of Chapter 17. For a discussion of the connection between EU citizenship and the four freedoms, see Eleanor Spaventa, From Gebhard to Carpenter: Towards a (non-)economic European Constitution, 41 C.M.L.R. 743, 768-71 (2004).

[460] Council Directive 93/109/EC, December 30, 1993, O.J. (L 329) 34.

[461] Id. at Art. 14(1). For example, if the 20 percent threshold has been exceeded, a minimum residency period of up to 5 years may be imposed on non-nationals who wish to vote, and up to 10 years on non-nationals who wish to stand for election to the European Parliament.

[462] Council Directive 94/80/EC, December 31, 1994, O.J. (L 368) 38.

[463] Id. at Arts. 10(1), 5(3).

The Lisbon Treaty enhances citizens' rights at the EU level, but none of its provisions undercut the Member State protections offered in the treaty provisions and directives described in the preceding paragraphs.

In the area of citizen rights, Article 288 of the EC Treaty states that a tort claim brought against the Community by an EU citizen or any other party will be subject not to Union law but to the "general principles common to the laws of the Member States." The substance of this provision is not altered by the Lisbon Treaty. Furthermore, EC Treaty Article 20 provides that the right to diplomatic or consular assistance from another Member State is subject to "the same conditions" as would apply to nationals of the assisting state. The implication is that the assisting Member State will be entirely free to set its own rules and procedures for granting diplomatic or consular assistance both to its own nationals and to those of other EU Member States. The substance of Article 20 is also preserved by the Lisbon Treaty.

As defined in the Treaties, EU citizenship is a carefully contained concept.[464] It supplements, but does not replace the national citizenship that is offered by the Member States. An EU citizen residing in a Member State where he or she is not a national citizen may enjoy many, but not all of the political rights granted to nationals of that state. Furthermore, the EU's ability to elaborate on the right to vote or stand for election in another Member State is subject to a unanimous vote on the Council, where any Member State can exercise a veto, and further subject to "derogations where warranted by problems specific to a Member State."[465] Likewise, the EU's ability to add to the rights granted in EC Treaty Articles 17-22 is subject to both a unanimous Council vote and the additional safeguard of separate ratification by each of the Member States.[466] The potential for derogations and the requirement of unanimity represent clear limits on the authority of the EU to define the rights of its citizens beyond the principles explicitly stated in the Treaties.[467]

3. THE BUDGET

3.1 The EU's budgetary independence

The European Union is not dependent on yearly contributions from its members. Rather, Article 268 of the EC Treaty calls for an annual budget, which must be in balance, and Article 269 requires the budget to be "financed wholly from own resources." These "own resources" include customs duties on goods entering the Union, a

---

[464] For an extended analysis of the rights attached to EU citizenship, see Dennis C. Mueller, Rights and Citizenship in the European Union, in Blankart, *supra* note 29, at 61-84.

[465] EC Treaty Art. 19(1), (2).

[466] Id. Art. 22.

[467] Jaap W. de Zwaan has commented that the EC Treaty's existing ratification requirement for expansion of citizen rights is "laborious" and comparable to the process of amending the treaty. Despite the sensitivity of these matters, De Zwaan states that "one could have hoped that a lighter procedure would have been included in the [Constitution]." De Zwaan 2005, *supra* note 452, at 246, n. 5.

value added tax, fines, and earned interest.[468] As is appropriate for an organisation whose primary business is business, Article 270 requires the EU to live within its budget. Articles 271 to 280 contain details about the process of adopting the budget.

The Lisbon Treaty adds a new sentence to Article 269: "The Union shall provide itself with the means necessary to attain its objectives and carry through its policies."[469] More concretely, the new treaty creates a multiannual financial framework that will establish the approved categories of expenditures and the annual appropriations ceilings for each category for periods of at least five years.[470] This framework is intended to provide more predictability and consistency in the EU's budgeting process. In addition, under the Lisbon Treaty the European Parliament becomes a full participant in approving all aspects of the budget and in proposing amendments to it.[471] Under the current EC Treaty the Parliament's right to amend was limited to compulsory expenditures.[472] The Lisbon Treaty adds a significant boost to the role of the Parliament.

Beyond actual creation of the budget, EC Treaty Article 280 calls for Member State cooperation in countering fraud relating to the Community's financial interests. The Lisbon Treaty adds a requirement that the Member States work with the Union to ensure proper use of budgeted monies.[473]

The European Union's budgetary independence, and in particular its ability to finance its activities through its own resources, are a critical distinction between the EU and a typical IGO. An IGO has no taxing power and is typically dependent upon subscriptions, assessments or contributions from its members. Payment of such contributions may be mandated by the IGO's constituent treaty, but revenue comes only from the treasuries of the member states. The EU's financial framework is a key indicator of its unique status and its state-like nature.

3.2   Elements of Member State control over EU finances

Article 269 of the EC Treaty requires that provisions "relating to the system of own resources of the Community" are subject to both a unanimous vote on the Council and approval by the Member States in accordance with their national constitutional requirements. The Lisbon Treaty amplifies on this provision by requiring unanimity and ratification for the creation of new categories of resources and for abolishing an existing category.[474] Furthermore, according to the Lisbon Treaty, each multiannual fi-

---

[468] See Council Decision 2000/597/EC, EURATOM of 29 September 2000 on the system of the European Communities' own resources, October 7, 2000, 2000 O.J. (L 253) 42-46.

[469] Lisbon Treaty Art. 2(259)(a).

[470] Id. Art. 2(261).

[471] Id. Art. 2(265).

[472] EC Treaty Art. 272(4), second subparagraph, provides that Parliament has a right "to amend the draft budget, acting by a majority of its Members, and to propose to the Council, acting by an absolute majority of the votes cast, modifications to the draft budget relating to *expenditure necessarily resulting from this Treaty or from acts adopted in accordance therewith.*" (emphasis supplied).

[473] Lisbon Treaty Art. 2(257)(c)(5).

[474] Id. Art. 2(259)(b).

nancial framework must be unanimously approved by the Council.[475] These unanimity requirements afford each Member State a veto over the budgeting process – in other words, a significant measure of protection and national control.

One commentator has criticised the unanimity requirement in budgeting as follows: "Unanimity is now required for all relevant decisions related to own resources. Majority voting only applies to implementing measures where specifically provided for in earlier unanimous decisions. In a Union of 25, with crucial decisions on financing on the horizon, this is far from satisfactory."[476] It might be that the unanimity requirements relating to the Union's budget and own resources arise from the fact that substantial portions of the EU budget are passed along to the Member States in the form of financial support for agriculture and other programmes, and each state has great incentive to protect its share of the payment stream from Brussels.[477] But regardless of the motives or history that may lie behind the necessity for unanimity, each Member State in the Union has a voice that must be heard in the process of determining categories of own resources. Neither the EU nor a majority of the other states can force a decision upon a member that has serious reservations. As a result, the financial independence that distinguishes the EU from a typical IGO is counterbalanced with a substantial protection left in the hands of each Member State.

4.   EXTERNAL ACTION

The Treaties mandate the Union to take action in a variety of international settings and for various purposes. To these specific provisions the Lisbon Treaty adds a reference to the fact that the EU will have "relations with the wider world."[478] The external action of the EU is examined in greater detail in Chapter 17, as one of the substantive areas of the Union's activity. It is briefly referenced here as one of the significant indicia of the EU's character, namely, that its Treaties endow it with the state-like authority to carry out relations with the nations of the world and with international organisations.

As the analysis in Chapter 17 action will demonstrate, the authority of the EU to act in external matters is carefully limited, both in the existing Treaties and in the Lisbon Treaty.

---

[475] Lisbon Treaty Art. 2(261)(2). However, note that this provision permits a unanimous vote of the European Council to change the Council's unanimity approval to a qualified majority vote.

[476] Giovanni Grevi, Light and shade of a quasi-Constitution – An Assessment, EPC Issue Paper No. 14, at 8-9 (June 23, 2004), available at www.theepc.net. Implementation measures decided by QMV are provided for in EC Treaty Art. 276(1). For a socio-economic analysis of the challenges facing the EU in setting its future budgets, see Charles B. Blankart & Christian Kirchner, The Deadlock of the EU Budget: An Economic Analysis of the Ways In and Ways Out, in Blankart, *supra* note 4, at 109-38.

[477] Agriculture subsidies consume nearly half the EU budget. Chronology – EU Common Agricultural Policy, Reuters, June 26, 2003, available at www. forbes.com/business/newswire/2003/06/26/rtr1011815. html.

[478] Lisbon Treaty Art. 1(4)(5).

5.   DESCRIPTION AND MANDATE OF THE EU INSTITUTIONS

5.1   **A state-like institutional framework**

a.   *Overview of the EU institutions*
EC Treaty Article 7(1) offers a formal list of the Community institutions, including the European Parliament, Council, Commission, Court of Justice and Court of Auditors. The Economic and Social Committee and the Committee of the Regions are mentioned in Article 7(2), but notably the European Council is not listed. As a later instrument that builds on the EC Treaty, the TEU arguably does not require a specific elaboration of the institutional framework, and a formal list is not included. However, at the beginning of the TEU, in its "Common Provisions," Article 3 states: "The Union shall be served by a single institutional framework." Article 3 also mentions the Council and Commission and their responsibilities with regard to the EU's external activities. Article 4 then describes the European Council and how it operates, although it is not labeled as an EU "institution" or "body." TEU Article 5 mentions the European Parliament, Council, Commission, Court of Justice and Court of Auditors, not as part of a description of an institutional framework, but to make clear that these institutions must "exercise their powers" under both the EC Treaty and the TEU.

It is Part Five of the EC Treaty, Articles 189 to 280, that contains most of the Treaties' detail on the EU institutions. The European Parliament is covered in Articles 189 to 201, the Council in Articles 202 to 210, the Commission in Articles 211 to 219, the Court of Justice in Articles 220 to 245 and the Court of Auditors in Articles 246 to 248. Articles 249 to 256 contain provisions common to the institutions, including the co-decision procedure for legislation (Art. 251) and the cooperation procedure (Art. 252). The Economic and Social Committee is described in Articles 257 to 262, the Committee of the Regions in Articles 263 to 265, and the European Investment Bank in Articles 266 and 267. Financial provisions relating to the Community are included as the final section of Part Five, in Articles 268 to 280.

The Lisbon Treaty transfers the institutional overview from the EC Treaty to the TEU,[479] effectively constituting the TEU as the introductory document to the EC Treaty. However, the extensive details on the institutions are left in the EC Treaty.[480] It is fair to criticise the authors of the Lisbon Treaty for dividing the institutional provisions between the TEU and EC Treaty, because this separation requires the reader to move back and forth between the two documents to get the complete picture. Nevertheless, the presentation of institutional provisions in the Lisbon Treaty is an improvement over the current Treaties' more random approach.

Each of the institutions is discussed in greater detail in Chapter 13 of this treatise.

---

[479] EC Treaty Art. 7 is deleted. Lisbon Treaty Art. 2(22). The institutional overview is inserted into the TEU through Lisbon Treaty Arts. 1(13)-1(21).

[480] Lisbon Treaty Arts. 2(177)-2(280i).

b. *Institutional mandate and functions*

Article 3 of the TEU requires the Union's institutions to "ensure the consistency and the continuity of the activities carried out in order to attain [the Union's] objectives while respecting and building upon the *acquis communautaire.*" Article 3 also mentions the need for consistency in the EU's external activities and the responsibilities of the Council and Commission toward that end. The EC Treaty also contains a number of general provisions that describe the responsibilities of the Union's institutions. These provisions refer to the Community rather than the Union, but the Union is brought in through Article 1 of the TEU.[481] EC Treaty Article 5 mandates the Community to act within its conferred powers and subject to the principles of subsidiarity and proportionality. These principles are discussed in Chapter 12 of this treatise.[482] Article 7 notes that the Community's tasks are entrusted to its institutions, each of which must act "within the limits of the powers conferred upon it by this Treaty." The identified institutions are the European Parliament, the Council, the Commission, the Court of Justice and the Court of Auditors. Articles 8 and 9 expand on the institutional mandate by mentioning the European Central Bank and the European Investment Bank. Article 10 calls on the Member States to support the institutions in their work. Part Five of the EC Treaty[483] contains most of the detail on the institutions and their responsibilities, and Part Six mentions various responsibilities of the Community in general or the Council and Commission acting on behalf of the Community.[484]

According to the Lisbon Treaty, the purpose of the EU institutions is "to promote its [the EU's] values, advance its objectives, serve its interests, those of its citizens and those of the Member States, and ensure the consistency, effectiveness and continuity of its policies and actions."[485] Each institution is further called upon to act "within the limits of the powers conferred upon it in the Treaties, and in conformity with the procedures and conditions set out in them," and all of them are required to practice "mutual sincere cooperation."[486] Specific responsibilities for each institution are discussed in Chapter 13 of this treatise. One of the Lisbon Treaty's chief mandates for the institutions is to create law for the Union, using a variety of legal instruments in the course of exercising their competences.[487] These legal instruments are discussed in detail in Chapter 14 of this treatise.

A new provision in the Lisbon Treaty requires that "the Union institutions, bodies, offices and agencies shall conduct their work as openly as possible."[488] This makes concrete an aspirational statement in Article 1 of the current version of the TEU that decisions in the Union "are taken as openly as possible and as closely as possible to

---

[481] TEU Art. 1 states: "The Union shall be founded on the European Communities, supplemented by the policies and forms of cooperation established by this Treaty."

[482] See Part 2 of Chapter 12.

[483] EC Treaty Arts. 189-267.

[484] Id. Arts. 281-314.

[485] Lisbon Treaty Art. 1(14)(1).

[486] Id. Art. 1(14)(2).

[487] Id. Art. 2(235)(a).

[488] Id. Art. 2(28)(a)(1).

the citizen."[489] Another provision added by the Lisbon Treaty states that the EU Parliament must meet in public, and the Council must do so when it is "considering and voting on a draft legislative act."[490] A third measure of openness is public access to Union documents. EC Treaty Article 255 currently offers access to Community documents, although the only institutions mentioned are the Parliament, Council and Commission. The Lisbon Treaty changes this list to "the Union institutions, bodies, offices and agencies," and documents include all items, "whatever their medium."[491] Interestingly, the Lisbon Treaty's broad provisions on access to documents would include for the first time the European Council, which has heretofore operated without being subject to any obligation of transparency.

Notwithstanding the differences in how the Lisbon Treaty describes the EU institutions, it is fair to say that – with the notable exceptions of the roles of the permanent European Council President and the High Representative of the Union for Foreign Affairs and Security Policy – the new document would change very little with respect to the institutions' overall functions. The differences, if any, are discussed in detail in Chapter 13 of this treatise. The Lisbon Treaty's method of organising and describing the broad institutional mandates is different from that of the Treaties, but the substance is the generally the same. One exception is that, as noted above, the public right of access to EU documents is expanded to include all EU institutions, bodies, offices and agencies. Furthermore, as described in Chapter 14 of this treatise, the forms of legislation and regulation available for use by the EU's institutions, as prescribed by the Lisbon Treaty, represent a simplification from the varieties available under the Treaties.[492]

c.   *Authorisations granted to the EU institutions*

To support the Union's activities, EC Treaty Article 284 permits the Commission to "collect any information necessary and carry out any checks required for the performance of the tasks entrusted to it," pursuant to a decision adopted by the Council. Since qualified majority voting on the Council is not mentioned in Article 284, by default the Council's decision will be taken by a majority vote of its members.[493] Article 285(1) allows the EU to compile statistics "necessary for the performance of the activities of the Community." However, the production of statistics is subject to certain guidelines and may not "entail excessive burdens on economic operators."[494] Articles 284 and 285 are not amended by the Lisbon Treaty.

Under EC Treaty Article 283 the Union may set the employment regulations for its own officials and employees. The Lisbon Treaty clarifies the procedures involved, but it preserves the substance of the provision.[495] It is useful to note that EU employees are

---

[489]   These words in TEU Art. 1 are preserved in the Lisbon Treaty. Lisbon Treaty Art. 1(2).
[490]   Lisbon Treaty Art. 2(28)(a)(2).
[491]   Id. Art. 2(28)(b).
[492]   See analysis in Part 1 of Chapter 14.
[493]   EC Treaty Art. 205(1).
[494]   Id. Art. 285(2).
[495]   Lisbon Treaty Art. 2(282).

subject to EU regulations and are thus outside the employment laws of the Member States where the employees work. Under the Treaties the EU is given complete autonomy in this area.

The members of EU institutions and committees, along with all other Union officials and employees, are prohibited by EC Treaty Article 287 from disclosing information "of the kind covered by the obligation of professional secrecy," and this obligation continues "even after their duties have ceased." Of particular concern is information "about undertakings, their business relations or their cost components." Article 287 is left intact by the Lisbon Treaty. Interestingly, the EC Treaty does not specify the source of the "obligation of professional secrecy." Unless further EU regulatory or legislative action is taken to identify the obligation, the source might be found in Member State law or some form of generally accepted principles.

The activities of the EU institutions are subject to review by a completely independent Ombudsman, who is first mentioned in Article 21 of the EC Treaty, which identifies the rights of EU citizens. Article 195 of the treaty contains additional details regarding the office, which represents both a sounding board for EU citizens and the power of the European Parliament, who appoints him or her. The Ombudsman is to receive complaints about maladministration of Community institutions and activities, and he or she must be completely independent in carrying out this mandate. The Lisbon Treaty offers only minor adjustments to Article 195.[496] The office of the Ombudsman reflects a measure of self-sufficiency in the EU institutions. The European Parliament has the ability to appoint the Ombudsman without consulting the Member States, and the appointed person can carry out his or her responsibilities without seeking the approval of the Member States. The Ombudsman's oversight of the EU institutions takes place exclusively at the Union level.

5.2 The EU's institutions must respect the Member States

Article 6 of the TEU requires the Union to "respect the national identities of the Member States." In addition, Article 10 of the EC Treaty, which requires Member States to fulfill their treaty obligations, has been interpreted to impose on the Community a reciprocal duty of "sincere cooperation" with the Member States.[497] EC Treaty Article 5 sets forth the principles of conferral, exclusivity, subsidiarity and proportionality as a check on EU power, and the test of subsidiarity is whether EU action "cannot be sufficiently be achieved by the Member States."

The Lisbon Treaty replaces TEU Article 6 with a broader mandate for the Union to respect "the equality of the Member States before the Treaties as well as their national identities."[498] The new treaty also makes textual reference to "sincere cooperation" and "full mutual respect" between the Union and Member States.[499] Furthermore, it re-

---

[496] EC Treaty Art. 2(183).
[497] See the Court of Justice ruling in Case C-2/88, *Zwartveld*, *supra* note 451.
[498] Lisbon Treaty Art. 1(5)(2).
[499] Id. Art. 1(5)(3).

quires the EU institutions to serve the interests of the Member States.[500] The Lisbon Treaty moves the principles of conferral, subsidiarity and proportionality from the EC Treaty to the TEU, while maintaining their substance.[501] However, the Treaties' protocols on national parliaments and on subsidiarity, which have been appended to the Treaties since the Treaty of Amsterdam in 1997, are revised to provide a greater role for the Member State parliaments. These protocols are further discussed in Chapter 12 of this treatise.[502]

Although the EU does have the power to run its own affairs, Articles 289 and 290 of the EC Treaty require that certain politically sensitive issues relating to Union institutions are subject to unanimous adoption. These include decisions on the seat of Union institutions, which must be approved by "common accord of the governments of the Member States,[503] and regulations governing the official use of languages within the institutions, which must be unanimously adopted by the Council.[504] The Lisbon Treaty preserves the substance of these provisions.[505]

There are two additional means by which the residual power of the Member States *vis-à-vis* the EU institutions is affirmed in the Treaties. First, the Union's activity is limited by the powers conferred on it in the Treaties.[506] Second, the Member States must unanimously agree to amend any part of the Treaties, including the institutional provisions.[507] The Lisbon Treaty adds new emphasis that the Union's powers are conferred by the Member States.[508] Furthermore, despite new "simplified" procedures to amend the Treaties, the Lisbon Treaty preserves the requirement that all Member States agree to any amendment.[509]

6.   STATE-LIKE ATTRIBUTES AND THE DIVIDING LINES

Of the subjects addressed this chapter, the matter most likely to impact the EU's dividing lines, at least in theory, is the enhanced legal status that the Lisbon Treaty offers to the Union. Lack of legal personality for the Union (as opposed to the Community) has not really caused the Union to refrain from acting as its membership has wished, but the Union's new personality might suggest an invigorated entity that may be better able to assert itself to the world and also to its members. But is this really a movement of dividing lines, or is it just an outward makeover? It is difficult to see any shift in the EU's competences as a result of these developments. Likewise, will

---

[500] Lisbon Treaty Art. 1(14)(1).
[501] Id. Arts. 1(6), 2(16).
[502] See Part 2 of Chapter 12.
[503] EC Treaty Art. 289.
[504] Id. Art. 290.
[505] For a minor wording change to EC Treaty Art. 290, see Lisbon Treaty Art. 2(284).
[506] EC Treaty Art. 5.
[507] TEU Art. 48.
[508] See, e.g., Lisbon Treaty Arts. 1(2), 1(6). See the discussion on conferral in Part 1 of Chapter 12 of this treatise.
[509] See the discussion on treaty amendments in Chapter 11 of this treatise.

the newly articulated ability of the Union to legally bind itself in international agreements mean that it will do so more frequently? And even if it does so, will this necessarily result in an infringement on Member State competences? Given the fact that other paths are currently open for the making of such agreements, there is little reason to conclude that the Lisbon Treaty's textual clarification will result in a significant increase in this type of activity or a threat to the Member States.

On the other side of the coin, does the Lisbon Treaty's new expression of the equality of the Member States somehow imply a limitation on EU competences? This must also be answered in the negative. In general, the same conclusions are appropriate with regard to the Lisbon Treaty's revised provisions addressing citizenship, budgetary affairs, external action and institutional matters.

In short, the state-like attributes of the Union under the Lisbon Treaty are clarified and improved-upon, but they do not represent a meaningful shift in the EU's dividing lines.

Chapter 9
THE EU AS A DEMOCRACY

Historically, the Union's values and objectives and its state-like attributes have been recurring themes in the Great Debate on whether the Union is (or should be) essentially intergovernmental in nature or a federation in-the-making. This chapter will expand our consideration of one of the EU's stated values – democracy – and we will examine the democratic features embedded in the Union's processes and institutions. In an organisation itself comprised of democratic states, one might not expect that elements of democracy at the EU level would be controversial. Nevertheless, this subject has proven to be of significant interest, and it has in fact engendered philosophical disagreement.

1.   IS DEMOCRACY REALLY NECESSARY AT THE EU LEVEL?

Article 6(1) of the TEU identifies democracy as a core value of the Union. But democracy at what level? Is the intention to respect democracy within the Member States, or does it mean that democracy should be practiced within the institutions and activities of the EU itself?

We can posit that proponents of a vigorous intergovernmental theory would contend the following: The EU is and should remain a project of the Member States, with centralisation only as absolutely necessary to coordinate national action. Since the Union should be little more than a limited pooling of certain national resources, citizens of the Member States should not be very concerned about influencing the EU processes except through their national governments. Thus, democracy within the Union should flow naturally – and exclusively – from and through the democratic features of the Member States.[510] In contrast, those who espouse the federal approach would see an increasing role for the Union in the lives of individual Europeans, and this would necessitate rights and procedures at the EU level to ensure citizen control. In other words, the new legal order developing in the EU demands a democratic approach, and the Union must be structured to enhance transparency, individual partici-

---

[510] Peter Lindseth urges that "we should not confuse formal democratisation of European institutions with democratic legitimacy. The Community remains, in essence, a supranational administrative body, the legitimacy of which derives from its ability to solve practical problems reasonably efficiently, as a regulatory agency of the Member States representing their particular national communities. Lindseth, *supra* note 6, at 683.

pation and a strong European Parliament.[511] Without these elements the system would suffer from a "democratic deficit."[512]

For an historical perspective, G.F. Mancini outlines four reasons why the European Community was not founded as a democratic institution. First, IGOs "do not normally provide for much direct democracy in their decision-making apparatus;" rather, a measure of democracy exists through national parliamentary control over the state's representatives to the IGO. Second, the Community's Member States were "anxious to circumscribe the surrender of national sovereignty within clearly defined limits." Third, a full national-style parliamentary system was not deemed feasible, and therefore the early version of the European Parliament was limited to a consultative role. Finally, an empowered parliament was seen as a hindrance to the desired IGO-inspired consensus approach to decision-making.[513] Nevertheless, the Community had its democratic underpinnings. Jan Muller has observed that "the initial constituent power was a plural one: the member states, represented by their governments, engaged in elite bargaining, and made the political decision to constitute the Community. Consequently, there was a deficit of direct democracy from the very start, but there was no lack of a democratically constituted, plural constituent power."[514] Muller's comments would be echoed by the intergovernmental camp, who would contend that the original democratic underpinnings of the Community are sufficient for the EU today and in the future. Mancini strongly articulates the contrary, federalist position:

> "Indeed, the Union is doomed never to be truly democratic as long as not only its foreign and security policies, which are openly carried out on an intergovernmental basis, but the very management of its supranational core, the single market, are entrusted, with or without a circumscribed control by the European Parliament, to diplomatic round tables. In other words, democracy will elude Europe as long as its form of government includes rules and legitimises practices moulded on those of the international community."[515]

Whether the European Union can or should manifest democratic elements depends both on the nature of the EU and the nature of democracy itself. The following section will examine first whether the Union possesses one of the basic building blocks of democracy, a *demos* – an identifiable people on which a democratic system can be

---

[511] Albert Weale, in his 1999 treatise on democracy, asserts that any "non-utopian" normative theory of democracy "is committed to the position that 'ought implies can.'" Christopher Lord, Assessing Democracy in a Contested Polity, 39 J. Common Mkt. Stud. 641, 644 (2001).

[512] The idea of a democratic deficit can be traced to David Marquand who in 1979 championed a strong European Parliament. See David Marquand, Parliament for Europe (1979). See also Yves Mény, De la democratie en Europe: Old Concepts and New Challenges, 41 J. Common Mkt. Stud. 1 (2002); Majone, *supra* note 48, at 6. For an extended analysis of the EU's democratic deficit and how the Constitution would have affected democratic rights and processes within the EU, see Stephen C. Sieberson, The Proposed European Union Constitution – Will it Eliminate the EU's Democratic Deficit?, 10 Colum. J. Eur. L. 173 (2004).

[513] Mancini, *supra* note 8, at 31-33.

[514] Muller, *supra* note 9, at 1790-91.

[515] Mancini, *supra* note 8, at 65.

based. Second, the analysis looks at whether there is an ideal form of democratic system to which the EU should aspire. Third, there is consideration of the practical issue of delegation as a necessary element of democracy in a complex society. After these inquiries, the Treaties will be examined to identify elements of democracy that exist at the EU level, as well as areas in which the national democracies of the Member States are emphasised.

2.   THE CHARACTER OF DEMOCRACY AT THE EU LEVEL

2.1   Is there a *demos* on which a democracy can be based?

In classic terms the basis for any democracy is the existence of a *demos*, an identifiable group of people with sufficient cohesiveness to agree on the principles of their self-governance.[516] Shared geography alone is not enough to create the common culture or values that can give rise to a *demos*. Rather, the people within the territory must share a deeper common identity. With respect to the existence of a *demos* at the core of the European Union, commentators generally fall into three camps. The first contends that such a *demos* can never develop, and thus a true pan-European democracy cannot be created. The second argues that Europeans do possess sufficient shared values to constitute a *demos* that will support an EU democracy. A third camp suggests that this debate is unnecessary, and that the Union does not need a traditional *demos* as a prerequisite to supporting a democratic system. We will briefly examine each of these theories.

The case against the existence of a European *demos* begins with the empirical observation that Europeans are a diverse people with diverse values. Andreas Føllesdal refers to the lack of "a shared history or gene pool among all Europeans, to create a common identity" and sees that "there is no 'demos', no shared sense of destiny or broad set of common values."[517] He also sees "no sufficiently widespread and appropriate political culture" and "little in the way of sufficiently clear and shared normative conceptions of what justice requires regarding the institutional distribution of political rights and material resources."[518] Andrew Moravcsik notes that multilateral bodies such as the EU "lack the grounding in a common history, culture and symbolism upon which most individual polities can draw."[519] One of the greatest concerns to some

---

[516] See general discussion in Neil MacCormick, Democracy, Subsidiarity, and Citizenship in the 'European Commonwealth', 16 Law & Phil. 331, 340-42 (1997). Democracy has been described as "the power of the demos." Yves Mény, *supra* note 512, at 3.

[517] Andreas Føllesdal, Citizenship and Political Rights in the European Union: Consensus and Questions, Institute for Advanced Studies, 1, 4, available at www.ihs.ac.at/public_rel/kbericht/ak1/fo.html (hereafter Føllesdal IAS).

[518] Id. at 12-13.

[519] Moravcsik 2003, *supra* note 66, at 38. Two constitutional Convention delegates from Malta, George Vella and Alfred Sant, have argued that "the diversity of cultures, languages, traditions, beliefs and historical backgrounds, found in the present and future member states of the EU, is the strongest factor against the claim that the EU should assume the structures of a federal superstate." Jesmond Bonello, Draft EU Constitu-

commentators is the absence of a common European language. Dieter Grimm, a justice of the German Federal Constitutional Court, sees the language problem as "the biggest obstacle to Europeanisation of the political substructure, on which the functioning of a democratic system and the performance of a parliament depends."[520] He asserts that effective democracy depends on effective communication, and that a shared language is critical.[521] G.F. Mancini agrees. He acknowledges that multi-language nations do exist, but he asserts that the size of the EU and the number of its languages create unprecedented challenges for democratisation.[522]

Population movement throughout history demonstrates that people are capable of shedding languages and nationalities while embracing new cultures. As an example, the Europeans who emigrated to the United States during the 19th century were generally successful in leaving the "Old World" behind and blending into the evolving American *demos*. But their willingness and ability to take on a new identity were spurred by the desperate economic or political conditions that led to emigration and by the dramatic impact of a physical relocation. It cannot be expected that today's Europeans who remain in their homelands during relatively comfortable economic circumstances will have the same motivation to let go of their national identities and personally accede to a pan-European *demos*. Joschka Fischer agrees that in these circumstances the nation states of Europe are "realities that cannot simply be erased" by the process of European integration.[523] Similarly, Alan Branthwaite sees "little evidence of European identity being able to offer a compensatory identity to replace na-

tion: MLP Sees Voluntary Withdrawal Clause as 'Interesting', Times Malta, May 28, 2003, at www.timesofmalta.com/core/article.php?id=127081. Joschka Fischer, an ardent proponent of further EU integration, likewise acknowledges that the Member States remain as the repository for citizens' identity and loyalty. Fischer, *supra* note 36, at 7.

[520] Dieter Grimm, Does Europe Need a Constitution?, 1 Eur. L.J. 282, 295 (1995). See also the analysis by G.F. Mancini, who observes that multi-lingual European states such as Belgium, Switzerland and Finland do exist, but are relatively small compared to the totality of the EU. In light of the Union's daunting language problem, Mancini concludes that the EU's democratic deficit "is therefore *inborn* and cannot realistically be removed within a time-frame which is other than geological or, at the very least, epochal." Mancini, *supra* note 8, at 56 (2000). Mancini notes that these temporal adjectives were used "ironically, but quite correctly in my opinion" by Joseph H.H. Weiler. Id. at 56 n. 29. See Joseph H. H. Weiler, Does Europe Need a Constitution? Demos, Telos and the German Maastricht Decision, 1 Eur. L.J. 219, 229 (1995).

[521] "Communication is bound up with language and linguistically mediated experience and interpretation of the world. Information and participation as basic conditions of democratic existence are mediated through language." Grimm, *supra* note 520, at 292.

[522] Mancini, *supra* note 8, at 56.

[523] In commenting on the "the transition from a union of states to full parliamentarisation as a European Federation" Fischer notes that such a level of integration is highly controversial: "Of course, this simple solution is immediately criticized as being utterly unworkable. Europe is not a new continent, so the criticism goes, but full of different peoples, languages and histories. The nation-states are realities that cannot simply be erased, and the more globalisation and Europeanisation create superstructures and anonymous actors remote from the citizens, the more the people will cling on to the nation-states that give them comfort and security." Fischer, *supra* note 36, at 7. Fischer states that he shares these objections, and therefore he endorses the idea that Member States should have a prominent role in an integrated Europe. Id. at 7.

tional identities."[524] He describes the EU as "an artificial entity for which there are no natural feelings or sympathy."[525] Likewise, it has been argued that "the average voter will always relate far more to his national political institutions" than to the EU.[526] In this vein Peter Lindseth has asserted that "as long as political identity continues to cling to the nation state . . . the status of the EC/EU as a self-legitimating 'constitutional' level of governance will remain tenuous."[527]

A number of observers have dismissed the "no *demos*" argument by asserting that Europeans in fact share certain deeply-held principles. Former French Prime Minister and current MEP Michel Rocard has described "the extraordinary community constituted by the intellectual and cultural patrimony that unites Europeans around recognised and accepted values."[528] Among these values are "respect for human life, the desire to protect the weak and the oppressed, equal treatment of women, the commitment to the rule of law" as well as liberty of thought, religious freedom and pluralism. Rocard heralds these principles as the nearly unanimously-accepted "pillars of political and institutional stability in today's Europe."[529] He might well have quoted Article 6(1) of the TEU, which states: "The Union is founded on the principles of liberty, democracy, respect for human rights and fundamental freedoms, and the rule of law, principles *which are common to the Member States.*" (emphasis supplied) Andreas Føllesdal refers to a "shared sense of justice,"[530] and social philosopher Jürgen Habermas has spoken of "the idea of Europe" being based on a "specific notion of justice" as manifested in "the social welfare state and the social market economy."[531] These ideas suggest that a deeper bond already exists among EU citizens.[532] The European Community itself in 1973 attempted to recognize this common ground in its "Declaration on the European Identity," which stated that the Member States at that time

---

[524] Alan Branthwaite, The Psychological Basis of Independent Statehood, in States in a Changing World 46, 60 (Robert H. Jackson & Alan James, eds., 1993).

[525] Id.

[526] Charlemagne, Europe's Forgotten President: Why It Matters Who Runs the European Parliament, Economist, January 12, 2002, at 49.

[527] Lindseth, *supra* note 6, at 644. Lindseth engages in an extensive analysis of democratic legitimacy and the "no demos" theory. Id. at 645-51, 672-83.

[528] Michel Rocard, Europe's Secular Mission, Taipei Times, May 28, 2003, at 9, available at www. taipeitimes.com/News/edit/archives/2003/05/28/2003053028.

[529] Id. Rocard notes the influence of Christianity on the development of these shared values, but he adds that "Europe also found a productive balance between church and state. In Europe, sovereignty belongs to the people and does not flow from a transcendent power . . ." Id.

[530] Føllesdal IAS, *supra* note 517, at 4.

[531] Jürgen Kaube, Espresso and Croissants, Frankfurter Allgemeine Zeitung, June 27, 2001, available at www.faz.com / IN / INtemplates/AZ/archive.asp?rub={B1311FFE-FBFB-11D2-B228-00105A9CAF88} &doc={7E646849-6AE3-11D5-A3B5-009027BA22E4}.

[532] It has also been argued that greater public participation in the EU's processes and institutions will engender a deeper European identity. Pascal Lamy and Jean Pisani-Ferry have suggested that formation of effective multi-national political parties within the Parliament may give rise to "a truly pan-European civil society that can bring life to pan-European debates." Pascal Lamy & Jean Pisani-Ferry, Europe's Future and the Centre-left, Fin. Times (London), March 8, 2002, at 19. In contrast, Andrew Moravcsik describes as "questionable" the proposition that "greater participation in European political institutions will generate a deeper sense of political community in Europe...". Moravcsik 2002, *supra* note 66, at 615.

shared "the same attitudes to life, based on a determination to build a society which measures up to the needs of the individual."[533]

A third approach is to suggest that the EU does not actually require a *demos* in the classic sense. Lothar Funk contends that the EU is a unique polity that "does not need citizens with a predominantly European identity" in order to be as legitimate as the Member States.[534] Eric Stein agrees and argues that since the EU is not a state in the traditional sense, "it does not need the underpinning of a single 'people.'"[535] Likewise, Peter Lindseth proposes that a redefinition of *demos* may be necessary for the concept of democracy to adequately apply to an institution such as the EU that exists outside the traditional concept of the nation-state.[536] Antonio Estella argues: "The important thing is not whether a *demos* exists; the important thing is that the pact is in equilibrium, that is, that a positive-sum game situation is created for all players."[537]

Reflecting on the debate, Stein questions whether the search for a *demos* may be a red herring, but he does recognise that something uniquely European is developing. In describing this "hopeful vision" he states: "Elements of what might emerge as a 'European identity' may be in place, but if this evolves, it will differ from, and will coexist with, the discrete identities of the peoples in the individual member states."[538] This idea of coexisting identities or attachments is explored by Joseph Weiler, who describes the concept as that of "multiple *demoi*."[539] He describes several versions of this theory, and they share the following characteristics: "[T]he invitation is to embrace the national in the in-reaching strong sense of organic-cultural identification and belongingness and to embrace the European in terms of European transnational affinities to shared values which transcend the ethno-national diversity."[540]

2.2   Can pure democracy exist in the EU?

Whether a *demos* exists in the EU or is even necessary, a second threshold question is whether there is an ideal form of democracy that can be identified for the European Union or for any society. Whether described with reference to the Greek *polis*, the

---

[533] Commission of the European Communities, Declaration on the European Identity, (1973) EC Bulletin 12, Cl. 2501, 118-127. For thoughts on the European identity from the perspective of a scholar from one of the new Central European Member States, see Priban, *supra* note 52.

[534] Funk, *supra* note 52.

[535] Eric Stein, International Integration and Democracy: No Love at First Sight, 95 Am. J. Int'l L. 489, 526 (2001).

[536] Lindseth, *supra* note 6, at 643. See also Kenneth Armstrong, Civil Society and the White Paper: Bridging or Jumping the Gap? (Harvard Jean Monnet Working Paper No.6/01, 2001), www.jeanmonnetprogram.org/papers/01/011601.html.

[537] Antonio Estella, Constitutional Legitimacy and Credible Commitments in the European Union, 11 Eur. L.J. 22, 26 (2005).

[538] Stein, *supra* note 535, at 528. See also Di Fabio, *supra* note 83, at 168. Note also Alan Branthwaite's reference to an EU identity that might be "complementary" to national identities. Branthwaite, *supra* note 524, at 60.

[539] Weiler, *supra* note 4, at 344-448.

[540] Id. at 346.

New England town or the Westminster model,[541] the pure majoritarian government "of the people, by the people, for the people" is proffered as a hope, an intention and a goal. But in the world of reality this magnificent aspiration is exposed as no more than an elusive abstraction. Yves Mény has branded Lincoln's famous Gettysburg phrase as a highly "misleading" motto that has unfortunately come to define "the ideal form of democracy conceived by citizens."[542] Joseph Weiler states that "democracy can not exist in a modern polity" as it might in the ideal community.[543] Giandomenico Majone has characterised the "pure majoritarian" model of democracy as one standard that the Union will not be able to meet,[544] but Mény insists that "all of today's democracies are 'impure'."[545] He contends that the EU's prospects for democracy should be viewed with no more scepticism than more recognized democratic systems.[546] In a further commentary, published after finalisation of the Constitution's text in the fall of 2004, Mény has observed: "The EU is not yet the traditional democratic polity that we have become used to (rather recently by the way!), but it is a democracy in the making. It is imperfect, to be sure. But then so is democracy itself."[547]

The impossibility of attaining the democratic ideal arises from the practical fact that democracies are institutions created by finite human beings operating under the constraints of culture, geography, time and the politics of the moment.[548] For Europe, one of its defining characteristics is its variety, from the rich diversity of ethnic and linguistic groups, to the dramatic differences in climate and topography and the ever-changing economic and geopolitical picture. Creating a widely accepted and stable system of government for such a continent is no small task. The fact that there are different governmental traditions within the EU only compounds the challenge for the Union. All of the Member States are democracies, but in different forms. Jan Muller observes that "in Britain, the Crown in Parliament is sovereign, in France, it is the state, representing the sovereign people, and its common national will. Finally, in Germany, the constitution is interpreted through the Federal Constitutional Court as

---

[541] "The Westminster model (which originated in Great Britain about three hundred years ago) concentrates power in the hands of cabinet ministers, and particularly the prime minister. The central attribute of this model of government is the individual and collective responsibility of ministers to Parliament (and of Parliament to the people)." W.T. Stanbury, Accountability to Citizens in the Westminster Model of Government: More Myth Than Reality, Fraser Inst. Digital Publication (February 2003), available at www.fraserinstitute.ca/admin/books/files/westminster.pdf. Also, for a useful historical analysis of the relationship between democracy and sovereignty, see Newman, *supra* note 13, at 4-15.

[542] Mény, *supra* note 512, at 3.
[543] Weiler, *supra* note 4, at 81.
[544] Majone, *supra* note 48, at 6.
Majone classifies current democratic deficit arguments into four groups, based on the underlying standards used: "Standards based on the analogy with national institutions; Majoritarian standards; Standards derived from the democratic legitimacy of the Member States; [and] Social standards." Id.
[545] Mény, *supra* note 512, at 3.
[546] Id. at 12.
[547] Yves Mény, The Achievements of the Convention, 14 J. Democracy 57, 70 (2003).
[548] Even the meaning of "democracy" is variable by era and location. "The very same word applies to the Athenian government, to de Tocqueville's America, to the British or continental parliamentary systems, to the new political systems emerging from the collapse of communism, etc." Mény, *supra* note 512, at 10.

the final arbiter."[549] Eric Stein describes "the consensual (consociational) pattern in the Netherlands [where it is known as the "polder model"[550]], Belgium, Austria and Switzerland...the strong regionalism in Spain... [and] the federal variants in Germany, Austria, Belgium, and Switzerland."[551] In the face of these divergent approaches, and against the backdrop of Europe's broad diversity, Yves Mény argues: "The legitimacy battle over who does what, at which level and according to which rules will be with us forever."[552] He sees an EU that will never be a "rational, well-ordered, uniform type of polity," but rather a system in constant motion.[553] He asserts that "we have to accept changes, disparities and differences over time and space, and not consider this a traumatic situation" and he adds that the Union can survive "only by accepting – and organising – these variations, be they beliefs, rules or institutions."[554]

Setting aside the ideal and embracing a flexible approach need not imply that there are no measurable standards for democracy in the European Union. Joseph Weiler asserts that "democracy can be measured by the closeness, responsiveness, representativeness, and accountability of the governors to the governed."[555] In similar terms, Michael Newman writes that "non-governmental opinion needs to be able to influence outcomes, expose injustice and incompetence, and offer alternative policies based on information about current policy failures."[556] These are useful concepts, but still abstract. Newman acknowledges that "such notions are exceedingly difficult to implement in *practice* in most political systems, and that there are particular problems involved in applying them within the EU."[557] More concrete standards and measurements are called for, and Andrew Moravcsik argues that in order to be fair, "any useful and realistic assessment of the EU's democratic performance must be based on a comparison with the actual functioning of national democracies."[558] In an elaborate analysis, Christopher Lord proposes two methods of creating appropriate standards. First, he suggests that "benchmarks for democratic performance used elsewhere [i.e., in other systems] should be adapted to the specific case of the EU."[559] Second, he examines self-assessments and peer reviews gleaned from a wide array of reports and

---

[549] Muller, *supra* note 9, at 1779.

[550] Historically, all elements of Dutch society needed to cooperate just to protect the country from the sea, to build dikes and to reclaim land (polder). More recently, the economic policy-setting cooperation among employers' organisations, labour unions and the government has been referred to as the polder model. Mark Kranenburg, The political branch of the polder model, NRC Handelsblad (July 1, 1999) available at www.nrc.nl/W2/Lab/Profiel/Netherlands/politics.html.

[551] Stein, *supra* note 535, at 489-95.

[552] Mény, *supra* note 512, at 12.

[553] Id. at 12.

[554] Id.

[555] Weiler, *supra* note 4, at 81.

[556] Newman, *supra* note 13, at 173.

[557] Id.

[558] Moravcsik 2003, *supra* note 66, at 38, 45.

[559] Lord, *supra* note 511, at 645. These benchmarks include: (1) distinguishing among "competing models of Euro-democracy" offered by academics and practitioners, including majoritarian, consensus and participatory classifications; (2) identifying indices of democratic performance for each model; (3) specifying units of assessment; and (4) setting standards of evidence. Id. at 645-48.

other documents issued by the various EU institutions.[560] Lord theorises that further studies utilising these two approaches will yield "a series of grounded and discriminating assessments of where in the EU's political system, and in relation to what democratic standards, problems are most acute or solutions most developed."[561]

2.3 Delegation and its impact on democracy

Regardless of the standards by which European Union democracy is to be measured, it is a certainty that delegation will be part of the system, as it is in any modern, functioning democracy. In a large and complex society it is a practical necessity to use elected and appointed representatives to carry out the task of governing, as an alternative to direct action by the citizenry.[562] There are two basic types of delegation. At the first level, individuals are elected by popular (democratic) vote to legislative bodies or executive positions, and these representatives carry out their responsibilities with the knowledge that they will in due course be required to stand again for election. At the second level, elected representatives appoint civil servants who carry out executive, administrative and judicial tasks and are subject, not to future elections, but to rules of administrative procedure and standards of good behavior.[563] It is this second type of delegation that engenders most of the debate about the democratic legitimacy of any system of government, and of the European Union in particular.[564]

Delegation to administrative agencies is both widespread and functional. Peter Lindseth has commented that "[t]he practice of delegation is so common in modern administrative states that one could probably describe it as 'universal.'"[565] Likewise, Giandomenico Majone asserts that "the pure majoritarian model of democracy is the exception rather than the rule" and that "most democratic polities . . . rely extensively on non-majoritarian principles and institutions."[566] Andrew Moravcsik explains that

---

[560] Id. at 648-56.

[561] Id. at 657.

[562] Yves Mény describes the "major intellectual shift" that occurred at the time of the American and French Revolutions: "Up until these major political changes, there was a general consensus about, on the one hand, the eminent quality of democracy (the best possible regime) and, on the other hand, its intrinsic limitation (democracy, it was argued, unfortunately can work only in tiny states and cities). The 'miracle' resulted from the combination of the representative principle with the democratic principle into something that was still called 'democracy', but had little to do with what the enlightenment had in mind." Mény, *supra* note 512, at 11. Joseph H.H. Weiler puts it succinctly: "Representative democracy replaces direct participation." Weiler, *supra* note 4, at 81.

[563] There are regional variations as to which governmental positions are elected and which are appointed. In the United States, for example, in some jurisdictions the offices of sheriff, city attorney and even trial and appellate judges may appointed, while in others they may be elected.

[564] Note that Arts. 202 and 211 of the EC Treaty specifically provide for the Council of Ministers (elected officials who represent the first level of delegation from the European citizens) to delegate to the Commission the right to adopt specific EU laws (the second level of delegation).

[565] Lindseth, *supra* note 6, at 645.

[566] Majone, *supra* note 48, at 11. Yves Mény writes: "An endless number of institutions which are at the heart of democratic systems are in fact not democratic (central banks, judiciaries, professional bodies with regulatory powers, etc.)...". Mény, *supra* note 512, at 9.

non-majoritarian bodies, insulated from public pressure, offer much-needed efficiency and expertise, impartial dispensation of justice, protection of minorities, and unbiased representation of majority interests.[567] Majone also sees delegation as a means of managing the "deep cleavages" in a system such as the European Union, where "a strict application of majoritarian standards would only produce deadlock and possibly even disintegration."[568] Beyond these practical benefits, Majone sees the delegation of authority as a manifestation of the delegating parties' commitment to the system.[569] In this view, the yielding of sovereignty from elected bodies to more independent administrative institutions ensures greater consistency and continuity of policy, and thus represents a greater endorsement by the electorate of their public officials.[570]

Common as it is, and useful as it may be, delegation is a two-edged sword. The very act of delegating to an administrative agency is a transfer of power away from individual citizens and a setting-aside of the principle of decision by majority vote. Inevitably there are times in any society when the electorate, the media and even other public officials will lash out at the "bureaucrats" who seem too removed from the people they are supposed to serve. Majone acknowledges the challenges posed by institutions "which by design are not directly accountable to the voters or to their elected representatives."[571] Lindseth has noted that despite the widespread practice of delegation in modern administrative states, "the power of unelected administrators to make regulatory norms – notably the power to make general rules in a quasi-legislative sense – is inescapably problematic from the standpoint of democratic legitimacy."[572] Within the European Union, the presence of non-majoritarian institutions has been described as "the conflict between bureaucracy and democracy, which is really at the heart of the present political and economic malaise across Europe."[573] The extent of delegation is thus a key point of contention in the debate over the proper structure for the European Union. A proper balance between efficient operation of

---

[567] Moravcsik 2002, *supra* note 66, at 613-14. Moravcsik also asserts that "non-majoritarian decision-making is justified in democratic theory not simply because it may be efficient, but because, ironically, it may better represent the long-term interests of the median voter than does a more participatory system – in distributive conflicts as well as matters of efficiency. Moravcsik 2000, *supra* note 36, at 311. Majone comments that "one of the important tasks of EC institutions has always been to protect the individual rights created by the Treaties, even against the majoritarian decisions of a Member State or the unanimous preference of all the Member States. EC competences [i.e., delegated authority] that serve to protect such rights are legitimated, and limited, by this function." Majone, *supra* note 48, at 23. Yves Mény concurs: "Power has to originate in the people. But, in a representative system, the minority has to be protected from the excesses of the majority." Mény, *supra* note 512, at 9.

[568] Majone, *supra* note 48, at 11. Majone describes the cleavages as "linguistic, geographical, economic, ideological and, especially, the division between large and small Member States." Id.

[569] Id. at 17.

[570] Majone states: "Because a legislature or a majority coalition cannot bind a subsequent legislature or another coalition, public policies are always vulnerable to reneging and hence lack credibility. Delegation to politically independent institutions is one method of achieving credible policy commitments." Id. at 17.

[571] Id. at 15. Majone also acknowledges the perception that independent regulatory agencies "do not fit well into the traditional framework of controls, checks and balances." Id.

[572] Lindseth, *supra* note 6, at 645.

[573] Anatole Kaletsky, EU Blueprint Spells the Demise of Democracy, Times London, October 31, 2002, at 24.

government and popular control over core policy decisions is sought by all sides,[574] but the precise form of that balance is where the divergence occurs. Those who would espouse a greater the role for the Commission must acknowledge that this will result in further removing decision-making from the European citizenry. On the other hand, those who would urge greater power for the European Parliament or Council must recognise that democratic procedures – and politics – are likely to yield a loss of efficiency. The picture is further complicated by the fact that in a complex system such as the EU, delegated administration and its oversight are spread among different levels of government,[575] and thus, the possibilities for adjusting the structure are seemingly endless.

3.   DEMOCRACY AT THE EU AND NATIONAL LEVELS

3.1   Democratic elements in the Union

The TEU identifies democracy as a core principle of the Union, but its references are aspirational rather than concrete. The treaty's preamble identifies democracy as a principle to which the people of Europe are attached, and it expresses their desire to "further the democratic and efficient functioning of the institutions." Article 1 refers to a union in which "decisions are taken as openly as possible and as closely as possible to the citizens." Article 6(1) declares that the Union is founded on the principle of democracy, along with "liberty" and "respect for human rights and fundamental freedoms, and the rule of law." Article 11(1) notes that development and consolidation of democracy is an objective of the EU's CFSP. The TEU does not contain any substantive provisions relating to the practice of democracy at the Union level.

The EC Treaty notes that fostering democracy is an objective of the Community's external relations,[576] but this treaty also addresses in concrete terms certain aspects of EU-level democracy. For example, EC Treaty Articles 189 and 190 include the right of direct representation in the European Parliament, and Article 191 includes recognition of the importance of EU-level political parties. Article 255 guarantees public access to documents of the Council, Commission and Parliament, and Article 207

---

[574] Peter Lindseth writes of the need for a "broader scholarly discussion of the appropriate means of controlling delegated normative power in any supranational body...." Lindseth, *supra* note 6, at 643. Francesca Bignami describes the challenges of achieving balance as follows: "A legislature that exercises too much oversight might very well slow down administrative action, render it partial, or compromise the scientific character of decision-making. Similar consequences follow from an administrative process that is too swift, relies too heavily on expert opinion, or is overly concerned with fairness. The aim is to achieve a balance, one that is not simply a matter of technocratic virtuosity but also depends on collective perceptions as what that balance should be." Francesca E. Bignami, The Democratic Deficit in European Community Rulemaking: A Call for Notice and Comment in Comitology, 40 Harv. Int'l L.J. 451, 460 (1999).

[575] Moravcsik 2003, *supra* note 66, at 42.

[576] EC Treaty Arts. 177(2) (regarding development cooperation), 181a(1) (regarding economic, financial and technical cooperation with third countries).

requires the Council to set rules for access to its documents. Protection of personal data is required of all EU institutions by Article 286.

Taking a page from the Constitution,[577] the Lisbon Treaty consolidates and amplifies concepts of democracy governing the EU. The treaty inserts into the TEU a new set of four articles under the heading "Provisions on Democratic Principles."[578] These are prefaced with a mandate for the Union to treaty all of its citizens equally.[579] The following article begins with a statement that the EU is founded on "representative democracy," and this includes a number of elements: direct representation in the European Parliament, representation on the Council and European Council by "democratically accountable" officials, the right to "participate in the democratic life of the Union," open decision-making, and the activities of pan-European political parties.[580] An additional article requires the EU institutions to maintain "open, transparent and regular dialogue with representative associations and civil society" and other "broad consultations." The new right of citizen initiative is also presented.[581] The final provision identifies the ways in which national parliaments (bastions of democracy that they are) participate in the "good functioning of the Union." These include the parliaments' role in reviewing EU legislation, monitoring certain Union activities and approving treaty amendments.[582]

In addition to these new TEU provisions, the Lisbon Treaty creates a complementary set of three articles in the EC Treaty. The first requires EU institutions to "conduct their work as openly as possible."[583] It also states that the European Parliament must meet in public, and the Council must do so when it is "considering and voting on a draft legislative act."[584] It further extends to all EU institutions the requirement that their documents must be made public.[585] The second provision offers a stronger statement regarding the right to personal data protection.[586] The third requires the Union to respect nationally recognised churches and similar organisations.[587]

The Lisbon Treaty thus offers new emphasis and new substance. The current Treaties do not contain a cohesive section on democratic principles of the Union and do not use the phrase "representative democracy." The Lisbon Treaty also recognises for the first time the rights and status in the EU of representative associations and civil society, as well as the national status of churches and other such groups. Open meetings of EU institutions are offered in some circumstances, and access to EU documents is increased. The right of public initiative is also introduced, although the

---

[577] See Constitution Arts. I-45 to I-52, a set of provisions entitled "The Democratic Life of the Union."

[578] Lisbon Treaty Art. 1(12).

[579] Id. Art. 1(12)(8).

[580] Id. Art. 1(12)(8A).

[581] Id. Art. 1(12)(8B). The initiative process requires at least one million signatures from a "significant number of Member States." The initiative will "invite" the Commission to propose specific EU legislation.

[582] Lisbon Treaty Art. 1(12)(8C).

[583] Id. Art. 2(28)(a)(1).

[584] Id. Art. 2(28)(a)(2).

[585] Id. Art. 2(28)(b).

[586] Id. Art. 2(29).

[587] Id. Art. 2(30).

editors of the *European Law Review* have expressed their "particular ire for the ridic-
ulous citizen initiatives" in the following terms:

> "This gimmick reeks of crass populism, as it allows minority interests representing less than
> a third of one per cent of the Union population to hijack Commission legislative resources.
> It forgets that the point of political institutions is that we pay them and hold them to account
> for exercising their judgment on these matters, not for kowtowing to newspaper editorial
> initiatives."[588]

A classic IGO does not offer citizenship, and neither does it offer its own democratic
rights and processes to the citizens of its member states. Certain of the benefits offered by an IGO to its member states may well pass through the states to their citizens, and the operating rules of the organisation may offer a measure of openness and
access to the public, but the organisation does not offer traditional rights at the IGO
level. The uniqueness of the European Union is emphasised by the fact that it has adopted a variety of democratic principles for the benefit of EU citizens and for improving their oversight of EU institutions. The Lisbon Treaty has absorbed the principles
previously included in the Treaties and both extended their substance and dramatically increased the prominence with which they are presented.

The expansion of democratic principles in the Lisbon Treaty is arguably one of its
most significant innovations, and the need for this development was a motivating factor behind the constitutional Convention.[589] When the Commission published its White
Paper on European Governance in 2001, it based its sweeping proposals for EU institutional reform on "principles of good governance," including openness, participation
and accountability.[590] These principles were described as the underpinning of democracy, not only for the Member States, but also for the Union.[591] The White Paper added: "Democracy depends on people being able to take part in public debate. To do
this, they must have access to reliable information on European issues and to be able
to scrutinise the policy process in its various stages."[592] The Commission insisted that
both the EU institutions and the Member States "need to communicate more actively
with the general public on European issues" and that information "should be presented in a way adapted to local needs and concerns, and be available in all official
languages."[593]

Later in 2001 the European Council met in Laeken, Belgium, and issued its Declaration on the Future of the European Union.[594] In mandating the constitutional Con-

---

[588] Editorial, A Constitution Whose Bottle is Definitely Half-Full and Not Half-Empty, 28 Eur. L. Rev.
449 (2003).

[589] The Laeken Declaration stated: "The first question is . . . how we can increase the democratic legitimacy and transparency of the present institutions." Laeken Declaration, *supra* note 114, at 23.

[590] White Paper, *supra* note 23, at 10.

[591] Id.

[592] Id. at 11. The Laeken Declaration also called on EU institutions to be more open. Laeken Declaration,
supra note 114, at 20.

[593] White Paper, *supra* note 23, at 11.

[594] Laeken Declaration, *supra* note 114, at 19, 20.

vention the Laeken Declaration noted that the EU "derives its legitimacy from the democratic values it projects, the aims it pursues and the powers and instruments it possesses" as well as from its "democratic, transparent and efficient institutions."[595] The Declaration described a need for the EU "to become more democratic, more transparent and efficient" and called on the Convention to resolve the challenge of "how to bring citizens . . . closer to the European design and the European institutions."[596] The Declaration also set forth a lengthy list of questions illustrating the need to "increase the democratic legitimacy" of the EU's institutions.[597]

The Laeken Declaration's demands for more democracy and transparency led the Convention to infuse the Constitution with new democratic trappings. These, in turn, were transferred into the Lisbon Treaty, particularly in provisions for open proceedings and for greater public access to Union documents.[598] The significance of the Lisbon Treaty's new provisions lies in the actual rights created, but also in the ambitious language and tenor of the democracy articles as drafted. Because of the dramatic scope of these articles, they will have an impact on any future debate over the EU's form. Under the Lisbon Treaty, democracy at the EU institutional level is guaranteed to all EU citizens. This is certainly a step away from classic intergovernmentalism, and it may well constitute a further step toward a more federal system.

3.2   The importance of democracy at the national level

In the Lisbon Treaty, the same provision that references citizens' direct representation through the European Parliament provides a reminder that the Member States themselves are represented on the European Council and Council, whose respective members are "democratically accountable either to their national parliaments, or to their citizens."[599] In the provision creating the new right of citizen initiative, the requirement for submission of an initiative is the signatures of at least one million citizens. Interestingly, however, the article also requires that the requisite number of citizens must represent "a significant number of Member States."[600] Another reminder of the Member States is found in the treaty's mandate for the Union to protect individuals' personal data. This requirement is also made applicable to the Member States

---

[595] Id. at 22-23.

[596] Id. at 21.

[597] Id. at 23.

[598] Kokott and Rüth have commented on "increasing democratic legitimacy and transparency of the Institutions" as follows: "The Constitution, in principle, maintains the present institutional design, which, in spite of its well-known deficiencies with regard to the separation of powers and democratic legitimacy, seems to be the most appropriate at the Union's current state of integration. Attempting a major overhaul of the institutional set-up would have not only been premature and therefore unlikely to lead to satisfying results, but would have endangered the whole project of a Constitution. It thus appears, for the time being, preferable, to bring about the necessary changes not by a single 'constitutional stroke', but through the European integration process of progressive reforms and adjustments of the Union's institutional architecture, all the while striving for the utmost transparency." Kokott & Rüth, *supra* note 87, at 1331. See their expanded analysis, id. at 1331-33.

[599] Lisbon Treaty Art. 1(12)(8A)(2).

[600] Id. Art. 1(12)(8B).

"when carrying out activities which fall within the scope of Union law."[601] There is no general requirement imposed on the Member States in all circumstances of their activities – only in their EU activities. Last, the statement in the Lisbon Treaty that the Union "respects and does not prejudice" the status of churches and non-confessional organisations is specifically tied to their status under the national laws of the Member States.[602]

In contrast to the Lisbon Treaty, the current Treaties primarily mention the EU and its institutions in those few treaty provisions that suggest democratic principles and processes. The Member States and their democracy are surely implied in the Treaties, but the only specific reference to them is TEU Article 6, which notes that liberty, democracy and other principles are "common to the Member States."

4.   DEMOCRACY AND THE DIVIDING LINES

Regarding the Lisbon Treaty's two sets of articles on democratic principles, it is important to note that these provisions are mainly about the EU and not about the Member States. The few references to the Member States, identified above, must be seen as little more than reminders of Member State democracy in the context of the EU system. The Lisbon Treaty's principal thrust is to illustrate how the *Union* is to be brought closer to its citizens.

As noted in the preceding analysis, an increased association of the EU and its institutions with the familiar democratic principles and processes that EU citizens expect at the national level is a calculated move to create greater popular appreciation for the Union. Such developments may also offer special appeal to those who would desire the EU to evolve into a democratic federal system. In contrast, those who prefer to preserve the Union's essential character as an IGO might well argue that the EU does not need to offer either its own citizenship or Union-level democratic concepts; national citizenship and the national democracy should be sufficient. The reality is that the trappings of democracy do not necessarily create or portend a superstate. The EU can indeed offer more direct rights to its citizens – and thus foster greater popular support for the Union – without necessarily altering its essential character as a blended entity that is neither intergovernmental in the traditional sense, nor fully federal.

With respect to the EU's existing dividing lines, greater transparency and more opportunities for citizen involvement do not obviously change anything. In the long run, greater citizen appreciation for the Union may open the door to expanded Union involvement in any number of substantive areas, and with that the dividing lines may well shift. But more trappings of Euro-democracy, by themselves, do not have that effect.

---

[601] Lisbon Treaty Art. 2(29)(2).
[602] Id. Art. 2(30)(1).

Chapter 10
A MALLEABLE ENTITY

The history of the European Union is one of steady enlargement. It has grown from the original six nations that formed the European Coal and Steel and Community to the group of 27 resulting after the accession of Bulgaria and Romania on January 1st, 2007.[603] This growth stands in contrast to the general geographical stability of the individual Member States during the same 50-year period.[604] The EU's expansion has been facilitated by accession provisions in the Treaties, and to these the Lisbon Treaty will add a formal withdrawal clause. Other evidence of the Union's malleability may be found in treaty provisions that permit suspension of the rights of a Member State that fails to live up to the Union's core principles. In addition, the Treaties tolerate activities by groups of Member States when the entire Union cannot agree to participate.

1.   FUTURE EXPANSION THROUGH ACCESSIONS

Article 49 of the TEU provides that any European state that respects the EU's core principles as set forth in TEU Article 6(1) may apply for membership in the Union.[605] The provision provides that the application must receive unanimous approval by the Council, following consultation with the Commission and "assent" by a majority vote of the European Parliament. After an accession agreement has been concluded, each of the existing EU Member States must ratify the agreement according to its national constitutional requirements. Further details on the accession process are presented in a Protocol on the Enlargement of the European Union.[606] The Lisbon Treaty perpetuates the accession process, although it adds an early notification to the national parliaments of the Member States.[607]

---

[603] The original six members were France, Germany, Italy, Belgium, the Netherlands and Luxembourg. Denmark, Ireland and the United Kingdom acceded in 1973, followed by Greece in 1981, Spain and Portugal in 1986, and Austria, Sweden and Finland in 1995. The 2004 "Big Bang" expansion took in Estonia, Latvia, Lithuania, Poland, the Czech Republic, Slovakia, Hungary, Slovenia, Cyprus and Malta.

[604] The principal geographical change among the Member States was the 1989 reunification of German, when the former East Germany merged into West Germany. A related development of political, but not geographical, significance was the attainment of political independence by Slovenia, Estonia, Latvia, Lithuania, Poland, the Czech Republic, Slovakia, Hungary, Bulgaria and Romania.

[605] For an analysis of the interplay between expansion of the EU through accessions and the development of the Union as a constitutional system, see Neil Walker, Constitutionalising Enlargement, Enlarging Constitutionalism, 9 Eur. L.J. 365 (2003). For a discussion of the linkage between accession to the EU and a candidate country's respect for human rights, see Cesare Pinelli, Conditionality and Enlargement in Light of EU Constitutional Developments, 10 Eur. L.J. 354 (2004).

[606] Protocol on Enlargement, *supra* note 443.

[607] Lisbon Treaty Art. 1(57).

The Union's further enlargement has recently proven to be a sensitive issue, as reflected in the "no" votes in the 2005 French and Dutch referenda on ratification of the Constitution. Whereas at one point it was generally assumed that the EU would eventually admit Turkey and others, the 2004 and 2007 accessions have caused something of an identity crisis within the Union as well as an administrative challenge.[608] Nevertheless, the provision for a formal accession process in the Treaties is based on the reality of the European Union as an entity whose geographical potential has not yet been reached.

2.   CONTRACTION – WITHDRAWAL OF A MEMBER STATE

A prominent article of the Constitution that has been retained in the Lisbon Treaty is a provision permitting a Member State to voluntarily withdraw from the Union.[609] No such provision exists in the current Treaties. The new provision calls for notification by the withdrawing state, negotiation of a withdrawal agreement, and, unless the parties agree otherwise, an exit date two years after first notification is given to the EU.[610] A state that has withdrawn may later apply to rejoin the Union pursuant to the ordinary accession procedure.[611] The inclusion of a withdrawal right in the Constitution was highly controversial at the Convention.[612] A number of proposals were made to delete the provision, and, failing that, to create more severe consequences for the withdrawing state. In the end, the prevailing sentiment was expressed by Convention President Valery Giscard d'Estaing, who noted that the European Union "is after all not a prison."[613] Thus, the withdrawal article requires procedures to be followed, but it imposes no penalties.

---

[608] Turkey has been approved as a candidate without a fixed accession timetable, but its possible accession has proven highly controversial, owing to a great extent to its overwhelmingly Muslim population. All future accessions may be in jeopardy, because the French and Dutch referenda have been seen in part as a reaction to the EU's expansion in 2004. Graham Bowley, EU teeters on edge of a broader crisis, Int'l Herald Trib., June 3, 2005; Katrin Bennhold, EU cuts expansion from its to-do list, Int'l Herald Trib., June 14, 2005. Other states considered as prospects for future accession include Norway, Iceland, Switzerland, Albania, Moldova, Ukraine and the Balkan states that were formerly Part of Yugoslavia.

[609] Lisbon Treaty Art. 1(58). See Constitution Art. I-60.

[610] Lisbon Treaty Art. 1(58)(2), (3). For a discussion of withdrawal from the Union, see Peter-Christian Müller-Graff, The Process and Impact of EU Constitution-making: 'Voice and Exit,' in The EU Constitution: The Best Way Forward? (Deirdre Curtin, Alfred E. Kellermann & Steven Blockmans, eds., 2005).

[611] Lisbon Treaty Art. 1(58)(5).

[612] Despite the controversy over a withdrawal provision, the European Union has experienced a type of withdrawal, not of a Member State, but of a constituent portion of a Member State. In 1985 Greenland, a Part of the Kingdom of Denmark, was permitted to withdraw from the European Community and change its status to that of an Overseas Country or Territory. For an analysis of this event and a comparative review of withdrawal rights and restrictions in several different governmental systems, see Raymond J. Friel, Providing a Constitutional Framework for Withdrawal from the EU: Art. 59 of the Draft European Constitution, 53 Int'l & Comp. L.Q. 407 (2004).

[613] Norman, *supra* note 123, at 215, 255.

George Bermann has described the EU's constitutional development as "highly untidy," and he notes that "the product at any given time will look highly unfinished."[614] He adds:

"This is all the more so when the only thing that has been predetermined is that these states will in principle continue to deliberate among themselves (and with other partner states they might pick up along the way), when each amendment will have to have been the product of the untidy political bargaining that strongly typifies intergovernmental decision-making, and when, by way of innovation under the new draft constitution, all States know that their partners have the express right to withdraw if they should ever become sufficiently disenchanted or come to look upon the EU as a sufficiently bad bargain."[615]

Secession of a constituent part from a federation, as the American Civil War demonstrated, is a threat to the very existence of the federal entity and is considered by some scholars to be illegal.[616] Furthermore, treaties are governed by the rule of *pacta sunt servanda* – the expectation that a treaty is a solemn undertaking and that a state will fulfill its treaty obligations.[617] However, even that venerable precept has its exceptions. International law does recognise a variety of grounds for revoking and withdrawing from a treaty.[618] Under the law of treaties the concept of state sovereignty would allow withdrawal either in accordance with the terms of the treaty itself or on the basis of an ultimate expression of self-interest. If the treaty itself does not provide for withdrawal, a party may withdraw on grounds such as supervening impossibility of performance or a fundamental change of circumstances.[619] The Lisbon Treaty's inclusion of a withdrawal clause underscores the fact that the EU Treaties are in fact treaties – their parties, the Member States, may assert their self-interest by withdrawing from the Union.[620] It can be argued that the new withdrawal provision pays homage to the deepest level of Member State sovereignty.

---

[614] Bermann, *supra* note 18, at 369.

[615] Id.

[616] The United States Supreme Court has decreed secession to be in violation of American federal law. *Texas* v. *White*, 74 U.S. 700, 724-26 (1869). Joseph H.H. Weiler has noted the "juridical" conclusion that under the current Treaties unilateral withdrawal from European Union would be illegal. Weiler, *supra* note 4, at 18. Cass Sunstein argues that provisions permitting secession may well endanger "ordinary democratic processes" and that they have no place in a constitution. Cass Sunstein, Constitutionalism and Secession, 58 U. Chi. L. Rev. 633, 669-70 (1991).

[617] Preamble, Vienna Convention on the Law of Treaties, May 23, 1969, 1155 U.N.T.S. 336, Art. 60 [hereafter Vienna Convention]; Ian Sinclair, The Vienna Convention of Treaties 84 (1984).

[618] Vienna Convention, *supra* note 617, Arts. 54-64. See also, Sinclair, *supra* note 617, at 181.

[619] Vienna Convention, *supra* note 617, Arts. 61, 62.

[620] Raymond Friel sees secession as a distinctly anti-federal concept, and he writes: "The degree to which secession is controlled tells us much about whether the Union is simply an association of States or a true federal Union." Raymond J. Friel, The Draft Constitution: Issues and Analyses: Secession from the European Union: Checking out of the Proverbial "Cockroach Motel," 27 U. Fordham Int'l L.J. 590, 641 (2004). Michael Dougan describes the withdrawal provision as "the ultimate constraint upon Union competence." Dougan, *supra* note 422, at 8.

3.   SUSPENSION OF RIGHTS

Article 7 of the TEU provides that the Council (meeting in the composition of the Heads of State or Government) may, after complying with strict procedures, determine that a Member State has committed a "serious and persistent breach" of the EU's core values.[621] The values are those expressed in TEU Article 6(1), namely, "liberty, democracy, respect for human rights and fundamental freedoms, and the rule of law." The suspension procedures include a preliminary determination by the Council and the assent of the European Parliament.[622] The decision by the Council must be unanimous, with the accused Member State ineligible to vote on the matter.[623] Upon such a determination, the Council may suspend certain of the violating State's rights under the Constitution, including its voting rights within the Council. However, despite such a suspension, the treaty requires that the Member State in question will continue to be bound by its obligations under the treaty.[624] EC Treaty Article 309(1) refers to and builds upon the TEU principles and the TEU suspension process, and it adds that a Member State whose voting rights have been suspended under the TEU will also lose its voting rights under the EC Treaty. Other rights under the EC Treaty may also be suspended, as the Council may determine.[625]

The Lisbon Treaty preserves the basic suspension procedures. One wording change is a new listing of the EU's core values: "human dignity, freedom, democracy, equality, the rule of law and respect for human rights, including the rights of persons belonging to minorities."[626] In addition, the new treaty has the actual suspension decision being made unanimously by the European Council rather than the Council "meeting in the composition of the Heads of State or Government."[627] The distinction is that the European Council of the Lisbon Treaty includes the new European Council President (who does not represent any Member State) and the President of the Commission, each sitting as a nonvoting member. The "Council" formation described in the TEU would not include the Commission President, but the "Council" President would obviously be present as one of the heads of state or government, and he or she would be a voting member of the formation.[628] Regardless of these technical differences, under the current Treaties and under the Lisbon Treaty the suspension of rights is essentially a political process assigned to the highest political levels within the Union.

---

[621] TEU Art. 7(2).

[622] Id. Art. 7(1).

[623] Id. Art. 7(2), (5).

[624] Id. Art. 7(3).

[625] EC Treaty Art. 309(2).

[626] Lisbon Treaty Art. 1(3).

[627] Id. Art. 1(9)(c).

[628] Note that the European Council is described in the second paragraph of TEU Art. 4, and this institution does include the President of the Commission. However, the suspension procedure of TEU Art. 7 does not involve the European Council as defined in Art. 4. As noted in the text, the suspension decision is to be made by the "Council, meeting in the composition of the Heads of State or Government." TEU Art. 7(2).

Given the harshness of an actual suspension of rights, it would seem unlikely that the procedure will ever be utilised.[629] However, if it ever is invoked, the citizens of the suspended state would be partially disenfranchised by having their national government incapable of fully representing them at the EU.[630] Thus, the Treaties direct the Council to "take into account the possible consequences of such a suspension on the rights and obligations of natural and legal persons."[631] The specific details on such "taking into account" are not provided.

In legal terms the employment of the suspension procedure would represent a form of counter-measure imposed by treaty partners on a state that has breached its treaty obligations. The aggrieved states reciprocate by denying the violating state the benefit of the treaty relationship.[632] The underpinnings of countermeasures are twofold: the sovereignty of the violating state and the corresponding inability of the other states to enforce treaty compliance. From this point of view, TEU Article 7 tacitly recognises that the Member States are sovereign entities within the Union, and in their sovereignty they may be immune to centrally imposed enforcement of their core responsibilities. In contrast, in a strong federal system the ability of the central government to enforce the system's foundational principles should not be in doubt.

4.   VARYING LEVELS OF COMMITMENT

4.1   Enhanced cooperation

The Treaties permit groups of Member States to engage in "enhanced cooperation" in areas where the Council has determined that the Union as a whole cannot be expected to participate. The procedure is provided for in Articles 11 and 11a of the EC Treaty with respect to the First Pillar, in TEU Articles 27a through 27e for the Second Pillar, and TEU Articles 40 through 40b for the Third Pillar. Procedural details for all types of enhanced cooperation are provided in Articles 43 to 45 of the TEU. Enhanced

---

[629] In January of 2000 the EU Member States imposed an informal "diplomatic isolation" on Austria after a far right political leader, Jörg Haider, joined the country's governing coalition. This situation, which did not constitute official EU action, lasted approximately 9 months before being withdrawn. However, the episode led directly to the later inclusion of TEU Art. 7 in the Treaty of Nice. See EurActiv.com, Austria's Haider affair gave the EU an "emergency brake," 7 August, 2006, www.euractiv.com/en/agenda2004/austria-haider-affair-gave-eu-emergency-brake/article-151443.

[630] Anticipating such fallout, the TEU provides that "the Council shall take into account the possible consequences of such a suspension on the rights and obligations of natural and legal persons." TEU Art. 7(3).

[631] TEU Art. 7(3); EC Treaty Art. 309(2).

[632] Vienna Convention, *supra* note 617, Art. 60. Notwithstanding the possibility of suspension of a Member State's voting rights, Joseph H.H. Weiler has argued that legal remedies available within the EU have largely eliminated "the most central legal artifact of international law: the notion (and doctrinal apparatus) of exclusive state responsibility and its concomitant principles of reciprocity and counter-measures." Weiler, *supra* note 4, at 29.

cooperation must further the objectives of the Union,[633] it must be undertaken as a "last resort,"[634] and the process may not undermine the internal market or cause trade discrimination between Member States.[635] A minimum of eight Member States must participate,[636] and the programme must be open to all Member States.[637] Enhanced cooperation activities must further the objectives of the Union.[638] It should be noted that under the Treaties enhanced cooperation as a formal process has not yet been utilised.[639]

The Lisbon Treaty consolidates the enhanced cooperation provisions into two sections, eliminating the differentiation among the Three Pillars. An introductory article is presented in the revised TEU,[640] with all of the "detailed arrangements" set forth in nine new articles in the revised EC Treaty.[641] Notable changes from the current Treaties include (1) a statement that enhanced cooperation may be carried out only in areas of the Union's "non-exclusive competences,"[642] (2) a requirement that nine Member States must participate,[643] and (3) elimination of the ability of a Member State to block enhanced cooperation in the area of the EU's CFSP on grounds of national policy.[644] Overall, the Lisbon Treaty's approach constitutes a simpler presentation of enhanced cooperation, with little change in substance.

4.2   Other forms of special cooperation

It should be noted that the EU is already a multi-track system with regard to monetary policy. Since Slovenia (2007) and Cyprus and Malta (2008) became full participants, there are 15 Member States within the euro-zone, nine new Member States which must enter the zone when economically qualified, two states (the U.K. and Denmark) which are permitted to remain outside the common currency, and one state (Sweden) which would qualify but has chosen not to take the necessary steps do so.[645] The euro

---

[633] TEU Art. 43(a).

[634] Id. Art. 43a.

[635] Id. Art. 43(e), (f).

[636] Id. Art. 43(g).

[637] Id. Art. 43b.

[638] Id. Art. 43(a).

[639] Dougan, *supra* note 422, at 12.

[640] Lisbon Treaty Art. 1(22).

[641] Id. Art. 2(278).

[642] Id. Art. 1(22)(1). The current Treaties do not clearly define whether EU competences are exclusive or not. The Lisbon Treaty does so. See Lisbon Treaty Art. 2(12). Also see the discussion in Part 4 of Chapter 12 of this treatise.

[643] Lisbon Treaty Art. 1(22)(2)

[644] TEU Arts. 27(c), 23(2). For further analysis of the changes to the enhanced cooperation procedures, as proposed in the Constitution (which are similar to those of the Lisbon Treaty), see Dougan, *supra* note 422, at 12-13.

[645] The current euro-zone countries are Finland, Ireland, The Netherlands, Belgium, Luxembourg, France, Germany, Spain, Portugal, Austria, Italy, Greece, Slovenia, Cyprus and Malta. The new Member States required to join are Estonia, Latvia, Lithuania, Poland, Czech Republic, Slovakia, Hungary, Bulgaria and Romania. Sweden has not yet created the necessary institutional independence for its central bank.

programme is a unique, treaty-based activity that contemplates non-participation by certain Member States; it is not being carried out under the enhanced cooperation provisions in the Treaties.[646] The Lisbon Treaty will carry forward the current programme, including its opt-outs.

Another treaty-based example of "flexible integration" relates to the integration into the EU legal order of the Schengen *acquis* on elimination of internal border controls, coordinated external border controls, certain visas, asylum and other related matters. When the European Community was unable to arrive at a mutually acceptable agreement on these issues, a core group consisting of France, Germany, Belgium, Luxembourg and the Netherlands entered into a 1985 agreement outside the Community process. The accord was eventually incorporated into EU law in 1999 through the Treaty of Amsterdam, which also transferred certain Third Pillar matters to the First Pillar.[647] As of the end of 2007 the Schengen area included 22 EU Member States plus Norway and Iceland.[648] However, through protocols the Treaties have recognised special treatment for Ireland and the United Kingdom.[649] The Lisbon Treaty will perpetuate these exceptional rights and the protocols.

Another programme similar to enhanced cooperation, but also technically outside the enhanced cooperation procedures, is the requirement in the Lisbon Treaty that certain Member States with superior military capabilities must engage in "permanent structured cooperation" in connection with the EU's CSDP.[650] This activity will be instituted in a fashion similar to enhanced cooperation, and a Member State initially outside the cooperation may subscribe at a later date.[651] Article 17 of the TEU anticipates cooperation between Member States in the field of armaments[652] and bilateral cooperation between states "in the framework of the Western European Union (WEU) and NATO,"[653] but these programmes and organisations exist outside the European Union. The WEU may serve as a model of structured cooperation, but the innovation in the Lisbon Treaty is that this form of cooperation is to be carried out "within the Union framework."[654]

---

[646] For further discussion of economic and monetary policy, see Part 1.2 of Chapter 17.

[647] Europa Website, The Schengen acquis and its integration into the Union, http://europa.eu.int/scadplus/leg/en/lvb/l33020.htm. See Protocol integrating the Schengen *acquis* into the framework of the European Union, November 10, 1997, O.J. (C 340) 93. Also see Pieter Jan Kuijper, The Evolution of the Third Pillar from Maastricht to the European Constitution: Institutional Aspects, 41 C.M.L.R. 609 (2004).

[648] The only EU Member States not included in Schengen as of the end of 2007 were Romania, Bulgaria and Cyprus (all of which will join when possible), plus the United Kingdom and Ireland. See http://ec.europa.eu/commission_barroso/president/focus/schengen/index_en.htm

[649] Protocol on the position of the United Kingdom and Ireland (1997), December 29, 2006, O.J. (C 321) E/198. This protocol is amended by the Lisbon Treaty. See Lisbon Treaty, December 3, 2007, CIG 14/07, TL/p/en 62. Also see Protocol on the position of Denmark (1997), December 29, 2006, O.J. (C 321) E/201, amended by Lisbon Treaty, December 3, 2007, CIG 14/07, TL/P/en 66. For critical commentary on the confusing results of flexible application of the Schengen regime, see Kuijper, *supra* note 647, at 624-26.

[650] Lisbon Treaty Art. 1(49)(c)(6).

[651] Id. Art. 1(50)(28E).

[652] TEU Art. 17(1).

[653] Id. Art. 17(4).

[654] Lisbon Treaty Art. 1(49)(c)(6).

One further example of the EU's tolerance for special relationships among its Member States is the explicit permission in EC Treaty Article 306 for ongoing "regional unions" among the Benelux countries. The Lisbon Treaty does not change this provision.

4.3   The implications of varying commitments

The multi-track characteristic of the European Union has been the subject of much analysis, undoubtedly because it creates confusion and may be seen as an inherent weakness in the system. In 2004 the think-tank Friends of Europe expressed their own concerns on this subject, tempered with a sense of realism:

> "Multi-speed solutions clearly generate anxiety. They raise difficulties of principle. Yet they are already part and parcel of EU reality. This is most notably the case with Schengen and the Eurozone. A defence group is beginning to form along similar lines. The Benelux customs union and the Belgo-Luxembourg currency union played the same role in the early days. Social opt-outs are also part of the practice. And the new member states will have only limited access to some important policies, including agricultural support, structural funds and the single market in labour.
>
> So the question is not whether or not to introduce multi-speed now. The real issue is whether the concept can be taken further in ways that are helpful to the Union as a whole."[655]

The Friends of Europe then identified three classes of varying commitment that might be considered:

> "– A full-scale *Political Union*, of perhaps the six founder states, binding themselves to act as one on all issues, taking the form of a federation or confederation, and effectively becoming a single state. Discussed some years ago, this hardly seems a real prospect today.
> – A clearly defined *Vanguard*, or hard core, of states agreeing to work together on a single list of specified issues. This has been frequently advocated in recent years.
> – A number of *Pioneer Groups* with different membership for different issues, but with a common core of France, Germany and some others."[656]

The opportunities for varying levels of commitment by the EU's Member States are uncharacteristic of a true federal system in which powers are divided vertically between the central government on the one hand and the states on the other.[657] In a federation, critical matters of policy are determined centrally and are applicable throughout the system. If there is insufficient support for a policy at the federal level,

---

[655] Keith Richardson & Robert Cox, Salvaging the Wreckage of Europe's Constitution, 2004 Friends of Eur. 3, 17.

[656] Id. at 18.

[657] Robert Senelle, Federal Belgium, in Federalism and Regionalism in Europe 27, 29 (Antonio d'Atena, ed., 1998).

either no action will be taken or, at best, separate action might be taken at the state level. However, groups of states will not undertake to do as a bloc what the central government could not accomplish. Action by smaller groupings reveals a lack of collective will to maintain policy consistency within the EU.[658] It is indisputable that if enhanced cooperation or other forms of group activity are utilised to a significant extent, the result will be a loss of coordination and an overall weakening of the EU. A multi-track Union would emphasise the continuing autonomy of the states and the intergovernmental character of the Union. The Lisbon Treaty's enshrinement of enhanced cooperation and similar vehicles, while perhaps a political necessity, reflects the continuing vitality and integrity of the Member States as separate nations.

5. MALLEABILITY AND THE DIVIDING LINES

Most of the concepts discussed in this chapter – accessions, suspension of rights and enhanced cooperation – describe a Union that is either creatively adjustable or frustratingly unstable, depending on one's enthusiasm for structural flexibility. These concepts are not changed in the Lisbon Treaty, and thus the relevant dividing lines are not affected. The remaining possibility – the withdrawal of a Member State – has been proposed for the first time in the Constitution and now in the Lisbon Treaty. One could argue that with the withdrawal provision a Member State's control over its EU membership (a particular dividing line) would shift dramatically toward the individual state. However, our analysis strongly suggests that the right of withdrawal in all likelihood already exists under the current Treaties, either as a legal proposition or as a political reality. Thus, the Union as a malleable entity and its related dividing lines will not appreciably change under the Lisbon Treaty.

---

[658] For a detailed review of "flexible integration" within the EU, both as to historical experiences and future possibilities, see Franklin Dehousse, Wouter Coussens & Giovanni Grevi, Integrating Europe: Multiple speeds – One direction? (EPC, Working Paper No. 9, 2004), available at www.theepc.net/en/default. asp?TYP=CE&LV=177&see=y&PG=TEWN/EN/detail&AI=353&l=. For an integrationist's perspective on the value of enhanced cooperation, see Fischer, *supra* note 36, at 9-12.

Chapter 11
AMENDING THE TREATIES – THE UNANIMITY REQUIREMENT

Every national legal system has a procedure for amending its constitution or other foundational legal acts. Every democratic system provides for such amendment to be carried out on the basis of majoritarian principles. On the other hand, international law provides that amending a treaty requires the approval of each nation that is a party to the instrument.[659] One of the striking characteristics of the European Union is its foundational basis as a treaty organisation, clearly manifested in the Treaties' provisions requiring unanimity for their amendment. The Lisbon Treaty will perpetuate this characteristic, while adding flexibility to the process of amendment.[660]

1.   THE STANDARD AMENDMENT PROCEDURE

The Treaties' only amendment provisions are found in Article 48 of the TEU, which refers to "the Treaties on which the Union is founded." Article 1 of the TEU explains that the EU "shall be founded on the European Communities, supplemented by the policies and forms of cooperation established by this Treaty." Thus, the EC Treaty is included in the TEU's amendment provision. One provision of the EC Treaty, Article 300(5), confirms this by providing that if an international agreement to be entered into by the Community would require an amendment to the EC Treaty, such amendment must be adopted pursuant to TEU Article 48. Procedurally, under Article 48 any Member State government or the Commission may submit an amendment proposal to the Council. The Council must "consult" with the European Parliament, and may consult with the Commission, and thereafter the Council may deliver "an opinion in favour" of calling an IGC into existence. The IGC is then convened by the Council President, and the conference's decision to approve the proposed amendment must be by common accord. If approved, the amendment must be ratified by all Member States in accordance with their respective national constitutional requirements, and the amendment will take effect when all of the states have ratified. Article 48 does not

---

[659] Vienna Convention, *supra* note 617, Art. 40. Art. 40 provides that unanimity is required unless the treaty itself provides otherwise.

[660] A frequently cited characteristic of the European Union is that, beginning with the Single European Act in 1985, the Treaties have been the subject of amendment every few years. In response to this phenomenon, various commentators have called for greater stability. One such critique was offered by Neil Walker, who suggested that the EU might benefit from a strict time limit of 10 years between amendments to the new Constitution, if it were ratified. To counter concerns about the rigidity of such a limitation, Walker asserts: "To design a constitution in the knowledge that it must remain untouched for 10 years would concentrate the minds of present IGC and future Convention members not only on the profound consequences of the results of their deliberations, but also on the question of what matters should be excluded from the 10-year embargo." Neil Walker, Europe's Constitutional Passion Play, 28 Eur. L. Rev. 905, 908 (2003).

provide for a Convention as a preliminary step to the IGC process, but the 2002-2003 Convention took place in any event.

The Lisbon Treaty expands TEU Article 48 in two ways. First, it refers to the current procedure as the "ordinary revision procedure," while adding greater detail to the process. Second, it adds an entirely new section entitled "simplified revision procedures."[661] These innovations are nearly identical to the amendment procedures proposed in the Constitution.[662]

In the ordinary revision procedure under the Lisbon Treaty, the European Parliament is added to the bodies that may submit an amendment proposal to the Council, which refers it to the European Council and notifies the national parliaments.[663] After consulting with the European Parliament and the Commission, the European Council by simple majority vote must either convene a Convention or an ICG to consider the proposed amendment.[664] Much like the Convention that wrote the Constitution, an amending Convention would consist of representatives of the Member State parliaments, heads of state or government of the Member States, the European Parliament and the Commission. If an IGC is convened instead of a Convention, the conference will simply consist of representatives of each of the Member States. A Convention must approve the amendment by "consensus," whereupon it is referred to an IGC.[665] Whether acting without a Convention or upon reference from a Convention, the IGC must approve a proposed amendment by "common accord."[666] After IGC approval and signing of the memorialising document by Member State representatives, the amendment will take effect only when it has been ratified by all of the Member States, acting in accordance with their own constitutional requirements.[667] If four fifths of the Member States have ratified the amendment within two years of its signature, but full ratification has not been achieved, the treaty provides that "the matter shall be referred to the European Council."[668]

The Lisbon Treaty's treatment of the ordinary amendment process is more sophisticated than the current TEU provision, and it recognises several political realities. First, the European Council is brought into the picture, as it should be. Second, there is consultation with national parliaments, a process that may forestall objections from the national capitals. Third, the Convention procedure is formalised. Finally, in light

---

[661] Lisbon Treaty Art. 1(56).

[662] Constitution Arts. IV-443 to IV-445.

[663] Lisbon Treaty Art. 1(56)(2).

[664] Id. Art. 1(56)(3).

[665] The editors of the Common Market Law Review have criticised the process of holding a Convention and then an IGC. They are concerned that the 2002-2003 Convention was not sufficiently representative of the Member States and that it exceed its Laeken Declaration mandate. One particular criticism related to the Convention's controversial (and ultimately unacceptable) new formula for QMV on the Council. The editors assert that "it is inconceivable that a Presidency would have put before an IGC, in which all the protagonists were represented and speaking with equal voices, a proposal so loaded with political dynamite." Editorial, The Failure to Reach Agreement on the EU Constitution – Hard Questions, 41 C.M.L.R. 1, 3 (2004).

[666] Lisbon Treaty Art. 1(56)(4).

[667] Id. Art. 1(56)(4). See comments on ratification in Part 3 of this chapter.

[668] Lisbon Treaty Art. 1(56)(5).

of the Constitution's demise, the Lisbon Treaty appropriately deals with a situation in which ratification is not proceeding smoothly.

2.   THE NEW SIMPLIFIED AMENDMENT PROCEDURES

The Lisbon Treaty offers two "simplified" procedures for particular types of treaty amendment, neither of which is found in the current Treaties. Under the first, EC Treaty provisions relating to the internal policies of the Union may be amended without a Convention or IGC. However, two forms of unanimous approval are required. The European Council must unanimously approve the amendment after consulting with the European Parliament and the Commission. Thereafter, the amendment is subject to ratification by all of the Member States.[669]

The second procedure provides a mechanism for changing unanimous Council voting requirements to qualified majority, both in the EC Treaty as a whole and in the external action provisions of the TEU. The latter include provisions in the CFSP, but not in matters "with military implications or those in the area of defence." Additionally, this procedure may be used to change special legislative procedures under the EC Treaty to the ordinary legislative procedure. Each of these changes can be adopted by the European Council without the necessity of a convention or IGC. However, prior to voting the European Council must notify the Member State parliaments of its possible action. Opposition by any parliament within six months of notification from the European Council will block the amendment, and the European Council may not proceed. If no opposition is expressed, the European Council may adopt the amendment unanimously after receiving the consent of the European Parliament through a majority vote of its members.[670]

Interestingly, the Lisbon Treaty offers several additional procedures that can effectively amend the EC Treaty:

– Special legislative procedures, requiring unanimous Council approval for "measures concerning family law with cross-border implications," may be changed to the ordinary legislative procedure.[671] However, such a change will require a unanimous Council decision after consultation with the European Parliament. Further, proposals for such changes must be notified to the Member State parliaments, and an objection by any of them within six months will veto the proposed procedural change.

– Unanimous Council voting on certain matters related to the fiscal aspects of environmental protection may be changed to QMV by a unanimous vote of the Council.[672]

---

[669] Lisbon Treaty Art. 1(56)(6).
[670] Id. Art. 1(56)(7).
[671] Id. Art. 2(66)(3).
[672] Id. Art. 2(144)(a).

– The requirement of unanimous Council approval to set the EU's multiannual financial framework may be changed to approval by a qualified majority. This change requires a unanimous decision of the European Council.[673]

– Qualified majority voting may replace unanimous Council decision-making within a programme of enhanced cooperation. Such change requires a unanimous decision of Council members, but only those representing the participating Member States.[674] Military and defence matters are excluded from this procedure.[675]

– Special legislative procedures within a programme of enhanced cooperation can be replaced with the ordinary legislative procedure. Such a change requires a unanimous decision of Council members representing the participating states only, and the European Parliament must be consulted prior to the decision.[676] Legislative procedures relating to military or defence matters may not be changed in this fashion.[677]

– In the CFSP a unanimous decision of the European Council will permit additional QMV exceptions to the general requirement of unanimity under current TEU Article 23.[678]

In all of the foregoing processes the Member States are protected by the requirement of a unanimous Council or European Council decision to institute the proposed changes.

Although the foregoing procedures are not found in the current Treaties, the TEU does include one special process that is effectively a treaty amendment. Under TEU Article 42 the Council (by unanimous vote) may move actions from the treaty's Third Pillar to Title IV of the EC Treaty (the First Pillar). However, like a full treaty amendment, such a decision must be approved by each of the Member State governments pursuant to their constitutional requirements. The streamlined aspect of this process is that an ICG under TEU Article 48 may be avoided.[679]

---

[673] Lisbon Treaty Art. 2(261)(2).

[674] Id. Art. 2(278)(280H)(1). The provision that restricts voting to participating Member States is Lisbon Treaty Art. 2(278)(280E). However, under that provision non-participating members may take Part in the Council's deliberations.

[675] Lisbon Treaty Art. 2(278)(280H)(3).

[676] Id. Art. 2(278)(280H)(2). The provision that restricts voting to participating Member States is Lisbon Treaty Art. 2(278)(280E). However, under that provision non-participating members may take Part in the Council's deliberations.

[677] Lisbon Treaty Art. 2(278)(280H)(3).

[678] Id. Art. 1(34)(b)(iv).

[679] Note that the Finnish Presidency in the second half of 2006 stated its intention to actively pursue the "community method" and greater use of qualified majority voting in Third Pillar matters, which would likely be brought about through the TEU Art. 42 procedure. See the published speech of Prime Minister Matti Vanhanen at the plenary session of the European Parliament on 5 July 2006, available at www.government.fi/ajankohtaista/puheet/puhe/en.jsp?oid=163080. These ideas had been introduced on May 10, 2006 by Commission President José Manuel Barroso, "A Citizen's Agenda – Delivering results for Europe, Speech/06/286, available at http://europa.eu/rapid/pressReleasesAction.do?reference=SPEECH/06/ 286&format=HTML&aged=0&language=EN&guiLanguage=en.

The Lisbon Treaty's simplified amendment procedures have been drawn from the Constitution.[680] Peter Norman reported that the constitutional Convention referred to the relevant constitutional articles as "bridge or *passerelle*" provisions "designed to eliminate the need for future treaty changes (with the attendant problems of ratification by all member states)."[681] Various versions of the provisions were hotly debated at the Convention,[682] but Norman saw the end result as something that "may offer an interesting way forward."[683] In particular, he asserted that the procedures for changing unanimous voting and special legislative procedures would constitute "a major relaxation" of the existing requirement of an IGC and Member State ratification. He expressed optimism that the procedures might be workable, even though they had been "criticised by integrationists as likely to remain inoperable in a Union of 25."[684] It is easy to agree with Norman that the simplified procedures will add variety and flexibility to the amendment process. Nevertheless, his optimism must be tempered by the fact that unanimity is preserved in all of the proposed procedures, regardless of how or where the consensus must be achieved. As discussed in Part 4 of this chapter, the retention of unanimity is of vital importance in assessing the impact of the new processes on the EU's dividing lines.

3.   THE RATIFICATION PROCESS

The focus in this chapter is on the treaty amendment process, and it bears reminding that the Lisbon Treaty is itself an amendment to the TEU and EC Treaty. Article 6 of the Lisbon Treaty calls for its ratification "by the High Contracting Parties in accordance with their respective constitutional requirements." It will become effective only when all Member States have ratified, but in any event no earlier than January 1, 2009. This approach is consistent with the Vienna Convention on the Law of Treaties. Article 24 of the Convention provides that unless a treaty specifically provides otherwise, "a treaty enters into force as soon as consent to be bound by the treaty has been established for all the negotiating States."[685]

Commenting on the Constitution, Herwig C.H. Hofmann observed that its ratification requirement "can be regarded as the last direct link between EU law and public international law principles . . . A strong intergovernmental aspect accompanies it."[686]

---

[680] See Constitution Arts. IV-444, IV-445.

[681] Norman, *supra* note 123, at 113.

[682] Id. at 286-97.

[683] Id. at 331.

[684] Id.

[685] Vienna Convention, *supra* note 617, Art. 24(2).

[686] Herwig C.H. Hofmann, A Critical Analysis of the New Typology of Acts in the Draft Treaty Establishing a Constitution for Europe (Eur. Integration Online Papers, Working Paper No. 9, 2003), available at http://eiop.or.at/eiop/pdf/2003-009.pdf. As noted in Chapter 1 of this treatise, the intergovernmental school of thought places emphasis on the ultimate power of the Member States. That power is especially evident when the states are called upon to ratify a treaty amendment.

With the retreat from the Constitution to a more traditional treaty amendment, that intergovernmental aspect is alive and well.

4. UNANIMITY REQUIREMENTS AND THE DIVIDING LINES

The Lisbon Treaty's unanimity requirements – both as to its own ratification and as to subsequent amendment – are a reflection that the new document retains the essential character of the existing Treaties as international compacts among sovereign nation states. For Rome, Maastricht, Amsterdam, Nice and now Lisbon, all of the High Contracting Parties have been required to approve each word of the treaty text at each stage of the document's development, and this indeed reflects standard treaty practice. The Lisbon Treaty is not subject to the previous debates over whether the Constitution was actually a treaty or not.

The unanimity rules offer clear evidence of a dividing line between the Union and the Member States that will not shift under the Lisbon Treaty. Of course, one could argue that because national ratification may be eliminated for some amendment procedures, the ultimate voice in the amendment process might be transferred from the national capitals to the Council chambers in Brussels. Doesn't this procedural change reflect something of a political shift and a modest centralising trend? While it is inarguable that the new amendment processes may be more efficient and more "centrally" carried out, one should not overlook the fact that the Council by its very nature consists of a group of ministers, each of whom is directly representative of and answerable to a national government and its sovereign interests. Except for the unlikely situation of a renegade minister, the national veto will always be available under the Lisbon Treaty, and no Member State should view the new amendment processes as a real transfer of power to Brussels.

At the Convention there were several attempts to permit constitutional amendments by less than a unanimous vote. However, even proposals for an easier path to amendment of provisions that "do not involve a shift of competences of the Union and member states" were rejected, despite the suggestion that such non-threatening amendments be approved by a five-sixths majority of the Member States.[687] Unanimity was retained, and it was criticised. Giovanni Grevi complained: "Considering the sometimes twisted dynamics of national politics in relation to Europe, this [unanimity] is absurd and seriously undermines the effectiveness of a very important procedure, allowing for a minimal degree of flexibility to overcome unanimity."[688]

With the unanimity requirement well preserved in the Lisbon Treaty, regardless of which amendment procedure is followed, each Member State effectively possesses a veto on even minor changes to the highly detailed Treaties. The need for flexibility could have been met much more efficiently if a majority vote were sufficient, but the

---

[687] See Norman, *supra* note 123, at 81, 293, 332.
[688] Grevi, *supra* note 476, at 11. For an analysis of the historical development and future prospects for the treaty/constitutional amendment process, see Smith, *supra* note 4, at 207-53.

framers of the Constitution and the Lisbon Treaty have conceded the point. The majoritarian ideal yields to the absolute right of each Member State to preserve intact what it has previously agreed to, including the Treaties' carefully drawn dividing lines. Any formal change in the competences of the Union and its institutions – even if minor – will be subject to procedural safeguards and full consensus. In acceding to EU membership and in choosing to remain in the Union, each Member State may expect the maintenance of the status quo unless it specifically consents otherwise. A Member State need not fear that its national powers will be eroded without its conscious and explicit approval. In the final analysis, the unanimity requirement protects each state from the unwanted imposition of an ultimate loss of sovereignty, which could occur if a majority or even super-majority of states were given the power to amend the Treaties. Such stability remains an integral part of the EU bargain.

Chapter 12
Principles Underlying EU Action

To complete this analysis of the basic character of the European Union, it is appropriate to examine several foundational principles that govern the EU's activities. These principles both reinforce and restrict Union power, and thus they reflect both the independence of the Union and its dependence on the Member States that created it.

1. CONFERRAL

The Treaties grant a wide range of power and authority to the European Union, the scope of which is discussed throughout this treatise. The EU's powers arise by conferral, which is in essence a principle of limitation.

In their current versions the TEU is silent as to the conferral principle, while the EC Treaty contains a single reference. EC Treaty Article 5 states: "The Community shall act within the limits of the powers conferred upon it by this Treaty and of the objectives assigned to it therein."[689] The Lisbon Treaty expands on this concept in two ways. First and foremost, the new treaty emphasises that Union competences are conferred *by the Member States*:

- Where Article 1 of the current TEU states that the High Contracting Parties enter into the treaty to establish the European Union, the Lisbon Treaty adds the phrase 'on which the Member States confer competences to attain the objectives they have in common.'[690]

- The new treaty also inserts the following declarations into the TEU: "The limits of Union competences are governed by the principle of conferral. . . . Under the principle of conferral, the Union shall act only within the limits of the competences conferred upon it by the Member States in the Treaties to attain the objectives set out therein. Competences not conferred upon the Union in the Treaties remain with the Member States."[691]

---

[689] Within the EC Treaty there are certain references to the treaty's conferral of powers on Community institutions. For example, EC Treaty Art. 7(1) notes that each of the institutions "shall act within the limits of the powers conferred upon it by this Treaty." Art. 5 is the only provision that mentions conferral of power on the Community as a whole.

[690] Lisbon Treaty Art. 1(2)(a).

[691] Id. Art. 1(6)(2). The statement regarding non-conferred competences remaining with the Member States bears a striking resemblance to the Tenth Amendment to the United States Constitution: "The powers not delegated to the United States by the Constitution, nor prohibited by it to the States, are reserved to the States respectively, or to the people." The doctrine of limited federal authority in the American system is complex and highly developed. Interestingly, Erwin Chemerinsky writes that from 1937 to 1995 not one

- A statement in the amended EC Treaty refers generally to the principle of conferral: "The Union shall ensure consistency between its policies and activities, taking all of its objectives into account and in accordance with the principle of conferral of powers."[692] Although conferral by the Member States is not specifically mentioned, the reference to "the principle of conferral of powers" surely refers back to the TEU's definition of that principle.

The Lisbon Treaty's second approach consists of statements that the Union's competences are conferred *in and by the Treaties*:
- A new TEU provision states: "The Union shall pursue its objectives by appropriate means commensurate with the competences which are conferred upon it in the Treaties."[693]
- The ordinary amendment procedure in the TEU may be used to "increase or reduce the competences conferred on the Union in the Treaties."[694]
- One of the simplified amendment procedures in the TEU may not "increase the competences conferred on the Union in the Treaties."[695]
- The EC Treaty provision describing exclusive EU competences begins with the words "When the Treaties confer on the Union exclusive competence in a specific area . . . .".[696]
- Similarly, the EC Treaty provision describing shared competences contains the following opening phrase: "When the Treaties confer on the Union a competence shared with the Member States in a specific area . . . ."[697]
- Another EC Treaty article on shared competence refers to circumstances in which "the Treaties confer [a competence on the EU]."[698]
- An EC Treaty provision on the EU's common commercial policy refers to the "exercise of the competences conferred by this Article."[699]

As illustrated above, the Lisbon Treaty defines conferral as flowing from the Member States, but it also refers to the Treaties themselves as a source of conferred powers. Whether this difference constitutes an inconsistency is debatable. On one hand, one could contend that conferral by the Treaties themselves suggests a communal origin, rooted in the peoples of Europe rather than in the Member States. The better argument would be that the authors of a treaty are none other than the states that are party

---

federal law was declared unconstitutional as violating the limits of Congressional power. However, since 1995 a more conservative Supreme Court "has revived the Tenth Amendment" and is beginning to indicate its willingness to declare limitations on the federal power. See Erwin Chemerinsky, Constitutional Law Principles and Policies 230-31 (2002).

   [692] Lisbon Treaty Art. 2(13).
   [693] Id. Art. 1(4)(6).
   [694] Id. Art. 1(56)(2).
   [695] Id. Art. 1(56)(6).
   [696] Id. Art. 2(12)(2A)(1).
   [697] Id. Art. 2(12)(2A)(2).
   [698] Id. Art. 2(12)(2C)(1).
   [699] Id. Art. 2(158)(6).

to it, that the treaty has no existence or character whatsoever without its parties, and that such a document by itself cannot confer any powers or competences.

It might at least be said that the various descriptions of conferral reflect a lapse in good drafting that might have been avoided. Nevertheless, it must be agreed that the Lisbon Treaty underscores the role of the Member States as parties with *inherent power* who have chosen to confer *limited powers* on the European Union. Two commentators have observed that this expression of conferral "underlines that Union competences derive from the Member States who remain the 'masters of the treaties'."[700] The ratification requirement relating to the Treaties augments this idea, because it is the Member States whose formal approval creates the Union and endows it with its powers.

2.   SUBSIDIARITY AND PROPORTIONALITY

The principles of subsidiarity and proportionality are limitations on EU action and thus a reservation of the rights of the Member States. The terms themselves have the sound of Euro-jargon, but they have been clearly defined. In Article 5 of the current EC Treaty subsidiarity is described as follows:

> "In areas which do not fall within its exclusive competence, the Community shall take action, in accordance with the principle of subsidiarity, only if and in so far as the objectives of the proposed action cannot be sufficiently achieved by the Member States and can therefore, by reason of the scale or effects of the proposed action, be better achieved by the Community."

Without using the term "proportionality," the third subparagraph of Article 5 adds: "Any action by the Community shall not go beyond what is necessary to achieve the objectives of this Treaty." TEU Article 1, which states that in the EU "decisions are taken . . . as closely as possible to the citizen," has been described as "a broader expression of subsidiarity."[701] In a similar vein, the preamble to the TEU notes the resolve of the Member States "to continue the process of creating an ever closer union among the peoples of Europe, in which decisions are taken as closely as possible to the citizen in accordance with the principle of subsidiarity." Article 2 of the TEU states the Union's objectives and notes that they are to be carried out "while respecting the principle of subsidiarity as defined in Article 5 of the [EC Treaty]."

The Lisbon Treaty moves the definitions from the EC Treaty to the TEU[702] and updates their wording. Subsidiarity is defined in the following terms:

---

[700] Lars Hoffmann & Jo Shaw, Constitutionalism and Federalism in the 'Future of Europe' debate: The German Dimension, The Federal Trust Online Paper 03/04, at 7, available at www.fedtrust.co.uk/uploads/constitution/03_04.pdf.

[701] P. W. Barber, The Limited Modesty of Subsidiarity, 11 Eur. L.J. 308, 312 (2005).

[702] Lisbon Treaty Art. 2(16).

"Under the principle of subsidiarity, in areas which do not fall within its exclusive competence, the Union shall act only if and insofar as the objectives of the intended action cannot
be sufficiently achieved by the Member States, either at central level or at regional and local level, but can rather, by reason of the scale or effects of the proposed action, be better
achieved at Union level."[703]

Proportionality is given a name and the following definition: "Under the principle of
proportionality, the content and form of Union action shall not exceed what is necessary to achieve the objectives of the Treaties."[704] Proportionality is not expressly limited to Union action outside the areas of its exclusive competence, and thus it arguably
applies even to matters of EU exclusivity. However, the very concept of exclusivity
would seem to entail the widest possible discretion as to the scope of action taken (always bearing in mind the "objectives of the Treaties").

In an article that compares the EU's concept of subsidiarity with its antecedent in
Catholic doctrine,[705] N. W. Barber notes three "operative elements" within EC Treaty
Article 5:

"First, the Article contains a preference for power to be allocated to the smaller unit: Member States . . . Second, this allocation of power is qualified by an efficiency test. Power
should be shifted downwards unless the centralization of power will result in efficiency
gains . . . Lastly, it is implicit in Article 5 that the power should be exercised by the Member State that will be affected by the power."[706]

The primary change in the Lisbon Treaty's formulation of the subsidiarity rule is that
Union action must be weighed against what could be achieved by the Member States
"either at central level or at regional and local level." The EC Treaty merely mentions action "by the Member States." In the matter of proportionality, the EC Treaty
states that "any action" by the Community must not "go beyond what is necessary" to
achieve the treaty's objectives. The Lisbon Treaty requires that "the *content and form*
of Union action shall not exceed what is necessary" to achieve the objectives of the
Treaties. (emphasis supplied)

Expanding on the revised definitions, the Lisbon Treaty adds that the EU institutions must apply the subsidiarity and proportionality principles in accordance with the
"Protocol on the application of the principles subsidiarity and proportionality" (Protocol on Subsidiarity).[707] This protocol requires each EU institution to "ensure constant

[703] Lisbon Treaty Art. 1(6)(3).
[704] Id. Art. 1(6)(4).
[705] The Catholic catechism defines subsidiarity as a concept by which "a community of a higher order
should not interfere in the internal life of a community of a lower order, depriving the latter of its functions,
but rather should support it in case of need and help co-ordinate its activity with the activities of the rest of
society, always with a view to the common good." Catechism of the Catholic Church, United States Conference of Catholic Bishops, Art. 1, ¶ 1883, available at www.usccb.org/catechism/text/pt3sect1chpt2.htm.
[706] Barber, *supra* note 701, at 311-12.
[707] Lisbon Treaty Art. 1(6)(4). See Protocol on Subsidiarity, *supra* note 328.

respect" for the principles,[708] it requires the Commission to "consult widely" before proposing legislation,[709] and it requires the institutions to forward both drafts and final legislation to the national parliaments of the Member States for review.[710] Proposed legislation must be accompanied by statements and substantiating data to demonstrate that it complies with the two principles.[711] The national parliaments may object to legislation on the grounds that it fails to meet the subsidiarity standard,[712] and in most instances if one-third of all votes allocated to the parliaments (two votes per nation, one per each legislative chamber in bicameral legislatures) concur in the objection, the legislation "must be reviewed" by the Commission or other institution that has proposed the act.[713] The parliaments that force such a review cannot actually block the legislation, but the initiating institution must give reasons for maintaining, amending or withdrawing the legislation.[714] The ECJ is granted jurisdiction to hear challenges based on violations of subsidiarity, and such challenges may be brought by Member States or the Committee of the Regions.[715] The Commission must submit annual reports on compliance with the subsidiarity requirements.[716]

Related to the Protocol on Subsidiarity is the "Protocol on the role of national parliaments in the European Union" (Protocol on National Parliaments).[717] This protocol requires the Commission and other EU institutions to forward reports, proposed legislation and other items to the national parliaments for review.[718] The protocol requires an eight-week review period between notification and adoption of proposed legislation[719] (six months in the case of certain proposed amendments to the Treaties),[720] but it refers to the Protocol on Subsidiarity for the procedures by which one or more parliaments may object to legislation on subsidiarity grounds.[721]

The Protocol on Subsidiarity and the Protocol on National Parliaments originated in 1997 in the Treaty of Amsterdam as additions to both the EC Treaty and TEU.[722] As appended to the Lisbon Treaty the two have been amended. The revised Protocol on Subsidiarity offers significant procedures and rights that were entirely absent in the treaty version. In particular, it offers the requirement of notifying national parliaments

---

[708] Protocol on Subsidiarity, *supra* note 328, Art. 1.

[709] Id., Art. 2.

[710] Id., Art. 4.

[711] Id., Art. 5.

[712] Id., Art. 6.

[713] Protocol on Subsidiarity, *supra* note 328, Art. 7. Certain legislation requires only one-fourth of the possible votes to comprise an objection that triggers a review.

[714] Id.

[715] Id., Art. 8.

[716] Id., Art. 9.

[717] Protocol on National Parliaments, *supra* note 328.

[718] Id., Arts. 1, 2, 5, 6, 7.

[719] Id., Art. 4.

[720] Id., Art. 6.

[721] Id., Art. 3.

[722] Protocol on the role of national parliaments in the European Union, November 10, 1997, O.J. (C 340) 113; Protocol on the application of the principles of subsidiarity and proportionality, November 10, 1997, O.J. (C 340) 105.

of proposed legislation, the opportunity for parliaments to object to legislation and force a review, and the right of a Member State to challenge legislation at the Court of Justice. The Lisbon Treaty's Protocol on National Parliaments also offers more than its predecessor. The new version expands the list of matters that must be forwarded to the national parliaments for review, references the objecting procedure in the Protocol on Subsidiarity, and offers an unprecedented six-month review period relating to certain proposed amendments to the Treaties.[723] Peter Norman reports that the two protocols were "beefed up somewhat" at the Convention (whose proposals have been carried over into the Lisbon Treaty) for the purpose of increasing Member State protections against "any centralising urges emanating from Brussels."[724]

Several observations can be offered regarding the Lisbon Treaty's refinements to subsidiarity and proportionality. First, the revised textual description of subsidiarity, referring to central, regional and local levels of the Member States rather than simply to the states, is at best a nuanced expansion in the concept of how potential state action is to be viewed. The new language does not suggest an actual shift in the definition or substance of subsidiarity. Second, the change in the textual description of proportionality, substituting "the content and form" of EU action for "any action," does not seem intended to alter the substance of the proportionality principle. Third, the Protocol on Subsidiarity is upgraded to a substantial extent. The rights of national parliaments to review, make objection and challenge EU legislation on subsidiarity grounds arguably put more teeth into the principle, although Michael Dougan has criticised this "early warning system on subsidiarity which suffers from almost enough operational flaws to undermine the arguments supporting its very existence."[725] Finally, the changes to the Protocol on National Parliaments are less dramatic, but they do offer somewhat more information to the Member States to enable them to review proposed EU legislation.[726]

Subsidiarity and proportionality may be seen as logical extensions of the conferral principle, in that they contribute to protecting the residuum of Member State power. With the EU limited to the competences specifically granted under the Treaties, and

---

[723] For a discussion on the general role of national parliaments within the EU, see Heidi Hautala, The Role of Parliaments in the EU Constitutional Framework: A Partnership or Rivalry? in The EU Constitution: The Best Way Forward? (Deirdre Curtin, Alfred E. Kellermann & Steven Blockmans, eds., 2005).

[724] Norman, *supra* note 123, at 252.

[725] Michael Dougan, The Convention's Draft Constitutional Treaty: Bringing Europe Closer to its Lawyers, 28 Eur. L. Rev. 763, 793 (2003).

[726] Two commentators have noted the EU has permitted expansion of the activities of national parliaments beyond the formal role provided in the protocols and beyond the concepts of subsidiarity and proportionality. First, "the EU has produced laws on topics considered beyond the traditional remit of national parliaments," and as a result the national governments have produced "new domestic laws in those areas that not only incorporate but also build upon EU law." Second, "the EU has facilitated communication and data sharing across Member States. The resulting knowledge has helped legislators and government officials design more effective legislative frameworks. This has confirmed national parliaments as viable regulatory institutions." Francesco Duina & Michael J. Oliver, National Parliaments in the European Union: Are There Any Benefits to Integration?, 11 Eur. L.J. 173, 174 (2005).

with all other authority reserved to the Member States, subsidiarity and proportionality support these concepts by requiring the Union to behave prudently even when it is permitted to act. Under the Lisbon Treaty the new procedures that provide a measure of enforcement to the subsidiarity rule clearly add more substance to the principle. Nevertheless, scepticism remains as to the rule's actual impact. For example, Lars Hoffmann and Jo Shaw assert that "in reality the [subsidiarity] principle itself is both unclear and widely regarded as rather toothless."[727] They contend that subsidiarity "has never been successfully invoked, for example, before the Court of Justice as a basis for finding that a measure should not have been adopted by the EU institutions."[728] P. W. Barber agrees that subsidiarity has not been credited with any overt decisions by the Court, but he nevertheless believes that the principle is deserving of respect:

> "The European principle of subsidiarity is important because it is one of the key constitutional principles that serve to set the character of the EU. As a legal principle, a justiciable constraint on the power of the Community Institutions, subsidiarity has had little obvious effect. Perhaps daunted by the complicated political assessments the principle entails, or, less charitably, perhaps disinclined to develop a principle that limits the centralization of power, the European Court of Justice has not made use of the principle. The degree to which subsidiarity has indirectly affected measures advanced by the Community is unclear. But the principle stands as a declaration of how the EU perceives itself, and as the sort of political community the authors of the Treaties intended it to be. In particular, it represents a commitment to democracy, to de-centralised power and, most importantly, opposition to nationalist ideals of state legitimacy."[729]

Michael Dougan asserts that the innovations in the Constitution (which are carried over into the Lisbon Treaty) "should help give more practical force to the principle of subsidiarity," but he argues that the EU still lacks "a truly coherent conception of the role national parliaments should play with the Union legislative process."[730] He contends that there are "major gaps" in the Member States' ability to function effectively, but he also argues that if the new provisions were inserted as mere "window dressing . . . to enhance the Union's democratic credentials," then the authors of the Constitution [and Lisbon Treaty as well] have run the risk of "complicating and prolonging still further the Union's legislative procedures."[731]

---

[727] Hoffmann & Shaw, *supra* note 700, at 6. For a recent wide-ranging criticism of subsidiarity, see Gareth Davies, Subsidiarity: The Wrong Idea, in the Wrong Place, at the Wrong Time, 43 C.M.L.R. 63 (2006).

[728] Id.

[729] Barber, *supra* note 701, at 324-25.

[730] Dougan, *supra* note 422, at 6.

[731] Id. For additional analysis of the subsidiarity principle and the role of national parliaments in EU legislation, see Anna Verges Bausili, Rethinking the methods of dividing and exercising powers in the EU – Reforming subsidiarity, national parliaments and legitimacy, in Shaw, *supra* note 4, at 95. See also Collignon, *supra* note 4, at 84-87.

Even without the innovations proposed in the Lisbon Treaty, the EU leadership has indicated its intention to pay greater attention to subsidiarity and proportionality. Conferences in The Hague in 2005 and in St. Pölten, Austria, in 2006 led the European Council in its June, 2006 Presidency Conclusions to endorse an ongoing examination of new approaches to application of these principles.[732] In addition the Conclusions welcomed the Commission's commitment to carry out greater consultation with national parliaments on new Union legislation, and the European Council specifically "invited" the Council, Parliament and Commission to "consistently check the correct application of the principles and guidelines laid down in the Protocol on subsidiarity and proportionality."[733]

3.   PRIMACY

The effectiveness of EU action within the Union, that is, within each of the Member States of the Union, has its legal basis in the principle of primacy.[734] The current Treaties do not explicitly use the term, but EC Treaty Article 10 imposes the following obligations on the Member States:

> "Member States shall take all appropriate measures, whether general or particular, to ensure fulfilment of the obligations arising out of this Treaty or resulting from action taken by the institutions of the Community. They shall facilitate the achievement of the Community's tasks. They shall abstain from any measure which could jeopardise the attainment of the objectives of this Treaty."

Furthermore, Article 249 of the EC Treaty defines a "regulation" of the Community as a measure that "shall have general application. It shall be binding in its entirety and directly applicable in all Member States." Although the Treaties do not explicitly state that EU law has primacy, the concept is implicit. For example, if a Member State has law that is inconsistent with EU law on the same subject, and if the state is required to "ensure fulfilment" of the EU law, then the Treaty obligation would require the state to follow EU law in preference to its national law. The practical result would be the superior force of Union law – indeed its primacy over the Member State's law.

Despite the imprecise manner in which the Treaties deal with primacy, case law interpreting the Treaties has firmly established the principle. The first decision was the 1963 ruling in the matter of *Van Gend en Loos* v. *Nederlandse Administratie der*

---

[732] 2006 Presidency Conclusions, *supra* note 132, at 13.

[733] Id. at 14.

[734] In American constitutional parlance, primacy is referred to as "supremacy," with Art. VI of the United States Constitution declaring that Constitution itself and federal law "shall be the supreme Law of the Land." Another term commonly used in American jurisprudence is "pre-emption," and the U.S. Supreme Court has declared that "under the Supremacy Clause, from which our pre-emption doctrine is derived, 'any state law, however clearly within a State's acknowledged power, which interferes with or is contrary to federal law, must yield.'" *Gade* v. *National Solid Wastes Management Association*, 505 U.S. 88, 108 (1992). See also Chemerinsky, *supra* note 691, at 376-401.

Belastingen.[735] In this case the Court of Justice ruled that the authority of the EC Treaty was not dependent upon any national implementing legislation or any other measure taken by a Member State. The second ruling was in the 1964 case of *Costa* v. *ENEL*,[736] in which the Court declared that Community law must be superior to national law because of the nature of the Community legal order:

> "[T]he law stemming from the [EC] Treaty could not, because of its special and original nature, be overridden by domestic legal considerations, however framed, without being deprived of its character as Community law and without the legal basis of the Community itself being called into question.
>
> The transfer by the States from their domestic legal system to the Community legal system of the rights and obligations arising under the Treaty carries with it a permanent limitation of their sovereign rights, against which a subsequent unilateral act incompatible with the concept of the Community cannot prevail."[737]

A further ruling in 1970 affirmed the primacy of Community law even over a national constitution. In *Internationale Handelsgesellschaft m.b.H* v. *Einfuhr- und Vorratsstelle für Getreide und Futtermittel* the Court declared:

> "[T]he validity of a Community instrument or its effect within a Member State cannot be affected by allegations that it runs counter to either the fundamental rights as formulated by the constitution of that State or the principles of a national constitutional structure."[738]

Notwithstanding these pronouncements from the Court, primacy has its boundaries. For example, primacy flows from the propriety of the action taken by the EU. Any act of the Union that exceeds its conferred authority would presumably lack legal validity and thus could not have primacy over Member State law. By way of illustration, EC Treaty Article 195 identifies two specific fields in which EU activity is curtailed: "The Treaty shall in no way prejudice the rules in Member States governing the system of property ownership." Similarly, Article 296 states that the treaty may not interfere with the right of a Member State to withhold information it considers vital to its national security, or the right of a state to protect its "production of or trade in arms, munitions and war material" as long as this protection does not have an anti-competitive effect in the internal market outside the military sphere. In these fields the Member States retain exclusive control, their laws enjoy absolute primacy, and their activities are exempt from interference by EU law.

Another limitation on primacy arises from the fact that certain EU law depends on implementation at the Member State level. EC Treaty Article 249 states that a "directive" is a Community act that "shall be binding, as to the result to be achieved, upon each Member State to which it is addressed, but shall leave to the national authorities

---

[735] Case 26/62, *Van Gend en Loos, supra* note 29.

[736] Case 6/64, *Costa* v. *ENEL*, 1964 ECR 585.

[737] Id. at 594.

[738] Case 11/70, *Internationale Handelsgesellschaft m.b.H* v. *Einfuhr- und Vorratsstelle für Getreide und Futtermittel*, 1970 ECR 1125, 1134.

the choice of form and methods." Simply stated, directives are subject to further action at the Member State level. They are by themselves binding only "as to the result to be achieved," but not as to the "form and methods" of achieving that result. The significance of this type of EU legislation is that if each Member State is permitted to determine the details for governing the regulated activity within its own territory, then it might be argued that the control over that activity – the primacy of authority, if you will – is shared between the EU and the state.

The drafters of the Constitution proposed a textual affirmation of the primacy principle by including as Article I-6 the following straightforward statement: "The Constitution and law adopted by the Union's Institutions in exercising competences conferred on it, shall have primacy over the law of the Member States."[739] This appealingly simple formulation set off a post-Convention flurry of speculation as to whether it should be taken at face value.[740] Paul Craig raised several concerns, including his assertion that the wording of Article I-6 would leave room to argue that EU law has primacy over national legislation, but not over national constitutions.[741] He also questioned whether EU regulations should have primacy equal to EU legislation, whether the Member States retain a residual competence (*Kompetenz-Kompetenz*) to decide issues of primacy,[742] and whether the principles of subsidiarity and proportionality limit the scope of primacy.[743] He assured the academic world that Article I-6 would not "signal the death of one of the staple topics in EU law courses."[744] Mattias Kumm likewise commented that "the supremacy clause does not by itself say who should settle the question whether EC legislation is or is not *ultra vires*, even though this is exactly the issue [that] has been the subject of disagreement between the Court of Justice and some national courts."[745] Michael Dougan also questioned "the merits of the Convention's attempt to codify a principle characterised by sophisticated nuance

---

[739] Constitution Art. I-6. In addition, Constitution Art. I-5(2) offered a statement similar to EC Treaty Art. 10 requiring the Member States to ensure fulfilment of EU law.

[740] For a review of the supremacy issue as the subject of long-standing judicial and academic attention, see Mattias Kumm, The Jurisprudence of Constitutional Conflict: Constitutional Supremacy in Europe before and after the Constitutional Treaty, 11 Eur. L.J. 262 (2005).

[741] Paul Craig, What Constitution does Europe Need? The Federal Trust, August 2003, at 8, www.fedtrust.co.uk/uploads/constitution/26_03.pdf.

[742] George Bermann notes: "[The] slowly growing number of Member States whose supreme or constitutional courts have, following the German example, in effect stated that, while they intend for them and their national judiciaries to show the highest degree of respect for the pronouncements of the Court of Justice (even on matters as sensitive and important as protection of human rights and fundamental freedoms), they will not in principle cede to that Court ultimate authority for determining the outer boundaries of the EU's legislative and policy powers. Under that view, *Kompetenz/Kompetenz* does not lie in Luxembourg (except of course for Luxembourg); it lies in the seats of the highest courts of the Member States, almost as if in the USA it lay, as it assuredly does not, in the state capitals." Bermann, *supra* note 18, at 367. For a general analysis of the Constitution and its impact on the sovereignty of the Member States' constitutional courts, see Anneli Albi & Peter Van Elsuwege, The EU Constitution, National Constitutions and Sovereignty: An Assessment of a "European Constitutional Order," 29 Eur. L. Rev. 741 (2004).

[743] Craig, *supra* note 741, at 8-9.

[744] Id. at 8.

[745] Kumm, *supra* note 740, at 296.

in the [EU] caselaw, and extensive debate among academics."[746] He suggested that "we should accept that this [Article I-6] is a largely hortatory provision which offers little of substance to the complex debate on relations between the Union and domestic legal orders."[747]

In the end, the Constitution's statement on primacy evidently proved to be too controversial to survive. The June 2007 IGC decided to omit the provision from the Lisbon Treaty, and in its place a declaration will state the following:

> "The Conference recalls that, in accordance with well settled case-law of the EU Court of Justice, the Treaties and the law adopted by the Union on the basis of the Treaties have primacy over the law of member States, under the conditions laid down by said case-law."[748]

Through its declaration the Lisbon Treaty thus offers both an affirmation of the primacy principle and a continuing opportunity for scholars to debate its limits. Regardless of the manner in which it is expressed, primacy serves as an essential and state-like means of ensuring the effectiveness of EU policies and programs.

4.   EXCLUSIVITY

The concept of exclusivity arises from the allocation of powers between the EU and the Member States. One of the perceived weaknesses of the current Treaties is that their approach to exclusivity is presented randomly. Competences in specific fields are found in the substantive provisions relating to that field, but the Treaties lack a set of overview provisions. The following are examples of how the Treaties deal with competences and exclusivity:

i.   EC Treaty Article 5 notes that in areas outside its exclusive competence, the Community may act only in accordance with the principle of subsidiarity. However, the treaty offers no definition as to which substantive matters fall within this exclusive competence.

ii. Article 127(1) of the EC Treaty permits the Community to encourage Member State cooperation in the field of employment policy, but it requires respect for "the competences of the Member States," and Article 129 states that the Community's measures "shall not include harmonisation of the laws and regulations of the Member States."

---

[746] Dougan, *supra* note 422, at 7.

[747] Id. at 8.

[748] 2007 Presidency Conclusions, *supra* note 146, Annex I at 16, n. 1. The Annex also refers to a legal opinion of the Legal Service of the Council entitled "Primacy of EC law," which states, in its entirety: "It results from the case-law of the Court of Justice that primacy of EC law is a cornerstone principle of Community law. According to the Court, this principle is inherent to the specific nature of the European Community. At the time of the first judgement of this established case-law (Costa/ENEL, 15 July 1964, Case 6/641) there was no mention of primacy in the treaty. It is still the case today. The fact that the principle of primacy will not be included in the future treaty shall not in any way change the existence of the principle and the existing case-law of the Court of Justice." Opinion of the Legal Service of the Council, 11197/07 (2007).

iii. EC Treaty Articles 131 to 134 govern the common commercial policy of the Community. Article 133(6) deals with negotiation of international trade agreements by the Community, but it states that an agreement "may not be concluded by the Council if it includes provisions which would go beyond the Community's internal powers, in particular by leading to harmonisation of the laws or regulations of the Member States in an area for which this Treaty rules out such harmonisation." Article 133(6) further designates certain subjects as falling within "the shared competence of the Community and its Member States."

iv. EC Treaty Article 137(4) states that Community activities in the field of social policy may not affect "the right of Member States" to define their own fundamental principles. Respect for the "responsibility" or "responsibilities" of the Member States is found in relation to Community support for education (Art. 149(1)), vocational training (Art. 150(1)) and public health (Art. 152(5)).

v. EC Treaty Article 174(4) speaks of the Community and Member States acting within "their respective spheres of competence" to cooperate with third countries and international organisations in the field of environmental protection, but any action must be "without prejudice to Member States' competence to negotiate in international bodies and to conclude international agreements." Similar statements are made in Article 181 with regard to Community activity in the field of development cooperation, and in Article 181a(3) in relation to economic, financial and technical cooperation with third countries.

vi. TEU Article 11 requires the Union to pursue a CFSP, and the Member States are required to support it. However, as further explained in Chapter 17 of this treatise, the Member States retain substantial power in this field.

vii. TEU Articles 29 to 42 call upon the EU to provide an AFSJ, but the focus of these provisions is on coordination of a field in which the Member States retain substantial power. This area is further examined in Chapter 16 of this treatise.

viii. TEU Article 43 permits "enhanced cooperation" among groups of Member States, but not in "the areas which fall within the exclusive competence of the Community."

As these provisions illustrate, the Treaties mention spheres of EU competence, shared competence and Member State competence without ever delineating clearly just where EU activity will run afoul of the authority reserved to the Member States. At best, the Treaties indicate what the Union is permitted to do in specific subject areas, but the big picture is lacking. This shortcoming was duly noted by the EU leadership in 2001. The ICG at Nice stated that a re-evaluation of the EU should include addressing "how to establish and monitor a more precise delimitation of powers between the European Union and the Member States, reflecting the principle of subsidiarity."[749] The Commission White Paper noted that the Union needs "clear principles identifying how competence is shared between the Union and its Member States."[750] The

---

[749] Nice Declaration, *supra* note 103, at 85.
[750] White Paper, *supra* note 23, at 34.

Laeken Declaration in late 2001, by which the IGC instituted the constitutional Convention, identified the critical need for the Convention to "clarify, simplify and adjust the division of competence between the Union and the Member States in light of the new challenges facing the Union."[751]

The Convention respond to these challenges, and the Constitution contained an unprecedented title called "Union Competences."[752] These articles identified different categories of competence,[753] including areas of exclusive EU competence,[754] areas in which competence would be shared between the Union and the Member States,[755] and areas in which the EU would provide support, coordination or supplementary action to activities of the Member States.[756] The Lisbon Treaty adopts this approach in a similar set of provisions inserted into the EC Treaty. Gathered under the heading "Categories and Areas of Union Competence,"[757] these articles include the following:

a.   The first provision provides basic definitions.[758] In areas of *exclusive EU competence*, only the EU may act. Member States may involve themselves only to implement Union acts or in response to specific permission from the EU. In matters of *shared competence*, both the Union and Member States have authority to act, but the states may act only if the EU does not. A third category is where the Union may *support, coordinate or supplement* Member State activities, as long as the EU does not encroach on the states' competences. Additional statements address the Union's implementation of the CFSP, as well as EU coordination of Member State economic and employment policies.

b.   The second article[759] lists the following areas as *exclusive* to the EU: the customs union, competition rules necessary for the functioning of the internal market, monetary policy for the euro-zone states, conservation of marine biological resources under the common fisheries policy and the common commercial policy (international trade policy of the Union). In addition, the EU possesses exclusive competence to conclude international agreements relating to these fields.

c.   The third provision[760] delineates the areas of *shared competence* as the following "principal" areas: the internal market; social policy as set forth in the EC Treaty; economic, social and territorial cohesion; agriculture and fisheries, excluding conservation of marine biological resources; environment; consumer protection; transport; trans-European networks; energy; the AFSJ; and common safety concerns

---

[751] Laeken Declaration, *supra* note 114, at 21. Also in 2001, Jürgen Habermas wrote that everyone could agree "that delimitation of the competences of federal, national and regional levels is the core political issue to be settled by any European constitution." Jürgen Habermas, Why Europe Needs a Constitution, 11 New Left Rev. 5, 26 (2001).

[752] Constitution Arts. I-11 to I-18.

[753] Id. Art. I-12.

[754] Id. Art. I-13.

[755] Id. Art. I-14.

[756] Id. Arts. I-15, I-17.

[757] Lisbon Treaty Art. 2(12).

[758] Id. Art. 2(12)(2A).

[759] Id. Art. 2(12)(2B).

[760] Id. Art. 2(12)(2C).

in public health matters as set forth in the EC Treaty. In shared competence both the EU and Member States may act, but Member States may legislate only "to the extent that the Union has not exercised, or has decided to cease exercising, its competence." However, there are exceptions to this general rule – the fields of research, technological development, space, development cooperation and humanitarian aid are identified as areas of shared competence, but Union action in these fields will not preclude Member State action.[761]

d.   In a fourth major provision[762] the Lisbon Treaty identifies the following areas in which the Union may carry out actions to *support, coordinate or supplement* the actions of the Member States: protection and improvement of human health; industry; culture; tourism; education, vocational training, youth and, sport; civil protection; and administrative cooperation. These are not fields of shared competence.[763] Rather, the EU's own actions are limited to supporting, coordinating or supplementing the activities of the Member States. Anything done by the Union may not supersede the underlying competence of the Member States, and Union acts may not "entail harmonisation of Member States' laws or regulations."[764]

The approach in the Lisbon Treaty represents a significant step toward helpful clarifying where the dividing lines lie. However, the new approach has several shortcomings. First, it is not comprehensive. The final provision of the overview article states: "The scope of and arrangements for exercising the Union's competences shall be determined by the provisions of the Treaties relating to each area."[765] In addition, two areas of shared competence identified in the Lisbon Treaty are limited by the phrase "for the aspects defined in this Treaty.[766] Furthermore, the introduction to the list of shared competences acknowledges that it is incomplete, by referring to "the following *principal* areas." (emphasis supplied)[767] Taken together, these references compel the reader to look beyond the overview provisions of the Lisbon Treaty and undertake a careful review of the substantive details of the Treaties. However useful, the overview is incomplete.

The second point of concern is that it is not clear as to why several subject areas are set apart from the three main types of EU competence. As noted above, matters of research, technological development and space are treated differently from the other shared-competence items. The same is true for development cooperation and humanitarian aid. Furthermore, economic and employment policies are placed into a separate

---

[761] Lisbon Treaty Art. 2(12)(2C)(3), (4).

[762] Id. Art. 2(12)(2E).

[763] The Lisbon Treaty states: "The Union shall share competence with the Member States where the Treaties confer on it a competence which does not relate to areas referred to in Articles 2B and 2E." Lisbon Treaty Art. 2(12)(2C). The referenced provisions are those on exclusive competence (2B) and on areas where of supporting, coordinating and supplementary EU action (2E).

[764] Lisbon Treaty Art. 2(12)(2A)(5).

[765] Id. Art. 2(12)(2A)(6).

[766] Id. Art. 2(12)(2C)(2)(b) (social policy), 2(12)(2C)(2)(k) (common safety concerns in public health matters).

[767] Lisbon Treaty Art. 2(12)(2C)(2).

provision calling for EU "coordination."[768] Activities in the CFSP are also segregated.[769] Apparently there is a case for affording special treatment to each of these areas, but one could just as well argue for including them in the three general categories of competence.

Third, there is an inherent paradox posed by the Union's coordinating action that on one hand may have an impact on the Member States, but on the other hand may not supersede Member State competence or require harmonisation of national law. Paul Craig has argued that the entire area of supporting, coordinating and supplementary action will prove to be "problematic."[770]

The preceding discussion illustrates that the matter of competences under the Lisbon Treaty includes a substantial role for the Member States. In areas of supporting, coordinating and supplementary activity the Member States are considered the primary actors, with the Union in a facilitating role. Shared competences anticipate that the Member States will act where the EU chooses not to. Even the areas of exclusive EU competence may involve Member State action if the Union so decides. Furthermore, regardless of whether competence is exclusive to the EU or shared with the Member States, in the case of an EU directive it will be left to the Member States to pass implementing legislation.[771] While directives are binding on the Member States "as to the result to be achieved,"[772] by their nature they require, rather than preclude, Member State action in the subject field. Finally, as noted in Part 1 of this chapter, under the principle of conferral there is a reservation to the Member States of all competences not conferred on the EU in the Treaties.

The allocation of competences, whether presented in a random fashion as in the current Treaties or more clearly as in the Lisbon Treaty, assists in defining what the European Union is and what its limits are. George Bermann describes the competence delineation as "an exercise whose evident purpose is to halt, or at least give the impression of halting, what has come in the trade to be known as the Union's competences 'creep'."[773] As illustrated above, the Lisbon Treaty's clearer expressions also offer ample evidence that the EU is a dual system. The Union has substantial power, but the Member States are vital actors in its activities.

5.   FLEXIBILITY

5.1   EU action beyond its designated competences

Even the highly detailed Treaties cannot anticipate every need for EU action. As a consequence the Member States have given the Union a flexibility clause, EC Treaty

---

[768] Lisbon Treaty Art. 2(12)(2D).
[769] Id. Art. 2(12)(2A)(4). Also see Lisbon Treaty Art. 1(27); TEU Art. 11(2).
[770] Craig, *supra* note 741, at 7-8. See the discussion in Part 1.4 of Chapter 17.
[771] EC Treaty Art. 249; Lisbon Treaty Art. 2(235).
[772] EC Treaty Art. 249.
[773] Bermann, *supra* note 18, at 368.

Article 308, which allows the Union in limited circumstances to take steps beyond its designated competences:

> "If action by the Community should prove necessary to attain, in the course of operation of the common market, one of the objectives of the Community, and this Treaty has not provided the necessary powers, the Council shall, acting unanimously on a proposal from the Commission and after consulting the European Parliament, take the appropriate measures."

The Lisbon Treaty has restated Article 308 in the following form:

> "If action by the Union should prove necessary, within the framework of the policies defined in the Treaties, to attain one of the objectives set out in the Treaties, and the Treaties have not provided the necessary powers, the Council, acting unanimously on a proposal from the Commission and after obtaining the consent of the European Parliament, shall adopt the appropriate measures. Where the measures in question are adopted by the Council in accordance with a special legislative procedure, it shall also act unanimously on a proposal from the Commission and after obtaining the consent of the European Parliament."[774]

Substantively, the Lisbon Treaty requires that any step taken under the flexibility clause must be "within the framework of the policies defined in the Treaties, to attain one of the objectives set out in the Treaties." Procedurally, the process begins with the Commission proposing an action and advising the Member State parliaments of the proposal.[775] Under the procedures described in the revised TEU and in the Protocol on Subsidiarity, the parliaments may issue a challenge if they believe that the proposal will violate the subsidiarity rule.[776] The next step is to obtain the consent of the European Parliament, and lastly the Council must vote unanimously to approve the action.[777] One further requirement is that actions taken under the flexibility provision "shall not entail harmonisation of Member States' laws or regulations in cases where the Treaties exclude such harmonisation."[778]

Note that the current EC Treaty refers to actions relating to "operation of the common market," while the Lisbon refers to the "framework of the policies defined in the Treaties." The Lisbon Treaty's realm of flexibility is thus more extensive. In addition, the Lisbon Treaty provides for consent by the European Parliament, rather than mere "consultation." The Lisbon Treaty's notification to Member State parliaments and its clarification regarding harmonisation of Member State law are also new. Both of these features constitute new protections for the Member States. However, the primary safeguard for the Member States in current Article 308 and in its Lisbon Treaty version is that Council decisions under the flexibility procedure must be taken unanimously. Each Member State has the opportunity at the Council to block the proposed action.

---

[774] Lisbon Treaty Art. 2(289)(1).

[775] Id. Art. 2(289)(2).

[776] See discussion of this challenge procedure in Part 2 of this chapter.

[777] Lisbon Treaty Art. 1(6)(3); Protocol on Subsidiarity, *supra* note 328.

[778] Lisbon Treaty Art. 2(289)(3).

The Constitution contained a flexibility clause nearly identical to the revised provision proposed in the Lisbon Treaty. Peter Ludlow described the Constitution's version as "a potentially far-reaching enabling clause . . . which, like [EC Treaty Article 308], can and should obviate the need for future IGC's as long as the Council can agree unanimously that changes are needed."[779] He argued that the new clause should be viewed in conjunction with the new simplified constitutional amendment procedures (which have been carried over into the Lisbon Treaty).[780] Ludlow noted that some critics have claimed that the unanimity requirement "negates the value" of these three articles,[781] but he believed that these criticisms were misleading. He contended:

> "In certain cases, such as these, which involve 'fast track' decisions regarding the scope and character of the EU system as such, the unanimity requirement seems both reasonable and necessary. Actual experience further suggests that it need not inhibit boldness."[782]

Ludlow noted that the "radical expansion of the European Community's agenda in the 1970s into areas such as environmental policy, regional policy and the [European Monetary System] was based on [EC Treaty Article 308] which also required unanimity."[783]

If EU officials determine that a law must be enacted or a decision taken that will enhance EU activity despite not being provided for in the Treaties, and if the matter is of a technical nature or does not infringe on any essential aspect of Member State sovereignty, then the flexibility clause should work in practice. Lack of controversy should lead to full cooperation and the necessary unanimity to see the matter through. Because of the procedural safeguards in the Lisbon Treaty, employment of the flexibility clause will not likely lead to any extension of EU competences. Michael Dougan has commented that the Constitution's flexibility clause "could not be used either to add new objectives to the Constitution, or to exceed the basic parameters of Union competence established in [the Constitution's Part III provisions governing its policies and functioning]."[784]

Peter Norman comments that the Constitution's revised flexibility clause and its simplified amendment procedures (both of which have survived in the Lisbon Treaty) "promise to put national parliaments on their mettle" because these provisions "have the potential to shift responsibilities from the member states to the Union."[785] He adds: "In both cases the national parliaments must be informed, giving them an opportunity to influence the decisions of their own governments." However, he warns that such "checks and balances" will be successful only if the Member State parliaments "pay

---

[779] Peter Ludlow, The Thessaloniki European Council, EuroComment Briefing Note, No. 2.3, July 3, 2003, at 28.

[780] Id. See the discussion in Chapter 11 of this treatise.

[781] For example, Michael Dougan observed that in an enlarged EU the unanimity requirement "automatically reduces the practical significance of the flexibility clause." Dougan, *supra* note 422, at 4.

[782] Id. at 28-29.

[783] Id. at 29.

[784] Id. at 4.

[785] Norman, *supra* note 123, at 328-29.

heed to what is happening at the European Union level."[786] An alert parliament might be able to influence its country's Council or European Council representative before a decision is taken.

5.2   The Open Method of Coordination

While EC Treaty Article 308 provides a mechanism for the EU itself to act beyond its designated competences, there are instances in which action in new areas may not be politically feasible due to the Article 308 unanimity requirement. In these circumstances, if there is a perceived need for centrally encouraged cooperation among the Member States, the EU has devised a process by which it can at least facilitate a common approach to national action. This process is known as the Open Method of Co-ordination (OMC). Because this activity does involve a measure of Union activity, a description of it is included in this section on the Union's flexibility.

The OMC was formally endorsed at the Lisbon IGC in March 2000, and it has been described as follows:

> "Its purpose was to spread legislative "best practices" across the Member States in areas where the EU has no competence for regulation. . . . Observers have described OMC as a clear effort on the part of the EU to encourage policy transfers among member states. OMC is in fact a compendium of mechanisms for cross-national communication."[787]

In the Open Method of Coordination the EU does not enact its own legislation or other measures. Rather, it carries out any of several different types of activity: (1) it collects National Action Plans from the Member States and makes them available for public review; (2) it evaluates the National Action Plans and issues Joint Reports (of the Council and Commission) including recommendations of best practices; (3) it creates statistical indicators and other measurements relating to the information it is evaluating; and (4) it creates and supports Peer Review Programmes such as conferences and exchanges among representatives of interested Member States.[788] In short, the OMC is an activity in which the EU fulfills the role of a facilitator, not a legislator or administrator.

The OMC has been controversial, and commentators David M. Trubek and Louise G. Trubek have summarised the debate as follows:

> "Both those who favour the OMC as a mode of governance and those who question its desirability compare the OMC, implicitly or explicitly, with the Community Method. The Community Method is thought of as 'hard law' because it creates uniform rules that Member States must adopt, provides sanctions if they fail to do so, and allows challenges for non-compliance to be brought in court. In contrast, the OMC, which has general and open-ended guidelines rather than rules, provides no formal sanctions for Member States that do

---

[786] Id. at 329.
[787] Duina & Oliver, *supra* note 726, at 183.
[788] Id. at 183-84.

not follow the guidelines, and is not justiciable, is thought of as 'soft law'. Proponents of the OMC argue that it can be effective despite – or even because of – its open-ended, non-binding, non-justiciable qualities. Opponents question that conclusion. They not only argue that the OMC cannot do what is needed to construct Social Europe and that "hard law" is essential, but also contend that use of the OMC could undermine efforts to build the hard law they think will be needed."[789]

Gráinne de Búrca has characterised the opposing "soft law" and "hard law" categories respectively as "new governance" and "traditional constitutionalism," and explains that new governance is necessary because the EU's "constitutional framework does not have a settled and embedded existence of the kind enjoyed by most national systems."[790]

Notwithstanding this theoretical debate, the EU has tackled employment issues through the OMC, and its European Employment Strategy was, after its first five years, judged a success by the Commission.[791] As a result, the OMC process has been applied under the current Treaties in additional subject areas, such as information technology, research and development, economic reforms, education, employment, social inclusion and pensions.[792] The OMC was described favorably in the Commission's White Paper on Governance with the following endorsement: "In some areas it sits alongside the programme-based and legislative approach; in others, it adds value at the European level where there is little hope for legislative solutions."[793]

The Treaties contain suggestions of the OMC, but process is not clearly defined. Article 99 of the EC Treaty permits the Community to draw up guidelines for the Member States' economic policies, and to assist in coordination of those policies. Article 127(1) permits the Community to encourage Member State cooperation in the field of employment policy, but it requires respect for "the competences of the Member States," and Article 129 states that the Community's measures "shall not include

---

[789] David M. Trubek & Louise G. Trubek, Hard and Soft Law in the Construction of Social Europe: The Role of the Open Method of Co-ordination, 11 Eur. L.J. 343, 344 (2005).

[790] Gráinne de Búrca, The Constitutional Challenge of New Governance in the European Union, 28 Eur. L. Rev. 814, 815-16 (2003). For additional relevant commentary, see Collignon, *supra* note 4, at 119-21.

[791] European Commission, Taking Stock of Five Years of the European Employment Strategy, COM (2002) 416 final. In a discussion entitled "Soft law may be harder than you think," commentators Trubek and Trubek identify several different ways in which the OMC actually results in compliance by the Member States: "shaming, diffusion through mimesis or discourse, deliberation, learning and networks." Trubek & Trubek, *supra* note 789, at 356-59.

[792] Duina and Oliver, *supra* note 726, at 183.

[793] White Paper, *supra* note 23, at 21-22. Despite its general endorsement, the Commission warned of necessary limitations: "The use of the open method of co-ordination must not dilute the achievement of common objectives in the Treaty or the political responsibility of the Institutions. It should not be used when legislative action under the Community method is possible; it should ensure overall accountability in line with the following objectives: – It should be used to achieve Treaty objectives. – Regular mechanisms for reporting to the European Parliament should be established. – The Commission should be closely involved and play a co-ordinating role. – The data information generated should be widely available [and] provide the basis for determining whether legislative or programme-based action is needed to overcome particular problems highlighted. Id. at 22.

harmonisation of the laws and regulations of the Member States." Articles 137 and 140 contemplate a variety of Union activities to coordinate the states' social policies. Several other substantive areas involve EU coordination as well.[794]

At the constitutional Convention the coordination process was the subject of much discussion,[795] and several provisions reflecting the OMC were proposed in the Constitution. As now presented in the Lisbon Treaty, these new articles are those that permit the EU to engage in "actions to support, coordinate or supplement the actions of the Member States, without thereby superseding their competence in these areas."[796] The primary areas for this Union activity are the protection and improvement of human health; industry; culture; tourism; education, youth, sport and vocational training; civil protection; and administrative cooperation.[797] In addition, the Lisbon Treaty provides for EU "guidelines" to assist Member States to coordinate their economic policies, "measures to ensure coordination" of Member State employment policies, and "initiatives to ensure coordination of Member States' social policies."[798] These EU coordinating activities have been discussed in Part 4 of this chapter in relation to the exclusivity of Union action.

Overall, it is fair to say that the Lisbon Treaty enhances the EU's ability to coordinate Member State activity in fields where the Union may not legislate. However, critics have argued that the Constitution's approach (mirrored in the Lisbon Treaty) is indirect, its results "murky," and its text "ambiguous."[799] As a consequence, it has been said that the OMC "is hardly given the robust endorsement and full-blown constitutional status some hoped for."[800]

6.   FOUNDATIONAL PRINCIPLES AND THE DIVIDING LINES

The principles discussed in this chapter do much to define the European Union, and they illustrate critical dividing lines between the Union and the Member States. Having said that, let us summarise the foregoing observations as to whether the Lisbon Treaty will impact these dividing lines:

–   *Conferral* by the Member States to the Union is more clearly emphasised in the Lisbon Treaty, but this does not appear to do anything other than state what was already the case. Thus, no shift in this dividing line.
–   *Subsidiarity* and *proportionality* are defined in the Lisbon Treaty essentially as they are in the current Treaties. However, the Protocol on Subsidiarity offers new opportunities for national parliaments to object to proposed EU legislation.

---

[794] See discussion in Part 1.4 of Chapter 17.
[795] Trubek & Trubek, *supra* note 789, at 344.
[796] Lisbon Treaty Arts. 2(12)(2A)(5), 2(12)(2E). See discussion in Part 4 of this chapter.
[797] Lisbon Treaty Art. 2(12)(2E).
[798] Id. Art. 2(12)(2D).
[799] Trubek & Trubek, *supra* note 789, at 354.
[800] Id. See also Myrto Tsakatika, The Open Method of Co-ordination in the European Convention: An Opportunity Lost?, in Dobson, *supra* note 4, at 90-102.

Here a dividing line between EU legislative competence and national oversight will shift toward the Member States. One may observe that this only undercuts the efficiency of EU lawmaking, but it is clear that the procedural rights of the Member States will be enhanced.

– The IGC's 2007 declaration on the *primacy* of EU law (in place of a clear textual affirmation) refers to primacy as developed in the case law of the Court of Justice. This is little more than a confirmation of the status quo and thus a preservation of the existing dividing line.

– The division of competences between the Union and the Member States, described above as the *exclusivity* principle, is much more clearly stated in the Lisbon Treaty than it is in the current Treaties. However, we have seen that clarity can cut both ways, and that it does not necessarily favor either the Union or the Member States. By itself, clarity is a good thing, but in this instance it does not appear to shift any of the EU's dividing lines.

– Finally, we have noted that the Lisbon Treaty's *flexibility* clause, which permits legislation in areas not clearly specified in the document's text, is somewhat broader than the current EC Treaty version. Nevertheless, the existing legislative unanimity requirements are preserved, and thus the new clause does not offer a meaningful shift of any competences to the Union.

All in all, the drafters of the Lisbon Treaty have confirmed these foundational principles without shifting any competences to the European Union. If anything, the Member States might have gained a bit in the right of their national parliaments to challenge EU legislation on the ground of subsidiarity. With that minor exception in favor of the Member States, the dividing lines illustrated in this chapter will stay in place.

Part Three
Institutions and Decision-Making

As we have observed in Part Two, the European Union's essential character is defined through its stated values and objectives, its structural features, and certain core principles. These elements work in combination to drive the Union's agenda, but also to limit its activities. We will now turn from the Union's basic identity to a review of the *means* by which EU policy is carried out. Chapter 13 will describe in detail the EU institutions, and Chapter 14 will analyse the instruments and procedures used by them in making EU law. Chapter 15 will focus on where the Lisbon Treaty will replace unanimous decision-making with qualified majority voting and where it will apply QMV to new subjects of EU activity. Throughout this analysis, the EU's dividing lines will reveal themselves. The Union's institutional structure reflects careful attention to the limits placed on EU competences, and the opportunities for individual Member State influence are readily discernible.

Chapter 13
THE EU INSTITUTIONS AND ORGANS

The EC Treaty identifies and describes the following institutions and organs:
- European Parliament
- Council
- Commission
- Court of Justice
- Court of Auditors
- European Central Bank
- European Investment Bank
- Advisory Committees: Committee of the Regions, Economic and Social Committee.[801]

In addition, the TEU describes the European Council.[802]

The Lisbon Treaty retains all of the foregoing. Moving the primary list from the EC Treaty to the TEU, the Lisbon Treaty identifies the Parliament, European Council, Council, Commission, Court of Justice, European Central Bank and Court of Auditors as the "institutional framework" of the Union. It also notes that the Parliament, Council and Commission will be assisted by the two advisory committees.[803]

The Lisbon Treaty also maintains the basic roles of all of the EU institutions with little variation from the Treaties. Nevertheless, certain institutional changes are proposed, and these changes have some potential to affect both the institutional balance among the institutions and the dividing lines between the Union and its Member States. The most notable developments are the new "permanent" European Council presidency and the new High Representative of the Union for Foreign Affairs and Security Policy.[804] These and other matters of structure are described in this chapter, with a focus on the institutions' existence, characteristics and competences. Their specific responsibilities in carrying out the EU's substantive activities are noted at various points throughout this treatise.

---

[801] EC Treaty Arts. 7-9. These provisions identify the institutions, while most details are set forth in EC Treaty Arts. 189 to 280.

[802] TEU Art. 4.

[803] Lisbon Treaty Art. 1(14).

[804] For the sake of brevity, this chapter will refer to the new position as the High Representative for Foreign Affairs or simply the High Representative.

1. EUROPEAN PARLIAMENT

1.1 A functioning parliament for the Union

Under the current Treaties the European Parliament bears reasonable resemblance to a traditional national parliament in its makeup and function. The EC Treaty offers detailed descriptions, and its Article 7 lists the Parliament first the EU institutions. Articles 189 to 201 provide structural and operational details: Article 189 introduces the Parliament; Article 190 provides that it is elected by popular vote of the EU citizens; Article 197 permits it to elect its own officers; and Article 192 permits it to participate in enacting legislation. Article 196 states that Parliament is to meet annually and may hold special sessions. Article 191 acknowledges that its members are affiliated with European-level political parties and notes that these parties "contribute to forming European awareness and to expressing the will of citizens of the Union." According to Article 199, the Parliament is to determine its own rules of procedure, although Article 198 mandates that decisions of the Parliament generally require a majority of the votes cast.

The Parliament is mentioned frequently in the TEU, with the most significant general reference being found in Article 5, where it is identified as one of the primary EU institutions.

With regard to inter-institutional relationships, EC Treaty Article 193 permits the Parliament to set up committees of inquiry to investigate improper implementation of EU law, and Article 195 assigns it the responsibility to appoint the permanent European Ombudsman to receive citizen complaints about EU institutions. Furthermore, under Article 214 the Parliament, upon a nomination by the Council, "approves" the President of the Commission and approves the slate of Commissioners nominated by the Council and the President-elect.[805] Under Article 201 it can force the resignation of the entire Commission.

The Lisbon Treaty inserts an overview of the Parliament into the TEU, leaving in the EC Treaty most of the institutional details.[806] The substantive changes from the EC Treaty to the Lisbon Treaty include the following: Article 190 of the current treaty provides for a Parliament of no more than 732 members, with no minimums or maxi-

---

[805] The appointment of the Commission in late 2004 illustrated that the Parliament's approval powers under EC Treaty Art. 214 can be significant. Because of controversy surrounding certain Commissioners nominated by incoming president José Manuel Barroso, the Parliament threatened to reject his entire slate. In the face of such unprecedented opposition, Mr. Barroso made adjustments to the slate, and the newly configured Commission was accepted by the Parliament on November 18, 2004. One commentator has observed: "This marked a new stage in the development of the powers of the European Parliament, not through Treaty revisions, or soft law, or recourse to the European courts, but instead through the constitutionally mandated procedure for approving the members of the European Commission. Naturally, in flexing its legal muscles, the European Parliament improved its position in inter-institutional politics, notably in relation to the Commission. But the most significant gain was not to a specific institution but instead to the EU's constitutional system: it strengthened representative, democratic EU government." Francis Snyder, Editorial: Enhancing EU Democracy, Constituting the European Union, 11 Eur. L.J. 131 (2005).

[806] Lisbon Treaty Arts. 2(15), 2(178)-2(188).

mums stated, but with the precise allocation indicated for each Member State. The Treaties' Protocol on the Enlargement of the European Union permits increases in that number to reflect new accessions to the Union.[807] The Lisbon Treaty provides for a maximum of 750 members, with a minimum of six and a maximum of 96 for any Member State, with Parliament's actual composition to be determined by a unanimous vote of the European Council.[808] The new treaty also expands the Parliament's role to full participation in the EU's budgeting process.[809] The little-used cooperation procedure under EC Treaty Article 252, by which the Parliament could affect the course of EU legislation but could not block a measure, is finally eliminated.[810] Under the Lisbon Treaty the "ordinary legislative procedure" is the co-decision procedure.[811] This procedure allows the Parliament full participation in the legislative deliberation, coupled with the power to prevent a legislative measure from taking effect.[812]

From a drafting perspective and political point of view, it is interesting that the European Parliament is the first body mentioned wherever the current Treaties and the Lisbon Treaty list the institutions.[813] This placement is reminiscent of the United States Constitution in which the Congress is the first institution described. The popular conception in the United States is that the Constitution's reference to Congress before the executive and judiciary implies that the Congress, as the body most representative of the people, is the premier branch of government. However, the political reality is otherwise – for the past 75 years the US has been dominated by its executive branch. In the European Union the legislative assembly also represents the broadest spectrum of the EU citizenry, but despite the fact that Parliament's legislative and budgetary competences have grown steadily,[814] the Council and Commission continue to drive the EU agenda.

---

[807] Protocol on Enlargement, *supra* note 443.

[808] Lisbon Treaty Art. 1(15)(2).

[809] Id. Art. 2(265). Under the Lisbon Treaty the Parliament must approve all aspects of the budget and may propose amendments to it. Under Art. 272 of the EC Treaty the Parliament's right to amend is limited to compulsory expenditures. Art. 272(4) states that Parliament has a right "to amend the draft budget, acting by a majority of its Members, and to propose to the Council, acting by an absolute majority of the votes cast, modifications to the draft budget relating to *expenditure necessarily resulting from this Treaty or from acts adopted in accordance therewith.*" (emphasis supplied)

[810] Lisbon Treaty Art. 2(240). The only instances in which the cooperation procedure is found after the Treaty of Nice relate to certain matters of economic and monetary union. See EC Treaty Arts. 99, 102, 103, 106.

[811] Lisbon Treaty Art. 2(239).

[812] For an overview of the development of the Parliament, see Ricardo Passos, The Expanding Role of the European Parliament, in The EU Constitution: The Best Way Forward? (Deirdre Curtin, Alfred E. Kellermann & Steven Blockmans, eds., 2005).

[813] TEU Art. 5; EC Treaty Art. 7(1); Lisbon Treaty Art. 1(14)(1).

[814] The Treaty of Rome created a Parliamentary Assembly with minimal supervisory powers over the Commission and a consultative role in legislation. Following a name change to European Parliament in 1962 and the first direct elections in 1979, the Parliament has gradually received greater supervisory, legislative and budgetary authority through subsequent treaties. The most significant step was TEU's grant of co-decision authority with the Council in specific areas of legislation. Expansion of these areas, more supervision over the Commission through censure and Committees of Inquiry, and more involvement in the Union's

It is particularly notable that the European Parliament lacks the traditional power of a national legislature to appoint and remove the highest political officials – in the Union, both the European Council and Council are beyond Parliament's control. Also significant is the fact that Parliament is denied the most basic competence of a legislature, namely, the right to initiate legislation. This power is generally reserved to the Commission,[815] although under the EC Treaty the Parliament may "request" the Commission to submit particular legislative proposals, and the Lisbon Treaty adds that the Commission must inform the Parliament of its reasons if it does not comply with the request.[816]

While the Parliament's lack of legislative initiative is often viewed as a weakness in the EU system, particularly as regards the democratic legitimacy of the Union's legislative process, at least one commentator has seen a positive side to the matter. John Temple Lang has observed:

> "One advantage of the "Community method" has been greatly underestimated. Since only proposals made by the Commission can be considered by the Council and the Parliament, it is impossible for lobbyists to get Members of the European Parliament to propose legislation. The "Community method" is a tremendous constraint on excessive legislation, and a valuable limitation on the powers of big business and vested interests. One has only to look at the United States to see how easily lobbyists can get Senators and Congressmen, anxious for re-election, to propose Bills on every conceivable subject. If the power of the Commission to influence policy is sometimes resented, its value as a safeguard against pressure groups should also be welcomed."[817]

Interestingly, although the Constitution does not offer a general legislative initiative to the European Parliament, the Lisbon Treaty creates an initiative procedure for EU citizens outside the normal institutional scheme. Carrying forward the Lang sentiments, this is arguably even worse than creating a parliamentary competence, and commentators have complained that this is a procedure that could "hijack" the Union's normal legislative processes.[818]

1.2   Elements of Member State control over the European Parliament

Under the current EC Treaty and the Lisbon Treaty, the system for electing the Parliament is subject to both a unanimous vote of the Council and separate ratification

---

budgetary procedures have enhanced Parliament's role as an important Union Institution. For a concise and useful analysis of the evolution of the Parliament, see Newman, *supra* note 13, at 174-83.

[815] EC Treaty Art. 251(2).

[816] EC Treaty Art. 192; Lisbon Treaty Art. 2(181). In certain instances legislation may be initiated by a group of Member States, the European Parliament or other EU bodies. Lisbon Treaty Art. 2(236)(249A) (4).

[817] John Temple Lang, The Commission: The Key to the Constitutional Treaty for Europe, 26 Fordham Int'l L.J. 1598, 1601 (2003).

[818] See Part 3.1 of Chapter 9 of this treatise.

by the Member State governments.[819] In addition, the Council must vote unanimously on any rules relating to taxation of Parliament's members or former members.[820] And while the Lisbon Treaty sets a maximum size of the European Parliament and minimum and maximum numbers of representatives per Member State, the actual composition of the Parliament will be subject to a unanimous vote of the European Council.[821] The primary difference between the EC Treaty and the Lisbon Treaty is that the former specifies the actual allocation of parliamentary seats to the Member States,[822] while the latter mandates that the Parliament's composition be determined by a unanimous vote of the European Council.[823] In both documents unanimity is required – to amend the allocations in the EC Treaty (via a treaty amendment) and to assign seats under the Lisbon Treaty.

The Parliament may determine the procedures for its own operation.[824] However, in those instances identified above where the Council or European Council must decide unanimously on the composition of the Parliament or the rules relating to its election or the taxation of its members, each of the Member States has the ability to block a decision or use the threat of a veto to influence the details of the decision. This is true of decisions made under the current EC Treaty or under the Lisbon Treaty.

The Parliament's inability to remove the European Council and Council carries with it two implications. First, it demonstrates the absence of a complete system of institutional checks and balances at the EU level. Second, it reflects a significant power residing in the Member States – representatives on the two Councils are officials of the national governments, and as such they are answerable to their national parliaments. On the other hand, the limits of Parliament's *legislative* power do not correlate to any broad reservation of authority in the Member States, because the power to initiate EU legislation is generally in the hands of the Commission.

2.   EUROPEAN COUNCIL

2.1   The European Council as the EU's highest authority

The position of the European Council is not clearly delineated in the current Treaties. From the earliest days of the Community the heads of state met from time to time, and formal recognition of this process eventually followed. The first textual mention of the body was included in the Single European Act in 1986,[825] but even with the

---

[819] EC Treaty Art. 190(4); Lisbon Treaty Art. 2(179)(b).

[820] EC Treaty Art. 190(5); Lisbon Treaty Art. 2(179)(c).

[821] Lisbon Treaty Art. 1(15)(2).

[822] EC Treaty Art. 190(2).

[823] Lisbon Treaty Art. 1(15)(2).

[824] EC Treaty Art. 190(5) permits the Parliament, after consulting with the Commission and obtaining QMV approval of the Council, to determine the "general conditions governing the performance of the duties of its Members." See Lisbon Treaty Art. 2(179)(c).

[825] Single European Act, *supra* note 89.

intervening treaty amendments the European Council is cited just eight times in the EC Treaty[826] and eight times in the Treaty on European Union.[827] Interestingly, it is not identified in Article 7 of the EC Treaty in the list of Community institutions, nor in the articles that extensively describe the institutions in Part Five of the treaty. The most prominent treaty reference may be found in TEU Article 4, which states that the European Council "shall provide the Union with the necessary impetus for its development and shall define the general political guidelines thereof." The same provision defines the group as consisting of the heads of state or government of the Member States, assisted by the foreign affairs ministers of the states and a Commission member. The European Council is to meet at least twice a year under the chairmanship of the head of state or government of the state that holds the Council's rotating presidency.[828] The European Council must report to the European Parliament annually and after each of its meetings.[829]

The remaining references to the European Council in the TEU relate to the EU's Second and Third Pillar. Article 13 requires the group to define principles, guidelines and common strategies in the Second Pillar, the CFSP.[830] Article 17 assigns the European Council the task agreeing on a "common defence" should it so desire. The only reference to voting on the European Council is found in TEU Article 23 which requires the Council to act unanimously in decisions with respect to the CFSP, but also permits the Council to refer decisions to the European Council "for decision by unanimity." The final mention of the European Council in the TEU is in the Third Pillar section, relating to police and judicial cooperation in criminal matters.[831] TEU Article 40a calls for a Council decision on programmes of enhanced cooperation within the Third Pillar, but permits any member of the Council to have the matter referred to the European Council, presumably for consultation only, because the article notes that the Council will nevertheless be responsible to act on the proposal.[832]

Since there is no mention of the European Council in the extensive institutional section comprising Part Five of the EC Treaty,[833] the treaty's few references seem almost random. Article 11(2) mentions the possibility of a reference from the Council to the European Council in cases of proposed enhanced cooperation, on the same terms as in TEU Article 40a. In the matter of economic and monetary union, EC Treaty Article 99 calls for the European Council to receive reports from the Council and then "discuss a conclusion on the broad guidelines of the economic policies of the Member States and of the Community." Similarly, Article 113 entitles the European Council to receive annual reports from the European Central Bank. In the matter of employment in the Community, EC Treaty Article 128 calls for the European Council

---

[826] See EC Treaty Arts. 11, 99, 113, 128.

[827] See TEU Arts. 4, 13, 17, 23, 40a.

[828] TEU Art. 4. See also EC Treaty Art. 203 (describing the rotating Council presidency).

[829] TEU Art. 4.

[830] See TEU Arts. 11-28 (provisions on the CFSP).

[831] See TEU Arts. 29-42 (provisions on the Third Pillar).

[832] See also TEU Arts. 43-45 (provisions on implementing enhanced cooperation).

[833] EC Treaty Arts. 189-280.

to receive reports from the Council and Commission,[834] and the European Council is expected to "adopt conclusions" on the employment situation.[835]

The Lisbon Treaty for the first time includes the European Council on the formal list of the Union's institutions. A new TEU provision will identify the body as part of the EU's "institutional framework."[836] An additional article replaces current TEU Article 4 and adds information about the group's President and its functions.[837] The Lisbon Treaty calls on the European Council to meet quarterly to set the "general political directions and priorities" of the Union.[838] The institution is mentioned more than 100 times in the document, in many instances with respect to taking decisions on policy matters. However, actual legislating is reserved to the Council and the European Parliament, because the new treaty mandates that the European Council "shall not exercise legislative functions."[839] Where decisions are taken, presumably outside the realm of actual legislation, the normal voting requirement is consensus.[840]

As described in the Lisbon Treaty, the European Council is composed of the heads of state or government of each of the Member States, a President, and the President of the Commission;[841] however, the latter two are not entitled to vote.[842] The High Representative for Foreign Affairs will also "take part" in the European Council's work.[843] The President of the European Council is a new position created by the Constitution to replace the half-yearly rotating presidency under the Treaties.[844] The President will serve a two and one-half year term, renewable once, and may not hold a national mandate during his or her term. In addition to chairing the European Council, the

---

[834] EC Treaty Art. 128(4).

[835] Id. Art. 128(1).

[836] Lisbon Treaty Art. 1(14).

[837] Id. Art. 1(16).

[838] Id. Art. 1(16)(1).

[839] Id. Art. 1(16)(1). The legislative responsibilities of the Council and Parliament are expressed in Lisbon Treaty Art. 1(17)(1).

[840] Lisbon Treaty Art. 1(16)(4). The Lisbon Treaty provides in specific instances for European Council decisions to be taken by less than unanimity. For situations calling for a qualified majority vote, see Lisbon Treaty Arts. 1(16)(5) (election of the European Council President); 1(189)(201b)(a) (establishing the list of Council configurations); 1(189)(201b)(b) (rotation of presidencies of Council configurations); 1(18)(7) (selection of the Commission President and final approval of the Commission); 1(19)(1) (appointment or removal of the Union Minister for Foreign Affairs). Also see the Lisbon Treaty's revisions to the Statute of the European Council for Small Business and Entrepreneurship (ECSB) and of the ECB, TL/P/en 42, Art. 11(j) (appointment of the Executive Board of the European Central Bank). Abstentions by a member of the European Council will not prevent unanimous decisions from being taken. Lisbon Treaty Arts. 2(189)(201a) (1), 2(291). Also see revisions to the Statute of the EIB, TL/P/en 46, Art. 12(i)(ii). The European Council may adopt its own procedural rules by simple majority vote. Lisbon Treaty Art. 1(189)(201a)(3). It may also decide by simple majority whether to examine proposed amendments to the Treaties and whether to convene a new amending convention. Lisbon Treaty Art. 1(56)(3).

[841] Lisbon Treaty Art. 1(16)(2).

[842] Id. Art. 2(189)(201a)(1),

[843] Id. Art. 1(16)(2).

[844] Id. Art. 1(16)(5), (6). See TEU Art. 4.

President will provide cohesive external representation for the European Union along with the High Representative.[845]

By virtue of the stature of its voting members, the European Council under the Lisbon Treaty will maintain and may even expand its role in representing the supreme executive and legislative authority within the European Union.[846] It is noteworthy that in the Lisbon Treaty the European Council is formally recognised as an EU institution for the first time, and its functions and responsibilities are spelled out more concretely than in the current Treaties. The Lisbon Treaty describes many instances in which the European Council will make policy decisions, and even if it must refrain from legislating in the technical sense, this institution certainly possesses the political power to instruct the Council on legislative matters. The new treaty's statement that the European Council sets policy but does not legislate is an apparent attempt to reduce confusion as to the differences between the competences of the Council and those of the European Council. Another important clarification is the Lisbon Treaty's specification that decisions on the European Council are normally to be taken by consensus.

Among the changes proposed for the European Council, it is the new office of the President that represents the most significant development, and it offers new evidence of the state-like nature of the Union. No longer will the President be the elected leader of a Member State government, and no longer will the President's term of office be based upon the six-month rotating Council presidency. Under the Lisbon Treaty the President may not hold a national mandate and he or she will serve a two and one-half year term, renewable once. The elimination of the national mandate coincides with the Lisbon Treaty's job description for the new High Representative for Foreign Affairs. This official, who will chair the Council's foreign affairs formation, will not be the foreign affairs minister from the Member State holding the Council's rotating presidency, but will be separately appointed by the European Council.[847]

Internally and externally the new European Council President will offer a more recognisable and consistent leadership presence than is offered by the Treaties' rotating presidency. However, this office has the potential to usurp the position of the Commission President (and even the High Representative for Foreign Affairs) as the day-to-day face of the Union. Will this necessarily be a positive development? Jürgen Schwarze is sceptical:

> "First, how much weight will the word of the President of the [European] Council have, and what will his position be among the Member States' Heads of State or Government? Second, who will be willing to accept this position, if the President of the [European] Council cannot occupy a position in the Member States simultaneously? Besides these issues, there may be some tension between the President of the [European] Council and the President of the Commission, but also between the President of the [European] Council and the – also

---

[845] Lisbon Treaty Art. 1(16)(5), (6).

[846] For a review of the increasing importance of the European Council, see Jan Werts, The Unstoppable Advance of the European Council, in The EU Constitution: The Best Way Forward? (Deirdre Curtin, Alfred E. Kellermann & Steven Blockmans, eds., 2005).

[847] Lisbon Treaty Art. 1(19).

new – [High Representative] for Foreign Affairs. This possibility arises especially with regard to the Union's foreign and security policy."[848]

In the same vein, Michael Dougan warns that the European Council President, especially if he or she is supported by a permanent professional staff, "could create a competing centre of executive power which might undermine the influence of the Commission, or at least create inefficiencies by setting the two institutions against each other."[849] Juliane Kokott and Alexandra Rüth suggest that the new President should "avoid conflicts by exercising his/her duties in the spirit of the political compromise that led to the creation of the post and by meticulously respecting the division of responsibilities within the institutional system without encroaching on the role of the Commission's President, the [High Representative] or even the Council."[850]

2.2 Members of the European Council represent the governments of the Member States

There are few textual references in the Lisbon Treaty that connect the European Council to the Member States, but few are really needed. The new treaty states the obvious, namely, that the members of the European Council are the heads of state or government of the Member States (assisted by a redefined President, the Commission President and the new High Representative for Foreign Affairs). Because the voting representatives on the European Council are chief officials of their nations, each member of this body will be expected to promote and protect the interests of his or her nation.[851] This is in contrast to other EU institutions such as the Commission, Court of Justice and European Central Bank, whose members have always been required to act independently and without regard to any national consideration.[852] It is fair to say that when the European Council meets, it looks less like an EU institution than an international summit meeting. Reinforcing the dominating presence of the Member States on the European Council is the fact that the default voting rule for decisions of this group is consensus, thus ensuring that the government of each Member State must be in accord with any steps taken to set broad policies for the Union.[853] Failing that, the European Council will be unable to act.

---

[848] Jürgen Schwarze, The Convention's Draft Treaty Establishing a Constitution for Europe, 40 C.M.L.R. 1037, 1039 (2003).

[849] Dougan, *supra* note 725, at 775.

[850] Kokott & Rüth, *supra* note 87, at 1338.

[851] Interestingly, the Lisbon Treaty mentions that members of the Council are to be ministerial level officials of each Member State who "may commit the government of the Member State in question and cast its vote." Lisbon Treaty Art. 1(17)(2). These words are not used in reference to the European Council. However, each of its members, as a head of state or government, is to an even greater degree expected by his or her constituents to represent the interests of the Member State's elected government and deliver the state's "vote" in achieving consensus within the European Council.

[852] Lisbon Treaty Arts. 1(18)(3) (Commission); 1(20)(2) (Court of Justice); 2(227)(3) (European Central Bank).

[853] Lisbon Treaty Art. 1(16)(4).

The qualities described above are also a legitimate way to characterise the European Council in its current embodiment under the Treaties. In fact, the European Council today looks even less like an EU institution than an intergovernmental gathering. The Lisbon Treaty's new institutional references might be seen as a helpful emphasis on this body's function as an EU organ, but the fact that all its decisions must be taken by consensus acts as a constant reminder of the power of each Member State. Despite the Lisbon Treaty changes, the European Council will remain a voice for the governments of the Member States in the most critical areas of EU policy and development.

3.   COUNCIL

3.1   A legislature and executive

The Council is mentioned throughout the TEU with respect to its involvement in a variety of Union programmes and processes. The only TEU provisions of a structural nature are Article 3, which refers to a "single institutional framework" for the Union, and Article 5, which lists the five primary Union institutions, including the Parliament, Council, Commission, Court of Justice and Court of Auditors.

As in the TEU, the EC Treaty refers to the Council numerous times with regard to Union programmes and processes, but the present focus is on those sections that describe the Council's structure and general competences, and the EC Treaty contains these important details. To begin, Article 7 of the EC Treaty lists the same five institutions as identified in the TEU, and it also refers to the two advisory committees of the Community.[854] Thereafter, Articles 202 to 210 add to the detail regarding the Council.

Article 202 describes the Council as having the power to "ensure coordination" of Member State economic policies, "take decisions," confer implementation powers on the Commission and "exercise directly implementing powers itself." EC Treaty Article 203 describes representation on the Council and the system of rotating presidencies, while Article 204 sets the terms for convening of Council meetings. Article 207 describes the offices that assist the Council, namely, Committee of Permanent Representatives (COREPER) and the General Secretariat. Although the Council may not itself initiate legislation, Article 208 allows it to request the Commission to do so. Article 209 permits the Council to set rules for the Community's advisory committees. Last, Article 210 grants the Council the authority to set salaries and benefits for members of the Commission, Court of Justice and Court of First Instance.

The critical matter of voting on the Council is covered in EC Treaty Article 205, which has several parts. First, Article 205(1) provides for Council decisions to be taken by "a majority of its Members" unless the Treaty provides otherwise. Second, Ar-

---

[854] The advisory committees are the Economic and Social Committee and the Committee of the Regions.

ticle 205(2) lists the population-weighted votes assigned to each Member State in qualified majority voting situations, and provides that 62 votes are required in all cases in which a matter has been proposed by the Commission. Third, Article 205(2) also requires 62 votes, but from at least 10 Member States, "in other cases." Finally, Article 205(3) provides that abstentions will not prevent a unanimous vote being taken, if such is required. Also in connection with voting, Article 206 notes that a Council member may accept a voting proxy from one other member.

EC Treaty Articles 249 to 254 describe in detail the creation of EU legislation and regulations, including the Council's critical role in the various processes. Likewise Articles 268 to 280 describe budgeting and fiscal procedures for the Community, again highlighting the Council's key participation in these processes.

The Lisbon Treaty offers an overview of the Council in a new article in the TEU.[855] The remaining provisions are left in the EC Treaty. Among the Lisbon Treaty's new details is an acknowledgment that the Council meets in various configurations.[856] It has always done so, but it is now mentioned in the treaty. The presidency of each configuration is chaired in six-month rotations, although the new High Representative for Foreign Affairs will permanently chair the Foreign Affairs configuration.[857] He or she will also serve as foreign affairs vice-chair of the Commission.[858] As provided in a Draft Decision of the European Council, the presidencies of all Council configurations other than Foreign Affairs are to be shared by groups of three States, serving collectively for 18 months, which each state holding the all of the presidencies for six months during the 18-month term. The groups are to be assigned on the basis of "equal rotation among the Member States, taking into account their diversity and geographical balance within the Union."[859] The Council is required to meet in public "when it deliberates and votes on a draft legislative act," although not when dealing with non-legislative activities.[860] Where Article 208 allows the Council to request the

---

[855] Lisbon Treaty Art. 1(17).

[856] Id. Art. 1(17)(6).

[857] The full title of the High Representative is "High Representative of the Union for Foreign Affairs and Security Policy." Lisbon Treaty Art. 1(19)(1). The High Representative will be an additional member of the Council, and he or she will chair the Foreign Affairs configuration. Lisbon Treaty arts. 1(17)(9), 1(19)(3). Another example of a configuration is General Affairs, which is mandated to "prepare and ensure follow-up to meetings of the European Council, in liaison with the President of the European Council and the Commission." Lisbon Treaty Art. 1(17)(6).

[858] Lisbon Treaty Art. 1(19)(4). Juliane Kokott and Alexandra Rüth have commented: "[T]his [High Representative], depending on the field, will continue to act according to different procedures. Only when exercising the responsibilities regarding current first pillar matters will he/she follow the regular Commission procedures. In contrast, within the ambit of CFSP, he/she will act 'as mandated by the Council'. This is all the more problematic as the role the Commission enjoyed so far with regard to CFSP will be taken over by the [High Representative]. Actual practice will prove whether the inherent dangers to this functional merger without a substantive harmonization will manifest themselves, or whether the aim of enhancing efficiency and overall coherence will be realized." Kokott & Rüth, *supra* note 87, at 1327.

[859] Draft Decision of the European Council on the exercise of the Presidency of the Council, Lisbon Treaty, Final Act, December 3, 2007, CIG 15/07, AF/TL/DC en 5.

[860] Lisbon Treaty Art. 1(17)(8).

Commission to initiate legislation, the Lisbon Treaty adds that the Commission must give reasons if it declines.[861]

In the basic description of the Council, the Lisbon Treaty states that this body "shall, jointly with the European Parliament, exercise legislative and budgetary functions."[862] Interestingly, the wording of EC Treaty Article 202 about the Council's right to "directly exercise implementing powers itself" – a phrase that helps define the Council as an executive as well as a legislative body – was not carried over into the Lisbon Treaty. In fact, Article 202 has been deleted, replaced by the new TEU overview provision.[863] The new TEU provision does add that Council "shall carry out policy-making and coordinating functions as laid down in the Treaties," but implementing powers are not mentioned. However, a Lisbon Treaty article that generally describes EU legislative procedures does contain the following statement:

> "Where uniform conditions for implementing legally binding Union acts are needed, those acts shall confer implementing powers on the Commission, or, in duly justified specific cases and in the cases provided for in Articles 11 and 13 of the Treaty on European Union [the common foreign and security policy], on the Council."[864]

A further indication that the Council would retain the right of direct implementation may be found in the Comitology Decision of 1999. It describes the various ways in which the Commission's implementing powers are to be carried out, and it explicitly refers to the Council's right in new legislation to reserve implementation for itself.[865] There is no indication that the Lisbon Treaty would override this decision.

The most significant Council-related developments in the Lisbon Treaty are the changes to the system of QMV. The Lisbon Treaty does two things. First, it declares QMV to be the ordinary decisional requirement for the Council.[866] Second, it abandons the EC Treaty's vote allocations for determining a qualified majority, in favor of a percentage formula. This formula was proposed in the Constitution, and it consists of the votes of 55 percent of the Member States, comprising at least 15 states and 65 percent of the EU population.[867] A blocking minority must include at least four mem-

---

[861] Lisbon Treaty Art. 2(193).

[862] Id. Art. 1(17)(1).

[863] Id. Art. 1(17). See Lisbon Treaty Art. 2(190).

[864] Id. Art. 2(236)(249C)(2).

[865] Council Decision of 28 June 1999 (1999/486/EC) laying down the procedures for the exercise of implementing powers conferred on the Commission, July 7, 1999, O.J. (L 184) 23, Art. 1. The 1999 Decision has been amended by the Council Decision of July 17, 2006 (2006/512/EC), O.J. (L 200) 11.

[866] Lisbon Treaty Art. 1(17)(3).

[867] Id. Art. 1(17)(4). The original voting scheme proposed for the Constitution by the Convention was that a qualified majority would consist of a majority of the Member States representing three-fifths of the EU's population, but this formula was rejected at the IGC meetings that took place in December, 2003, and approval of the Constitution was postponed. The chief problem was that Spain and Poland wished to protect the favorable weighting of their Council votes as assigned to them in the Treaty of Nice, and the proposed QMV percentage formulas negated the special advantage they had come to expect. The Irish presidency invested a great deal of energy in solving the problem, and the result was a revised voting scheme approved at the June, 2004 IGC. This is the formula that carried over into the Lisbon Treaty. Fuller, *supra* note 79. For an

bers. This formula will take effect on November 1, 2014, although between that date and March 31, 2017, special requests by groups of states not sufficient to form a blocking minority may force the Council to reconsider a close vote.[868]

Qualified majority voting is, by definition, a majoritarian procedure that on one hand resembles the democratic process within a typical nation state and on the other hand undercuts the autonomy of the Member States in the European Union.[869] Under the Lisbon Treaty's version of QMV no single Member State will have the ability to block EU legislation. Likewise, because more 55 percent of the Member States would be represented in a prevailing vote under the new QMV formula, no small group of the largest Member States will be able to dictate decisions. However, because of the requirement that 65 per cent of the EU population be represented, a small group of the largest states will be able to prevent a successful vote, although the treaty requires at least four states to form a "blocking minority." Giovanni Grevi has observed that the requirement of four States to form a blocking minority would "prevent Germany, the UK, France or Italy from forming a blocking coalition of three."[870]

The Lisbon Treaty's public meeting requirement for the Council is also noteworthy. The new treaty requires the Council to meet in public when it "deliberates and votes on a draft legislative act," but not when it considers "non-legislative activities."[871] It is interesting that no open-meeting requirement is imposed on the European Council, and the Lisbon Treaty's admonition that the European Council "shall not exercise legislative functions"[872] appears to be designed in part to justify insulating its activities from public scrutiny. Nevertheless, by requiring the Council to conduct its legislative business in public, the Lisbon Treaty offers a response to public demands for more EU transparency and to the Commission's White Paper challenge to take concrete steps to boost public confidence in the Union. However, the effectiveness of an open-meeting requirement is questionable. A Council desiring secrecy could easily declare a "non-legislative" session and conduct its deliberations behind

---

extensive historical review of QMV formulas and an assessment of the positions of Spain and Poland under the Nice Treaty, see Edward Best, What is Really at Stake in the Debate over Votes? 2004/1 Eipascope 14, available at http:// www.eipa.nl/cms/repository/eipascope/Art_2(2).pdf.

[868] Draft Decision of the Council, Lisbon Treaty, Final Act, December 3, 2007, CIG 15/07, AF/TL/DC en 2.

[869] For a detailed analysis of QMV formulas and suggestions for alternative allocations of voting power, see Bela Plechanovová, Draft Constitution and the Decision-Making Rule for the Council of Ministers of the EU – Looking for an Alternative Solution (Eur. Integration Online Papers, Working Paper No. 12, 2004).

[870] Grevi, *supra* note 476, at 8. For a detailed analysis of the various majority and blocking formulas possible under the Constitution and its predecessors, see Janis A. Emmanouilidis, Historically Unique, Unfinished in Detail – An Evaluation of the Constitution, Centre for Applied Policy Research, 2004/3 EU Reform 5-8, 12-13. For an earlier review of coalition-forming and negotiations that have led to QMV decisions on the Council, see Madeleine O. Hosli, Coalitions and Power: Effects of Qualified Majority Voting in the Council of the European Union, 34 J. Common Mkt. Stud. 255 (1996).

[871] Lisbon Treaty Art. 1(17)(8). Note that in response to the difficulties in the process of ratifying the Constitution, the European Council in June 2006 chose to implement this reform on its own initiative (and under its general authority under the Treaties), rather than to wait for the Constitution or its replacement to take effect. See notes 134-137, *supra*, and accompanying text.

[872] Lisbon Treaty Art. 1(16)(1).

closed doors. Its members could also conduct extensive, but informal discussions in corridors or other venues away from the Council chamber. Such tactics would undermine the spirit of openness.

The revision to the system of rotating the Council presidencies is arguably a modest change from the present form of cooperation, in which the current presidency may informally receive assistance and coordination from the Member States representing the immediately preceding presidency and the one to follow.[873] Whether joint coordination and cooperation among the same three Member States for an 18-month period will result in more operational and policy consistency remains to be seen. It might be argued that the disruption caused by a complete replacement of the presidency team every year and a half would be greater than that caused by informally adding and removing a cooperating member every six months. However, even under the Lisbon Treaty's proposed system it should be expected that out-going and incoming presidencies would be available for consultation. Furthermore, under the Lisbon Treaty the High Representative for Foreign Affairs will be in a position to provide continuity in the face of Council presidency rotations,[874] and COREPER will remain fully active in providing ongoing bureaucratic support for the Council.

Beyond these structural and procedural changes, certain areas in which the current Treaties require unanimous Council decisions are changed in the Lisbon Treaty to a QMV. These matters are analysed in Chapter 15 of this treatise.

3.2   The Council serves as an additional voice for the Member States

There is little question that members of the Council, like their counterparts on the European Council, are expected to represent the separate interests of the Member States. In fact, the Lisbon Treaty speaks of Council representatives as having the authority to "commit the government of the Member State in question and cast its vote."[875] Also, as suggested in the previous section, the influence of each state is to some extent protected by the "equal rotation" language of the new treaty: "The Presidency of Council configurations, other than that of Foreign Affairs [which is chaired by the High Representative for Foreign Affairs], shall be held by Member State representatives in the

---

[873] In the area of the common foreign and security policy, the cooperative arrangement has been referred to as a "troika," although Art. 18(4) of the TEU says only that the current Council presidency "shall be assisted in these tasks if need be by the next Member State to hold the Presidency."

[874] Jürgen Schwarze has commented: "Notwithstanding all the difficulties, the creation of the position of [High Representative] for Foreign Affairs is a sound decision. Yet, from an idealistic point of view, the improvements in the field of foreign and security policy remain unsatisfactory. With the principle of unanimity still in effect, the strength of Europe's foreign policy will remain rather limited. Realistically, the claim for national sovereignty, especially in the field of foreign policy, seems difficult to overcome in the near future. The office of the [High Representative] for Foreign Affairs and the proposed solution of a 'double hat' both reflect the current situation with regard to the different positions on foreign policy existing in the Member States. At the moment, a greater extent of common policy in this field does not seem achievable." Schwarze, *supra* note 848, at 1040.

[875] Lisbon Treaty Art. 1(17)(2).

Council on the basis of equal rotation,"[876] with the system of rotation to be determined by a qualified majority decision of the European Council.[877]

The primary changes relating to the Council, as described in the preceding section (the new QMV formula, the open-meeting requirement, the new High Representative for Foreign Affairs, and the new presidency rotation scheme) will not appreciably affect the influence of the Member States within the Council. The change in QMV formulas might impact the individual influence of Spain and Poland, but in general the Lisbon Treaty's new approach preserves the existing majoritarian basis for Council action. It is uncertain whether the requirement for open meetings will cause Council members to act in a more collegial, EU-focused manner than they might have in private. Overall, the Member States will not gain or lose essential power as a result of the Lisbon Treaty's structural changes to the Council. The impact of any movement from unanimous Council voting to QMV in matters of substance will be addressed in Chapter 15.

4.   COMMISSION

4.1   **The central and essential Union institution**

The Commission acts as the permanent executive and chief administrative body of the European Union. In the current Treaties the Commission is identified in Article 5 of the TEU and in Article 7(1) of the EC Treaty as one of the primary EU institutions. The institutional detail is found in EC Treaty Articles 211 to 219. The Commission's general mandate in Article 211 is to "ensure the proper functioning and development of the common market." The same provision considers the Commission the guardian of the EC Treaty, because it must "ensure that the provisions of this Treaty and the measures taken by the institutions pursuant thereto are applied." The provision adds that the Commission must "exercise the powers conferred on it by the Council for the implementation of the rules laid down by the latter."

The EC Treaty does not state that the Commission alone may initiate legislation. However, Article 211 mandates the Commission to "participate in the shaping of measures taken by the Council and the European Parliament." Furthermore, the two primary forms of legislative procedure, co-decision under Article 251 and cooperation under Article 252, are initiated only upon the Commission's submission of a proposal.[878] The Commission's right of initiative is further strengthened by Article 250, which requires a unanimous vote of the Council of Ministers to amend a Commission proposal[879] and permits the Commission to amend proposed legislation "at any time during the procedures leading to the adoption of a Community act."[880] In addition, Ar-

---

[876] Lisbon Treaty Art. 1(17)(9).
[877] Id. Art. 2(189)(201b)(b).
[878] EC Treaty Arts. 251(2), 252(a).
[879] Id. Art. 250(1).
[880] Id. Art. 250(2).

ticle 251(3) requires a unanimous Council vote to approve a Parliament-proposed legislative amendment if the Commission has delivered a "negative opinion" on the amendment. Article 274 calls on the Commission to "implement the budget," and the Commission has a prominent role throughout the entire budgeting process under the treaty.[881] Regarding enforcement powers, Article 226 permits the Commission to take steps against a Member State that has "failed to fulfil an obligation" under the treaty.

Under Article 213(1) of the EC Treaty, the Commission is to consist of one national of each Member State. Pursuant to the Protocol on Enlargement, upon expansion of the EU to 27 states (which occurred in January of 2007) the Commission should be reduced to less than one Commissioner per Member State, with the actual number to be set by a unanimous Council vote, and with the rotation to be unanimously agreed, subject to the "principle of equality."[882] The Lisbon Treaty postpones the reduction to 2014,[883] and the Commission currently consists of 27 members.

In keeping with the Commission's status as the central organ of the EU, members of the Commission and its President are appointed by other EU institutions. EC Treaty Article 214(2) provides that the Commission President is nominated by the Council, meeting in the composition of heads of state or government, and then approved by the European Parliament. The Council and President-nominee by "common accord" then "adopt the list" of Commissioners on the basis of candidates proposed by the Member States. The Parliament must then approve the slate, after which the Council "appoints" the Commission. The term is five years.[884] Once the Commission is approved, EC Treaty Article 217 empowers the President to determine its internal organisation, while the Commission adopts its own rules of procedure.[885] Commission decisions are taken by majority vote.[886]

EC Treaty Article 213(2) requires the Commission to be independent at all times, and its members may not "seek nor take instructions from any government or other body." Member States are required to respect the Commissioners' independence and "not seek to influence the Members of the Commission in the performance of their tasks." The Commission is, however, answerable under Article 201 to the European Parliament, which may censure the Commission and force its resignation.

The Lisbon Treaty places an overview of the Commission into the amended TEU, while retaining certain details in the EC Treaty.[887] The reworded general mandate for the Commission is to: (1) promote the general interest of the Union; (2) ensure and oversee application of the Treaties and EU law; (3) exercise the budget and manage programmes; (4) exercise coordinating, executive and management functions; (5) en-

---

[881] EC Treaty Arts. 268 to 280.

[882] Protocol on Enlargement, *supra* note 443, Art. 4(2), (3).

[883] Lisbon Treaty Art. 1(18)(5).

[884] EC Treaty Art. 214(1). A Commissioner must resign if so requested by the Commission President, or upon the order of the Court of Justice. EC Treaty Arts. 217(4), 216. A replacement will be selected by the Council. EC Treaty Art. 215.

[885] EC Treaty Art. 218.

[886] Id. Art. 219.

[887] Lisbon Treaty Arts. 1(18), 2(196)-2(203).

sure the EU's external representation (with exceptions); and (6) initiate annual and multiannual programming.[888] The Lisbon Treaty also states clearly that "Union legislative acts may only be adopted on the basis of a Commission proposal, except where the Treaties provide otherwise."[889] The exceptions to this rule include acts adopted "at the initiative of a group of Member States or of the European Parliament, on a recommendation from the European Central Bank or at the request of the Court of Justice or the European Investment Bank."[890]

Under Lisbon Treaty the Commission President is nominated by a QMV decision of the European Council (rather than the heads-of-state composition of the Council[891]) and "elected" by the European Parliament.[892] The European Council, with the consent of the Commission President-elect, also "appoints" the High Representative for Foreign Affairs by QMV.[893] After election of the President-elect, the new treaty provides that each of the Member States will "suggest" its candidate to the Council and President-elect, who by common accord then adopt the list of candidates. The entire slate of President, High Representative and Commissioners is then submitted for approval by the Parliament and is thereafter appointed by a QMV decision of the European Council.[894]

Overall, the following are the most noteworthy developments in the Lisbon Treaty with respect to the Commission:

- The Commission's eventual reduction in size has been controversial, even though the EC Treaty already contemplates some measure of reduction after the EU reaches 27 Member States. The paring down under the Lisbon Treaty in 2014 will undoubtedly increase the Commission's operating efficiency, but its political outreach within the "unrepresented" Member States may be undermined.
- The new High Representative for Foreign Affairs will both preside over the Foreign Affairs formation of the Council and serve as a vice-president of the Commission.[895] This will undoubtedly create confusion from time to time as to which hat the Minister is wearing at any given moment, and to whom he or she is answerable.
- The Lisbon Treaty transfers from the Council to the European Council the unanimous decisions as to the Commission's eventual size and its system of rotation.[896] This seems unlikely to cause any procedural difficulties or political challenges.
- In the matter of legislative initiative, the Lisbon Treaty both adds and detracts. In the AFSJ, the Lisbon Treaty identifies matters on which one-fourth of the

---

[888] Lisbon Treaty Art. 1(18)(1).

[889] Id. Art. 1(18)(2).

[890] Id. Art. 2(236)(249A)(4).

[891] The difference between the European Council and this special formation of the Council is the non-voting presence on the European Council of its permanent President and the Commission President.

[892] Lisbon Treaty Art. 1(18)(7).

[893] Id. Art. 1(19)(1).

[894] Id. Art. 1(18)(7).

[895] Id. Art. 1(19)(3), (4).

[896] Id. Art. 1(18)(5).

Member States may initiate legislation.[897] The counterpart provisions in Articles 34(2) and 42 of the TEU permit a single state to initiate the legislative process.[898] Arguably, this change will reduce Member State authority and correspondingly strengthen the Commission. On the other hand, the unprecedented right of citizen initiative under the Lisbon Treaty may serve as a potential challenge to the Commission's legislative competence.

Despite these changes, under the Lisbon Treaty the Commission and its basic competences are essentially carried over from the Treaties.[899] Through its independence and its method of operation the Commission remains the embodiment of the "Community method" – a distinct contrast with the intergovernmental approach that prevails in the Council and European Council.[900]

4.2   The Member States have limited influence over the Commission

In general, both the current Treaties and the Lisbon Treaty create institutional separation between the Member States and the Commission. The existing Protocol on Enlargement contains the requirement of a unanimous Council decision to determine the size of the Commission after the EU reaches 27 Member States, as well as the consensus voting requirement for the Council to determine the Commission's rotation after the Commission has been reduced in size.[901] EC Treaty Article 215 contains the requirement for a unanimous Council decision not to fill a vacant Commission seat, while Articles 250(1) and 251(3) express the requirement of a unanimous Council decision to amend or approve amendments to certain legislative proposals from the Commission. Last, Article 214(2) establishes each Member State's exclusive right to name its candidate for a seat on the Commission.

    Under the Lisbon Treaty the only Commission-related matters subject to a national veto are (1) the requirement of a unanimous European Council decision to change the size of the Commission after it has been reduced in size commencing in 2014,[902] (2) the consensus voting requirement for the European Council to determine the Commission's rotation after 2014,[903] (3) the need for a unanimous Council decision not to

---

[897] Lisbon Treaty Art. 2(64)(61I).

[898] Under Title IV of Part Three of the EC Treaty, during a 5-year transitional period expiring on May 1, 2004, a single Member State was permitted to initiate legislation on matters of visas, asylum, immigration and other related policies. EC Treaty Art. 67(1).

[899] For a review of the development of the Commission, see Michel Petite and Clemens Ladenburger, The Evolution in the Role and Powers of the European Commission, in The EU Constitution: The Best Way Forward? (Deirdre Curtin, Alfred E. Kellermann & Steven Blockmans, eds., 2005).

[900] For a comparison of the Community method with alternative means for managing the European Union, along with an analysis of the value of the Commission to the ongoing success of the EU project, see Lang, *supra* note 817.

[901] Protocol on Enlargement, *supra* note 443, Art. 4(3).

[902] Lisbon Treaty Art. 1(18)(5).

[903] Id. Art. 1(18)(5).

fill a vacant Commission seat,[904] and (4) the requirement of a unanimous Council decision to amend or approve amendments to certain legislative proposals from the Commission.[905] Furthermore, each Member State possesses the exclusive right to name its candidate for a seat on the Commission.[906]

The prospect of reducing the size of the Commission has raised concerns,[907] with many of the smaller Member States protesting that they need to be represented on the Commission at all times to maintain a better link between their people and the operations of the EU. Although the Commission must act completely independently of Member State influence, a seat on the Commission carries with it an emotional appeal and a special means of communicating developments in Brussels back to the "represented" Member State. Thus, the eventual temporary loss of representation may create a further separation of this EU institution from the Member States and their citizens.

5.   EUROPEAN COURT OF JUSTICE

5.1   **Expanded jurisdiction for the Court**

The Court of Justice is listed among the EU's primary institutions in TEU Article 5 and in EC Treaty Article 7. There are numerous additional references in the TEU to the scope and limitation of the Court's jurisdiction,[908] but the principal institutional descriptions are found in EC Treaty Articles 220 to 245. The Court is granted the authority under EC Treaty Article 226 to hear cases brought against a Member State by the Commission, while under Article 227 it may hear cases brought by one Member State against another if the ground for action is that the accused state "has failed to fulfil an obligation under this Treaty." Although Article 227 actions are rare, "infringement actions" under Article 226 are regularly brought by the Commission. Article 228 adds significant coercive power to judgments of the Court by permitting it to require a defendant State to comply with a Court decision, or, failing that, to pay a "lump sum or penalty payment."

Three levels of court are provided in Articles 220 and 225a. These include the Court of Justice, the Court of First Instance, and specially created "judicial panels." Members of the courts and panels must be persons "whose independence is beyond doubt."[909] Under Article 221 the Court may sit as a full court (Grand Chamber) or in smaller chambers. Article 225a provides for appeals from judicial panels to the Court

---

[904] Lisbon Treaty Art. 2(200)(a).

[905] Id. Art. 2(238).

[906] Id. Art. 1(18)(7).

[907] European Commission, Eurobarometer 59: Public Opinion in the European Union (Eur. Opinion Res. Group, June 2003), at 10-11, 32. See also Conference of the Representatives of the Governments of the Member States, Presidency Note, Brussels, 11 December 2003, CIG 60/03 ADD 2.

[908] See, e.g., TEU Art. 46.

[909] EC Treaty Arts. 223, 224, 225a.

of First Instance, on points of law only, or on points of fact and law, depending on the mandate that establishes the panel. Appeals from the Court of First Instance to the Court of Justice are generally limited by Article 225 to points of law.

Under the Lisbon Treaty the name of the Court of First Instance is changed to the "General Court," and judicial panels are called "specialised courts."[910] In most other respects, the Lisbon Treaty maintains the Court's basic characteristics. It will remain an institution that is both central to the operations of the EU and independent of the other Union institutions. In carrying out its work the Court will remain independent of the governments and courts of the Member States. Its basic competences and procedures will not change. However, several developments are of interest.

The Lisbon Treaty adopts an innovation proposed in the Constitution that extends the Court's jurisdiction into the sensitive area of the CFSP, the Second Pillar under the TEU.[911] As a general matter TEU Article 46 limits the Court's jurisdiction under the TEU to a specific list of subjects, which do not include any aspects of the CFSP. The Lisbon Treaty specifically states that the Court shall have no jurisdiction with respect to the CFSP (which includes the CSDP), with two new exceptions.[912] First, the Court may "monitor compliance" with a new TEU provision which states that (1) CFSP activities may not affect the Union's general exercise of its competences, and (2) the Union's exercise of those its competences may not affect the CFSP.[913] The Court will thus be empowered to referee disputes over the interface of the Union's general authority and its specific authority relating to the CFSP. Second, the Lisbon Treaty permits the Court to review "the legality of decisions providing for restrictive measures against natural or legal persons adopted by the Council.[914]

The second area of extension of the Court's jurisdiction relates to those portions of the AFSJ that formerly comprised the Union's Third Pillar under the TEU.[915] Simply stated, the Lisbon Treaty will transfer the Third Pillar to the EC Treaty's First Pillar, and, except as noted below, all of the AFSJ will be subject to the Court's ordinary jurisdiction, under EC Treaty Article 230 (action for annulment), EC Treaty Article 232 (complaint for failure to act), and EC Treaty Article 241 (plea of illegality). These types of proceedings are maintained in the Lisbon Treaty. The exception to this general jurisdiction over the transferred AFSJ provisions is that the Lisbon Treaty states that the Court has no authority to review "the validity or proportionality of operations carried out by the police or other law-enforcement services of a Member State" or the

---

[910] Lisbon Treaty Art. 1(20)(1).

[911] For a discussion on the Constitution's potential impact on the Court's jurisdiction, see Ad Geelhoed, The Expanding Jurisdiction of the EU Court of Justice, in The EU Constitution: The Best Way Forward? (Deirdre Curtin, Alfred E. Kellermann & Steven Blockmans, eds., 2005).

[912] Lisbon Treaty Art. 1(27)(a)(1), 2(223)(240a).

[913] Id. Art. 1(45)(25b), 2(223)(240a).

[914] Id. Art. 1(27)(a)(1), 2(223)(240a).

[915] TEU Arts. 29-42; Lisbon Treaty Arts. 1(51), 2(63)-2(68). For a delineation of those provisions in the AFSJ that have their basis in the Third Pillar, see Chapter 16 of this treatise.

activities of a Member State "with regard to the maintenance of law and order and the safeguarding of internal security."[916]

The approach of the TEU in the Third Pillar is quite different. TEU Article 46 states that the powers of the Court in the Third Pillar are specifically *limited* to those enumerated in TEU Article 35. That provision identifies three areas in which the Court may act:

– Article 35(1) states that the Court may give preliminary rulings on the "validity and interpretation" of EU Third Pillar measures, but Article 35(2) makes subparagraph (1) applicable only to those Member States that have affirmatively accepted such jurisdiction.

– Article 35(6) permits the Court to hear EC Treaty Article 230 actions for annulment brought by a Member State or the Commission to challenge a Third Pillar framework decision or decision.

– Article 35(7) authorises the Court to rule on disputes between Member States regarding the interpretation of Third Pillar acts, as well as disputes between the Commission and Member States regarding "conventions" adopted under the Third Pillar.

Any other acts relating to the Third Pillar are outside the Court's jurisdiction, and TEU Article 35(5) contains specific prohibitions on the tribunal's authority in matters of Member State police and law enforcement services, maintenance of law and order and safeguarding of internal security.[917] These restrictions are the same limits that have been carried over into the Lisbon Treaty

A third jurisdictional extension for the Court is that actions for annulment of an EU regulatory act may be brought by an individual under Lisbon Treaty if the act "is of direct concern to him or her and does not entail implementing measures."[918] The corresponding provision in Article 230 of the EC Treaty requires that an action can be brought only if the regulatory act is of "direct and individual concern" to the plaintiff. This extension lacks the political impact of expanded jurisdiction in the CFSP and AFSJ, but its practical impact might be significant.[919]

Beyond these jurisdictional matters, two phrases in the Lisbon Treaty affirm the role of the Court as guardian of EU law. The Lisbon Treaty's new overview provision in the TEU requires the Court to "ensure that in the interpretation and application of the Treaties the law is observed."[920] This replaces a similar statement in EC Treaty Article 220 that is deleted by the Lisbon Treaty.[921] In addition, where the Lisbon Treaty describes the Commission and its responsibilities, it states that the Commis-

---

[916] Lisbon Treaty Art. 2(223)(240b).

[917] EC Treaty Art. 68(2) contains a similar restriction on the Court's jurisdiction in "any measure of decision taken pursuant to Article 62(1) relating to the maintenance of law and order and the safeguarding of internal security."

[918] Lisbon Treaty Art. 2(214)(d).

[919] See the discussion in Piris, *supra* note 359, at 14.

[920] Lisbon Treaty Art. 1(20)(1).

[921] EC Treaty Art. 220 is deleted by Lisbon Treaty Art. 2(205).

sion "shall oversee the application of Union law under the control of the Court of Justice."[922] This is a statement not found in either of the current Treaties. The Constitution's two phrases may not constitute an actual endorsement of the Court's historically activist approach, but they certainly do not support any curtailment of the Court's role.

An additional item worthy of note is that the Lisbon Treaty partially subjects the Court to the treaty's expanded public access provision.[923] This article requires each EU institution to make its documents available to the public. The Court is not included in the EC Treaty's corresponding Article 255(1).[924] However, the Lisbon Treaty states that the Court (and the European Central Bank and European Investment Bank as well) "shall be subject to the [public access] provisions . . . only when exercising their administrative tasks."[925] Administrative tasks are not defined, but the limitation is obviously intended to maintain the confidentiality of the Court's deliberations on pending cases.

5.2   The Member States' interaction with the Court

The Treaties offer several areas in which each Member State has direct input into matters relating to the Court of Justice. First, under EC Treaty Articles 221 and 223 the Court is to be comprised of one judge from each of the Member States, and the appointment of judges is to be accomplished by "common accord" of the states.[926] Second, Article 240 of the EC Treaty provides that the Court's jurisdiction in suits against the Union is exclusive only to the extent that jurisdiction is specifically conferred by the treaty, and thus in other situations the courts of the Member States will have concurrent jurisdiction. Third, the Court's jurisdiction is limited, as described above, in matters of the CFSP, certain aspects of police operations, maintenance of law and order, and matters of internal security. Finally, the Statute of the Court of Justice is appended as a protocol to the EC Treaty and TEU,[927] and according to EC Treaty Article 245, amendments to the Statute require a unanimous Council decision. Furthermore, Title I of the Statute may be amended only through the treaty amendment procedure, requiring ratification by the Member States.[928]

The Lisbon Treaty changes the unanimous Council decision to amend the Statute to the "ordinary legislative procedure," which would entail a QMV of the Council.[929] A procedural change from the current Treaties is that the Lisbon Treaty mandates a

---

[922] Lisbon Treaty Art. 1(18)(1).

[923] Id. Art. 2(28)(b).

[924] The Lisbon Treaty moves EC Treaty Art. 255 and expands its scope. Lisbon Treaty Arts. 2(244), 2(28).

[925] Lisbon Treaty Art. 2(28)(d).

[926] Advocates-General and members of the Court of First Instance are also chosen by common accord of the Member States. EC Treaty Arts. 223, 224.

[927] Protocol on the Statute of the Court of Justice, December 12, 2002, O.J. (C 325) 167.

[928] See TEU Art. 48 (the treaty amendment procedure).

[929] Lisbon Treaty Art. 2(226). However, this provision also adds Statute Art. 64 (language arrangements) to the items that must be amended through the treaty amendment procedure.

new panel to give an "opinion" on the suitability of nominees to the Court. This panel will be appointed by the Council of Ministers and will consist of seven members who must be former judges of the Court of Justice, the General Court or a national supreme court, or "lawyers of recognised competence." One of the panel members "shall be proposed by the European Parliament."[930]

The most notable development in the Lisbon Treaty is the expansion of the Court's jurisdiction in the CFSP and the AFSJ. Except for this, the current Treaties' provisions affecting the interface between the Member States and the Court of Justice have been transferred into the Lisbon Treaty with little substantive change. The new panel to review nominees to the Court might offer some further input from the Member States as to the Court's composition, but the Member States' primary contribution would arise in the process of nominating members to the Court and then reaching common accord on the full membership of the Court. Through concurrent jurisdiction, the current EC Treaty and the Lisbon Treaty both allow substantial involvement of the Member State courts in dealing with matters of EU law.

6.   OTHER INSTITUTIONS AND ORGANS

The European Central Bank, Court of Auditors, European Investment Bank, Committee of the Regions and Economic and Social Committee are dealt with in detail in the EC Treaty. However, these institutions will not be changed under the Lisbon Treaty in any manner impacting the EU's dividing lines. The Central Bank will retain its independence from Member State influence. The Court of Auditors will retain its largely internal role, also independent of Member State influence, although Member States will still be required to cooperate when the Court audits national activities relating to EU revenues and expenditures. The Members of the European Investment Bank will remain the Member States themselves.

The advisory committees are just that – advisory bodies with little power. However, the Lisbon Treaty does offer them somewhat more than they possess under the Treaties. Article 8 of the Lisbon Treaty's revised Protocol on Subsidiarity grants the Committee of the Regions the right to commence an action with the Court of Justice to challenge any new EU legislative act on the ground that it violates the principle of subsidiarity.[931] This is similar to the right granted to Member State governments in the same section of the Protocol. Article 9 of the Protocol provides that the Commission must also provide annual reports to both of the committees (as well as to the Member States and the major EU institutions) regarding the compliance of new EU laws with the subsidiarity principle.[932] Neither the right of action nor the right to receive reports is found in the current Treaties or their protocols.

---

[930] Lisbon Treaty Art. 2(209).
[931] Protocol on Subsidiarity, *supra* note 328, Art. 8.
[932] Id. at Art. 9.

7.   INSTITUTIONAL CHANGES AND THE DIVIDING LINES

This chapter has explored the principal institutions and has noted that the Lisbon Treaty does propose some changes to their structure and their responsibilities. Let us consider whether the most prominent of these innovations would affect the EU's dividing lines.

– The *European Parliament's* role in legislation (co-decision) and in budgetary matters will be expanded, but no major institutional change (such as the right of legislative initiative) is offered. Overall, the Lisbon Treaty's provisions relating to the Parliament would not impact the dividing lines.
– The *European Council* and its responsibilities will be more clearly identified, and its new President will be a visible development. However, the prominence of the President is not accompanied by any competence-shift to Brussels. A more coherent voice for the Union does not constitute the movement of a dividing line *vis-à-vis* the Member States.
– The *Council of Ministers* will receive a new formula for qualified majority voting, a new High Representative for Foreign Affairs, and a mandate to meet in public when legislating. The QMV formula may be seen as merely a technical adjustment, and the new High Representative may offer greater coherence. Neither of these changes affects the dividing lines.
– The *Commission* will be reduced in size in 2014. Arguably, the elimination of representation by all Member States will reduce somewhat the ability of the states to influence the course of EU activity, thus creating a minor shift in one of the dividing lines. In legislation, the more demanding requirements for Member State initiatives in the AFSJ arguably strengthen the Commission, while the citizen initiative may undercut the Commission's right of initiative, but these dividing line movements are of relatively little consequence.
– The jurisdiction of the *Court of Justice* will be extended into new areas in the CFSP and AFSJ. This is arguably a real dividing-line shift, because where the Court gains power, the national courts generally lose. However, even this development must be seen as relatively incremental. This is not a wholesale increase in the Court's competence, nor an overt reduction in the powers of the national courts. This shift represents a thoughtful attempt to provide greater accountability in the CFSP and greater efficiency and predictability in the AFSJ.

In light of the above summaries, it is fair to conclude that in broad terms the institutions under the Lisbon Treaty will maintain their essential character, functions and mandates. It might be speculated that the structural changes to the institutions could lead to their increased strength and effectiveness, and that these qualities could result in a stronger Union that will better be able to draw power away from the Member States. However, this is a theoretical possibility at best. In general, the Lisbon Treaty's treatment of the EU institutions does not appear intended to significantly shift the Union's dividing lines.

Chapter 14
INSTRUMENTS AND PROCEDURES AVAILABLE TO THE EU

This chapter addresses the techniques that may be employed by the EU institutions in the process of making laws and decisions. The primary focus here will be on the EU's legal instruments and acts, although we will also briefly address the matter of co-decision by the European Parliament and the ongoing role of Member State law in EU affairs. As noted at the end of this chapter, the Lisbon Treaty's proposed changes in these matters appear to have minimal impact on the EU's dividing lines. Nevertheless, this analysis is included to provide a fuller description of the Lisbon Treaty and to provide information relevant to the workings of the EU institutions and to the subjects discussed in Chapters 15, 16 and 17.

1.   TYPES OF LEGAL ACT

1.1   The Union may use a variety of legal acts

a.   *The primary acts*
Article 249 of the EC Treaty identifies five principal types of legal acts to be used by the Community:
i.   A *regulation* has "general application" and is "binding in its entirety and directly applicable in all Member States." This constitutes the most basic form of EU law.
ii.   A *directive* is "binding, as to the result to be achieved, upon each Member State to which it is addressed, but shall leave to the national authorities the choice of form and methods."
iii. A *decision* is to be "binding in its entirety upon those to whom it is addressed."
iv.   A *recommendation* has "no binding force."
v.   An *opinion* likewise has "no binding force."

The Lisbon Treaty preserves the names and substance of these basic legal acts.[933] However, it adds further details in a new section in the EC Treaty entitled "The Legal Acts of the Union."[934] This section contains a revised Article 249 plus four new articles. In Article 249 the primary change is to restate the definition of a decision as follows: "A decision shall be binding in its entirety. A decision which specifies those

---

[933] In contrast, the Constitution would have changed the names of several of the acts and added a sixth act to the list. See Constitution Arts. 1-33 to 1-39.
[934] Lisbon Treaty Art. 2(234)-2(236).

to whom it is addressed shall be binding only on them."[935] The first new article defines the "ordinary legislative procedure" and the alternative "special legislative procedure." It also classifies "legal acts adopted by legislative procedure" as "legislative acts."[936] These definitions are not contained in the current Treaties. The second new provision describes the process by which a legislative act may "delegate to the Commission the power to adopt non-legislative acts of general application to supplement or amend certain non-essential elements of the legislative act."[937] In national terms, the described Commission activities might be termed "administrative rule-making." The third new article notes that the Member States are required to "adopt all measures of national law necessary to implement legally binding Union acts." It also describes the implementing powers of the Commission and, in certain cases, the Council.[938] The final new provision describes the adoption of recommendations by the Council, Commission or European Central Bank.[939]

b.   *Acts in the Second and Third Pillars*

The complexity of the approach in the current Treaties arises from the fact that Article 249 applies only to First Pillar activities carried out under the EC Treaty. Activities under the TEU relating to the CFSP (the TEU's Second Pillar) and police and judicial cooperation in criminal matters (Third Pillar) do not fit within the five categories of Article 249. Rather, the TEU contains its own types of legal act, such as "general guidelines," "common strategies," "joint actions" and "common positions" in the Second Pillar,[940] and "common positions," "framework decisions" (similar to directives), "decisions" and "conventions" in the Third Pillar.[941]

In the Second Pillar the Lisbon Treaty emphasises the adoption of "decisions" to define actions and positions to be taken by the Union.[942] It preserves the concept of "general guidelines," but it replaces all references to "common strategies," "joint actions," and "common positions" with references to decisions that will accomplish the same purpose.[943] Since "decisions" are part of the standard list of legal acts, these changes are obviously intended to bring Second Pillar activity into a framework similar to that of the First Pillar.

The Lisbon Treaty's transfer of the Third Pillar from the TEU to the EC Treaty effectively merges the Third Pillar into the First. The Lisbon Treaty does refer to "strategic guidelines" to be set by the European Council "for legislative and operational

---

[935] Lisbon Treaty Art. 2(235)(b).
[936] Id. Art. 2(236)(249A).
[937] Id. Art. 2(236)(249B).
[938] Id. Art. 2(236)(249C).
[939] Id. Art. 2(236)(249D).
[940] TEU Arts. 12-15.
[941] Id. Art. 34.
[942] Lisbon Treaty Art. 1(28)(b).
[943] Id. Arts. 1(29), 1(31), 1(32).

planning"[944] in the entire AFSJ (including the matters transferred from the Third Pillar), but these are policies that guide legislation and not substitutes for legislation. In the former Third Pillar provisions the TEU's special forms of action are eliminated, and all activity is subject to the "ordinary legislative procedure."[945]

c.   *Additional forms of activity*
Further complicating the current arrangement is the fact that the current EC Treaty refers to several additional forms of action for use in the First Pillar. These include the following:

i.   Article 3 requires the Community to engage in the "promotion of coordination" relating to Member State employment policies, and Article 127(1) states that the Community must "contribute" to high employment by "encouraging cooperation," "supporting" and "complementing" the actions of the states. Article 128(2) mandates that the Community draw up "guidelines for employment." The Lisbon Treaty deletes the referenced portion of Article 3,[946] but the remaining employment provisions are preserved.

ii.   EC Treaty Article 99(2) calls on the Council to draft "broad guidelines" for the economic policies of the Member States, and Article 202 requires the Council to "ensure coordination" of these policies. The Lisbon Treaty preserves Article 99(2), although it eliminates Article 202 and its mandate to the Council.

iii. Community action to "support," "coordinate" or "supplement" Member State action is provided in various provisions of the EC Treaty.[947] This random approach is formalised in the Lisbon Treaty's new EC Treaty section defining the Union's ability to "carry out actions to support, coordinate or supplement the actions of the Member States" in a variety of fields.[948]

iv.   Several articles in the EC Treaty permit the Community to enter into agreements with third countries and international organisations. This form of action is preserved throughout the Lisbon Treaty.[949] In fact, the Lisbon Treaty adds a new title called "International Agreements" to define the procedures by which the Union may enter into such agreements.[950]

v.   EC Treaty Article 310 contemplates the Community entering into "association agreements" with third countries or international organisations." The Lisbon Treaty renumbers but preserves this provision.[951]

---

[944] Lisbon Treaty Art. 2(64)(61A).
[945] Id. Arts. 2(67), 2(68).
[946] Id. Art. 2(14).
[947] See, e.g., EC Treaty Arts. 149(1) (regarding education policy), 150(1) (vocational training), 151(2) (culture), 152(2) (public health), 153(3) (consumer protection), 155(1) (trans-European networks), 157(3) (industry), 159 (economic and social cohesion) and 163(2) (research and technological development).
[948] Lisbon Treaty Art. 2(12)(2E). Also see discussion in Part 4 of Chapter 12 of this treatise.
[949] See, e.g., EC Treaty Art. 174(4) (international agreements relating to environmental matters). This is maintained in Lisbon Treaty Art. 2(143). Also see EC Treaty Art. 181a(3) (agreements relating to economic, financial and technical cooperation with third countries). This is maintained in Lisbon Treaty Art. 2(166).
[950] Lisbon Treaty Arts. 2(170)-2(174).
[951] Id. Art. 2(172).

vi. The Commission is granted administrative, investigative and enforcement powers to ensure the proper application of EU law.[952] Because this activity is technically not law-making, the use of these powers may well involve actions that do not fall within the primary forms of act described in EC Treaty Article 249. Under the Lisbon Treaty the Commission will retain such powers.[953]

The foregoing are illustrative of the fact that under the current Treaties and under the Lisbon Treaty the Union has a wider range of motion than covered by its five primary legal acts. Even the Lisbon Treaty's movement of the Second and Third Pillars into the basic procedures has not eliminated the flexibility available to the Union.

d.   *Choosing a form*
If the current Treaties do not specify which type of instrument must be used on a particular subject matter, the involved institutions presumably have the right to choose the appropriate form. When the Commission initiates legislation – or when any other institution takes action – it is logically left to them to decide which available form of action they will take under the circumstances. The only treaty provisions related to this issue are EC Treaty Article 253, which states that regulations, directives and decisions must be accompanied by a statement of "the reasons on which they are based," and Article 254, which mandates that most acts must be formalised and published prior to taking effect.

The Lisbon Treaty addresses the choice of form by stating: "Where the Treaties do not specify the type of act to be adopted, the institutions shall select it on a case-by-case basis, in compliance with the applicable procedures and with the principle of proportionality."[954] The same provision calls on the Parliament and Council to "refrain from adopting acts not provided for by the relevant legislative procedure in the area in question."

e.   *Comment*
As described above, the Lisbon Treaty improves the Treaties' presentation of the legal acts available to the Union. Furthermore, it brings Second and Third Pillar activities into the same set of acts that are currently applicable to the First Pillar. The new treaty's classification of certain acts as "legislative" is also new. Furthermore, although Community action to "support," "coordinate" or "supplement" Member State action is provided in various provisions of the EC Treaty, the Lisbon Treaty's overview of areas in which the EU may "carry out actions to support, coordinate or supplement the actions of the Member States" has no precedent in the Treaties.

The EU is a complex organisation with wide-ranging responsibilities. Variety in its array of potential acts is necessary for its successful operation. The Lisbon Treaty

---

[952] See, e.g., the Commission's extensive role in enforcing EU competition law. EC Treaty Art. 85.
[953] See, e.g., Lisbon Treaty Art. 2(76).
[954] Lisbon Treaty Art. 2(241).

simplifies the unnecessarily confusing arrangement under the existing Treaties in which the Three Pillars each have their own distinct types of legislative and regulatory act. However, despite some improvement offered by the Lisbon Treaty, it has been noted above that other forms of action will be possible, and thus the picture will be more complicated than suggested by the new section on "The Legal Acts of the Union."

Prior to the advent of the Lisbon Treaty, Herwig C. H. Hofmann published a detailed analysis of the "typology of acts" in the Constitution, which proposed many of the reforms incorporated into the Lisbon Treaty.[955] He noted that the constitutional changes emerged from a longstanding debate that included concerns about "the democratic legitimacy of EC/EU decision-making," whether EU legislation should be modeled after Member State forms of law, the balance of power among the EU institutions, and the lack of "elegance or clarity" displayed in the Treaties.[956] Hofmann described the subtleties of EU legislation, and he recognised that the system proposed in the Constitution was not without its faults.[957] Nevertheless he concluded that the Constitution's provisions represented a "very welcome step in reducing the intransparencies of the EU's legal system and adding to its overall maturity."[958] The same may be said of the Lisbon Treaty.

1.2   Member State participation in EU law-making

Article 10 of the EC Treaty requires the Member States to "take all appropriate measures, whether general or particular, to ensure fulfilment of the obligations arising out of this Treaty or resulting from action taken by the institutions of the Community." This means that the governments of the Member States must cooperate with EU institutions in their regulatory and enforcement activities. The Lisbon Treaty transfers this provision to the TEU and broadens its application to the Treaties and the Union.[959] As an example of Member State cooperation, the national governments must assist the Commission in enforcing Community competition law.[960] In addition, the rules of procedure and the appropriate authorities of the Member States may be used to enforce "pecuniary obligations" imposed by Community law on "persons other than States."[961] Both of these responsibilities are retained in the Lisbon Treaty.

If the Union issues a directive, Article 249 of the EC Treaty states that a directive "shall be binding, as to the result to be achieved, upon each Member State to which it is addressed, but shall leave to the national authorities the choice of form and methods." The actual means of implementation will depend upon national or local law and

---

[955] Hofmann, *supra* note 686.

[956] Id. at 1-2.

[957] Id. at 25.

[958] Id. at 24. For an additional analysis of the Constitution's simplification of legal instruments, see Kokott & Rüth, *supra* note 87, at 1340-43.

[959] Lisbon Treaty Art. 1(5)(3).

[960] EC Treaty Arts. 85, 88.

[961] Id. Art. 256.

the particular legal mandates for national or local officials. However, the results achieved by each state must be consistent with the EU mandate. The nature of directives and the responsibilities of the Member States are carried over into the Lisbon Treaty.

TEU Articles 34 and 42 provide that the Council may act in the Third Pillar on the initiative of any Member State. Article 34 relates to Union acts to promote police and judicial cooperation in criminal matters, while Article 42 contemplates the transfer of certain Third Pillar matters to the First Pillar. The Lisbon Treaty eliminates the Member State initiative in favor of the "ordinary legislative procedure" on matters covered in Article 34.[962] Furthermore, as a result of the wholesale shift of the Third Pillar to the EC Treaty, Article 42 is no longer relevant and is deleted by the Lisbon Treaty.[963]

Under TEU Article 48 an amendment to the Constitution may be initiated by a proposal from any Member State to the Council. The Lisbon Treaty preserves this right with regard to the ordinary amendment procedure and one of its simplified amendment procedures.[964]

A specific reservation in favor of the Member States is found in a new provision in the Lisbon Treaty, which provides that in cases where the Union acts to "support, coordinate or supplement the actions of the Member States," EU involvement may not supersede Member State competence in the field, and Union acts may not require harmonisation of Member State law.[965] This provision has no precedent in the Treaties.

In general, the responsibility of Member States to cooperate in enforcing and implementing EU law and their right to trigger the treaty amendment process do not change from the current Treaties to the Lisbon Treaty. However, the Member States do lose the right of initiative in the Third Pillar. On the other side of the coin, the Lisbon Treaty offers new emphasis that Union action to "support, coordinate or supplement the actions of the Member States" may not supersede Member State competence in the pertinent field of activity.

In his commentary on the Constitution, Herwig C. H. Hofmann contended that the "structure of the typology of acts and the allocation of decision-making procedures is at the heart of the relation between the Member States . . . and the EU powers."[966] This cannot be contested, because law-making procedures both reflect and determine the roles that various institutions will play. As the above analysis indicates, the Lisbon Treaty will change very little in regard to the Member States' role in EU law-making or enforcement. Interestingly, Andreas Føllesdal, also commenting on the Constitution, expressed concern about "the allocation of enforcement authority, which is still largely left with the Member States."[967] Citing the ongoing dispute over the Stability and Growth Pact, he warned that "partial compliance" by certain states "may unravel

---

[962] See discussion in Part 1.1(b) of this chapter.
[963] Lisbon Treaty Art. 1(53).
[964] Id. Art. 1(56)(2), (6).
[965] Id. Art. 2(12)(2A)(5).
[966] Hofmann, *supra* note 686, at 1.
[967] Føllesdal TFT, *supra* note 388, at 7.

trust among citizens and officials."[968] A greater enforcement role at the central level – most likely through the Commission – would create more uniformity in the application of EU law, and it would offer less opportunity for individual Member States to arbitrarily apply Union law for their own purposes or to their exclusive benefit.

2. CO-DECISION AS THE ORDINARY PROCEDURE

The EC Treaty contains the co-decision procedure for legislation in Article 251. Under co-decision the European Parliament and Council must both approve a measure for it to be adopted. On the other hand, EC Treaty Article 252 contains an alternative "cooperation" procedure, in which the European Parliament is consulted but has no final authority to block the legislation. Cooperation has been steadily excised from the EC Treaty, and today its use is limited to a few provisions relating to economic and monetary union.[969] Under the Lisbon Treaty co-decision is the "ordinary legislative procedure," and cooperation is entirely eliminated.[970] The Lisbon Treaty also contemplates certain legislative acts being adopted "by the European Parliament with the participation of the Council, or by the latter with the participation of the European Parliament," but these instances will be considered exceptional circumstances specifically provided for in the Treaties, and their procedures are considered "special legislative procedures."[971]

Although the cooperation procedure has been retired, the text of the Lisbon Treaty does contain many instances in which the Parliament must merely be "consulted" by the Council in connection with a Council decision.[972] As a result, Parliament may be a co-legislator, but it does not enjoy the status of a co-decider on all matters.

The movement toward full co-decision under the Lisbon Treaty will have an obvious inter-institutional impact within the EU, but it will not affect the balance of competences and powers of the Union *vis-à-vis* those of the Member States.

3. A PLACE FOR MEMBER STATE LAW

As previously discussed in Chapter 8, EC Treaty Article 282 grants the Community capacity as a legal person under the laws of the Member States, and in particular, the

---

[968] Id.

[969] The only instances in which the cooperation procedure is found after the Treaty of Nice relate to certain matters of economic and monetary union. See EC Treaty Arts. 99, 102, 103, 106.

[970] Lisbon Treaty Art. 2(239), 2(240).

[971] Id. Art. 2(236)(249A)(2).

[972] See, e.g., Lisbon Treaty Arts. 1(30)(3), 1(47)(d), 1(56)(3), 1(56)(6), 2(35), 2(36), 2(60), 2(64)(61G), 2(65)(62)(3), 2(65)(63)(3), 2(66)(3), 2(68)(69F)(3), 2(68)(69H), 2(84), 2(89), 2(91)(c), 2(92)(b), 2(116)(a), 2(144)(a), 2(147)(3), 2(153), 2(173)(6)(b), 2(174)(a), 2(200)(a), 2(213), 2(259)(b), 2(278)(280G), 2(278)(280H)(2), 2(287)(b). For a list of approximately 30 instances under the current Treaties in which decisions or other acts may be taken by the Council without participation by the Parliament or after consultation with the Parliament, see Piris, *supra* note 359, at 209, Annex 2.

rights to own property and to be a party to legal proceedings.[973] Likewise, under Article 288 the Community is specifically made subject to the contract law of individual Member States and to tort law based on "the general principles common to the laws of the Member States." The TEU, which does not create legal capacity for the EU, also does not contain any provisions relating to the Union's relationship to Member State law. The Lisbon Treaty will expand the scope of the current Treaties and bring the entire EU into a direct relationship with Member State law.

Although Articles 282 and 288, as extended by the Lisbon Treaty, reinforce the legal capacity of the EU, they also underscore the vitality of Member State law. Wherever the EU has a physical presence within any of its states, it will be subject to a host of local and national laws relating to its movable and immovable physical property. Also, in contracting for goods and services, the Union will be subject to "the law applicable to the contract in question."[974] Strictly speaking, this need not be local contract law, because the EU and its contracting party could select a different jurisdiction's law, but national contract law of some sort will likely be a factor. In the area of "non-contractual liability" (tort), the Union will be required to "make good any damage" it causes, with its liability to be determined "in accordance with the general principles common to the laws of the Member States."[975] This perhaps might not lead immediately and directly to the local law where the incident occurs, but it seems unlikely that the EU in a proceeding before a local court would try to assert its rights on the basis of principles established in other Member States.

As this analysis has shown, in certain matters of contract and tort the Lisbon Treaty will preserve and actually broaden the EU's subjection to Member State law. The existing dividing lines in these areas will be maintained and made even brighter.

4.   INSTRUMENTS, PROCEDURES AND THE DIVIDING LINES

The Lisbon Treaty offers a more widely applicable set of acts to be used in EU lawmaking, and on the surface this is a noteworthy improvement over the complex legislative scheme of the Treaties with their Three Pillars. As noted, however, the updated system is actually more complex than it appears at first blush. In any event the question remains as to whether the Lisbon Treaty's new approach will have any impact on the dividing lines. Do simplification and more transparency result in any net gains for Brussels? It is difficult to imagine any such gain, and thus our conclusion is that the dividing lines are not affected.

It is noteworthy that the Member States are called upon in the Lisbon Treaty to work side-by-side with the Union to "ensure fulfillment" of EU law. In the case of directives, national implementing laws are required, with each state being free to choose

---

[973] The discussion in Part 1.1 of Chapter 8 points out that this capacity may be referred to as "private law personality," in contrast to the "public law personality" granted to the Community under EC Treaty Art. 281.

[974] EC Treaty Art. 288

[975] Id. Art. 288.

the form and method of implementation. This role for the national governments is significant, signaling a partnership between the Member States and the EU, but the character of this relationship does not change from that described in the current Treaties.

The Lisbon Treaty's elimination of the cooperation procedure in favor of co-decision in all cases may represent a slight inter-institutional shift of power to the European Parliament, but this will not affect the dividing lines between the EU and the Member States.

The Lisbon Treaty's expansion of the affect of Member State law to include the full Union, rather than merely the European Community, is a slight extension of the impact of national law on the institutions of the EU. However, this is at best a technical change, and it does not appear that it will affect the dividing lines as they are described in this treatise.

In concluding this brief analysis of instruments and procedures, we do well to recall several procedural concepts that have a bearing on all EU legislation. First, Member State parliaments must be advised of all proposed EU legislation, and they may object, force reconsideration or bring a challenge to the Court of Justice if they feel that the law will violate the subsidiarity principle. Second, a citizen initiative may propose legislation where the Union institutions have chosen not to. Third, the requirement for unanimous Council decisions in many instances and the general necessity for consensus on the European Council create a veto right for each Member State in many critical areas of EU activity. Fourth, where the EU is unable to legislate due to lack of sufficient consensus, groups of Member States may bypass the Union by engaging in some form of enhanced cooperation. These principles are beyond the technical focus of this chapter, but no discussion of legislative procedures should overlook their significance.

Chapter 15
WHERE QMV REPLACES UNANIMOUS VOTING
OR APPLIES TO NEW SUBJECTS

A recurring theme in this treatise is the fact that the Lisbon Treaty will preserve the two primary voting requirements that have been available to the Council, namely, unanimity and the QMV. The Lisbon Treaty's preference for QMV at the Council – where most EU legislation must be approved – is clear enough.[976] However, many critical decisions will remain subject to approval by all Council representatives.

This chapter offers a detailed description of where the Lisbon Treaty embraces QMV decision-making either as a departure from unanimity required under the current Treaties or in a new field of EU activity. This analysis will be divided into four sections. Part 1 provides a brief perspective on why the European Union would choose unanimity or QMV. Part 2 identifies those instances in which a requirement of unanimity in the current Treaties will be changed to qualified majority voting under the Lisbon Treaty. These areas are seen to represent a diminishment of the national blocking power. Part 3 describes the *new* subjects of legislation in the Lisbon Treaty for which the QMV will be the means of Council action. These are areas which could have been designated for unanimous Council voting, but QMV has been selected. Finally, to illustrate the continuing vitality of unanimous voting in certain fields, Part 4 introduces the Addendum, which identifies all of the Lisbon Treaty articles in which unanimity or another form of unity will be required at the Council and European Council. These provisions highlight the substantial number of policy areas in which the Member State veto power will be retained.

It should be noted that the primary purpose of this chapter is to evaluate whether the Lisbon Treaty significantly shifts voting on the Council from unanimity to qualified majority. The mechanics of QMV, especially the voting formulas, have been addressed in Part 3 of Chapter 13.

1.   THE SIGNIFICANCE OF UNANIMOUS DECISION-MAKING

As discussed in Chapter 11, a foundational principle of international law is that all parties to a treaty must consent to its initial ratification and its subsequent amendment.[977] Likewise, when a group of nations has contracted to form an international or-

---

[976] Lisbon Treaty Art. 1(17)(3) states: "The Council shall act by a qualified majority except where the Treaties provide otherwise." The policy-making European Council must generally act by consensus. Lisbon Treaty Art. 1(16)(4) states: "Except where the Treaties provide otherwise, decisions of the European Council shall be taken by consensus."

[977] Vienna Convention, *supra* note 617, Arts. 24, 40.

ganisation, history indicates that they have expected unanimity to be the general rule for decision-making within the new entity. Stephen Zamora has observed:

> "Under traditional international law, as exemplified by early diplomatic conferences, two basic truths controlled the question of voting: every state had an equal voice in international proceedings (the doctrine of sovereign equality of states), and no state could be bound without its consent (the rule of unanimity). These rules were bound together, and were extensions of the general principle of the state's sovereign immunity from externally imposed legislation."[978]

The straightforward expectation of unanimity has a major flaw, however. It inhibits the actual achievement of results. Zamora adds:

> "The disadvantage of the rule of unanimity, of course, is that international agreement is impossible to obtain when any single participant can block a decision; to achieve unanimous consent, the strength of a decision must be diluted so as to please everyone. Either result is unsatisfactory for an effectively functioning international organization that is charged with making and implementing decisions to meet urgent, practical problems."[979]

Andreas Føllesdal concurs. Referring to voting patterns within the European Union he notes that the presence of "multiple veto points ensuring stability easily leads to stagnation, preventing common action even where required."[980] Even worse than inaction, according to Føllesdal, is that a nation may threaten a veto to exact concessions in its favor: "Thus many hold that this safety valve has been abused by some Member States to extort unfair benefits from cooperation."[981] The EU Commission White Paper of 2001 echoed this concern, noting that a consensus requirement often "holds policy-making hostage to national interests."[982] The consequence of this reality is, according to Zamora, that a number of international organisations have gradually abandoned unanimity in favor of majority rule.[983] But this trend has led to inevitable conflicts,[984] and the European Union has reflected this tension.

According to Youri Devuyst, the founders of the European Community were determined to avoid the shortcomings of previous organisations. He quotes Paul-Henri Spaak as having stated that "unanimity formulae are the formulae of impotence."[985] To avoid the "unanimity trap" Devuyst describes Spaak as urging the Community's initial members to "leave ancient notions of sovereignty behind and accept the principle

---

[978] Stephen Zamora, Voting in International Economic Organizations, 74 Am. J. Int'l L. 566, 571 (1980).

[979] Id. at 574.

[980] Føllesdal TFT, *supra* note 388, at 5.

[981] Id.

[982] White Paper, *supra* note 23, at 29.

[983] Zamora, *supra* note 978, at 574.

[984] Id. at 566.

[985] Devuyst, *supra* note 39, at 30.

of majority voting."[986] This was not to be grounded in mere idealism, but in recognition that a successful Community would advance the "substantive political and economic preferences" of the Member States.[987]

Notwithstanding the practical appeal of majority voting, the force behind it was by no means irresistible as the EU developed.[988] To the contrary, national interests at times appeared to be an immovable object, as in the 1965 episode of the French "empty chair" to protest the Treaty of Rome's phase-in of qualified majority voting in certain policy fields. French representatives simply boycotted Community activities for a seven-month period, until the Luxembourg Accord was adopted to allow any Member State to halt Community action that might threaten its vital interests.[989] Paul Craig comments that this was "the prime example of negative inter-governmentalism."[990] Twenty years later the Single European Act finally overcame the Accord to enable the decision-making efficiency necessary for completion of the Community's internal market.[991]

Despite much progress toward qualified majority voting in the past 20 years, the path has been marked with many concessions toward preserving Member State sovereignty. For one matter, under the Treaties a qualified majority has always been defined in such a manner as to provide extra protection to the smallest states. In addition, there is a continuing attempt to reach consensus on the Council even on matters for which a QMV decision may be taken. Edward Best describes these phenomena as follows:

> "[T]he 'Founding Fathers' of Europe explicitly rejected 'objective' keys and population, in favor of a distribution of votes reflecting a balancing act between the states. This balance was conceived in terms of clusters of states and responded to a general principle of 'degressive proportionality' . . . by which the larger units are under-represented compared to the smaller ones. This in turn has loosely reflected the belief that, in such a diverse and sensitive union as the European Community, the pursuit of consensus and the protection of minorities are more important principles than simple majority rule."[992]

Other concessions have included opt-outs, derogations and transition periods for new policies,[993] and Volker Röben notes: "The trend to qualified majority voting in the Council of Ministers at the center is counter-balanced by the ever-increasing role on

---

[986] Id.

[987] Id. at 8.

[988] It is appropriate to note that qualified majority voting as a means of making decisions among the Member States is a step well short of full delegation of authority to the EU institutions. Andrew Moravcsik describes QMV as an example of "pooling" of sovereignty, as contrasted with the delegating of sovereignty that takes place when Union institutions (the Commission being one example) are given the power to make and carry out law without consulting the Member States. Andrew Moravcsik, The Choice for Europe: Social Purpose and State Power from Messina to Maastricht 67 (1998).

[989] Devuyst, *supra* note 39, at 31.

[990] Paul Craig, The Community Legal Order, 10 Ind. J. Global Legal Stud. 79, 86 (2003).

[991] Id. at 89-100. The Single European Act is cited in note 89, *supra*.

[992] Best, *supra* note 867, at 17.

[993] Devuyst, *supra* note 39, at 20-21.

the periphery of the European Council."[994] Finally, despite the expansion of QMV, there remain many areas in which unanimity has been preserved, leaving much room for what Pavlos Eleftheriadis has termed "discretionary state action."[995]

The following sections will identify precisely where the Lisbon Treaty will increase the opportunities for qualified majority voting, and where it will preserve the unanimity requirement. Please note that this chapter provides only a brief description of the identified matters. Greater elaboration and fuller context for certain fields may be found in the subject matter analyses offered in Chapters 16 and 17.

2.   WHERE UNANIMOUS VOTING WILL CHANGE TO QMV

The Lisbon Treaty contains a number of provisions in which voting or decision-making will change from a unanimity requirement in the current Treaties to qualified majority voting. Each of these instances may be seen as a loss of Member State power, in that the states lose their right to block these decisions. This section identifies these new QMV subject matters and their predecessor provisions in the current Treaties.

For the Lisbon Treaty provisions described, the QMV requirement will arise, unless otherwise noted, as a result of the decision being subject to the "ordinary legislative procedure," which entails a QMV decision of the Council and co-decision with the European Parliament.[996] However, this analysis will not focus on the role of the Parliament, but solely on the Council's voting requirements.

2.1   **Institutional matters**

a.   *Council presidencies.* The Lisbon Treaty provides for a qualified majority decision of the European Council to determine the system for rotation of the Council formation presidencies other than Foreign Affairs.[997] This is a rare instance in which the European Council would vote by QMV. Under Article 203 of the current EC Treaty the rotation of Council presidencies is to be determined by the Council itself, acting unanimously. Under the current treaty, the Foreign Affairs formation is treated like all other formations, whereas under the Lisbon Treaty it is to be headed by the new High Representative for Foreign Affairs.

b.   *Commission.* The Lisbon Treaty provides for regulations to "lay down in advance the rules and general principles concerning mechanisms for control by Member States of the Commission's exercise of implementing powers."[998] These regulations will require a QMV decision of the Council under the ordinary legislative procedure.

---

[994]   Volker Röben, Constitutionalism of the European Union After the Draft Constitutional Treaty: How Much Hierarchy, 10 Colum. J. Eur. L. 339, 359 (2004).

[995]   Eleftheriadis, *supra* note 56, at 38-39.

[996]   Lisbon Treaty Art. 2(239).

[997]   Id. Arts. 1(17)(9), 2(189)(201b)(b).

[998]   Id. Art. 2(236)(249C)(3).

There is not a directly parallel provision in the current Treaties that addresses how the Member States may exert control over the Commission's implementing authority. Instead, EC Treaty Article 202 generally permits the Council to confer on the Commission the power to implement "rules which the Council lays down." The Council may "impose certain requirements in respect of the exercise of these powers," presumably including any assignment of authority to the Member States. In any event the Commission must act according to "principles and rules to be laid down in advance by the Council, acting unanimously on a proposal from Commission and after obtaining the opinion of the European Parliament." Thus, in at least one respect the unanimous approval required under the EC Treaty will be changed to a QMV decision under the Lisbon Treaty.

c.   *Statute of ESCB and European Central Bank (ECB).* The Lisbon Treaty permits regulations to amend specified provisions in the Statute of the European System of Central Banks and of the European Central Bank, relating to monetary policy. These regulations will require a QMV decision of the Council.[999] In contrast, Article 107(5) of the current EC Treaty identifies the same provisions in the Statute, and if an amendment to any of them is proposed by the Commission, the Council's vote on the matter must be unanimous. If such an amendment is proposed by the ECB itself, the Council may vote by QMV. The Lisbon Treaty thus offers a shift to QMV for Commission-proposed amendments only. Arguably this will be an inter-institutional change that will remove a measure of protection for the ECB against unwanted adjustments to its Statute.

d.   *ECB Executive Board.* The Lisbon Treaty permits the Executive Board of the European Central Bank to be appointed by a QMV of the European Council (euro-zone Member State representatives only).[1000] This is a change from current EC Treaty Article 112(2) which requires the appointment to be made by the *common accord* of the heads of state or government of the euro-zone Member States.

e.   *Court of Justice Statute.* The Lisbon Treaty allows a regulation (requiring only a QMV of the Council) to amend the Statute of the Court of Justice, excluding Title I and Article 64.[1001] The corresponding provision in the current EC Treaty is Article 245, which requires a *unanimous* Council decision for amendments to the Statute, with Title I (but not Article 64) excepted. Amendment to Article 64 actually becomes more demanding under the Lisbon Treaty, requiring a treaty amendment rather than a mere Council vote. With the exception of Title I and Article 64, the Lisbon Treaty offers a broad shift to qualified majority voting for changes to the Statute.

---

[999]   Lisbon Treaty Art. 2(93)(c).

[1000]   Id. Arts. 2(98), 2(228)(b).

[1001]   Id. Art. 2(226). Title I sets the basic rights and duties of judges, while Art. 64 governs the language arrangements at the Court, and amendments to these provisions will require an amendment to the treaty.

f.   *Specialised courts.* The Lisbon Treaty permits regulations to create specialised courts to be attached to the General Court (currently called the Court of First Instance) and also to determine their fields of jurisdiction. These laws will require a QMV of the Council,[1002] whereas similar provisions in Article 225a of the current EC Treaty require a unanimous Council decision. Interestingly, the Lisbon Treaty retains the EC Treaty's current requirement that members of specialised courts be appointed by unanimous vote of the Council, and both the current treaty and Lisbon Treaty permit a QMV Council vote to approve rules of procedure for the special panels.

2.2   Resources and revenues

a.   *Own resources.* The Lisbon Treaty permits regulations approved by a QMV Council decision to implement measures relating to the Union's own resources.[1003] However, such implementing regulations must be based on a policy previously approved by a unanimous Council vote that is approved by all of the Member States. EC Treaty Article 269 requires unanimity for all "provisions" without differentiating between the basic policy and subsequent implementing measures. Because the budget is a politically sensitive area, it is apparently necessary under the Lisbon Treaty to preserve the veto power of each Member State at the critical policy-setting stage. Any state that is concerned about subsequent implementation can in principle withhold its vote at the policy stage until any controversial aspects of implementation are agreed in advance.

b.   *Revenues.* The Lisbon Treaty permits the Council to adopt by QMV a European regulation governing how EU budget revenues will be made available to the Commission.[1004] This is a change from EC Treaty Article 279(2), which requires unanimity for this action.

2.3   Internal market

a.   *Social security.* The Lisbon Treaty permits regulations, approved by a QMV decision of the Council, to protect the social security of workers moving from one state to another within the Union.[1005] This provision deletes a unanimity requirement in the existing provision, EC Treaty Article 42. Despite this potentially significant change, the Lisbon Treaty provides an "emergency brake" by which a Member State may refer the question to the European Council (for a unanimous decision) on grounds that a proposed EU law might "affect important aspects of its social security system."[1006]

[1002] Lisbon Treaty Art. 2(211)(a).
[1003] Id. Art. 2(259)(b).
[1004] Id. Art. 2(273)(b).
[1005] Id. Art. 2(51).
[1006] Id. Art. 2(51)(b).

b.   *Freedom to provide services.* The right of establishment and freedom to provide services are covered by Articles 43 to 48 of the EC Treaty. Under the treaty, EU legislation in these areas is governed by the general rule of QMV decision-making on the Council. One change is that in relation to the taking-up and pursuit of activities as self-employed persons the Lisbon Treaty consistently provides for QMV decisions,[1007] while Article 47(2) of the Treaty requires a unanimous Council decision "on directives the implementation of which involves in at least one Member State amendment of the existing principles laid down by law governing the professions with respect to training and conditions of access for natural persons." The Lisbon Treaty's elimination of this one unanimity requirement reflects a specific shift to QMV, the result of which could be more efficient EU decision-making on the matter of professional licensing.

2.4   Policies in other areas

a.   *Structural Funds and Cohesion Fund.* Under the Lisbon Treaty regulations relating to the Structural Funds and Cohesion Fund may be approved by the Council using QMV.[1008] This is a change from EC Treaty Article 161, under which QMV would replace unanimity only if a multiannual financial perspective and an Interinstitutional Agreement have been adopted. The Lisbon Treaty will implement QMV even if these conditions have not been met.

b.   *Transport.* European legislation to support a common transport policy is permitted by the Lisbon Treaty, and the Council's decision on these new laws will be determined by QMV.[1009] The new treaty does require that these laws take account of "cases where their application might seriously affect the standard of living and level of employment in certain regions, and the operation of transport facilities." In contrast, EC Treaty Article 71(2) states that where these special circumstances exist the EU legislation is subject to a unanimous Council vote. The Lisbon Treaty's provision thus eliminates the veto of a Member State that might be concerned about the standard of living within one of its own regions or that of a different state.

2.5   Area of freedom, security and justice

The Lisbon Treaty provides for a wide variety of EU laws in the AFSJ, and in most instances the decisions of the Council will be made by QMV.[1010] On the surface this appears to be a major shift from the Treaties. For example, under TEU Article 34(2) the Council is required to act unanimously in a number of AFSJ matters. Furthermore, EC Treaty Article 67(1) generally requires unanimity for decisions on AFSJ matters

---

[1007] Lisbon Treaty Art. 2(54).
[1008] Id. Art. 2(133).
[1009] Id. Art. 2(70).
[1010] Id. Arts. 2(63)-2(68).

found within Articles 61 to 69 of that treaty. EC Treaty Article 67(2) contemplates a move away from unanimity in this field, but it does require a unanimous Council decision to shift certain decisions to QMV.[1011] Despite the fact that a Council decision in December, 2004, did institute QMV for certain matters under Articles 62 and 63,[1012] the Lisbon Treaty will generate greater movement in this direction.

There is, however, a theoretical catch to all of this. A new article in the Lisbon Treaty requires the European Council to "define the strategic guidelines for legislative and operational planning within the area of freedom, security and justice."[1013] Such action, of course, will require consensus. These guidelines should ordinarily be on the broadest level, and the European Council should not ordinarily insert itself into the details of lawmaking. However, as a political matter, a Member State with concerns as to the ultimate nuts and bolts of AFSJ legislation theoretically could object at the strategic guideline stage. Such an objection might be asserted to avoid future legislation that would be initiated by the Commission and ultimately voted upon by the Council through QMV. This scenario might be highly unlikely, but the Lisbon Treaty creates the possibility.[1014]

The specific voting changes relating to the AFSJ are as follows:

a.   *Administrative cooperation.* The Lisbon Treaty permits the Council, by QMV, to adopt regulations relating to administrative cooperation in the area of AFSJ.[1015] TEU Article 34(2), although not specifically referring to administrative cooperation, requires unanimity for actions of this type.

b.   *Border controls.* The Lisbon Treaty provides for regulations, with the Council voting by QMV, to set forth a policy on border controls.[1016] This is a change from EC Treaty Article 62, in which measures on border controls are subject to the unanimity requirement of EC Treaty Article 67(1) unless the Council under Article 67(2) unanimously decides that QMV is to be employed. In fact, such a Council decision was made in December, 2004,[1017] but the Lisbon Treaty will enshrine the QMV.

[1011] See Chapter 16 of this treatise (analysing the AFSJ).

[1012] Decision of the Council of 22 December 2004 providing for certain areas covered by Title IV of Part Three of the Treaty establishing the European Community to be governed by the procedure laid down in Art. 251 of that Treaty, December 22, 2004, O.J. (L 396) 45 (hereafter 22 December 2004 Council Decision). The Decision approves QMV decisions on (i) the crossing of internal EU borders (EC Treaty Art. 62(1)), (ii) standards and procedures for checking persons crossing external EU borders (art. 62(2)(a)), and (iii) measures relating to third country nationals traveling within the EU (art. 62(3)). The Decision leaves intact the unanimous voting requirement for rules on the issuance of visas to third country nationals (EC Treaty Art. 62(2)(b)).

[1013] Lisbon Treaty Art. 2(64)(61A).

[1014] For an extensive analysis of the AFSJ and for further references to the European Council's strategic guidelines, see Chapter 16 of this treatise.

[1015] Lisbon Treaty Art. 2(64)(61G).

[1016] Id. Art. 2(65)(62).

[1017] 22 December 2004 Council Decision, *supra* note 1012.

c.   *Asylum.* The Lisbon Treaty permits EU laws to determine a "common policy on asylum," with the Council approving the measures by a QMV.[1018] This is a departure from EC Treaty Article 63, which contemplates such measures,[1019] but under which Community action is subject to the unanimity provisions of EC Treaty Article 67(1). However, note that under Article 67(2) the December 2004 Council decision has partially shifted Article 63 to QMV.[1020] The Lisbon Treaty will complete the shift.

d.   *Immigration.* European regulations (with a QMV Council approval) to provide for a common immigration policy are mandated by the Lisbon Treaty.[1021] This deviates from EC Treaty Article 63, whose corresponding measures[1022] are subject to the unanimity provisions of EC Treaty Article 67. However, note that the December 2004 Council decision has partially shifted Article 63 to QMV.[1023]

e.   *Cooperation in criminal matters.* The Lisbon Treaty permits EU directives, approved by a QMV decision of the Council, to establish minimum rules for cooperation on recognition of judgments and judicial cooperation in criminal matters.[1024] This is a change from TEU Article 31(1), in which legislation is subject to the unanimity requirements of TEU Article 34(2). Note, however, that certain of the Lisbon Treaty provisions are subject to an "emergency brake" by which by which a Member State may refer the question to the European Council (for a unanimous decision) on grounds that a proposed EU law might "affect fundamental aspects of its criminal justice system."[1025] This is a highly significant protection for the Member States, and it dramatically undercuts the effectiveness of the shift to QMV.

f.   *Definition of criminal offences.* Directives to define certain criminal offences having cross-border dimensions are permitted by the Lisbon Treaty.[1026] The Council would approve such directives by a QMV. The corresponding TEU provision, Article 31(1)(e), subjects such legislation to the unanimity requirements of TEU Article 34(2). However, the Lisbon Treaty once again provides an "emergency brake," per-

---

[1018] Lisbon Treaty Art. 2(65)(63).

[1019] EC Treaty Art. 63(1), (2).

[1020] 22 December 2004 Council Decision, *supra* note 1012. The Decision moves to QMV all decisions on measures aimed at balancing the efforts among Member States with regard to receiving and caring for refugees (EC Treaty Art. 63(2)(b)). The Decision leaves in place the setting of standards and mechanisms for asylum (Art. 63(1) and setting standards relating to temporary protection to displaced persons (Art. 63(2)(a)).

[1021] Lisbon Treaty Art. 2(65)(63a).

[1022] EC Treaty Art. 63(3).

[1023] 22 December 2004 Council Decision, *supra* note 1012. The Decision permits QMV decisions immigration measures relating to immigration and illegal residence, including repatriation of illegal residents (EC Treaty Art. 63(3)(b)). The Decision does not change the unanimity requirement for measures on conditions of entry and residence, and standards for issuance of long-term visas and residence permits (Art. 63(3)(a)).

[1024] Lisbon Treaty Arts. 2(67).

[1025] Id. Art. 2(67)(69A)(3).

[1026] Id. Art. 2(67)(69B).

mitting any Member State to move a directive to the European Council for a unanimous decision. The only justification required for such a referral is the Member State's belief that a proposed EU law might "affect fundamental aspects of its criminal justice system."[1027]

g.   *Eurojust.* The Lisbon Treaty mandates EU regulations (with the Council approving by QMV) to determine the structure of Eurojust, its field of activities and its responsibilities.[1028] Under the Treaties this is governed by TEU Article 31(2), under which such activity is subject to the unanimity requirements of TEU Article 34(2).

h.   *Non-operational police cooperation.* EU legislation on non-operational aspects of police cooperation is permitted under the Lisbon Treaty, with such legislation to be approved by the Council on a QMV.[1029] Under TEU Article 30(1) all aspects of legislation relating to police cooperation are subject to the unanimity requirement of TEU Article 34(2).

i.   *Europol.* The Lisbon Treaty requires EU regulations to determine Europol's structure and responsibilities.[1030] Once again the ordinary procedure would have the Council voting by qualified majority, whereas under TEU Article 30(2) all aspects of legislation relating to Europol are subject to the unanimity requirement of TEU Article 34(2).

2.6   Areas of supporting, coordinating or supplementary action

The only voting change with regard to the Union's actions to support, coordinate or supplement Member State activities is found in a Lisbon Treaty provision that addresses EU action to "contribute to the flowering of the cultures of the Member States." This provision authorises the Council to adopt recommendations to the Member States by a QMV.[1031] The same activity under EC Treaty Article 151(5) specifically requires unanimous Council approval.

2.7   External action

a. *Certain CFSP decisions.* The Lisbon Treaty identifies certain decisions in the field of CFSP that may be made by the Council through a QMV.[1032] This expands a list of QMV decisions permitted under Article 23(2) of the TEU. However, several safeguards under the TEU are preserved in the Lisbon Treaty. First, under TEU Article 23 a Member State may invoke national policy and force referral of a Council matter to

---

[1027] Lisbon Treaty Art. 2(67)(69B)(3).
[1028] Id. Art. 2(67)(69D)(1).
[1029] Id. Art. 2(68)(69F)(1), (2).
[1030] Id. Art. 2(68)(69G).
[1031] Id. Art. 2(126).
[1032] Id. Art. 1(34)(b).

the European Council for a unanimous vote. Second, under TEU Article 23 a Member State may abstain from a Council vote and declare its intention not to be bound by the decision. Finally, under TEU Article 13(1) the general guidelines for the CFSP are to be determined by the European Council, acting unanimously.

2.8   Assessing the changes

A legitimate question is whether the identified items remove the national veto power in any areas of policy that are critical to Member State sovereignty. Brendan Donnelly and Lars Hoffmann have described the Constitution's additional areas for QMV (which carry over into the Lisbon Treaty) as "technical policy areas with cross-border implications."[1033] Andreas Føllesdal comments that the EU's movement toward more QMV decision-making "requires a well-developed trust in other Europeans and officials," and that it is "unsurprising that the default procedure [QMV] does not apply in a number of key cases involving legislation on matters close to national sovereignty."[1034]

The items described above indeed consist primarily of non-critical areas relating to the functioning of the EU and its current programmes. However, several of the changes arguably will go beyond the category of technical adjustment. Foremost among these is the change to qualified majority voting in many aspects of the AFSJ. The Member States will retain certain veto rights, but a significant shift would occur in the AFSJ.[1035] The analysis in Chapter 16 examines these areas more closely. Another change of interest is the broadening of QMV on EU laws that support free movement of professional services. The loss of the limited unanimity requirement under EC Treaty Article 47(2) might be narrow in scope, but it arguably will affect Member State control over professional training and licensing. A third item of note relates to EU support for culture. The partial elimination of unanimity in this area might raise concerns in countries of particular cultural sensitivity, such as France. It is fair to predict that cultural affairs will not become a major EU programme in the near future, if ever, but the field has the potential to be classified as more than mere technical cross-border policy.

It is also interesting to consider whether the Lisbon Treaty will lead toward more qualified majority voting in the future. As noted in Chapter 11,[1036] the Lisbon Treaty contains a "simplified" amendment process, not found in the Treaties, to change the Council's voting procedures in any area of EU activity. However, even this streamlined procedure will require a unanimous decision by the European Council and the

---

[1033] Brendan Donnelly & Lars Hoffmann, All change or no change? Convention, constitution and national sovereignty, The Federal Trust Policy Brief No. 1, at 3 (November 2003), available at www.fedtrust.co.uk/admin/uploads/PolicyBrief1.pdf.

[1034] Føllesdal TFT, *supra* note 388, at 5.

[1035] As noted in Part 2.5 of this chapter, there is the theoretical possibility that the shift to QMV could be affected by the European Council's right to (unanimously) set strategic guidelines in matters of the AFSJ.

[1036] See Part 2 of Chapter 11 of this treatise.

right of any national parliament to block the change.[1037] Each Member State will thus have two opportunities to exercise its veto over any attempt to change to QMV any of the remaining treaty provisions that require a unanimous vote by the Council.

There are several additional articles in the Lisbon Treaty that permit increased qualified majority voting on the Council, without the treaty amendment process. These *passerelle* provisions include the following:

– A unanimous European Council decision may permit additional QMV certain areas of the CFSP.[1038]
– A unanimous European Council decision may approve QMV in place of unanimity when the Council determines the EU's multiannual financial framework.[1039]
– A unanimous Council decision may permit QMV where unanimity is required in relation to AFSJ measures affecting family law with cross-border implications. Any national parliament may block such a decision.[1040]
– A unanimous Council decision (participating Member States only) may permit additional QMV within a programme of enhanced cooperation.[1041]
– A unanimous Council decision (participating Member States only) may change a special legislative procedure to the ordinary legislative procedure within a programme of enhanced cooperation.[1042]
– A unanimous Council decision may permit additional QMV within EU programs on environmental protection.[1043]

These bridging provisions are without precedent in the Treaties. However, each decision to permit more qualified majority voting on the Council requires a unanimous decision of the European Council or Council. In the case of a programme of enhanced cooperation, only participating Member States will take part in the unanimous decision.

How should these proposed new areas of qualified majority voting be viewed? There will indisputably be some movement toward more QMV, and a positive comment (relating to the Constitution) is offered by Janis A. Emmanouilidis:

"The extension of decisions taken by majority in the Council of Ministers is a step forward for the enlarged EU's ability to act efficiently. It is also positive that decisions in the Council of Ministers taken on the grounds of the ordinary legislative procedure will as a rule be decided by qualified majority. Exceptions to this rule, when Council decisions are to be taken on the basis of unanimity, will have to be explicitly listed. In the end, this will not only substantially improve the enlarged EU's ability to act. It will also help prevent unjustified crossover deals, for example, between milk quotas and tax issues."[1044]

[1037] Lisbon Treaty Art. 1(56)(7).
[1038] Id. Art. 1(34)(b)(iv).
[1039] Id. Art. 2(261)(2).
[1040] Id. Art. 2(66)(3).
[1041] Id. Art. 2(278)(280H)(1), (280E).
[1042] Id. Art. 2(278)(280H)(2), (280E).
[1043] Id. Art. 2(144)(a).
[1044] Emmanouilidis, *supra* note 870, at 5.

Nevertheless, as the above analysis demonstrates, it is difficult to conclude that the Lisbon Treaty's new areas of qualified majority voting represent a major shift toward greater centralisation and away from the existing, critical reservations of Member State sovereignty.

3.   NEW SUBJECTS FOR APPLICATION OF QMV

This section addresses those provisions in the Lisbon Treaty that will create new areas of EU legislative activity subject to qualified majority voting on the Council. Under the Treaties these new matters would either (1) fall outside the EU's competence, in which case action would not be possible, or (2) if relating to "the operation of the common market," be subject to EC Treaty Article 308, which permits legislation in new internal market fields outside the Community's specified powers, but always subject to a unanimous vote on the Council.[1045] The new subjects identified below are addressed explicitly and affirmatively in the text of the Lisbon Treaty, and thus there is no need to resort to the special requirements of Article 308.

In instituting these new fields of EU activity, the drafters of the Lisbon Treaty could have selected a unanimous voting requirement as a reflection of what the EC Treaty would have required under Article 308. However, a new treaty amendment provides an opportunity to update the text of the Treaties and to provide for efficient management of new subjects that fit within the current and anticipated needs of the Union. Therefore, in addressing these new fields the drafters have chosen to permit qualified majority voting on the Council, and the Lisbon Treaty's approval by the IGC has endorsed that choice.

In the following list, unless there is a specific mention of the required voting method, the utilisation of qualified majority voting by the Council would stem from application of the Lisbon Treaty's ordinary legislative procedure.[1046] Also note that one identified item (number 3.1(a) below) calls for a QMV decision by the European Council.

3.1   **Institutional and general Union matters**

a.   *New Council configurations.* The Lisbon Treaty permits the European Council to decide by QMV the list of Council configurations other than Foreign Affairs.[1047] This coincides with the European Council's mandate to determine by QMV the rotation of the Presidencies of Council formations. Article 203 of the current EC Treaty requires

---

[1045] The Lisbon Treaty contains an expanded version of Art. 308, and it likewise requires unanimous Council action to approve lawmaking on subjects not specifically covered in the document's text. The Lisbon Treaty's flexibility clause is not limited to matters of the common market, but covers all subjects addressed in the Treaties.

[1046] Lisbon Treaty Art. 2(236).

[1047] Id. Arts. 1(17)(6), 2(189)(201b)(a).

a unanimous vote of the Council to set the Presidency rotations, but it does not address how configurations are to be created.

b. *Representation on advisory committees.* Under the Lisbon Treaty the Council may adopt decisions regarding the types of representatives who will comprise the Committee of the Regions and the Economic and Social Committee. Adjustments are contemplated to reflect "economic, social and demographic developments within the Union."[1048] Actual composition of the committees – the number of members allocated to each Member State – is subject to a unanimous Council vote.[1049] The EC Treaty specifies the allocation of members by country, but it is silent as to adjusting the segments of society represented.

c. *Citizen initiatives.* The Lisbon Treaty requires regulations to determine the procedures and conditions for citizen initiatives.[1050] These initiatives are not contemplated in the Treaties.

d. *Withdrawal agreement.* If a Member State wishes to withdraw from the Union under the Lisbon Treaty, the withdrawal provision requires the Council, acting by QMV, to conclude an agreement with the withdrawing state.[1051] There is no withdrawal provision in the Treaties.

e. *Services of general economic interest.* The Lisbon Treaty permits EU regulations to establish principles and conditions relating to services of the general economic interest to be provided by the Union.[1052] Article 16 of the EC Treaty addresses these services, but there is no provision for any EU legislation on the matter.

f. *Diplomatic and consular protection.* A new provision in the Lisbon Treaty permits EU directives to facilitate Member State diplomatic and consular protection of Union citizens in third countries.[1053] EC Treaty Article 20 contemplates such protection, but with no provision for EU legislation on the subject.

g. *EU administration.* Regulations to support "open, efficient and independent European administration" of the EU institutions are mandated by the Lisbon Treaty.[1054] There is no precedent for this provision in the Treaties.

[1048] Lisbon Treaty Art. 2(246)(5).

[1049] Id. Arts. 2(248), 2(252).

[1050] Id. Arts. 1(12)(8B)(4), 2(37).

[1051] Id. Art. 1(58)(2).

[1052] Id. Art. 2(27)(c).

[1053] Id. Art. 2(36).

[1054] Id. Art. 2(243).

3.2   Internal market

Intellectual property. The Lisbon Treaty permits legislation to create European intellectual property rights.[1055] This is a new field, not covered in the Treaties.

3.3   Policies in other areas

a.   *Space.* Legislative measures to create a European space programme are permitted by the Lisbon Treaty.[1056] Space is not a subject of the Treaties.

b.   *Energy.* The Lisbon Treaty permits legislation to support a Union policy on energy.[1057] Although Article 3(1)(u) of the EC Treaty mentions energy as one of a long list of Community activities, there are no specific provisions for legislation in the field.

c.   *Climate Change.* The Lisbon Treaty adds "combating climate change" to EC Treaty Article 174, which permits EU action in the field of environmental protection.[1058] There is no mention of climate change in the Treaties.

3.4   Area of freedom, security and justice

Crime Prevention. A new provision in the Lisbon Treaty permits EU legislation to support Member State efforts in crime prevention.[1059] TEU Article 31 generally supports cooperation in criminal matters through judicial cooperation and through Eurojust.[1060] However, it does not specifically mention crime prevention measures. Although this is best considered as a new matter that would be subject to the unanimity requirement under Article 308 of the EC Treaty, it could also be argued that it falls within the scope of TEU Article 31, in which case it would be subject to the general unanimity requirement of TEU Article 34(2). In any event, the Lisbon Treaty's permission for legislation through the ordinary legislative procedure is an extension of what is possible under the Treaties.

3.5   Areas of supporting, coordinating or supplementary action

a.   *Public health.* The Lisbon Treaty permits the Union to take action supplementary to national policies aimed at improving public health and preventing disease.[1061] In general, the terms of the Lisbon Treaty article are carried over from EC Treaty Article 152, but there is a noteworthy change. The Lisbon Treaty expands upon the Treaty's

---

[1055] Lisbon Treaty Art. 2(84).
[1056] Id. Art. 2(142)(2).
[1057] Id. Art. 2(147)(2).
[1058] Id. Art. 2(143)(a).
[1059] Id. Art. 2(67)(69C).
[1060] TEU Art. 31(1), (2).
[1061] Lisbon Treaty Art. 2(127)(d).

list of Community activities by mandating the Union to take action for the purpose of setting standards for medicines and medical devices, combating cross-border threats to health, and dealing with the use of tobacco and alcohol.

Interestingly, "common safety concerns in public health matters" are described in the Lisbon Treaty as part of the Union's shared competence,[1062] but at the same time "protection and improvement of human health" are identified as matters of supporting, coordinating or supplementary action.[1063] This creates potential confusion as to whether EU activity may preclude Member State activity or not. The Union possesses the primary right to exercise its competence if an area is "shared," and such EU acts enjoy primacy over Member State. On the other hand, in areas of supporting action the Union's acts may not supersede Member State competence.

b.   *Tourism.* The Lisbon Treaty permits EU legislation to promote European tourism.[1064] The EC Treaty mentions tourism in Article 3(1)(u) as a subject of Community activity, but no separate provision is made for legislation in the field.

c.   *Sport.* EU legislation to promote and support sporting activities is added by the Lisbon Treaty to existing EC Treaty Article 149 provisions on education.[1065] Sport is not currently mentioned in these provisions.

d.   *Civil protection.* The Lisbon Treaty provides for Union legislation to support Member State cooperation in "preventing and protecting against natural or man-made disasters."[1066] Civil protection is mentioned in Article 3(1)(u) of the EC Treaty, but its inclusion as a Community "activity" is not accompanied by any specific call for legislation.

e.   *Administrative cooperation.* The Lisbon Treaty permits EU regulations to assist Member States in improving their administrative capacity to implement EU law.[1067] There is no counterpart to this provision in the Treaties.

3.6   External action

a.   *European Defence Agency.* The Lisbon Treaty permits the Council to adopt a decision by qualified majority to define the "statute, seat and operational rules" of the European Defence Agency, a body not contemplated in the Treaties.[1068] It should be noted that the Council's ability to act by QMV is limited to the statute, seat and op-

---

[1062] Lisbon Treaty Art. 2(12)(2C)(2)(k).
[1063] Id. Art. 2(12)(2E)(a).
[1064] Id. Art. 2(148).
[1065] Id. Art. 2(124).
[1066] Id. Art. 2(149).
[1067] Id. Art. 2(150).
[1068] Id. Art. 1(50)(28D)(2).

erational rules. Actual creation of the Agency and its mandate would be subject to a unanimously adopted European Council decision.[1069]

b.   *Permanent structured cooperation.* The Lisbon Treaty permits a decision of the Council, pursuant to a QMV, to establish a permanent structured cooperation in the area of defence and to determine which Member States will participate. In addition, the treaty contemplates a QMV decision (by Council members of participating states only) that a particular Member State qualifies to be engaged in the cooperation, and a similar decision may end a state's participation.[1070] Although the word "cooperation" is used frequently in the CFSP provisions of the Treaty on European Union,[1071] the precise concept of "permanent structured cooperation" is not presented. This is a new construct under the Lisbon Treaty, and the provision for certain QMV Council decisions is a departure from the Lisbon Treaty's general requirement of unanimity with regard to decisions on permanent structured cooperation.[1072]

c.   *Access to defence appropriations.* The Lisbon Treaty permits the Council to adopt a decision as to how to provide EU budget appropriations relating to urgent policies under the CSDP.[1073] The Treaties do not address these matters.

d.   *Start-up fund.* The Lisbon Treaty permits a decision on the creation and administration of a defence start-up fund, which is to be made up of contributions by the Member States.[1074] The start-up fund is not addressed in the Treaties.

e.   *Urgent financial assistance.* Under the Lisbon Treaty the Council may make decisions when "the situation in a third country requires urgent financial assistance from the Union."[1075] There is no counterpart to this provision in the Treaties.

f.   *Humanitarian aid.* The Lisbon Treaty mandates EU legislation to determine the framework within which the Union's humanitarian aid operations will be implemented.[1076] TEU Article 17(2) makes reference to "humanitarian and rescue tasks" as part of the CFSP, but a formal, ongoing programme of humanitarian aid is not mentioned.

g.   *Aid Corps.* A European Voluntary Humanitarian Aid Corps is contemplated in the Lisbon Treaty, and EU legislation may determine its operating rules.[1077] This is an entirely new programme, not contemplated in the Treaties.

[1069] Lisbon Treaty Art. 1(49)(b)(i).
[1070] Id. Art. 1(50)(28E)(2)-(4).
[1071] TEU Arts. 11-28.
[1072] Lisbon Treaty Art. 1(50)(28E)(6).
[1073] Id. Art. 1(47)(d).
[1074] Id. Art. 1(47)(d).
[1075] Id. Art. 2(167).
[1076] Id. Art. 2(168)(3).
[1077] Id. Art. 2(168)(5).

h. *Solidarity clause.* The Lisbon Treaty contains a new solidarity clause, which requires the Union and all Member States to support any Member State that becomes a victim of a terrorist attack or a natural or man-made disaster.[1078] Decisions on EU action are to be made by a QMV of the Council, although decisions with "defence implications" are subject to unanimity.[1079] While solidarity is mentioned as a political ideal in the Treaties, the Lisbon Treaty provision is unprecedented.

3.7   No major shift in EU competences

Many of the matters described in this section are intriguing, and a few may even be dramatic. Citizen initiatives and the withdrawal clause have been controversial. Expansion of EU activity into space, public health, tourism, sport, climate change and energy could potentially extend the impact of the Union in people's lives and imaginations. A European Peace Corps could help young people further identify with the EU as a whole. However, it is difficult to conclude that these activities will meaningfully expand the competences of the Union. Perhaps the greatest attention will be paid to those proposed changes in the EU's external activities, which are always matters of heightened national sensitivity. However, the CFSP even under the Lisbon Treaty will generally be subject to unanimity requirements, so Member States should feel assured that the approved new areas of QMV-based activity in external affairs will not lead to unapproved expansion into other areas.

Overall, it is fair to suggest that most of the Lisbon Treaty's new subjects are either technical subjects that are tied to existing Union activity, or fields that pose no threat to essential Member State sovereignty.

4.   WHERE THE LISBON TREATY REQUIRES UNANIMITY

To conclude this analysis of voting requirements, it is useful to identify all of the points in the Lisbon Treaty in which a unanimous vote, consensus or common accord – by all Member States or their representatives – would be required to enact EU legislation, make decisions or otherwise carry out EU law. Because these matters are rather numerous, the list of such provisions is placed in the Addendum. A review of these items reveals that most references are to decisions of the Council, for which unanimity is the exception rather than the rule. However, the Addendum also identifies each instance in which the Lisbon Treaty mentions a decision of the European Council, either specifying that it must be taken by consensus or unanimous vote, or not specifying a voting procedure, in which case the default consensus require-

---

[1078] Lisbon Treaty Art. 2(176)(1), (2).
[1079] Id. Art. 2(176)(3).

ment will govern.[1080] In addition to acts of the two councils, the Addendum identifies several provisions in which the unanimous consent of the Member State governments is specifically mandated.

The retention of unanimity is may be characterised as positive or negative,[1081] depending on one's feelings about whether the European Union should be federal or intergovernmental in character. Nevertheless, unanimous decision-making remains an important feature of the Union landscape. As noted in previous discussions, the unanimity requirements in the Lisbon Treaty in many ways offer the essential protection and preservation of Member State sovereignty within the EU. These provisions mark the brightest dividing lines between majoritarian-based Union authority and the ability of each Member State to prevent Union encroachment in matters of vital national interest.

5.   UNANIMITY, QMV AND THE DIVIDING LINES

Some critics of the Constitution complained of a wholesale shift of decision-making on the Council from unanimity to QMV. Section 2 of this chapter identifies all such changes in the Lisbon Treaty, which essentially adopts the Constitution's proposals. The pertinent question is: if each of these changes represents the shift of one of the EU's dividing lines, what is their overall impact? Added together, it does not appear to be cause for alarm. At best there is evidence of further incremental movement of the sort that has characterised the course of the EU throughout its history. This development is both logical and measured, fashioned to make the Union more effective in light of today's challenges. It is not designed as an assault on the general competence or sovereignty of the Member States.

Similarly, the new areas of EU activity for which QMV is specified, as described in Section 3 of this chapter, appear to be carefully contained. Overall, they would enhance existing and related Union responsibilities. They certainly lack the drama of the changes instituted by TEU. These new areas demonstrate an attempt to continue the evolution of an organisation that must respond to the times and meet the needs of its members. The proposed new competences for the Union represent a shifting of the dividing lines, but not in a manner that should strike fear in the hearts of anyone but the most dedicated of Euro-sceptics.

[1080] Those few situations in which the European Council may vote by less than unanimity have been described in note 840, *supra.*

[1081] Janis A Emmanouilidis has commented on the Constitution's requirements of unanimity, which are carried over into the Lisbon Treaty: "In the case of the extension of majority decision-making in the Council of Ministers, it is unfortunate that the Constitution provides for a large number of areas where decisions will still be taken unanimously. Most prominent among these are tax harmonization, questions of social security, some areas of trade in services and intellectual property, some areas of environmental policy, anti-discrimination measures, . . . some areas of immigration policy, and – with a few exceptions – the Common Foreign and Security Policy." Emmanouilidis, *supra* note 870, at 7.

Part Four
The Subject Matters of EU Activity

Although the Lisbon Treaty has inserted a number of overview provisions into the TEU, the amended EC Treaty remains the document that contains most of the detail about the EU's activities. Chapters 16 (the AFSJ) and 17 (internal activities and external action) examine the subjects of EU programmes. The AFSJ is addressed first, because it would be most significantly affected by the Lisbon Treaty. Because of the great amount of text devoted to the Union's other internal, the analysis in Chapter 17 is generally limited to the Lisbon Treaty provisions that may impact the EU's dividing lines.

Chapter 16
THE AREA OF FREEDOM, SECURITY AND JUSTICE

The Lisbon Treaty's AFSJ comprises subject matter that is covered partly in the TEU (the Third Pillar of the Treaties) and partly in the EC Treaty's First Pillar.[1082] The provisions have been described as a grouping that "brings together the already 'communitarized' provisions on border checks, asylum and immigration and on judicial cooperation in civil matters with the third pillar provisions on police and judicial cooperation in criminal matters."[1083] As this chapter will demonstrate, the regrouping of the AFSJ provisions has ramifications well beyond mere organisational convenience. The transfer of the Third Pillar provisions into the realm of ordinary legislative procedure also shifts unanimous Council decision-making to qualified majority voting, thus adjusting one of the EU's dividing lines in the direction of centralised administration.

The Lisbon Treaty introduces the AFSJ in a reworded TEU provision that states:

"The Union shall offer its citizens an area of freedom, security and justice without internal frontiers, in which the free movement of persons is ensured in conjunction with appropriate measures with respect to external border controls, asylum, immigration and the prevention and combating of crime."[1084]

In terms of exclusivity, the AFSJ is designated by the Lisbon Treaty as a matter of shared competence.[1085] Furthermore, under the Lisbon Treaty the AFSJ will be subject to the ordinary forms of EU legislation, while the current TEU provides for a separate set of instruments (common positions, framework decisions, decisions and conventions).[1086]

The Lisbon Treaty's title on the AFSJ is divided into five chapters. Interestingly, the entire title is restated as a consolidated version of the current TEU and EC Treaty provisions.[1087] This is in contrast to many articles in the Lisbon Treaty that refer to existing treaty provisions and state which words of those provisions are being amended.

[1082] TEU Arts. 29-42 (police and judicial cooperation in criminal matters); EC Treaty Arts. 61-69 (visas, asylum, immigration and other matters).

[1083] Kokott & Rüth, *supra* note 87, at 1325. Kokott and Rüth were referring to these combined provisions as presented in the Constitution. For a general analysis on the AFSJ, including the tensions between public order and individual rights within the European Union, see Hans Lindahl, Finding a Place for Freedom, Security and Justice: The European Union's Claim to Territorial Unity, 29 Eur. L. Rev. 461 (2004). For a history of the evolution of the AFSJ from its beginnings to its treatment in the Constitution (which is mirrored in the Lisbon Treaty), see Kuijper, *supra* note 647, at 609. Kuijper's topics include "The evolution of the Third Pillar and the intergovernmental method," "Transition to the Community method," "Variable geometry," and "Integration of the Schengen Acquis."

[1084] Lisbon Treaty Art. 1(4)(2). This is substantively identical to TEU Art. 2.

[1085] Id. Art. 2(12)(2C)(j).

[1086] TEU Art. 34(2).

[1087] The Lisbon Treaty's new title is nearly identical, chapter-by-chapter and article-by-article, to the presentation of the AFSJ in the Constitution. See Constitution Arts. III-257 to III-277.

As a result, the AFSJ title is easier to read by itself, but it is correspondingly awkward to compare specific provisions to their existing counterparts. Fortunately, each chapter in the Lisbon Treaty begins with a recitation of which EC Treaty and TEU provisions are being replaced. The ensuing analysis will address the five new chapters in sequence, noting where their substance varies significantly from the existing Treaties.

1.   SETTING THE STAGE – GENERAL PROVISIONS

The first chapter in the Lisbon Treaty contains ten articles that replace various introductory provisions in the EC Treaty and TEU.[1088] Notable provisions include the following:

a.   *Another overview.* The first article expands on the revised TEU's overview of the AFSJ, quoted above. The provision states the main thrust of the AFSJ title.[1089]

b.   *Member State legal traditions.* The first article mandates that Union action must take into account "the different legal traditions and systems of the Member States."[1090] There is no counterpart to this provision in the TEU or EC Treaty, but this new emphasis appears to be merely rhetorical.

c.   *Preventative measures.* The Lisbon Treaty calls upon the Union to exert efforts to ensure security through "measures to prevent and combat crime, racism and xenophobia," as well as through measures to coordinate police and judicial cooperation, mutual recognition of criminal judgments and, as necessary, approximation of criminal laws.[1091] These goals and activities have their antecedent in Articles 29 and 31(1) (a) of the TEU.[1092]

d.   *Strategic guidelines.* A new provision requires the European Council to develop "strategic guidelines for legislative and operational planning within the area of freedom, security and justice."[1093] In accordance with the general requirement for European Council decisions, the adoption of these guidelines will require a consensus decision. This is a significant reflection of intergovernmentalism, and for each of the AFSJ matters addressed in the following analysis there is the theoretical potential that the necessity for strategic guidelines could undercut any use of qualified majority voting on the Council. The strategic guidelines requirement has no direct antecedent

---

[1088] The replaced articles are identified in the introduction to Lisbon Treaty Art. 2(64).

[1089] Lisbon Treaty Art. 2(64)(61).

[1090] Id. Art. 2(64)(61)(1).

[1091] Id. Art. 2(64)(61)(3).

[1092] For an extended analysis of how the EU and its Member States can cooperate to fight crime within the constitutional constraints of the Treaties and the Constitution, see Elspeth Guild, Crime and the EU's Constitutional Future in an Area of Freedom, Security, and Justice, 10 Eur. L.J. 218 (2004).

[1093] Lisbon Treaty Art. 2(64)(61A).

in the TEU, although the European Council has in fact set strategic guidelines for the AFSJ,[1094] and the Lisbon Treaty's provision may be seen as a codification of the institution's existing practice. Neither is the unanimity requirement a new development. TEU Article 34(2) generally requires that *all action* in the field of the Third Pillar must be adopted unanimously, albeit by the Council and not the European Council. Under TEU Article 42 a unanimous Council vote may also move EU competence into Title IV of the EC Treaty and change the requisite voting requirements. Furthermore, EC Treaty Article 67(1) generally requires unanimity for decisions under Title IV of Part III of the treaty, while Article 67(2) permits a unanimous Council decision to shift certain decisions to QMV. In fact, the Council decision in December, 2004, did employ the Article 67(2) procedure to shift the majority of decisions under EC Treaty Articles 62 and 63 to QMV.[1095] After the 2004 decision only a few areas remain subject to unanimity under Article 67(1).[1096]

e.   *Subsidiarity.* The Lisbon Treaty requires national parliaments to ensure that certain EU legislation will respect the principle of subsidiarity.[1097] The legislation referred to is that relating to the transferred Third Pillar (judicial cooperation in criminal matters, as well as police cooperation), which forms the subject matter Chapters 4 and 5 of the new AFSJ title). There is no corresponding provision in the TEU, and the Lisbon Treaty's mandate injects a reminder of the Union's limitations in this field. Sceptics might contend that subsidiarity is an aspiration without any force behind it,[1098] but intergovernmentalists are given some support for expecting the EU to proceed carefully, with the national parliaments monitoring each legislative move.

f.   *Cooperation.* The Lisbon Treaty emphasises "mutual recognition" between EU and Member State authorities,[1099] and it also speaks of "operational cooperation" and "coordination" among the Member States.[1100] These are reflective of TEU Article 34(1), which states that "Member States shall inform and consult one another within the Council with a view to coordinating their action." The same provision urges the states to "establish collaboration between the relevant departments of their administrations." As with the principle of subsidiarity, mutual recognition and cooperation may prove to be toothless concepts, but the Member States are offered grounds to argue that they must play a significant role in AFSJ legislation.

[1094] See, e.g., the European Council's Tampere Conclusions of 15 and 16 October, 1999, available at http://europa.eu.int/council/off/conclu/oct99/oct99_en.htm, and their successor guidelines, the Hague Programme, of 5 November, 2004, available at http://ec.europa.eu/justice_home/doc_centre/doc/hague_programme_en.pdf.

[1095] 22 December 2004 Council Decision, *supra* note 1012.

[1096] The remaining subjects for unanimity are identified in notes 1012, 1020 and 1023, *supra.*

[1097] Lisbon Treaty Art. 2(64)(61B).

[1098] See the discussion of subsidiarity in Part 2 of Chapter 12 of this treatise.

[1099] Lisbon Treaty Art. 2(64)(61C).

[1100] Id. Art. 2(64)(61D).

g.   *National responsibility.* According to the Lisbon Treaty, EU efforts in the AFSJ may not affect the ultimate responsibility of each Member State "with regard to maintenance of law and order and the safeguarding of internal security."[1101] This is a direct carryover from Article 33 of the TEU, and it maintains one of the Third Pillar's emphases on national sovereignty.

h.   *Administrative cooperation.* The Lisbon Treaty permits the Council to adopt legislation to "ensure administrative cooperation" among the Member States and between the states and the Commission in the areas covered by the AFSJ title.[1102] These measures will be approved by a QMV, and this represents a procedural change. TEU Article 29 mentions various forms of cooperation, and Article 34 provides for the Council to take a variety of measures to achieve these objectives.[1103] Under the TEU the Council must act unanimously.

i.   *Restricting flow of capital.* Article 60 of the current EC Treaty permits the Council to take "necessary urgent measures" against third countries to restrict payments and flow of capital. The Lisbon Treaty moves this provision into the AFSJ title and expands it to include freezing of assets. The potential targets of this action under the Lisbon Treaty are not third countries, but natural or legal persons, groups or non-State entities. The thrust is "preventing and combating terrorism and related activities."[1104]

j.   *Legislative initiative.* In one of the relatively rare instances in which the proposing of EU legislation is not reserved to the Commission, the Lisbon Treaty states that Union acts pertaining to chapters 4 and 5 of the AFSJ title (the former Third Pillar) may be initiated by one-fourth of the Member States.[1105] This actually weakens somewhat the rights of individual states, because Articles 34(2) and 42 of the TEU permit a single Member State to initiate a Council decision in the Third Pillar. If individual states lose this right, a measure of power will transfer to the only other entity that may initiate legislation – the Commission. Possibly increasing the loss to the Member States is the fact that under the TEU a Council decision in the Third Pillar must be taken unanimously, whereas under the Lisbon Treaty the general rule is qualified majority voting. However, the discussions below also identify certain surviving requirements for unanimous decision-making, as well as "emergency brakes" that permit reference of legislative matters to the European Council for a unanimous vote.

k.   *Form of legal acts.* Under the Lisbon Treaty all activity in the revised EC Treaty (including the AFSJ) will be subject to the EU's normal legal acts. In contrast, under TEU Article 34(2) EU activity in the Third Pillar is subject to its own set of instruments, including common positions, framework decisions, decisions, and conven-

---

[1101]   Lisbon Treaty Art. 2(64)(61E).
[1102]   Id. Art. 2(64)(61G).
[1103]   TEU Arts. 34(1), 34(2).
[1104]   Lisbon Treaty Art. 2(64)(61H).
[1105]   Id. Art. 2(64)(61I).

tions.[1106] While the Lisbon Treaty's approach is more straightforward, it does not suggest any substantive movement away from or toward Member State influence within the Union.

1. *Recapping the major changes.* From the above comparisons it can be noted that the general treatment of the AFSJ in the Lisbon Treaty contains several significant changes from the TEU. First and foremost, the Third Pillar of the current TEU will disappear, with its provisions merged into the EC Treaty's First Pillar. As a result, all AFSJ activity under the Lisbon Treaty will take place as the ordinary working of the European Union. Second, under the TEU Article 34 all EU legislation and decisions in the Third Pillar must be adopted unanimously by the Council. In contrast, the Lisbon Treaty will require unanimity only for certain guidelines adopted by the European Council (but see the comment below). Third, the Lisbon Treaty will permit one-fourth of the Member States to initiate AFSJ legislation in the former Third Pillar, while the TEU permits any single Member State to do so. Fourth, the Lisbon Treaty will do away with the special set of legislative instruments that the TEU specifies for the Third Pillar. Finally, as analysed in Part 5 of Chapter 13, the Lisbon Treaty will expand the jurisdiction of the ECJ within the former subjects of the Third Pillar.

The reduction in the unanimity requirement for legislation and decision-making in the former Third Pillar is significant. However, the impact of the Lisbon Treaty's "strategic guidelines" provision remains to be seen. If all new AFSJ legislation is dependent on the European Council unanimously approving "strategic guidelines for legislative and operational planning," there remains at least the theoretical possibility that new AFSJ activity could be blocked at the policy-setting stage.[1107] However, the opportunity for a Member State to use its seat on the European Council to hold up further AFSJ development is not the only shield for national interests. As this discussion has demonstrated, and as further illustrated in the following analyses, there are other, more straightforward protections for the Member States.

2.   BORDER CHECKS, ASYLUM AND IMMIGRATION

Chapter 2 consists of four articles that are for the most part a restatement of Articles 62 to 64 of the current EC Treaty.[1108] These are not a part of the Third Pillar provisions transferred from the TEU. The four Lisbon Treaty provisions and their EC Treaty counterparts are as follows:

[1106] See discussion in Part 1 of Chapter 14 of this treatise.
[1107] The possible impact of Art. III-258 is introduced for consideration in Section 1.1(d) of this chapter and in Section 2.5 of Chapter 15 of this treatise.
[1108] The replaced articles are identified in the introduction to Lisbon Treaty Art. 2(65).

– The first article requires the EU to develop open internal borders and a uniform system of managing external borders, along with common policies relating visas for non-EU nationals.[1109] This restates EC Treaty Article 62.

– Under the second article the Union is expected to develop a common asylum policy.[1110] This corresponds with parts (1) and (2) of EC Treaty Article 63.

– The third article calls for a common approach to immigration.[1111] This restates EC Treaty Articles 63(3) and 64(2).

– The final article, which has no antecedent in the EC Treaty, states that in all of these EU programmes the Union must seek "solidarity and fair sharing of responsibility" among the Member States, including the financial costs.[1112]

Although much of the substance of the Lisbon Treaty is transferred from the EC Treaty, the existing treaty contains a number of transitional articles whose time periods have by now expired.[1113]

It is significant that the Lisbon Treaty's general change from unanimity to qualified majority voting on the Council in the AFSJ affects these provisions, even though Chapter 2 is not taken from the unanimity-based Third Pillar of the TEU. Article 67 of the EC Treaty also generally requires the Council to act unanimously under Articles 61 to 69 unless the Council unanimously decides to apply QMV to a particular matter.[1114] A Council decision in December, 2004, did indeed shift most (but not all) decisions under Articles 62 and 63 to QMV,[1115] but the Lisbon Treaty nevertheless represents a further broadening of majority voting.

Interestingly, the Lisbon Treaty's Chapter 5 contains several protections for Member States not found in the EC Treaty or the TEU. The first provision states that despite the goal of common border controls, the Member States retain the competence to determine the "geographical demarcation of their borders, in accordance with international law."[1116] Another article declares that an EU-wide immigration policy "shall not affect the right of Member States to determine volumes of admission of third-country nationals coming from third countries to their territory in order to seek work, whether employed or self-employed."[1117] These provisions represent at least a clarification of Member State rights, and they arguably strengthen the position of the Member States. Beyond this, the "fair sharing" requirement of the fourth article in Chapter 5[1118]

[1109] Lisbon Treaty Art. 2(65)(62).

[1110] Id. Art. 2(65)(63).

[1111] Id. Art. 2(65)(63a).

[1112] Id. Art. 2(65)(63b).

[1113] See, e.g., EC Treaty Arts. 61(a), 62, 63, 67(1).

[1114] See EC Treaty Art. 67(2).

[1115] 22 December 2004 Council Decision, *supra* note 1012, Art. 1. The changes are described in Part 1 of this chapter, in the text accompanying notes 1095-96, and are specifically identified in notes 1012, 1020 and 1023, *supra*.

[1116] Lisbon Treaty Art. 2(65)(62)(4).

[1117] Id. Art. 2(65)(63a)(5).

[1118] Id. Art. 2(65)(63b).

reflects a newly articulated ideal of parity among the Member States in these vital matters of national sovereignty.[1119]

3.   JUDICIAL COOPERATION IN CIVIL MATTERS

Judicial cooperation in civil matters has been part of the EC Treaty, and so it is not part of the transferred Third Pillar. Chapter 3 of the Lisbon Treaty consists of a single article[1120] that is an expansion of Article 65 in the current EC Treaty. This provision permits the EU to enact measures to promote "judicial cooperation in civil matters having cross-border implications."[1121]The Lisbon Treaty expresses a number of goals for EU legislation in this field, including the following goals that are not expressed in EC Treaty Article 65:
–   "effective access to justice,"
–   "the development of alternative methods of dispute settlement," and
–   "support for the training of the judiciary and staff."[1122]

Measures instituted by the Union may include requirements for the approximation of Member State laws, but any policies affecting family law must be unanimously adopted by the Council. However, family law decisions may be converted to QMV on the basis of a unanimous Council decision and notification to the Member State parliaments. Opposition from any parliament will prevent the change to QMV.[1123] Under current EC Treaty Article 67(5), the Council may act by QMV in matters governed by current Article 65, "with the exception of aspects relating to family law." The current treaty contains no *passerelle* procedure to shift the family law decisions to QMV.

4.   JUDICIAL COOPERATION IN CRIMINAL MATTERS

Chapter 4 consists of five articles that expand on a single Third Pillar provision, Article 31 of the TEU. Article 31 briefly mentions a number of activities that will support judicial cooperation in criminal matters: administrative cooperation, facilitation of extradition, rules compatibility, prevention of jurisdictional conflicts, and coordination of criminal laws and procedures.[1124] The descriptions in Chapter 4 are broad and richly detailed in comparison.[1125] Three significant provisions include the following:

[1119] Note again that the final position of these dividing lines could theoretically be affected by the role of the European Council in setting strategic guidelines. See discussions in Sections 1.1(d) and 1.1(l) of this chapter and in Section 2.5 of Chapter 15.

[1120] Lisbon Treaty Art. 2(66).

[1121] Id. Art. 2(66)(1).

[1122] Id. Art. 2(66)(2).

[1123] Id. Art. 2(66)(3).

[1124] TEU Art. 31(1).

[1125] Lisbon Treaty Art. 2(67)(69A)-(69E).

- The Lisbon Treaty describes an ambitious EU programme of developing uniform standards for crimes with a cross-border dimension, such as drug trafficking, trafficking in persons and money laundering.[1126] This provision is based on TEU Article 29, which speaks generally of "preventing and combating" such activities, and on Article 31(1)(e).
- The second provision authorises EU legislation "to promote and support the action of Member States in the field of crime prevention," albeit without the right of requiring harmonisation of national laws.[1127] TEU Article 29 speaks of crime prevention as a goal, but with no legislative programme described.
- The third provision anticipates the creation of a European Public Prosecutor's Office from Eurojust.[1128] While Eurojust is described in TEU Articles 29 and 31, the prosecutor is not mentioned.

The EU is granted wide authority in Chapter 4 to legislate the details of judicial cooperation. In these activities the basic decisional requirement on the Council is a qualified majority, which does represent a significant change to the unanimity requirements of the Third Pillar.[1129] However, there are a number of inherent limitations on EU action. For example, EU promotion of crime prevention is merely supportive of national action and may not require approximation of Member State laws.[1130] Furthermore, Eurojust is a centralised EU program, but it is an office that supports and coordinates, but does not supplant, the efforts of national investigating and prosecuting authorities.[1131] Finally, Member States in some instances may adopt higher levels of protection of individual rights than are mandated by EU law.[1132]

Unanimity also serves as a restraint on EU activity. For example, uniform rules of criminal procedure beyond those listed in the treaty must be adopted unanimously by the Council.[1133] In addition, the expansion of the EU's list of serious cross-border crimes requires a unanimous Council decision.[1134] Furthermore, the Lisbon Treaty permits the Council to establish a European Public Prosecutor's Office, but it must act unanimously in establishing the office, and the European Council must act unanimously in granting extended powers to the prosecutor.[1135] Finally, under certain provisions a Member State which believes that a proposed directive – one that can be approved by a QMV Council decision – might "affect fundamental aspects of its criminal justice system" can force the proposal to be referred to the European Coun-

---

[1126] Lisbon Treaty Art. 2(67)(69B).

[1127] Id. Art. 2(67)69C).

[1128] Id. Art. 2(67)(69E).

[1129] One example of a concrete shift is that any laws relating to Eurojust may be approved by QMV under Lisbon Treaty Art. 2(67)(69D),while similar laws under the current TEU would require unanimity under TEU Art. 34(2).

[1130] Lisbon Treaty Art. 2(67)(69C).

[1131] Id. Art. 2(67)(69D).

[1132] Id. Art. 2(67)(69A)(2).

[1133] Id. Art. 2(67)(69A)(2).

[1134] Id. Art. 2(67)(69B)(1).

[1135] Id. Art. 2(67)(E)(1), (4).

cil, where unanimous approval will be required.[1136] Whether subject to a unanimous vote or an "emergency brake" referral to the European Council, these matters of EU competence are subject to significant Member State protections.

As a reflection of the relative lack of detail in TEU Article 31, all of the areas identified above as requiring unanimous Council action or offering special protections to the interests of the Member States are innovations in the Lisbon Treaty. However, the new treaty's selective use of the unanimity requirement may be somewhat deceiving. Since Article 31 is part of the Third Pillar title in the TEU, it is subject to the general requirement of TEU Article 34 that all EU legislation and decisions in the field must be adopted unanimously by the Council. Under the Lisbon Treaty the default rule for Council voting in the entire field of AFSJ (including the former Third Pillar) is the QMV. Thus, the specific Lisbon Treaty provisions requiring unanimity may be seen not as new restrictions on AFSJ activities, but as the retention of some unanimity in the face of a general move to QMV.[1137]

5.   POLICE COOPERATION

Chapter 5 contains three articles that also represent Third Pillar provisions transferred from the TEU.[1138] The three provisions and their TEU counterparts are as follows:
-   Under the first article the EU may enact legislation to require cross-border police cooperation, but such laws relating to *operational* cooperation are subject to unanimous vote on the Council.[1139] These provisions are drawn from Article 30(1) of the TEU.
-   The second provision allows the Union to create Europol to assist in these efforts, but national parliaments are expected to monitor its activities, it must work with Member State authorities, and any "application of coercive" measures is reserved to national authorities.[1140] This article is a restatement of TEU Article 30(2).
-   The final article provides that any EU law permitting police officials from one Member State to operate in another Member State is subject to unanimous vote on the Council.[1141] This is a carryover from TEU Article 32.

[1136] Lisbon Treaty Arts. 2(67)(69A)(3), 2(67)(69B)(3). Jean-Claude Piris comments that this "emergency brake" is accompanied by an "accelerator" provision to avoid a stalemate on the proposed framework law. If certain time periods have expired without satisfactory action, Member States wishing to proceed with the proposed framework law may do so under a programme of enhanced cooperation. Lisbon Treaty Arts. 2(67)(69A)(3), 2(67)(69B)(3). See Piris, *supra* note 359, at 169.

[1137] Note again the theoretical possibility of strategic guidelines from the European Council under Art. III-258. See discussions in Section 1.1 of this chapter and in Section 2.5 of Chapter 15. If such guidelines were to be restrictive on future legislation, the opportunities for QMV decisions on new legislation would be reduced.

[1138] The replaced articles are identified in the introduction to Lisbon Treaty Art. 2(68).

[1139] Lisbon Treaty Art. 2(68)(69F).

[1140] Id. Art. 2(68)(69G).

[1141] Id. Art. 2(68)(69H).

In general, the Lisbon Treaty provisions mirror the TEU articles, although the Lisbon Treaty eliminates a five-year time period mentioned in the existing treaty,[1142] and the new treaty contains updated language referring to information collection, analysis and exchange.[1143] Significantly, areas of police cooperation *other than* operational cooperation may be decided by the Council by QMV under the Lisbon Treaty,[1144] where TEU Article 30(1) requires unanimity for all forms of cooperation. Furthermore, EU laws relating to Europol will be subject to a QMV Council vote under the new treaty,[1145] in contrast to the unanimity required under TEU Article 30(2).[1146]

The primary wording changes in the Lisbon Treaty are those described above that require unanimity on the Council or protect Member State competences. However, as noted in the previous section, TEU Articles 30 and 32 are already subject to unanimous voting on the Council. Thus the Lisbon Treaty's "new" references to unanimity are actually a means of maintaining the status quo in the subject provisions.

6.   THE SIGNIFICANCE OF THE AFSJ

Several recent commentaries have addressed the importance of the European Union's continuing development as an AFSJ. A supportive argument is presented by Dario Melossi, who notes the global threats confronting the EU, such as "the evil-doing of wayward States, . . . domestic enemies, terrorists, *narcotraficantes*, common criminals and, of course, 'undocumented' or 'irregular' migrants," and he contends:

> "In view of such global developments, we Europeans have to proceed with the greatest urgency and decision toward the creation of an actual common area of 'freedom, security and justice', but this should not be an area of conversation among a few government functionaries preoccupied with defending what has been named the 'fortress Europe'. Rather, it should be a crucial part of that construction, or indeed 'constitution', of a European democracy that is increasingly becoming the order of the day."[1147]

In contrast, Pieter Jan Kuijper injects a note of pessimistic realism into the discussion of the AFSJ, by describing the diverse ways in which several states have participated in EU programmes.[1148] These have included Member States who have opted out of certain activities, as well as non-members who have opted in. Kuijper comments:

[1142] TEU Art. 30(2).

[1143] Lisbon Treaty Art. 2(68)69F)(2).

[1144] Id. Art. 2(68)(69F)(2).

[1145] Id. Art. 2(68)(69G)(2).

[1146] However, note that any future legislative activity in the field of police cooperation could theoretically be affected by the role of the European Council in setting strategic guidelines. See discussions in Sections 1.1(d) and 1.1(l) of this chapter and in Section 2.5 of Chapter 15.

[1147] Dario Melossi, Security, Social Control, Democracy and Migration within the 'Constitution' of the EU, 11 Eur. L.J. 5, 21 (2005).

[1148] Kuijper, *supra* note 647, at 620-23.

"Variable geometry is *not* a success. The non-participants may be free riders in the decision-making, and may not even intend to participate. The fact that they must declare their intentions is not sufficient. Even combined with qualified majority, the Member States have a right to opt to have, in practice, too much influence on decision-making when the others attach importance to their participation. In the field of external relations variable geometry creates untold technical complications which will make the Union's international life only more miserable."[1149]

7.   THE AFSJ AND THE DIVIDING LINES

While dispensing with the Third Pillar, the drafters of the Lisbon Treaty have proposed more than the conversion of the AFSJ into an activity subject to the new set of ordinary legislative instruments. They have offered two more profound consequences: First, a shift from unanimity to QMV at the Council is incorporated into this field. Second, the jurisdiction of the Court of Justice in the AFSJ is significantly expanded. Together, these developments are potentially far-reaching – a relatively profound shifting of the EU's dividing lines. There are safeguards in the Lisbon Treaty, but one should acknowledge that its most significant substantive legacy may lie here.

Is this really cause for alarm? Are the sceptics correct in seeing a major movement toward Brussels? To respond to these questions, we should reflect on the subject matter represented in the AFSJ. As discussed in Section 6 of this chapter, the authors of the Lisbon Treaty did not fabricate a need for greater EU efficiency and oversight in these matters. Rather, the need already exists, and it is urgent. The arguments for greater integration and coordination in the AFSJ predated the Lisbon Treaty, and the case grows stronger each year. There is little doubt that absent a new treaty the representatives of the Member States would be pursuing these initiatives through EU legislation, or, failing that, cooperation outside the Union mechanisms. In other words, the drafters of the Lisbon Treaty have merely responded to the vital requirements of the Member States. Yes, the Lisbon Treaty proposes a shift in the EU's dividing lines, but the shift would happen in any event.

[1149] Id. at 626.

Chapter 17
THE UNION'S INTERNAL ACTIVITIES AND EXTERNAL ACTION

This chapter will address how the Lisbon Treaty may affect the EU's dividing lines in all of the subjects of European Union activity except the AFSJ. Most of this material is found in the revised EC Treaty,[1150] and it includes both internal activities within the EU and the Union's external action. However, a part of the external affairs, namely, the CFSP, is retained in the TEU. As a consequence, this chapter will be divided into two parts, the first dealing with the revised EC Treaty and all of its subjects. The second will address the CFSP as presented in the revised TEU.

1.   UNION POLICIES AND EXTERNAL ACTION

The revised EC Treaty retains its basic structure under the Lisbon Treaty, although it will be divided into seven parts, rather than six. The Lisbon Treaty's parts are as follows:

(1) Part One[1151] is entitled "Principles." It retains certain overview provisions, and it adds the new delineation of EU and Member State competences.

(2) The title of Part Two[1152] is changed from "Citizenship of the Union" to "Non-Discrimination and Citizenship of the Union." Two articles prohibiting discrimination are transferred into this section, and certain rights of EU citizens are clarified.

(3) Part Three[1153] will be titled "Union Policies" instead of "Community Policies." As amended, this part contains the EU's internal market provisions, the AFSJ, and new areas of activity added by the Lisbon Treaty.

(4) Part Four[1154] retains the title "Association of the Overseas Countries and Territories," and it receives only a few technical amendments.

(5) The Lisbon Treaty creates a new Part Five[1155] entitled "External Action by the Union." The contents of this part are consolidated from provisions previously scattered throughout the treaty, plus several new fields. The subjects include the common commercial policy, cooperation with third countries, humanitarian aid, development cooperation, restrictive measures,

---

[1150] The EC Treaty will be renamed the Treaty on the Functioning of the European Union (TFEU).

[1151] Lisbon Treaty Arts. 2(11)-2(30). Part One of the current treaty consists of Arts. 1-16.

[1152] Id. Arts. 2(31)-2(39). Part Two of the current treaty consists of Arts. 17-22.

[1153] Id. Arts. 2(40)-2(150). Part Three of the current treaty consists of Arts. 23-181a.

[1154] Id. Arts. 2(151)-2(153). Part Four of the current treaty consists of Arts. 182-188.

[1155] Id. Arts. 2(154)-2(176). See the individual Lisbon Treaty provisions to identify their counterparts, if any, in the current EC Treaty.

international agreements, international organisations, and solidarity. The CFSP is not included here, but remains in the TEU.

(6)   Part Six of the Lisbon Treaty, titled "Institutional and Financial Provisions," is a restatement of Part Five of the existing EC Treaty.[1156] This part updates the institutional provisions, legislative procedures and budgeting processes. It also consolidates the articles governing enhanced cooperation.

(7)   Part Seven is a renumbering of the current treaty's Part Six, entitled "General and Final Provisions."[1157]

Previous chapters have addressed matters covered in Parts One, Two, Six and Seven of the amended EC Treaty. Therefore, the analysis in the first part of this chapter will focus on Parts Two, Three, and Four, excluding the title in Part Three that addresses the AFSJ. The analysis will be limited to those matters in which the EU's dividing lines may be affected.

1.1   Internal market

From its earliest days and continuing to the present, one of the principal successes of the European Union has been its creation and management of the internal market.

The Lisbon Treaty describes the Union's management of the internal market (including its critical "four freedoms"[1158]) as a "shared competence."[1159] In addition the new treaty grants the Union exclusive competence in the customs union and in competition rules "necessary for the functioning of the internal market."[1160] As previously discussed, in areas of exclusive competence only the Union may act, while in matters of shared competence the EU is free to act, and Member States may legislate only to the extent the Union has not done so.[1161] In all cases the authority granted to the EU includes the right act within the Union and externally as necessary to support the Union's internal programmes.[1162] Under the Lisbon Treaty the Member States will continue their active role in the functioning of the internal market, and the Lisbon Treaty's delineation of competences establishes the basic parameters for both EU and Member State action.

The current EC Treaty lacks a delineation of exclusive and shared competences. However, certain broad principles are stated. Article 2 explains that the Community "shall have as its task, by establishing a common market and an economic and mone-

---

[1156]   Lisbon Treaty Arts. 2(177)-2(278). Part Five of the current treaty consists of Articles 189-280.

[1157]   Id. Arts. 2(279)-2(295). Part Six of the current treaty consists of Arts. 281-314.

[1158]   The freedoms include free movement of persons, goods and capital, as well as services and the related right of establishment. For a review of recent case law development of the four freedoms, see Spaventa, *supra* note 459.

[1159]   Lisbon Treaty Art. 2(12)(2C)(1).

[1160]   Id. Art. 2(12)(2B)(1).

[1161]   See discussion in Part 4 of Chapter 12 of this treatise.

[1162]   Lisbon Treaty Art. 2(12)(2B)(2).

tary union and by implementing common policies or activities referred to in Articles 3 and 4, to promote [economic development and other goals] throughout the Community." However, it is not made clear whether the Community's task is exclusive or shared with the Member States. Also without reference to exclusivity, Article 3 sets out a long list of tasks for the Community, all of which are dealt with in specific treaty articles, and all of which will be discussed below. Article 3 also refers to approximation of Member State laws as part of the activity "required for the functioning of the common market."[1163] Article 4 mentions activities of the Member States as well as the Community in relation to adoption of a Community economic policy "which is based on the close coordination of Member States' economic policies."[1164]

EC Treaty Article 5 does not refer to the internal market or any other subject area, but it most explicitly refers to competences. It begins with an attribution principle that affirms the Community's mandate to "act within the limits of the powers conferred upon it by this Treaty and of the objectives assigned to it therein." It then states that where activities "do not fall within its exclusive competence" the Community must abide by the principle of subsidiarity, and in any event it must adhere to the concept of proportionality. However, as noted, there is no list of which activities – whether related to the internal market or not – actually are exclusive to the Community. The fact that the Lisbon Treaty fills in this gap arguably represents a significant improvement. On the other hand, one might contend that the Lisbon Treaty also removes an element of flexibility permitted under the Treaties, replacing it with more clarity but also more rigidity.

The following are specific changes of interest relating to the internal market, as proposed in the Lisbon Treaty:

a.   *Multi-state social security calculations.* The free movement of workers is governed by Articles 39 to 42 of the EC Treaty. They provide the Community with broad authority to override Member State law as necessary to promote worker mobility. However, within this broad mandate Article 42 of the treaty always requires a unanimous Council vote in relation to multi-state social security calculations. The Lisbon Treaty revises Article 42 to create a presumption that decisions on such calculations will be taken by QMV at the Council. However, the new treaty also provides an "emergency brake" by which a Member State fearing potential disruptions to its social security system may move decisions in the field from the Council to the European Council, where unanimity will be required.[1165] Thus, a dividing-line shift will occur, but it will be carefully contained.

[1163] EC Treaty Art. 3(1)(h).

[1164] Id. Art. 4(1), (3). There are several other overview provisions in the EC Treaty. Art. 6 states environmental protection to be a Community goal. Art. 14 mentions the broad objective of establishing the internal market. Art. 15 anticipates temporary derogations from internal market policies to take into consideration the special economic needs of certain Member States. Arts. 297 and 298 commit the Member States to work to preserve the internal market even in the face of wars and other threats to internal security.

[1165] Lisbon Treaty Art. 2(51).

b.   *Professional licensing.* EC Treaty Articles 43 to 48 (plus Article 294) permit wide-ranging Community activity to ensure that nationals of one Member State may set up establishments or engage in self-employment in other Member States. Subsection 2 of Article 47 provides for a unanimous Council decision "on directives the implementation of which involves in at least one Member State amendment of the existing principles laid down by law governing the professions with respect to training and conditions of access for natural persons." The Lisbon Treaty deletes subsection 2, thus permitting all decisions under Article 47 to be taken by QMV of the Council.[1166] The Lisbon Treaty thus offers a small shift from unanimity to QMV with regard to the licensing of professionals, permitting QMV decisions of the Council to create more uniformity in this field at the expense of an objecting Member State.

c.   *Free flow of capital.* Articles 56 to 60 of the EC Treaty establish Community competence in supporting a free flow of capital. The Lisbon Treaty introduces two changes of note:

First, EC Treaty Article 60(1) refers broadly to restrictions on movements of capital and payments to and from third countries in matters described in Article 301 as "relating to the common foreign and security policy." The Lisbon Treaty replaces Article 60 with a new provision that provides more specific grounds for restrictions on capital flow, namely, "preventing and combating terrorism and related activities." The new article also provides a more specific list of measures that may be taken, such as freezing of assets, and the broad reference to third countries is more precisely described as "natural or legal persons, groups or non-State entities." The language of the Lisbon Treaty represents a narrowing of EU's options compared to those under the treaty.[1167]

The second change relates to the ability of a Member State to act unilaterally if the EU has not done so. Article 60(2) of the treaty permits a Member State "for serious political reasons and on grounds of urgency" to take action against a third country to restrict capital and payment flow. However, the Council by QMV may override the state's action. The Lisbon Treaty deletes Article 60(2),[1168] thus removing the right of unilateral action. However, the new treaty adds a new, more limited provision that allows a Member State to unilaterally institute "restrictive tax measures" against a third country.[1169] The Member State may (but apparently is not required to) request a decision of the Council approving the unilateral action that has been taken. Such decision must be taken unanimously, and the Lisbon Treaty does not explain what happens if the Council fails to approve the request. Presumably, the Member State will not be permitted to act. The narrower focus of the Lisbon Treaty (tax measures instead of restrictions on capital and payment flow) may be seen as a loss of national competence – a movement of one dividing line away from the Member States.

[1166] Lisbon Treaty Art. 2(54).

[1167] Note the Lisbon Treaty preserves the EC Treaty Art. 59 possibility of restrictions on movement of capital to or from third countries if there is a threat to the EU's economic and monetary union.

[1168] See Lisbon Treaty Arts. 2(62), 2(64)(61H).

[1169] Lisbon Treaty Art. 2(61).

d.   *EU intellectual property rights.* EC Treaty Articles 94 to 97 are a chapter that addresses the means by which Member State laws must be harmonised to support the internal market. The Lisbon Treaty offers a significant addition to this chapter, a new article that permits the Union to create EU intellectual property rights and to provide for Union-wide protection of such rights.[1170] This represents an expansion of Union competences in a matter vital to cross-border commerce. Interestingly, the new provision reflects some sensitivity to national interests by requiring a unanimous Council vote in regard to establishing "language arrangements" relating to European IP rights.

e.   *Tax law harmonisation – the change that didn't happen.* It is noteworthy that an early draft of the Constitution contained a provision that would have allowed qualified majority voting at the Council on certain aspects of company tax law harmonisation. Under EC Treaty Article 93, "turnover taxes, excise duties and other forms of indirect taxation" may be subject to EU harmonising legislation, albeit only through a unanimous Council vote. Any form of Union authority on direct taxation has to this point been outside the EU's competence. The harmonisation proposal coming out of the Convention was ultimately rejected by the IGC at the insistence of the United Kingdom and others. Giovanni Grevi has commented that tax harmonisation constitutes a "red line" that has been "drawn by a few Member States,"[1171] and under the Lisbon Treaty this dividing line will stay in place.

1.2   Economic and monetary policy

The economic and monetary union, popularly characterised by Europe's common currency, is a significant and highly visible accomplishment of the European Union. The current provisions on economic and monetary policy are found in EC Treaty Article 4 and Articles 98 to 124, and the Lisbon Treaty offers no changes that will affect the EU's dividing lines.

1.3   Areas of shared competence

Under the Lisbon Treaty's new classification of EU competences, all activities identified as matters of "shared competence"[1172] are areas in which the Union is free to legislate. Member States are permitted to legislate only to the extent that the EU does not.[1173] The subjects of shared competence have been identified in Part 4 of Chapter 12 of this treatise.

Under the current EC Treaty there is no definition of shared competences, and one might argue that under the treaty a Member State retains the right to act even after the EU has stepped in. If so, then the Lisbon Treaty theoretically weakens the compe-

---

[1170] Lisbon Treaty Art. 2(84).
[1171] Grevi, *supra* note 476, at 10.
[1172] Lisbon Treaty Art. 2(12)(2C).
[1173] Id. Art. 2(12)(2A)(2).

tences of the Member States. However, current Article 10 of the EC Treaty requires Member States to "abstain from any measure which could jeopardise the attainment of the objectives of this Treaty," and this limits any national action in areas where the Union is active. Thus the Lisbon Treaty may be seen as sensibly defining a concept that was already implied in the EC Treaty. It does not so much propose a *shift* in the EU's dividing lines as the *articulation* of lines that are lurking beneath the surface of the Treaties.

Beyond these general comments, there are several specific developments that will affect EU competences, and they are described below.

a. *Space.* For the first time the EU will be permitted to include matters of space on its agenda. Articles 163 to 173 of the EC Treaty allow the Community to carry out programmes in research and technological development. The Community may "encourage" and "support" such development,[1174] but may also implement its own programmes, "complementing the activities carried out in the Member States."[1175] The Community is required to "coordinate" its activities with the Member States and cooperate with them.[1176] In some matters of research the Community may establish "supplementary programmes . . . involving the participation of certain Member States only."[1177]

The primary change is the Lisbon Treaty's addition of space as a field of activity. The provisions in the current EC Treaty are gathered in a title named "Research and Technological Development," and the Lisbon Treaty adds the reference to space in the title of its section.[1178] In addition, a new article is added to the section, and it will permit the Union to draw up a European space policy and implement a European space programme, as well as establishing relations with the non-EU European Space Agency.[1179] This is obviously an expansion of EU competence, but one that is hardly controversial.

Curiously, although research, technological development and space are classified by the Lisbon Treaty as areas of shared competence, the Lisbon Treaty states that in these fields the Union's exercise of competence "shall not result in Member States being prevented from exercising theirs."[1180] Thus, this field constitutes its own class of EU competence, not purely one of shared competence, but something more than merely supporting, coordinating or supplementary action.

b. *Energy.* The current Treaties mention energy only in passing. Article 3(1)(u) of the EC Treaty refers to "measures in the spheres of energy, civil protection and tour-

---

[1174] EC Treaty Art. 163(2).
[1175] Id. Art. 164.
[1176] Id. Art. 165.
[1177] Id. Art. 168.
[1178] Lisbon Treaty Art. 2(135).
[1179] Id. Art. 2(142).
[1180] Id. Art. 2(12)(2C)(3).

ism" among the intended Community activities. The treaty also makes reference to energy in its provisions on trans-European networks[1181] and environment,[1182] and energy may be included in Article 86(1), which mentions "public undertakings and undertakings to which Member States grant special or exclusive rights." However, there is no stand-alone provision on energy.[1183]

The Lisbon Treaty adds a new article on energy.[1184] In this provision the Union is mandated to set an overall Union energy policy tied to the functioning of the internal market and to environmental protection. The EU must aim to ensure the functioning of the energy market and the security of the energy supply, and the Union is required to promote energy efficiency and renewable forms of energy. Energy is an area of shared competence, but there are two primary reservations in favor of the Member States. First, EU action may not affect each state's right to "determine the conditions for exploiting its energy resources, its choice between different energy sources and the general structure of its energy supply."[1185] Second, any energy laws "of a fiscal nature" will be required to receive the unanimous approval of the Council.[1186]

The Lisbon Treaty's unprecedented approach may spur greater EU activity in this field, and if so, the level of Member State action may be correspondingly diminished. Furthermore, the classification of energy as a shared competence may prevent national action where it had previously been permitted. However, the Lisbon Treaty will leave in Member State control the critical choice and structure of their energy sources, and it will require that fiscal measures relating to energy be unanimously approved on the Council. The Lisbon Treaty may shift the energy dividing line toward Brussels, but it also offers important safeguards for national sovereignty in this field.

c.   *Climate change.* The current EC Treaty contains three provisions relating to a Community environmental policy.[1187] One of the Community's mandates is "promoting measures at international level to deal with regional or worldwide environmental problems."[1188] To the end of this phrase the Lisbon Treaty simply adds "and in particular combating climate change."[1189] One might call this a new EU competence, but it is just as well considered a clarification that one aspect of environmental protection is the fight against global warming and climate change.

[1181] EC Treaty Art. 154(1).

[1182] Id. Art. 175(2)(c).

[1183] Although energy programmes as such are not addressed in the Treaties, energy matters have been the subject of numerous competition decisions of the Commission, and significant harmonisation of energy standards in relation to the internal market has taken place under Arts. 94 and 95 of the EC Treaty.

[1184] Lisbon Treaty Art. 2(147).

[1185] Id. Art. 2(147)(2).

[1186] Id. Art. 2(147)(3).

[1187] EC Treaty Arts. 174-176.

[1188] Id. Art. 174(1).

[1189] Lisbon Treaty Art. 2(143)(a).

1.4 Areas of supporting, coordinating or supplementary action

The Lisbon Treaty for the first time identifies a group of activities in which the Union may take supporting, coordinating or supplementary action.[1190] There are two restrictions imposed: EU action may not supersede Member State competences, and EU legislation may not require harmonisation of Member State law.[1191] The subjects of in this area have been identified in Part 4 of Chapter 12 of this treatise. Among these fields a number of innovations in the Lisbon Treaty are of interest to our examination of the EU's dividing lines.

a. *Public health.* A "high level of human health protection" is stated as an EU goal in EC Treaty Article 152. Community action "shall complement national policies" and Member States' action in this area. The Community is to "encourage cooperation between the Member States . . . and, if necessary, lend support to their action." The Member States are expected to "coordinate among themselves their policies and programmes," while the states and the Community together must cooperate with third countries and international health organisations. The Community must "respect the responsibilities of the Member States" for the "organisation and delivery of health services and medical care." Article 152 does identify a number of specific subjects in which the Community may legislate, although even in these areas there are limitations in favor of the Member States.

The Lisbon Treaty contains several additions. For example, the term "human illness" is expanded to "physical and mental illness," and a new area of EU action will be "monitoring, early warning of and combating serious cross-border threats to health."[1192] The Union is also called upon to adopt new measures in "setting high standards of quality and safety for medicinal products and devices for medical use."[1193] In addition, the Lisbon Treaty mentions for the first time the adoption of EU measures relating to (i) cross-border health scourges; and (ii) "the protection of public health regarding tobacco and the abuse of alcohol, excluding any harmonisation of the laws and regulations of the Member States."[1194]

In addition to adding to the EC Treaty, the Lisbon Treaty creates an inconsistency in this field. The general matter of "protection and improvement of human health" is a subject for supporting, coordinating or supplementary action by the EU,[1195] while the Union also enjoys *shared competence* in the area of "common safety concerns in public health matters."[1196] It may be possible to navigate through revised Article 152 and assign some of its provisions to human health in general and others (such as pandemics) to safety concerns in public health matters, but it can also become a game of se-

---

[1190] Lisbon Treaty Art. 2(12)(2E).
[1191] Id. Art. 2(12)(2A)(5).
[1192] Id. Art. 2(127)(a).
[1193] Id. Art. 2(127)(d).
[1194] Id. Art. 2(127)(d).
[1195] Id. Art. 2(12)(2E).
[1196] Id. Art. 2(12)(2C).

mantics. Nevertheless, the nuances may be important, since shared competence permits full EU legislation (and thus EU dominance over Member State law), while supporting, coordinating and supplementary action will significantly limit Union action (thus preserving a greater measure of Member State competence).

b.   *Culture.* The Community is required under EC Treaty Article 151 to "contribute to the flowering of the cultures of the Member States," and it must encourage expression of "the common cultural heritage." At the same time it must respect the "national and regional diversity of the Member States." The Community is to encourage cooperation among the states, and work with them to cooperate with third countries and international organisations. In its other activities the Community must consider cultural aspects, but "in particular in order to respect and promote the diversity of its cultures." The Community may legislate to create "incentive measures," but this action may not require harmonisation of national laws. The Council may also adopt recommendations.

The Lisbon Treaty preserves substantive coverage of Article 151, but it changes certain voting rules. Article 151 currently contains two mandates for a unanimous vote on the Council, while the Lisbon Treaty drops both of these requirements. The first is found in the provision permitting the Council to create incentive measures, and the second relates to the Council's adoption of recommendations. The elimination of unanimity as a voting requirement in the matter of culture is curious, since culture is a particularly emotional matter for some Member States and their political leaders. However, the basic protection remains, because EU action may do no more than support, coordinate or supplement national action. Further, harmonisation of Member State laws will still be prohibited. Thus, even with the Lisbon Treaty's voting changes, there is little risk to a Member State that its cultural heritage will be infringed upon by the Union. Indeed, the Union has more important matters to attend to.

c.   *Tourism.* In the area of tourism promotion, a new article in the Lisbon Treaty will permit the EU to encourage "a favourable environment" for tourism and promote cooperation among the Member States.[1197] However, any EU measures in this field may not require harmonisation of Member State laws. Article 3 of the current EC Treaty mentions the possibility of Community action in the area of tourism,[1198] but neither of the current Treaties contains any substantive provision on the subject. Thus, the Lisbon Treaty provision is novel. Nevertheless, there will not likely be a surge in Union activity in this field. Due to EU budget constraints and more pressing needs for centralised action, tourism promotion will likely be left to the Member States, with the Union playing no more than a minor supportive role.

[1197] Lisbon Treaty Art. 2(148).
[1198] EC Treaty Art. 3(1)(u).

d. *Sport and education.* The Lisbon Treaty for the first time includes sport as a subject of EU activity, by adding sport to matters of education and youth that are addressed in Article 149 of the current EC Treaty. The expansion of Article 149 will have the EU contributing to "the promotion of European sporting issues" and "developing the European dimension in sport."[1199] The addition of sport to the EU agenda has been controversial, resulting in a softening of the Constitution's original language on this subject, with the apparent intention of preventing the EU from injecting itself into regulation of sports.[1200] In any event, EU laws may not entail any harmonisation of Member State laws, and EU activity will be merely supportive and supplementary, leaving the Member States in charge.

e. *Civil protection.* Under the subject of civil protection, the Lisbon Treaty requires the EU to "encourage cooperation between Member States in order to improve the effectiveness of systems for preventing and protecting against natural or man-made disasters."[1201] EU action will entail supporting, coordinating and supplementing Member State action, promoting cooperation and promoting consistency. Union laws in this area may not require harmonisation of national laws. There is no corresponding provision in the Treaties. However, as defined in the Lisbon Treaty, the area of civil protection will not relate to actual responses to disasters. Rather, the new provision deals only with planning and prevention. A new solidarity clause, included in the Lisbon Treaty's external action section, deals with EU activity after a natural or man-made disaster has occurred.[1202]

f. *Administrative cooperation.* The Lisbon Treaty adds an article that promotes the effective implementation of EU law by the Member States.[1203] The EU may "support the efforts of the Member States to improve their administrative capacity to implement Union law," and it may offer information and training to the states. If the EU does offer assistance, any Member State may decline to accept such support, and any EU action may not require harmonisation of national laws. However, the foregoing flexibility on accepting administrative assistance does not undercut the Member States' responsibility to implement EU law and cooperate with the Union where the Treaties so require.

[1199] Lisbon Treaty Art. 2(124).

[1200] One commentary noted: "This is the first time the EU has claimed power over sport in its basic legal documents. UEFA [the body that regulates soccer in Europe] was alarmed that it might herald a fresh barrage of legislation. So it launched an energetic lobbying campaign that has now managed to get the phrase 'taking account of its special nature, its structures based on voluntary activity and its social and educational function' inserted into a new draft [of the Constitution]. The hope is that this phrase will provide a legal basis to argue that sport can, in certain circumstances, be exempted from the usual strictures of the EU's single-market rules." How special interests infiltrate the European Union Constitution, Economist, May 22, 2004. The referenced insert into the Constitution has been included in the Lisbon Treaty with the exception that the introductory words are "taking account of the specific nature of sport." Lisbon Treaty Art. 2(124)(a).

[1201] Lisbon Treaty Art. 2(149).

[1202] See discussion in Part 1.6 of this chapter.

[1203] Lisbon Treaty Art. 2(150).

1.5   Overseas countries and territories

Part Four of the EC Treaty, "Association of the Overseas Countries and Territories,"[1204] deals with matters that seem to fall somewhere between "internal policies and action" and "external action." It relates to EU relations with non-European countries and territories having special relations with Denmark, France, the Netherlands and the United Kingdom. The Lisbon Treaty preserves these provisions with no substantive changes.[1205]

1.6   External action

As noted at the beginning of this chapter, the EC Treaty contains provisions on the EU's external action, while the TEU addresses the CFSP. To complete the review of substantive changes in the EC Treaty, we now address its external action provisions. The EC Treaty creates a new Part Five titled "External Action by the Union,"[1206] and it consolidates provisions from throughout the existing treaty. It also adds several new provisions. This new part is divided into seven brief titles, as follows:
- Title I is a new provision serving to introduce Part Five.
- Title II governs the EU's common commercial policy.[1207]
- Title III covers cooperation with third countries and humanitarian aid.[1208]
- Title IV addresses restrictive measures.[1209]
- Title V governs EU participation in international agreements.[1210]
- Title VI deals with the Union's relations with international organisations and third countries, include its delegations abroad.[1211]
- Title VII creates a new solidarity clause.

Among the subjects covered in the Lisbon Treaty, a number of amendments and innovations are relevant to the EU's dividing lines.

a.   *Common commercial policy.* The introductory provision of Title III contains a new reference to abolishing restrictions on "direct foreign investment," thus reflecting recent emphasis in discussions at the World Trade Organisation. In addition, the goal of lowering of customs barriers is expanded to "customs and other barriers."[1212] Other updating includes expanding on the subjects for which the Council must act

---

[1204]   EC Treaty Arts. 182-188.
[1205]   Lisbon Treaty Arts. 2(151)-2(153).
[1206]   Id. Arts. 2(154)-2(176).
[1207]   These provisions are based on EC Treaty Arts. 131-134.
[1208]   These provisions are based on EC Treaty Arts. 177-181a. The provision on humanitarian aid is new.
[1209]   This provision is based on EC Treaty Art. 301.
[1210]   These provisions are based on EC Treaty Arts. 111, 300 and 310.
[1211]   These provisions are based on EC Treaty Arts. 302-304.
[1212]   Lisbon Treaty Art. 2(157).

unanimously when negotiating international agreements. These new subjects include "trade in cultural and audiovisual services" if cultural and linguistic diversity might be threatened, and "trade in social, education and health services" if EU agreements might encroach on Member State involvement in such activity.[1213] These latter provisions must be seen as new protections for Member State interests.

b.   *Cooperation with third countries and humanitarian aid.* In the EC Treaty, cooperation with developing countries has its own title,[1214] and a separate title addresses economic, financial and technical cooperation with "third countries."[1215] The Lisbon Treaty adds to the latter (renamed a "chapter") a reference that the assistance is to be provided to countries "other than developing countries."[1216] In addition, a new article is added permitting the EU to take action when "the situation in a third country requires urgent financial assistance from the Union."[1217] There is no counterpart to this provision in the Treaties.

Another new Lisbon Treaty provision mandates EU legislation to determine the framework within which the Union's humanitarian aid operations will be implemented.[1218] TEU Article 17(2) makes reference to "humanitarian and rescue tasks" as part of the CFSP, but a formal, ongoing programme of humanitarian aid is not mentioned. The new provision includes a mandate for the Union to create a European Voluntary Humanitarian Aid Corps, and EU legislation may determine its operating rules.[1219] This is an entirely new programme, not contemplated in the Treaties.

The Lisbon Treaty broadens somewhat the EU's horizons in its relations with third countries. Currently, the Union is not clearly authorised to enter these new areas, and thus the Lisbon Treaty may be described as modestly shifting these dividing lines.

c.   *Restrictive measures.* Article 301 of the EC Treaty permits legislation to carry out a mandate under the CFSP to adopt restrictive measures against third countries. The Lisbon Treaty's restatement of this provision permits measures against "natural or legal persons and groups or non-State entities," if the TEU decision so specifies.[1220] This simply confirms the ability of the EU to make practical application of a unanimous decision under the TEU. If all the Member States want to take action of any sort, the current terms of EC Treaty Article 308 would permit it, and thus the Lisbon Treaty provision described here cannot be seen as an expansion of EU competences.

d.   *Solidarity clause.* The Lisbon Treaty contains a new solidarity clause, which requires the Union and all Member States to support any Member State that becomes

---

[1213] Lisbon Treaty Art. 2(158)(4).
[1214] EC Treaty Arts. 177-180; Lisbon Treaty Arts. 2(159)-2(164).
[1215] EC Treaty Art. 181a; Lisbon Treaty Arts. 2(165)-2(167).
[1216] Lisbon Treaty Art. 2(166)(a).
[1217] Id. Art. 2(167).
[1218] Id. Art. 2(168)(3).
[1219] Id. Art. 2(168)(5).
[1220] Id. Art. 2(169)(2).

a victim of a terrorist attack or a natural or man-made disaster.[1221] The Union is also required to help prevent terrorist attacks. While solidarity is mentioned as a political ideal in the Treaties, the Lisbon Treaty provision is unprecedented. Technically, this represents a new competence for Brussels, but it is obviously one that the Member States demand.

2.   COMMON FOREIGN AND SECURITY POLICY

The field of external action has always been a subject of controversy for the European Union and its Member States. The desire for Europe to take concerted action in foreign affairs is offset by an insistence that Member States maintain their sovereignty in the international arena. In its mandate for the constitutional Convention, the Laeken Declaration asked for consideration of Europe's role in a "fast-changing, globalised world," and it stated: "Europe needs to shoulder its responsibilities in the governance of globalisation."[1222] It noted that EU citizens "want to see Europe more involved in foreign affairs, security and defence, in other words, greater and better coordinated action to deal with trouble spots in and around Europe and in the rest of the world."[1223] Ultimately, it asked "How . . . should a more coherent common foreign policy and defence policy be developed?"[1224] It offered no guidance, however, as to how these questions should be answered. Thus, the Convention possessed wide latitude to consider dramatic new programmes and procedures in the EU's external action, but its response to this opportunity was, at best, conservative. The Constitution's substantive treatment of external action, now reflected in the Lisbon Treaty, is not significantly at variance with the approach of the Treaties. As a result, only a few points of interest will be described here.

A new overview provision in the Lisbon Treaty assumes that the European Union will have "relations with the wider world."[1225] In addition the entire TEU title on external action is introduced with two new overview provisions that set goals for the Union overall, and in particular for the CFSP.[1226] These new statements of objectives that are broader than those found in current TEU Articles 3 and 11. However, in general the Lisbon Treaty's approach to the CFSP is more a matter of emphasis than substance.

[1221] Lisbon Treaty Art. 2(176).

[1222] Laeken Declaration, *supra* note 114, at 20. Note that the Declaration of Nice, which preceded the Laeken Declaration, called for a "deeper and wider debate about the future of the European Union" but did not specifically mention external relations. Nice Declaration, *supra* note 103, at 85.

[1223] Laeken Declaration, *supra* note 114, at 21.

[1224] Id. at 22.

[1225] Lisbon Treaty Art. 1(4)(5).

[1226] Id. Art. 1(24).

2.1   Common foreign and security policy

Several additions to the CFSP by the Lisbon Treaty are of interest with respect to the EU's dividing lines:

a.   *Unanimous decision-making and exceptions.* Article 23(1) of the current TEU provides that decisions on CFSP matters are to be taken unanimously by the Council, but Article 23(2) offers three exceptions – three instances in which the Council may act by QMV. The first and second of these involve implementing prior (unanimously adopted) common strategies or common positions. The third relates to appointment of a special representative based on a prior unanimous decision of the Council. The Lisbon Treaty refines these concepts, but preserves their basic substance.[1227] It also adds a fourth exception, by which QMV decisions can be made on a proposal from the new High Representative for Foreign Affairs. However, such a proposal must be requested by the European Council (which must act by consensus).[1228] Thus, no meaningful shift to QMV is offered by this Lisbon Treaty innovation.

b.   *Increasing QMV.* Additional increases in QMV decision-making are offered in the Lisbon Treaty's amendments to TEU Article 23. A new subparagraph will permit the European Council to extend QMV to areas beyond the Article 23(2) exceptions.[1229] This is a *passerelle*, because it will permit a change in the TEU voting requirements without resorting to an amendment to the document. The procedure is not provided in the current TEU. The obvious limitation on any significant movement under the new provision is that the European Council will be required to act unanimously in any decision to alter the rules. Thus, existing national protections will be maintained.

c.   *Extended ECJ jurisdiction.* As analysed in Chapter 13, The Lisbon Treaty offers a limited, but significant extension of the jurisdiction of the ECJ into the CFSP.[1230]

d.   *Limits on EU competences.* The Lisbon Treaty adds a provision to the TEU, stating that the implementation of the CFSP "shall not affect the application of the procedures and the extent of the powers of the institutions laid down by the Treaties for the exercise of Union competences [as described in the revised EC Treaty.]"[1231] The provision adds that exercising the other Union competences may not affect the carrying out of the CFSP. These statements, which have no antecedents in the Treaties, are reminders that under the Lisbon Treaty the EU's competences are carefully drawn.

[1227] Lisbon Treaty Art. 1(34)(b).

[1228] Marise Cremona describes the new exception as follows: "This is likely to apply where the European Council, by specifically requesting a [High Representative] proposal, has given a clear indication of the policy line to be adopted on a specific issue." Marise Cremona, The Draft Constitutional Treaty: External Relations and External Action, 40 C.M.L.R. 1347, 1358 (2003).

[1229] Lisbon Treaty Art. 1(34)(b)(iv).

[1230] See discussion in Part 5.1 of Chapter 13 of this treatise.

[1231] Lisbon Treaty Art. 1(45)(25b).

The CFSP will have defined limits. The activities in the CFSP may not be used to affect the powers and rights reserved to the Member States.

The conclusion to be drawn from these Lisbon Treaty developments is that except for an incremental extension of the ECJ's jurisdiction, the dividing lines in the CFSP will be preserved.

2.2   Common security and defence policy

A common defence policy is referred to in the Preamble to the TEU and in Article 2 of the treaty. In Article 13 defence is mentioned as part of the CFSP, but details are provided in only one provision, Article 17. Decisions on defence are to be made by unanimity on the Council, pursuant to Article 23(1) and revised Article 17.[1232] The QMV exceptions in Article 23(2) are not applicable in the case of decisions "having military or defence implications." Furthermore, according to Article 17(1), the seminal decision to establish the common defence will require a unanimous decision of the European Council and approval by the member States.

The Lisbon Treaty expands TEU Article 17, offering a greater overview of the CSDP.[1233] It also adds four new articles to paint a much fuller picture of the possible programmes that will comprise the common defence.[1234] These new provisions contain a number of activities that are not mentioned in the current Treaties:

–   *Operational capacity.* The Union is to develop its own operational capacity in defence.[1235]

–   *Peace-keeping missions.* The EU may use its civilian and military assets in peacekeeping activities outside the Union.[1236] Peace-keeping is mentioned in TEU Article 17(2), with no operational details provided.

–   *Member State assets.* The Member States are required to make civilian and military assets available to the Union to implement the CSDP. They are also required to progressively improve their military capabilities.[1237]

–   *European Defence Agency (EDA).* An EU agency will be created for research and development toward improving Member State and Union capabilities.[1238] Participation in the EDA will be optional.[1239] The Lisbon Treaty permits the Council to adopt a decision by qualified majority to define the "statute, seat and operational

---

[1232] Lisbon Treaty Art. 1(49)(c)(4).
[1233] Id. Art. 1(49).
[1234] Id. Art. 1(50).
[1235] Id. Art. 1(49)(a).
[1236] Id. Art. 1(49)(a).
[1237] Id. Art. 1(49)(c)(3).
[1238] Id. Arts. 1(49)(c)(3), 1(50)(28D).
[1239] Id. Art. 1(50)(28C)(2).

rules" of the EDA,[1240] but QMV is limited to those specific matters. Actual creation of the Agency and its mandate will be subject to a unanimously adopted European Council decision.[1241]

– *Initiative.* Both the High Representative and individual Member States may propose CSDP decisions.[1242]

– *Fulfilment.* Union tasks may be assigned to a group of Member States.[1243]

– *Permanent structured cooperation.* Member States with higher military capabilities must enter into "permanent structured cooperation" within the EU framework.[1244] Decisions concerning which Member States will participate may be made by a QMV vote on the Council.[1245] The provision for structured cooperation resembles "enhanced cooperation" under the Treaties, but without the requirement for participation by a certain number of Member States.

– *Aid and assistance.* Consistent with existing NATO obligations, Member States must assist each other in case of armed aggression against any of them.[1246] Article 17(2) mentions NATO and the WEU without stating an affirmative requirement of aid and assistance within the Union context.

– *Access to defence appropriations.* The Council may adopt by unanimity a decision as to how to offer rapid access to EU budget appropriations relating to urgent financing of initiatives in the CSDP.[1247]

– *Start-up fund.* The Council, acting by QMV, may create and administer a defence start-up fund, which is to be made up of contributions by the Member States.[1248]

The far more elaborate approach of the Lisbon Treaty with regard to EU defence matters is not matched with commensurate new Union assets and powers to institute and implement a defence policy. It is also not accompanied by any real EU power. In terms of dividing lines, the status quo will be maintained, with all but a few minor defence decisions still requiring Member State consensus. Thus, the actual expansion of EU activity in the area of CSDP will likely continue to be a process of gradual development.

[1240] Lisbon Treaty Art. 1(50)(28D)(2).
[1241] Id. Art. 1(49)(b)(i).
[1242] Id. Art. 1(49)(c)(4).
[1243] Id. Arts. 1(49)(c)(5), 1(50)(28C).
[1244] Id. Arts. 1(49)(c)(6), 1(50)(28E).
[1245] Id. Art. 1(50)(28E).
[1246] Id. Art. 1(49)(c)(7).
[1247] Id. Art. 1(47)(d).
[1248] Id. Art. 1(47)(d).

3.   SUBSTANTIVE MATTERS AND THE DIVIDING LINES

In matters of the EU's substantive activity it is important to note that a detailed analysis of the Lisbon Treaty's articles governing internal activities and external action reveals a significant rearrangement of the existing treaty provisions. However, the substance of the existing Treaties is largely preserved, and it is beyond the scope of this treatise to recite each Lisbon Treaty provision and its current treaty counterpart. In Chapter 16 and in this chapter we have reviewed all of the internal and external provisions of the Lisbon Treaty that arguably might have an impact on the Union's dividing lines. With the notable exception of the AFSJ, discussed in Chapter 16, a wholesale reworking of the substantive competences of the European Union was clearly not on the agenda. Looking at the items identified in this chapter, none of them individually amounts to a significant dividing-line shift. Even taken collectively, they should not raise any concern. These items represent either relatively minor adjustments, or relatively cautious innovations.

Part Five
Conclusion

Conclusion
A FINAL REVIEW – HOLDING THE MIDDLE GROUND

Among those who follow developments in the European Union, a question always near the surface is: "Will the Creation come to dominate its Creators?" Federalists might be tempted to answer: "It must, and it will." Intergovernmentalists would counter: "No, never." Realists could then raise their hands and urge: "Stop! There is a middle ground, and we are standing on it. The European Union can be a significant force in Europe and the world, but the Member States need not slide into oblivion or irrelevance." The intergovernmental and federal camps are entitled to press their agendas, but this treatise has demonstrated that the Lisbon Treaty will maintain the EU as a blended entity, carefully preserving most of the dividing lines that exist under the current Treaties. The Union will continue to possess competences considerably more sweeping than those granted to a typical IGO, but it will stop far short of becoming a United States of Europe.

Our review of the Lisbon Treaty, however, demands that we conclude with a more nuanced summation. Three points should be stressed. First, the stated motivations behind the Constitution (and presumably behind the Lisbon Treaty as well) were that Europe's foundational documents should be clearer and that the EU should be managed more efficiently. Deepening the process of integration was not an expressed goal. As a result, most of the changes proposed in the Lisbon Treaty will not entail any shift of competence or power to the Union. Second, some movement of the EU's dividing lines has indeed been proposed. Third, this shift has been offset somewhat by renewed emphasis on the Member States and their sovereignty. Let us briefly elaborate on these propositions.

Many changes will not shift the dividing lines

If we review the broad list of significant changes proposed in the Lisbon Treaty, which are identified in Chapter 4, we are reminded that most of them are merely structural. The merger of the Community into the Union will end unnecessary redundancy, but it will not create any new programmes. The scheduled reduction in the size of the Commission will arguably create a measure of further separation between it and the Member States, but the Commission's mandate as the Union's professional executive will remain the same. The EU's senior legislature, the Council, will make greater use of the QMV, but few matters of critical policy will lose their current requirement of unanimous approval. The new posts of a permanent European Council President and High Representative for Foreign Affairs may offer the EU a cohesiveness and stature it has not yet enjoyed, but neither post appears intended to possess executive powers beyond those already assigned to existing Union officials. The identification of the European Council as an institution of the EU is little more than articulation of the status quo under the current Treaties. The expanded requirements of open meetings and greater access to documents will increase the transparency of the institutions, but they will not change their functions. All of these changes offer new coherence and efficiency, but they do not by themselves add a single Union competence.

The TEU presents new overviews of the Union's foundational concepts. These provide a more coherent picture, but they are primarily restatements of existing principles. The TEU's highly innovative section on democratic principles speaks of more transparency and accountability in EU affairs, but its most significant new programme is the citizens' right of legislative initiative. Other TEU developments such as simplified treaty amendment procedures and expanded potential for a Union defence policy are limited by a continuing requirement of Member State unanimity in one form or another. In the amended EC Treaty, the delineation of EU competences by itself does not add any competences. Likewise, the simplification of the Union's legislative instruments – by eliminating many special forms of action in the Second and Third Pillars – is notable, but it offers no new powers in any field. Re-definition of the ordinary legislative procedure (including full participation by the European Parliament) is also an internal matter, not affecting the relationship between the Union and its Member States.

Some shifting will occur

While many changes proposed in the Lisbon Treaty will have no impact on the EU's dividing lines, it is clear that the existing lines will not be preserved absolutely intact.[1249] Upon closer inspection one can identify certain innovations that arguably will strengthen the Union – perhaps at the expense of the Member States. For example, by granting legal personality to the Union, the presents an entity with enhanced stature. This entity will be more cohesive through utilisation of a single set of legislative instruments. The elimination of the Third Pillar will arguably instill a more supranational character for the Union. Overall, these changes signal more than mere style. There is new substance in the Lisbon Treaty, indeed some form of new legal order. And if this new regime does not pose an immediate threat to the sovereignty of the Member States, its new character may prove to be at least the *beginning* of such a threat. New coherence may portend new dimensions for the future.

The elevation of the Charter of Fundamental Rights to treaty status is a significant development. But is this an increase in Union competence? We recall that the Union has already subscribed to the Charter as a "solemn proclamation," and that the current Treaties contain a variety of similar – if differently organised – statements about fundamental rights. Thus, increasing the stature of the Charter may be no more than a reaffirmation of basic principles to which the Union is already bound. One could even argue that on its face the affirmation of the Charter will draw no power from the Member States in favor of central authority in Brussels. However, one weakness of

---

[1249] For a summary of the movement in the dividing lines, see Chapter 6.

this position is in the fact that the integration of the Charter into the treaty realm likely will offer greater jurisdictional power to the ECJ in matters of human rights. Depending on the Court's behaviour in future cases, the national courts may well experience an erosion of their authority in this field. The Lisbon Treaty's derogation in favor of the United Kingdom regarding the relationship between the Charter and U.K. national law is an indication that at least the British are of the opinion that the new status of the Charter represents a shift in favor of Brussels.

We have also noted a potential shifting of the dividing lines in areas of substance other than human rights. These include, for example:

- Incremental extensions of the Council's ability to make decisions by QMV in a number of substantive areas. In general, these fields include matters such as transport, social security and professional licensing, which are closely connected to the EU-dominated internal market. The most significant of the affected matters is the Third Pillar, although limited new QMV decision-making in the Second Pillar is also provided.
- Expansion of EU activity into new fields, including intellectual property rights, space, energy, tourism, sport, civil protection and administrative cooperation.
- The extension of the jurisdiction of the Court of Justice into the CFSP and the AFSJ.

We have argued that none of these changes by itself should be cause for alarm. We have further proposed that these changes, even when added together, do not represent a dramatic competence-shift to Brussels. Rather, they must be seen as the enhancement of existing Union activities and the continued evolution of commitments previously made by the Member States. In reality, the Lisbon Treaty will do far less than TEU to deepen European integration. Nevertheless, persons concerned about "creeping federalism" are appropriately on the alert, and the true Eurosceptic may remain wary.

Bolstering the position of the Member States

A fascinating feature of the European Union is that its foundational coin always has two distinct sides. Notwithstanding the significant central features built into the EU system, the power of the Union has always been carefully contained. The drafters of the Lisbon Treaty have actually gone beyond the current Treaties in emphasising both the limits on EU action and the sovereignty of the Member States.

Like the current Treaties, the Lisbon Treaty is permeated with language that speaks to the Member States' integrity and competence within the EU system. However, much of the Lisbon Treaty's language is more forcefully expressed. Also, the new treaty's clarification of EU competences cuts both ways – it confirms the propriety of certain Union action, while at the same time defining the limits of such action and offering clearer definition of the Member States' own competences. Under the principle of conferral, which is more clearly articulated in the Lisbon Treaty, the Union will be permitted to act only within the limits of authority granted to it by the Member States. Competences not conferred upon the Union will remain with the national governments. A related principle is that the Lisbon Treaty mandates the Union to respect the integrity of the Member States as sovereign nations. In matters of foreign policy and defence, such respect translates into permitting the Union to act only when there is full consensus by the Member States. These areas, which could be employed to enhance the Union's stature as a world power, have traditionally been left to the Member States, and the Lisbon Treaty offers no significant challenge to this approach.

Institutionally, the European Council is the over-arching voice of the Member States in setting EU policy, and under the Lisbon Treaty it will remain so. Its members are the heads of state or government of all the Member States, along with its own permanent President (an innovation) and the President of the Commission, and when they convene it is more a summit meeting than a board of directors. The group takes its decisions by consensus – a principle understood under the current Treaties but now clearly articulated in the Lisbon Treaty. The Lisbon Treaty will also maintain the character of the Council, whose members represent their respective Member States. Many of the Council's most critical policy decisions are subject to full consensus, and so they will remain. Unanimity and consensus are distinctly anti-majoritarian, allowing a single Member State to block a decision or exact concessions as the price for its vote. To avoid gridlock, opt-outs or derogations may be necessary. The ultimate expression of the unanimity principle is that the Lisbon Treaty, like the current Treaties, cannot be amended without the consent of each Member State. The majoritarian ideal will continue to yield to the absolute right of each state to preserve what it has previously agreed to, including the Lisbon Treaty's careful balancing of authority. Unanimity protects each Member State from the unwanted imposition of an ultimate loss of sovereignty.

Four procedures highlight how the Lisbon Treaty will perpetuate the intergovernmental nature of the EU project. First, the new treaty offers a greater role to national parliaments in reviewing proposed EU legislation, along with greater standing for a parliament to raise objections to the new laws. The second procedure is enhanced cooperation, a carryover from the current Treaties, by which groups of Member States may proceed to act on their own where the EU is unable to achieve the consensus necessary for Union action. Enhanced cooperation is classified in the Lisbon Treaty as an EU activity, but it evidences a certain weakness at the central level and a measure of autonomy left to the Member States. The third procedure, also taken from the current Treaties, is the Lisbon Treaty's provision for the Union to suspend a Member State's voting rights on the Council if the state fails to adequately support the EU's core values. Such suspension underscores the fact that the Union lacks ultimate coercive power over its members and that the amended Treaties will remain treaties. Finally, the Lisbon Treaty will for the first time permit a Member State to withdraw from the Union. Under this right, should a Member State ever become dissatisfied to the point of wanting back the competences it has already yielded to the Union, or should it conclude that its vital interests are no longer being protected within the EU, it may lawfully resign its membership. This is a singular concept. Although the economic and political ramifications of withdrawal will likely inhibit this provision from ever being invoked, its presence in the Lisbon Treaty is a bold affirmation of national sovereignty.

A broader perspective on the dividing lines

As part of this summing up, we now return to the broad questions posed in the Introduction. The analysis presented in this treatise offers a number of responses.

What institutions are necessary to ensure that the EU reaches its potential, and what authority should they be granted? What is the role of the Member States in those institutions? The institutions created at the very beginning by the Treaties of Paris and Rome have proven to be remarkably effective for the Union. The Commission, possessing the right of legislative initiative and operating with the legislative approval of the Council, offers continuity and professional management. The European Parliament provides popular input, the Council represents the interests of the Member States, and the European Council serves as a summit meeting to set broad policy guidelines. The Court of Justice has served as an effective arbiter and, occasionally, as a mover of European integration. In all of these institutions the individual interests of the Member States are heard to varying extents, and overall the institutional framework displays relatively clear dividing lines between the Union and the Member States. This is a success, and the Lisbon Treaty will maintain the basic arrangements.

What instruments and decision-making procedures should be employed, and which institutions (including those of the Member States) should participate in particular actions? The hodge-podge of instruments and procedures under the current Treaties begs for simplification, and the drafters of the Lisbon Treaty have correctly set out to improve this state of affairs. The increasing influence of the national parliaments on EU legislation poses a more interesting challenge. On the one hand, the broadening of Union activity carries a risk of marginalising the national legislatures. On the other, the expanded rights of review and objection for national parliaments may prove – especially in an EU of 27 members – to hinder the ability of the Union to act efficiently.

In an expanding Union, how should the internal market be managed, and should there be a role for the Member State governments in its management? The internal market is literally and figuratively the bread and butter of the EU, and its success is a result of central management and the relinquishment of national control in favor of efficiency and equality. However, one of the brilliant strokes of the European Union is its use of central legislation that must be nationally implemented. This promotes efficiency in Brussels and active engagement by national parliaments and authorities. This balance has been highly successful, and it need not be changed. The Lisbon Treaty does not propose to do so.

At what level should social policy be determined? Should key concepts be uniform throughout the EU, or should the Member States maintain local control? This is certainly the point at which strains can develop in the Union. Social policy is a two-edged sword. On the one hand, market-related social policy – for example, worker mobility – demands a measure of central coordination to create a level playing field within the internal market. On the other hand, nothing will create more suspicion and ill will with the average citizen and the average national parliamentarian than situations in which policies impacting daily life are dictated by institutions outside the country. With each extension of EU activity into new areas – for example, health policy – feelings of alienation with regard to Brussels are bound to intensify. Likewise, the increasing diversity in the EU population arising from EU enlargement and internal migration creates seemingly insoluble challenges. Although the Lisbon Treaty has not proposed any bold moves in social policy initiatives – no major shift in the relevant dividing lines – further legislative adjustments and treaty changes are undoubtedly in store.

How should foreign affairs and defence be conducted? Should they be the central responsibility of the Union or the separate responsibility of each Member State? This is another dilemma, although perhaps less problematic than social policy. The simple observation is that the EU would be far more effective on the world stage if it could speak with a single voice in foreign affairs and defence. However, at the current time this is not in the cards. These matters are a key indicator of nationhood, a primary facet of sovereignty. As a bloc, the Union will not achieve a unified approach any time soon, and the Lisbon Treaty has not suggested any significant shift in these critical dividing lines. The best that can be expected in the near future is that some sort of core group of Member States might be able to pool their resources to create a more closely united foreign policy or defence.

The foregoing inquiries relate to political power and institutional authority within the EU, but we also raised questions that relate more deeply to the intrinsic character of the Union. To these questions the Lisbon Treaty suggests the following answers:

Should the Member States continue to enjoy their status as sovereign nations within the world community? There is no indication whatsoever that any of the Member States wishes to form a true federation with supreme central authority. The original members and the later-acceding states appear fully committed to retaining their sovereignty. The Lisbon Treaty will respect this reality, and the line between the current hybrid Union and a federal superstate will not be crossed.

Where is the loyalty and attachment of the individual European citizen to be focused? The rights to live, work and invest in other Member States do create a European-ness that did not exist 50 years ago. EU citizenship has value, and it is appreciated. However, for linguistic, cultural and historical reasons, the vast majority of Union citizens identify first and foremost with their separate nations. The EU does well to foster a fealty to the Union, but Brussels must accept the fact that national attachment today is infinitely stronger than regional identification. The Constitution proposed greater recognition of EU symbols to enhance European identity, but these proved to be controversial, and the Lisbon Treaty omits them. What appeared to be a small shift of a symbolic dividing line will be avoided.

Where are the manifestations of democracy to be found – at the national level only, the Union level, or both? Here it may well be said that more democracy within the Union system is a good thing. EU citizens should have rights of information and participation with respect to Brussels, and the Lisbon Treaty will enhance these rights. However, even in a more open Union, true democracy remains rooted more in national practice than in international practice. Thus it seems unnecessary to promote a Union that offers all of the democratic rights that EU citizens enjoy at the national level. To the extent that there is a dividing line between full democratisation at the national level and modest democratisation at the Union level, the EU is moving closer toward the national approach, but it need not go all the way.

How much integration is necessary, and where should it stop? It is never a good thing to doubt the capacity of EU leaders to push the Union to new heights. New programmes in new areas will likely develop, even if it takes unanimity to create them. However, in structural and programmatic terms it is eminently reasonable to argue that some kind of limit has been reached. The Constitution may have challenged that limit, at least in the perception of some Europeans, and the Lisbon Treaty may represent a modest retreat toward the status quo. After 50 years the EU has developed to a point at which further integration might well encroach on the residual sovereignty of the Member States, and this is a dividing line that few are willing to cross. Some (who we have referred to as federalists) will always seek "ever closer union," but many others will assert that the Union was born as an intergovernmental organisation, so it must remain, and further integration would threaten that status.

A Laeken scorecard

To conclude our analysis, it is useful to recall the challenges posed in the Laeken Declaration[1250] and to gauge whether the Lisbon Treaty offers a satisfactory response:

1.   *The challenge:* "Simplifying the existing Treaties without changing their content. Should a distinction between the Union and the Communities be reviewed? What of the division into three pillars?" *The result:* Some restructuring of the Treaties and consolidation of certain sections (such as enhanced cooperation) is proposed in the Lisbon Treaty, but its restructuring is modest in comparison to the Constitution. The substance of the EC Treaty and TEU will generally be preserved. The Community will merge into the Union. The Three Pillars will be reduced to two.

2.   *The challenge:* "The possible reorganisation of the Treaties. Should a distinction be made between a basic treaty and the other treaty provisions? Should this distinction involve separating the texts? Could this lead to a distinction between the amendment and ratification procedures for the basic treaty and for the other treaty provisions?" *The result:* The TEU has been re-fashioned to provide some overview of itself and the EC Treaty. No distinction has been made between a basic treaty and a

---

[1250] See text accompanying notes 114-119, *supra.*

more easily amended "other" treaty. The new, somewhat simpler amendment procedures for certain provisions[1251] are an exceedingly modest step.

3.   *The challenge:* "Thought would also have to be given to whether the Charter of
Fundamental Rights should be included in the basic treaty and to whether the European Community should accede to the European Convention on Human Rights." *The
result:* The Charter is elevated to treaty status, and the EU is mandated to accede to
the ECHR. However, because of the manner in which these steps are handled, the
overall treatment of human rights and their sources is unduly complicated.

4.   *The challenge:* "The question ultimately arises as to whether this simplification
and reorganisation might not lead in the long run to the adoption of a constitutional
text in the Union. What might the basic features of such a constitution be? The values
which the Union cherishes, the fundamental rights and obligations of its citizens, the
relationship between Member States in the Union?" *The result:* A constitution was
proposed and rejected. The Lisbon Treaty preserves and amplifies statements on the
Union's values, and it also maintains the sensitive political balance between the EU
and its Member States.

Overall, it is incontestable that the Lisbon Treaty offers an improvement over the
existing Treaties. It will meet many of the goals set at Laeken. Nevertheless, what
of the broader goals of simplification and making EU law more accessible and easily
understood? It is perhaps wishful thinking to expect that the average EU citizen could
ever readily grasp any treaty document, but the Lisbon Treaty will be scarcely more
approachable than the treaties it will amend.

Will the Lisbon Treaty be successful?

Given the constantly shifting winds of global affairs, regional politics and national
sentiment, it is impossible to predict whether any revision to the Union's current
Treaties will be successful or long-lived. The Constitution never took its first breath,
and so we look ahead to the Lisbon Treaty. Will the new document's balance of
power be workable? Can its political compromises be sustained? Will there be continuing pressure to hand more power to Brussels, or will there be a trend toward disintegration or a drift toward special cooperation among groups of Member States? In
short, will the dividing lines set forth in the Lisbon Treaty or any other treaty revision
withstand the political strains that will inevitably follow?

The challenge presented to those who seek acceptance of any treaty revision is to
sell the new arrangements to national officials, but also to the European citizenry. The
difficulty in doing so is directly tied to the fact that the European Union does not resemble any other existing governmental or intergovernmental structure. The editors
of the Common Market Law Review have well articulated the task as follows:

[1251]   See Part 2 of Chapter 11 of this treatise.

"It would be easy to build a super-state or to transform the Union into an international cooperation organization, but it is difficult to regulate the workings of a machine which is based on an association of sovereign States and their peoples, aiming at exercising a part of their sovereignty jointly. The difficult task of the political leaders now is to explain in a clear way what they wanted to create, so that their citizens do not decide on the basis of propagandist clichés, but rather on the Union as they wanted it."[1252]

It is clear that the Lisbon Treaty will set the course of a European Union that is foundationally similar to the current version. The next version of the Treaties will maintain the EU's current duality, with the Member States retaining their status as sovereign nations in a union with significant central features. Under the Lisbon Treaty the United States of Europe is not about to be born. The dividing lines between the EU and its Member States will largely be maintained, and thus the middle ground between intergovernmentalism and federalism will be held.

[1252] Editorial Comments, *supra* note 360, at 907.

Addendum

Addendum

Where the Lisbon Treaty Requires Unanimous Voting,
Consensus or Common Accord

[This addendum is referenced in Chapters 5 and 15 of the treatise]

Chapter 15 details those instances in which the Lisbon Treaty either offers QMV as a change from unanimity under the current Treaties or assigns QMV to new fields of EU activity. The focus is on the shifting dividing lines – where Member States may lose their veto or blocking rights. The purpose of this addendum is to list all of those subjects under the Lisbon Treaty which will require unanimous voting, consensus and common accord. These are generally matters for which unanimity is required under the current Treaties, but they may also represent variations brought about by the new amendments. The material in this addendum is arranged as unanimity provisions appear in the revised Treaties, first the TEU and then the EC Treaty (which will be renamed). NOTE: for shorthand reference, the EC Treaty will be designated "ECT" and the Lisbon Treaty will be designated "LT." Articles will be indicated by numbers only.

1. UNANIMITY UNDER THE AMENDED TEU

NOTE: Current TEU Title VI (Third Pillar) (TEU 29-42) is transferred to ECT.

FURTHER NOTE: The subheadings below are those presented in the TEU as amended by the Lisbon Treaty.

a. Title I: Common provisions: LT 1(2)-1(10); current TEU 1-7

Breach of EU values. LT 1(9)(c) provides for a unanimous decision that a Member State has breached the EU's core values. The decision is to be made by the European Council. The offending Member State does not participate in the vote.
– Current TEU 7(2) provides for a unanimous decision by the Council "meeting in the composition of the Heads of State or Government." The difference is that the European Council also has the Commission President and the permanent European Council President as non-voting members.

b. Title II: Provisions on democratic principles: LT 1(12); no current TEU counterpart

– No unanimity is referenced in these Lisbon Treaty provisions.

c. Title III: Institutions: LT 1(13)-1(20); current TEU 4

European Parliament composition. LT 1(15)(2) provides for a unanimous decision of the European Council to set the Parliament's composition.

- Current ECT 190(2) defines the composition of the Parliament, allocating a number of parliamentarians to each Member State. No decision is involved, because the composition is specified in the treaty text.

European Council decisions in general. LT 1(16)(4) provides that all European Council decisions, except where the Treaties provide otherwise, are to be taken by consensus.
- Current TEU 4 does not mention any consensus requirement.

Commission composition. LT 1(18)(5) and 2(196) require a unanimous European Council decision to determine the rotation of Commission members after the body has been reduced to less than one representative per Member State.
- Current ECT 213(1) and Article 4(3) of the Protocol on Enlargement of the European Union provide for unanimity on these matters, but the decisions are to be taken by the Council.[1]

d.   Title IV: Enhanced cooperation: LT 1(22); current TEU 43-45

- No unanimity is mentioned in this Lisbon Treaty provision. Unanimity provided for in current TEU 44 and 44a is reflected in the enhanced cooperation provisions in the amended ECT. See LT 2(278) as discussed in Part 2(f) below.

e.   Title V: External action and CFSP: LT 1(23)-1(50); current TEU 11-28

Strategic interests and objectives. LT 1(24)(10B)(1) mandates the European Council to make decisions on the EU's strategic interests and objectives in the CFSP and other areas of external action. These decisions are to be made unanimously.
- Current TEU 13(1) and (2) call for similar decisions, without specifying unanimity. However current TEU 23(1) generally calls for unanimity.

CFSP definition and implementation. LT 1(27)(a)(1) states that the CFSP will be "defined and implemented" by the European Council and Council acting unanimously, except if the Treaties provide otherwise.
- There is no counterpart in the current Treaties.

CFSP strategic interests, objectives and guidelines. LT 1(29)(a) requires the European Council to "define" the strategic interests, objectives and guidelines for the CFSP. Unanimity is not specified, and thus the general unanimity requirement would govern.
- Current TEU 13(1) and (2) call for similar decisions, without specifying unanimity. However current TEU 23(1) generally calls for unanimity.

CFSP decisions in general. LT 1(34)(a) provides that all CFSP decisions by the European Council or Council in the security policy are to be taken unanimously, unless otherwise provided in the CFSP chapter.
- Current TEU 23(1) contains the same requirement, although only the Council is mentioned.

---

[1] Protocol on Enlargement, *supra* note 443, Art. 4(1).

Unanimity in vital matters. LT 1(34)(b)(iii) permits a QMV vote of the Council to refer what would have been a QMV Council decision to the European Council for a decision by unanimity. This will triggered by a Member State's declaration that it is opposed to an impending QMV decision for vital and stated reasons of national policy.
– This procedure is taken from current TEU 23(2).

Passerelle to QMV in the CFSP. LT 1(34)(b)(iv) requires unanimity for a European Council decision to allow more QMV on the Council in the area of CFSP.
– There is no counterpart in the current Treaties.

Expenditures. LT 1(47)(c) requires that non-defence expenditures in the CFSP be charged to the EU budget, unless a unanimous Council decision is made to the contrary.
– This provision is taken from current TEU 28(2).

Common defence establishment. LT 1(49)(b)(i) mandates a unanimous European Council decision establishing a common defence.
– Current TEU 17(1) is similar, but unanimity is not specified, and there is no general provision requiring the European Council to vote by unanimity. However, unanimity may be presumed under current TEU 23(1).

Common defence policy. LT 1(49)(c)(4) requires unanimity for all Council decisions relating to the common security and defence policy.
– Current TEU 23(1) and (2) contain the same requirement.

Permanent structured cooperation in defence. LT (1)(50)(28E)(6) requires unanimous Council decisions within the framework of permanent structured cooperation in the field of defence, except in matters for which QMV is specified. Only the participating Member States may take part in this decision-making.
– TEU Article 17 deals with related matters, but not permanent structured cooperation as such. Unanimity in defence is generally provided in current TEU Article 23(1).

f. Title VI: Final provisions: LT 1(54)-(61); TEU 46-53

Amendment recommendation by convention. LT 1(56)(3) requires that in the ordinary procedure to amend the Treaties, a convention (if convened) must approve a proposed amendment by consensus before it is referred to an intergovernmental conference for further consideration.
– The current Treaties do not provide for a convention.

IGC and Member State approval of an amendment. LT 1(56)(4) requires an IGC (acting with or without a prior convention) to approve a proposed treaty amendment by common accord. The same article requires that all amendments be ratified by all Member States.
– Current TEU 48 contains these same requirements, although with no reference to a post-convention IGC.

Amendment of internal policies. LT 1(56)(6) permits the European Council by unanimity to approve an amendment to the amended ECT in regard to internal policies and action of the Union. After such a vote of the European Council, the amendment must be ratified by all Member States.
– The current Treaties do not contain such a procedure.

Simplified amendment. LT 1(56)(7) permits the European Council to unanimously decide to change (1) any unanimous Council voting requirement in the amended EC Treaty or the CFSP title of the amended TEU to a qualified majority voting requirement and (2) any special legislative procedure in the amended EC Treaty to the ordinary legislative procedure. After such a decision by the European Council the matter must be referred to the national parliaments of the Member States, and any opposition expressed within six months will nullify the amendment.
–   The current Treaties do not contain such a procedure.

New EU member. LT 1(57)(b) requires a unanimous Council decision to approve a new EU member. Such a decision must be ratified by all Member States.
–   Current TEU 49 contains the same requirement.

Extension of withdrawal period. LT 1(58) provides for a unanimous European Council decision to extend the two-year withdrawal period of a withdrawing Member State.
–   There is no withdrawal provision in the current Treaties and thus no counterpart to the extension provision.

2.   UNANIMITY UNDER THE AMENDED EC TREATY

NOTE: The parts and titles indicated below are those presented in the EC Treaty as amended by the Lisbon Treaty.

a.   Part One: Principles: LT 2(11)-2(30); current ECT 1-16

–   No unanimity is referenced in these Lisbon Treaty provisions or their current treaty counterparts. But see LT 2(33) below.

b.   Part Two: Citizenship: LT 2(31)-2(38); current ECT 17-22

Discrimination. LT 2(33) provides for a unanimous vote of the Council on legislation to combat discrimination on the basis of sex, race, religion, disability, age or sexual orientation.
–   Current ECT 13 contains the same requirement.

Free movement of persons. LT 2(35)(b) requires a unanimous Council vote on legislation on social security or social protection.
–   Current ECT 18(3) does not specify unanimity, but states that ordinary Council action (QMV) does not apply to these subjects.

Right to vote and stand for election. Current ECT 19 requires the Council to vote unanimously on EU legislation detailing the right of an EU citizen to vote and stand for election in another Member State.
–   The Lisbon Treaty does not amend this provision.

Citizenship rights. LT 2(38) mandates a unanimous Council vote on legislation to add to the citizenship rights described in the EC Treaty.
–   Current ECT 22 is nearly identical.
–   The Lisbon Treaty and current EC Treaty require approval by all of the Member States in accordance with their constitutional requirements.

c. Part Three: Community policies: LT 2(39)-2(150); current ECT 23-181a. NOTE: Part Three includes the transferred Third Pillar: LT 2(63)-2(68)

Title I: Internal market: LT 2(40)-2(45); current ECT 23-31, 135

– No unanimity is referenced in these Lisbon Treaty provisions or their current treaty counterparts.

Title II: Agriculture and fisheries: LT 2(46)-2(49); current ECT 32-38

– No unanimity is referenced in these Lisbon Treaty provisions or their current treaty counterparts.

Title III: Free movement of persons, services and capital: LT 2(50)-2(62); current ECT 39-60

Social security calculations. LT 2(51)(b) provides for a European Council decision regarding the impact of a draft EU law relating to multi-state social security calculations. The provision initially provides for a QMV Council vote, but permits any Member State to demand that the matter be referred to the European Council. A unanimous decision by the European Council is not specified, but unanimity would be required under the general consensus requirement LT 1(16)(4).
– Current ECT 42 requires a unanimous Council vote in all instances.

Restrictions on capital flow. LT 2(60)(2) requires a unanimous vote of the Council on legislation restricting the movement of capital to or from third countries.
– Current ECT 57(2) contains the same requirement.

Support for restrictive measures. LT 2(61) provides for a unanimous Council decision affirming that a Member State's restrictive tax measures against a third country are acceptable.
– This is an addition to current ECT 58, but there is no counterpart to this type of decision in the Treaties.

Title IV: Area of freedom, security and justice: LT 2(63)-2(68); current ECT 61-69 and current TEU 29-42

AFSJ strategic guidelines. LT 2(64)(61A) requires the European Council to "define" the strategic guidelines for legislative and operational planning within the AFSJ. Unanimity or QMV is not specified, and therefore the general consensus requirement for the European Council would apply.
– There is no direct counterpart in the Treaties, but current TEU 34(2) specifies unanimous Council decisions within the Third Pillar, which is part of the Lisbon Treaty's broader field of AFSJ.

Personal identification. LT 2(65)(62)(3) requires a unanimous Council decision on EU measures relating to passports, identity cards and the like.
– Current ECT 18(3) does not specify unanimity, but states that ordinary Council action (QMV) does not apply to these subjects.

Family law. LT 2(66)(3) mandates a unanimous Council vote on legislation regarding measures concerning family law with cross-border implications. It also requires a unanimous Council decision to shift certain of these matters to QMV, and any Member State parliament may block such a decision.

– Current ECT 67(5) permits the Council to act by QMV in matters governed by current ECT 65 (a listing of items relating to judicial cooperation in civil matters), "with the exception of aspects relating to family law." There is no counterpart to the *passerelle* provision of the Lisbon Treaty.

Criminal procedure. LT 2(67)(69A)(2) requires unanimity for Council decisions relating to certain aspects of Member States' mutual recognition of criminal procedures.

– There is no direct counterpart in the current Treaties, but current TEU 34(2) generally requires unanimity in the current Third Pillar, which represents this part of the Lisbon Treaty's expanded AFSJ.

Referral of fundamental matters. LT 2(67)(69A)(3) permits a Member State to refer to the European Council a draft EU law relating to judicial cooperation in criminal matters, if the Member State believes that the legislation will affect fundamental aspects of its criminal justice system. Where the Council might have taken a vote by qualified majority, the European Council must make a decision on the matter. Since the method of European Council voting is not specified, its decision must be made under its normal consensus rule.

– There is no direct counterpart in the current Treaties, but current TEU 34(2) generally requires unanimity in this aspect of the AFSJ, which is currently part of the Third Pillar.

New areas of cross-border crime. LT 2(67)(69B)(1) requires a unanimous Council decision to identify areas of cross-border crime beyond those listed in the treaty.

– There is no direct counterpart in the current Treaties, but current TEU 34(2) generally requires unanimity in this aspect of the AFSJ, which is currently part of the Third Pillar.

Referral of fundamental matters. LT 2(67)(69B)(3) permits a Member State to refer to the European Council a draft EU law relating to the definition of criminal offences and sanctions, if the Member State believes that the legislation will affect fundamental aspects of its criminal justice system. Where the Council might have taken a vote by qualified majority, the European Council must make a decision on the matter. Since the method of European Council voting is not specified, its decision must be made under its normal consensus requirement.

– There is no direct counterpart in the current Treaties, but current TEU 34(2) generally requires unanimity in this aspect of the AFSJ, which is currently part of the Third Pillar.

Prosecutor's Office. LT 2(67)(69E)(1) requires a unanimous Council decision to establish European Public Prosecutor's Office.

– There is no direct counterpart in the current Treaties, but current TEU 34(2) generally requires unanimity in this aspect of the AFSJ, which is currently part of the Third Pillar. Otherwise, this type of decision might require unanimity under the EC Treaty flexibility clause, current ECT 308, because this is an area of activity not otherwise covered in the current Treaties.

Extension of prosecutor's powers. LT 2(67)(69E)(4) mandates a unanimous European Council decision to extend the powers of the European Prosecutor.

– There is no direct counterpart in the current Treaties, but current TEU 34(2) generally requires unanimity in this aspect of the AFSJ, which is currently part of the Third Pillar. Otherwise, this type of decision might require unanimity under the EC Treaty flexibility clause, current ECT 308, because this is an area of activity not otherwise covered in the current Treaties.

Police operational cooperation. LT 2(68)(69F)(3) requires a unanimous vote of the Council on legislation concerning operational cooperation between police authorities of the Member States. If unanimity is not obtained, the matter may be referred to the European Council for a consensus decision.

– Current TEU 30(1)(a) contains language regarding operational cooperation, but unanimity comes through the general unanimity requirement of current TEU 34(2).

Police operations in another state. LT 2(68)(69H) requires a unanimous Council vote on legislation regarding operations of one Member State's authorities in another Member State.

– Current TEU 32 contains counterpart language, but unanimity comes through the general unanimity requirement of current TEU 34(2).

Title V: Transport: LT 2(69)-2(75); current ECT 70-80

Transport. LT 2(71) requires a unanimous Council decision to permit a derogation in the area of transport legislation.

– EC Treaty Article 72 is nearly identical.

Title VI: Competition, taxation and approximation of laws: LT 2(76)-2(84); current ECT 81-97

Approval of aid granted by a state. Current ECT 88(2) mandates a unanimous Council decision to affirm that aid granted by a Member State is acceptable.

– This requirement is not changed in the Lisbon Treaty.

Tax harmonisation. Current ECT 93 requires a unanimous vote of the Council on EU legislation to harmonise certain taxes.

– This requirement is not changed in the Lisbon Treaty.

Approximation of laws. Current ECT 94 provides for the Council to vote unanimously on legislation to require harmonisation of Member State laws relating to the internal market.

– The Lisbon Treaty does not change the unanimity requirement.

Language for EU intellectual property rights. LT 2(84) provides for a unanimous Council vote on legislation establishing language arrangements for European intellectual property rights.

– There is no provision in the current Treaties for EU intellectual property rights, and thus no counterpart to this unanimity requirement.

Title VII: Economic and monetary policy: LT 2(85)-2(110); current ECT 98-124

Economic policy guidelines. Current ECT 99(2) requires the European Council to "discuss a conclusion" on broad guidelines of the economic policies of the Member States. The Council will then act (by QMV) to adopt a recommendation based on this conclusion.

- The Lisbon Treaty does not amend this provision. However, under the Lisbon Treaty the European Council is subject to a general consensus rule.

Replacement of budget deficit protocol. Current ECT 104(14) provides for a unanimous vote of the Council on legislation to replace the protocol on excessive budget deficits.
- The Lisbon Treaty does not change this requirement.

Expansion of ECB powers. Current ECT 105(6) mandates unanimity on the Council with respect to legislation to expand powers of the European Central Bank.
- The Lisbon Treaty does not change this requirement.

New euro-zone member. LT 2(102)(c) and 2(109) require an agreement to approve decisions or regulations fixing the euro exchange rate of the currency of a Member State that will be permitted to join the euro-zone. A unanimous Council vote of members from the euro-zone states and the new member will be required.
- ECT 123(5) contains essentially the same requirement.

Title VIII: Employment: LT 2(111); current ECT 125-130

Employment situation. Current ECT 128(1) calls for European Council "conclusions" on the employment situation in the EU. Unanimity is not specified, nor is QMV.
- The Lisbon Treaty does not change this provision, and under the Lisbon Treaty the European Council's general consensus requirement will apply.

Title IX: Social policy: LT 2(114)-2(120); current ECT 136-145

Social policy. LT 2(116)(a) requires a unanimous vote of the Council on EU legislation in certain areas of EU supporting action relating to social policy; a unanimous Council decision is also required to change certain of those areas to QMV.
- Current ECT 137(2) contains the same requirements.

Labor-management agreements. LT 2(118)(b) requires a unanimous vote of the Council to adopt regulations or decisions relating to certain EU-facilitated labor-management agreements.
- Current ECT 139(2) contains the same requirements.

Title X: European Social Fund: LT 2(121)-2(122); current ECT 146-148

- No unanimity is referenced in these Lisbon Treaty provisions or their current treaty counterparts.

Title XI: Education, vocational training, youth and sport: LT 2(123)-2(125); current ECT 149-150

- No unanimity is referenced in these Lisbon Treaty provisions or their current treaty counterparts.

Title XII: Culture: LT 2(126); current ECT 151

- No unanimity is referenced in this Lisbon Treaty provision or its current treaty counterpart.

Title XIII: Public health: LT 2(127); current ECT 152

- No unanimity is referenced in this Lisbon Treaty provision or its current treaty counterpart.

Title XIV: Consumer protection: LT 2(128); current ECT 152

- No unanimity is referenced in this Lisbon Treaty provision or its current treaty counterpart.

Title XV: Trans-European networks: No LT provisions; current ECT 154-156

- No unanimity is referenced in these EC Treaty provisions, which are preserved intact in the Lisbon Treaty.

Title XVI: Industry: LT 2(129); current ECT 157

- No unanimity is referenced in this Lisbon Treaty provision or its current treaty counterpart.

Title XVII: Economic, social and territorial cohesion: LT 2(130)-2(134); current ECT 158-162

- There are no unanimity requirements in the Lisbon Treaty, and QMV replaces two instances of unanimity in current ECT 161.

Title XVIII: Research, technological development and space: LT 2(135)-1(142); current ECT 163-173

- No unanimity is referenced in these Lisbon Treaty provisions or their current treaty counterparts.

Title XIX: Environment: LT 2(143)-2(144); current ECT 174-176

Environment. LT 2(144)(a) provides for a unanimous vote of the Council on EU legislation pertaining to certain environmental matters; a unanimous Council decision is also required to institute limited QMV decision-making in these areas.
- Current ECT 175(2) contains the same requirements.

Title XX: Energy: LT 2(147); no current ECT counterpart

Energy. LT 2(147)(3) mandates a unanimous vote of the Council on legislation of a fiscal nature relating to energy policy.
- The Treaties contain no counterpart to this requirement, and energy is merely mentioned in a long list of Community activities in current ECT 3.

Title XXI: Tourism: LT 2(148); no current ECT counterpart

- There is no unanimity requirement in this Lisbon Treaty provision, which has no counterpart in the current EC Treaty.

Title XXII: Civil protection: LT 2(149); no current ECT counterpart

- There is no unanimity requirement in this Lisbon Treaty provision, which has no counterpart in the current EC Treaty.

Title XXIII: Administrative cooperation: LT 2(150); no current ECT counterpart

- There is no unanimity requirement in this Lisbon Treaty provision, which has no counterpart in the current EC Treaty.

d.   Part Four: Overseas countries and territories: LT 2(151)-2(153); current ECT 182-188

Terms of association. Current ECT 187 mandates a unanimous vote of the Council on legislation regarding rules and procedure for the association of overseas countries and territories with the EU. Current ECT 186 provides that matters of freedom of movement of workers are to be "governed by agreements to be concluded subsequently with the unanimous approval of Member States."
- LT 2(152) and 2(153) preserve these unanimity requirements.

e.   Part Five: External action: LT 2(154)-2(176); various current ECT articles

Common commercial policy. LT 2(158) requires unanimous Council decisions on international agreements in certain fields.
- Current ECT 133(5)-(7) contains the similar requirements.

International agreements. LT 2(173)(8) requires unanimity for Council decisions relating to the making of international agreements in fields where internal EU decisions would require unanimity. Unanimity is also required for association agreements with countries that are candidates for accession, and for the EU's accession agreement on the European Convention on Human Rights.
- The general unanimity requirement is found in current ECT 300(2) and current TEU 24(2).

Euro exchange rate agreements. LT 2(174)(a) requires a unanimous Council decision on euro exchange rates with third countries.
- Current ECT 111(1) contains the same requirement.

f.   Part Six: Institutions and financial provisions: LT 2(177)-2(278); current ECT 189-280

Institutions:

Parliament election procedures. LT 2(179)(b) mandates a unanimous vote of the Council on legislation setting uniform procedures for electing members of the European Parliament.
- This is based on the requirements of current ECT 190(4).

– The Lisbon Treaty and current EC Treaty require Member States to ratify these procedures in accordance with their own constitutional requirements.

Taxation of parliamentarians. LT 2(179)(c) mandates a unanimous decision of the Council on taxation of members and former members of the European Parliament.
– This is based on the requirements of current ECT 190(5).

Commission vacancy. LT 2(200)(a) requires a unanimous Council decision not to fill a vacancy on the Commission.
– Current ECT 215 contains the same requirement.

Advocates General. Current ECT 222 requires a unanimous decision of the Council to increase the number of Advocates General.
– The Lisbon Treaty does not change this requirement.

Appointment of Court positions. Current ECT 223 requires common accord of the governments of the Member States to appoint judges and to the Court of Justice, as well as Advocates-General.
– The Lisbon Treaty does not change this requirement. See LT 2(207).

Appointments to General Court. Current ECT 224 requires common accord of the Member States to appoint Judges to the General Court (currently called the Court of First Instance).
– The Lisbon Treaty does not change this requirement. See LT 2(208).

Appointments to specialised courts. Current ECT 225a mandates unanimity in a Council decision to appoint members to specialised courts (currently called judicial panels).
– The Lisbon Treaty does not change this requirement. See LT 2(211).

Extended ECJ jurisdiction. LT 2(213) allows a unanimous Council decision to extend the jurisdiction of the Court into matters of EU intellectual property rights.
– Current ECT 229a has a similar requirement.
– Both the Lisbon Treaty and the current EC Treaty require such decisions to be ratified by all Member States.

Legal acts of the Union:

Recommendations. LT 2(236)(249D) requires unanimity by the Council if it makes recommendations in cases in which a legislative act would require unanimity.
– Recommendations are permitted by current ECT 249, but there is no counterpart to the Lisbon Treaty's unanimity requirement.

Amendment of Commission proposal. LT 2(238) requires unanimity on the Council to amend most legislative proposals from the Commission.
– Current ECT 250(1) contains the same requirement.

Legislative amendments. LT 2(239)(b)(9) requires a unanimous Council vote to approve legislative amendments proposed by the European Parliament if the Commission has given a negative opinion on the amendments.
– This retains the unanimity requirement of current ECT 251(3).

Other bodies:

Economic and Social Committee. LT 2(248) mandates a unanimous Council decision to determine the composition of the Economic and Social Committee.
– Current ECT 258 does not contain such a requirement. However, no decision is necessary under the treaty, because the composition of the committee is specified in this treaty article. Any amendment to the specified composition will require and amendment to the EC Treaty, which will involve ratification by all of the Member States.

Committee of the Regions. LT 2(263)(b) provides for a unanimous Council decision to determine the composition of the Committee of the Regions.
– Current ECT 263 does not contain such a requirement. However, no decision is necessary under the treaty, because the actual composition of the committee is specified in this treaty article. Any amendment to the specified composition will require an amendment to the EC Treaty, which will involve ratification by all of the Member States.

European Investment Bank. LT 2(265) requires a unanimous vote of the Council on EU legislation to amend the Statute of the European Investment Bank.
– Current ECT 266 deals with the EIB Statute, but only certain provisions of the Statute are specified for amendment by unanimous Council action.

Resources and budgets:

System of own resources. LT 2(259)(b) requires a unanimous vote of the Council for EU legislation relating to the system of own resources.
– Current ECT 269 contains the same requirement.
– The Lisbon Treaty and current EC Treaty also require approval by all Member States in accordance with their respective constitutional requirements.

Multiannual financial framework. LT 2(261)(2) requires a unanimous vote of the Council to approve a regulation establishing the multiannual financial framework.
– There is no counterpart to this provision in the Treaties.

Passerelle to QMV on the multiannual framework. LT 2(261)(2) mandates a unanimous European Council decision to allow QMV on the Council relating to the multiannual financial framework.
– There is no counterpart to this *passerelle* in the Treaties.

Enhanced cooperation:

Enhanced cooperation in CFSP. LT2(278)(280D)(2) requires a unanimous Council decision permitting a programme of enhanced cooperation in the area of the CFSP.
– Current TEU 27c and 23(2) permit Council decisions to be taken by QMV.

Permission to join a programme in progress. LT 2(278)(280F)(2) requires a unanimous Council decision (participating Member States only) to allow a new Member State to join a programme of enhanced cooperation in the CFSP that is already in progress.
– Current TEU 27e and 23(2) provide for such Council decisions to be taken by QMV (participating Member States only, under current TEU 44(1)).

Programme costs. LT 2(278)(280G) mandates unanimity for a Council decision (all Member States) to charge the Union budget with the costs (other than administrative costs) arising from a programme of enhanced cooperation.
– Current TEU 44a contains the same requirement.

Passerelle to QMV. LT 2(278)(280H)(1) requires a unanimous decision of the Council (participating Member States only) to shift voting within a programme of enhanced cooperation from unanimity to QMV.
– There is no counterpart to this *passerelle* in the Treaties.

Passerelle to ordinary legislative procedure. LT 2(278)(280H)(2) mandates a unanimous Council decision (participating Member States only) to shift the legislative procedure within a programme of enhanced cooperation from a special procedure to the ordinary legislative procedure.
– The Treaties do not contain such a *passerelle*.

g. Part Seven: General and final provisions: LT 2(279)-2(295); current ECT 281-312

Location of EU institutions. Current ECT 289 requires a common accord decision of the governments of the Member States with respect to the location of EU institutions.
– The Lisbon Treaty does not change this requirement.

Languages of the EU institutions. Current ECT 290 mandates a unanimous Council decision to adopt a regulation setting the rules for use of languages in the EU institutions other than the European Court of Justice.
– The Lisbon Treaty retains this unanimity requirement. See LT 2(284).

List of arms, munitions and war material. Current ECT 296(2) requires a unanimous Council decision to change a 1958 list of arms, munitions and war materials that qualify for Member State protective measures.
– The Lisbon Treaty does not change this requirement.

Flexibility clause. LT 2(289) mandates that all legislation under the flexibility clause will require a unanimous vote of the Council.
– Current ECT 308 contains the same requirement.

Change of status. LT 2(293)(e) permits the European Council to unanimously adopt a decision changing the status of one of the overseas countries or territories.
– This is an addition to current ECT 299, but there is no counterpart provision in the Treaties.

Lisbon Treaty Art. 6:

Ratification. LT 6(1) requires ratification of the Lisbon Treaty by all Member States.
– Current ECT 313 and TEU 52 contain the same unanimity requirement for their respective ratifications.

BIBLIOGRAPHY

A. PRIMARY SOURCES

EU Treaties; Other Constitutions, Treaties and International Agreements
Agreement between the European Union and Canada establishing a framework for the partici-
pation of Canada in the European Union crisis management operations, December 1, 2005
(L 315) 20.
Agreement between the European Union and the Swiss Confederation on the participation of
the Swiss Confederation in the European Union Monitoring Mission in Aceh (Indonesia),
December 31, 2005, O.J. (L 349) 30.
Charter of Fundamental Rights of the European Union, December 18, 2000, O.J. (C 364) 1.
Draft Treaty establishing a Constitution for Europe, July 18, 2003, O.J. (C 169) 1.
European Convention for the Protection of Human Rights and Fundamental Freedoms, Novem-
ber 4, 1950, 213 U.N.T.S. 221 (entered into force Sept. 3, 1953).
Single European Act, February 7, 1986, O.J. (L 169) 1.
Treaty establishing a Constitution for Europe, December 16, 2004, O.J. (C 310) 1.
Treaty establishing a Single Council and a Single Commission of the European Communities
(Merger Treaty), April 8, 1965, O.J. (L 152) 2.
Treaty establishing the European Atomic Energy Community, March 25, 1957, 298 U.N.T.S.
167.
Treaty establishing the European Coal and Steel Community, April 18, 1951, 261 U.N.T.S.
140.
Treaty establishing the European Economic Community, March 25, 1957, O.J. (C 340) 173.
Treaty of Amsterdam amending the Treaty on European Union, The Treaties Establishing the
European Communities and Certain Related Acts, October 2, 1997, O.J. (C 340) 1.
Treaty of Nice amending the Treaty on European Union, the Treaties Establishing the Europe-
an Communities and Certain Related Acts, February 26, 2001, O.J. (C 80) 1.
Treaty on European Union (Maastricht), February 7, 1992, O.J. (C 191) 1.
United States Constitution.
Vienna Convention on the Law of Treaties, May 23, 1969, 1155 U.N.T.S. 336.

Protocols to EU Treaties
Protocol integrating the Schengen *acquis* into the framework of the European Union, Novem-
ber 10, 1997, O.J. (C 340) 93.
Protocol on protection and welfare of animals, November 10, 1997, O.J. (C 340/110).
Protocol on the application of the Charter of Fundamental Rights of the European Union to Po-
land and to the United Kingdom, Lisbon Treaty, December 3, 2007, CIG 14/07, TL/P/en
17.
Protocol on the application of the principles of subsidiarity and proportionality, November 10,
1997, O.J. (C 340) 105.
Protocol on the application of the principles of subsidiarity and proportionality, Lisbon Treaty
December 3, 2007, CIG 14/07, TL/P/en 6.
Protocol on the enlargement of the European Union, December 24, 2002, O.J. (C 325) 163.
Protocol on the position of Denmark (1997), December 29, 2006, O.J. (C 321) E/201.

Protocol on the position of the United Kingdom and Ireland (1997), December 29, 2006, O.J. (C 321) E/198.

Protocol on the privileges and immunities of the European Communities, (1965), December 29, 2006, O.J. (C 321) E/318.

Protocol on the role of national parliaments in the European Union, November 10, 1997, O.J. (C 340) 113.

Protocol on the role of national parliaments in the European Union, Lisbon Treaty, December 3, 2007, CIG 14/07, TL/P/en 2.

Protocol on the Statute of the Court of Justice, December 12, 2002, O.J. (C 325) 167.

EU Directives, Decisions, Declarations and Other Documents

Commission of the European Communities, Declaration on the European Identity (1973) EC Bulletin 12, Cl. 2501, 118-127.

Conference of the Representatives of the Governments of the Member States, Presidency Note, Brussels, December 11, 2003, CIG 60/03 ADD 2.

Council Decision of 28 June 1999 laying down the procedures for the exercise of implementing powers conferred on the Commission, July 7, 1999, O.J. (L 184) 23.

Council Directive 93/109/EC, December 30, 1993, O.J. (L 329) 34.

Council Directive 94/80/EC, December 31, 1994, O.J. (L 368) 38.

Decision of the Council of 22 December 2004 providing for certain areas covered by Title IV of Part Three of the Treaty establishing the European Community to be governed by the procedure laid down in Article 251 of that Treaty, December 22, 2004, O.J. (L 396) 45.

Declaration on the ratification of the Treaty Establishing a Constitution for Europe, December 16, 2004, O.J. (C 310) 464.

Draft Council Decision relating to the implementation of Article I-25 (previously Article I-24), December 16, 2004, O.J. (C 310) 421.

Draft Decision of the Council, Lisbon Treaty, Final Act, December 3, 2007, CIG 15/07, AF/TL/DC en 2.

Draft Decision of the European Council on the exercise of the Presidency of the Council, Lisbon Treaty, Final Act, December 3, 2007, CIG 15/07, AF/TL/DC en 5.

European Commission, Eurobarometer 59: Public Opinion in the European Union (Eur. Opinion Res. Group, June 2003).

European Commission, Taking Stock of Five Years of the European Employment Strategy, COM (2002) 416 final.

European Council, Declaration by the heads of state or government of the Member States of the European Union on the ratification of the Treaty Establishing a Constitution for Europe, June 18, 2005, SN 117/05.

European Council, Declaration on the future of the Union (Nice Declaration), March 10, 2001, O.J. (C 80) 85.

European Council, Declaration on the ratification of the Treaty Establishing a Constitution for Europe, December 16, 2004, O.J. (C 310) 464.

European Council, Laeken Declaration on the Future of the European Union, in Presidency Conclusions: European Council Meeting in Laeken, 14 and 15 December 2001, Annex I, SN 300/1/01 REV 1, available at http://europa.eu.int/futurum/documents/offtext/doc151201en.htm.

European Council, Presidency Conclusions, June 16, 2006, CONCL 2, 10633/06.

European Council, Presidency Conclusions, June 23, 2007, CONCL 2, 11177/07.

European Union on the ratification of the Treaty Establishing a Constitution for Europe, June 18, 2005, SN 117/05.

European Governance: White Paper from the Commission to the European Council, July 25, 2001, COM (2001) 428.

Praesidium, Updated Explanations relating to the text of the Charter of Fundamental Rights, July 18, 2003, CONV 828/1/03 REV 1.

Praesidium of The European Convention, Preliminary Draft Constitutional Treaty, October 28, 2002, CONV 369/02.

Press Release, Committee of the Regions, Committee of the Regions wants a greater role in EU decision-making (July 10, 2003), available at www.cor.eu.int.

Cases

Case 26/62, *Van Gend en Loos* v. *Nederlandse Administratie Der Belastingen*, 1963 ECR 1.

Case 6/64, *Costa* v. *ENEL*, 1964 ECR 585.

Case 11/70, *Internationale Handelsgesellschaft m.b.H* v. *Einfuhr- und Vorratsstelle fur Getreide und Futtermittel*, 1970 ECR 1125.

Case 22/70, *Commission* v. *Council (ERTA)*, 1971 ECR 263.

Case C-2/88, *J.J. Zwartveld and others*, 1990 ECR I-3365.

Case 2/94, *Accession by the Community to the European Convention for the Protection of Human Rights and Fundamental Freedoms*, Advisory Opinion, 1996 ECR I-1759.

Gade v. *National Solid Waste Management Association*, 505 U.S. 88 (1992).

Texas v. *White*, 74 U.S. 700 (1869).

Speeches

Barroso, José Manuel, "A Citizen's Agenda – Delivering results for Europe, Speech/06/286 (May 10, 2006), available at http://europa.eu/rapid/pressReleasesAction.do?reference=SPEECH/06/286&format=HTML&aged=0&language=EN&guiLanguage=en.

Dehaene, Jean-Luc, Understanding Europe: The EU Citizen's Right to Know, Speech Before the Conference Organized by the Friends of Europe in Brussels (Apr. 3, 2003), available at http://european-convention.eu.int/docs/speeches/8285.pdf.

Fischer, Joschka, From Confederacy to Federation: Thoughts on the Finality of European Integration, Speech at the Humboldt University in Berlin (May 12, 2000), available at www.auswaertiges-amt.de/www/de/infoservice/download/pdf/reden/redene/r000512b-r1008e.pdf.

Giscard d'Estaing, Valery, Introductory Speech to the Convention on the Future of Europe (February 26, 2002) available at http://european-convention.eu.int/docs/speeches/1.pdf.

Vanhanen, Matti, Speech at the plenary session of the European Parliament (July 5, 2006), available at www.eu2006.fi/news_and_documents/ speeches/ko27/en_GB/1152081630727.

B. SECONDARY MATERIALS

Books

A Constitution for the European Union (Charles B. Blankart & Dennis C. Mueller, eds., 2004).

Chemerinsky, Erwin, Constitutional Law Principles and Policies (2002).

Collignon, Stefan, The European Republic: Reflections on the Political Economy of a Future Constitution (2003).

Constitution-Building in the European Union (Brigid Laffan, ed., 1996).

De Zwaan, Jaap W., The Permanent Representatives Committee: Its role in the decision-making of the European Union (T.M.C. Asser Institute – The Hague, Elsevier – North Holland 1995).

Developing a Constitution for Europe (Erik Oddvar Eriksen, et al. eds., 2004).

Forsyth, Murray, Unions of States (1981).

Jurisprudence or Legal Science? (Coyle, Sean & Pavlakos, George, eds., 2005).

Mancini, G.F., Democracy and Constitutionalism in the European Union: Collected Essays 65 (2000).

Marquand, David, Parliament for Europe (1979).

Moravcsik, Andrew, The Choice for Europe: Social Purpose and State Power from Messina to Maastricht (1998).

Newman, Michael, Democracy, Sovereignty and the European Union (1996).

Norman, Peter, The Accidental Constitution – The Story of the European Convention (2003).

Nugent, Neill, The Government and Politics of the European Union (2003).

Piris, Jean-Claude, The Constitution for Europe – A Legal Analysis (2006).

Political Theory and the European Constitution (Lynn Dobson & Andreas Føllesdal, eds., 2004).

Shaw, Jo, et al., The Convention on the Future of Europe: Working Towards an EU Constitution (2003).

Sinclair, Ian, The Vienna Convention of Treaties (1984).

Smith, Brendan P.G., Constitution Building in the European Union (2002).

The Constitution for Europe and an Enlarging Union: Unity in Diversity? (Kirstyn Inglis & Andrea Ott, eds., 2005).

The EU Constitution: The Best Way Forward? (Deirdre Curtin, Alfred E. Kellermann & Steven Blockmans, eds., 2005).

The Post-Nice Process: Towards a European Constitution (Peter A. Zervakis & Peter J. Cullen, eds., 2002).

Weiler, Jospeh H.H., The Constitution of Europe: "Do the New Clothes Have an Emperor?" and Other Essays on European Integration (1999).

Law Review & Journal Articles

Albi, Anneli, & Van Elsuwege, Peter, The EU Constitution, National Constitutions and Sovereignty: An Assessment of a "European Constitutional Order," 29 Eur. L. Rev. 741 (2004).

Alpa, Guido, The Meaning of "Natural Person" and the Impact of the Constitution for Europe on the Development of European Private Law, 10 Eur. L.J. 734 (2004).

Attucci, Claudia, An institutional dialogue on common principles – Reflections on the significance of the EU Charter of Fundamental Rights, in Political Theory and the European Constitution (Lynn Dobson & Andreas Føllesdal, eds., 2004).

Backer, Larry Cata, The Extra-National State: American Confederate Federalism and the European Union, 7 Colum. J. Eur. L. 173 (2001).

Barber, P. W., The Limited Modesty of Subsidiarity, 11 Eur. L.J. 308 (2005).

Bausili, Anna Verges, Rethinking the methods of dividing and exercising powers in the EU – Reforming subsidiarity, national parliaments and legitimacy, in Jo Shaw, et al., The Convention on the Future of Europe: Working Towards an EU Constitution (2003).

Best, Edward, What is Really at Stake in the Debate over Votes? 2004/1 Eipascope 14 (2004), available at www.eipa.nl/cms/repository/eipascope/Art_2(2).pdf.

Bignami, Francesca E., The Democratic Deficit in European Community Rulemaking: A Call for Notice and Comment in Comitology, 40 Harv. Int'l L.J. 451 (1999).

Birkinshaw, Patrick, A Constitution for the European Union? – A Letter from Home, 10 Eur. Pub. L. 57 (2004).

Blankart, Charles B., & Kirchner, Christian, The Deadlock of the EU Budget: An Economic Analysis of the Ways In and Ways Out, in A Constitution for the European Union (Charles B. Blankart & Dennis C. Mueller, eds., 2004).

Branthwaite, Alan, The Psychological Basis of Independent Statehood, in States in a Changing World 46 (Robert H. Jackson & Alan James eds., 1993).

Bermann, George, Editorial: The European Union as a Constitutional Experiment, 10 Eur. L.J. 363 (2004).

Breyer, Stephen, Constitutionalism, Privatisation, and Globalisation: Changing Relationships Among European Constitutional Courts, 21 Cardozo L. Rev. 1045 (2000).

Coyle, Sean and Pavlakos, George, Introduction, in Jurisprudence or Legal Science? (Coyle, Sean and Pavlakos, George, eds., 2005).

Craig, Paul, The Community Legal Order, 10 Ind. J. Global Legal Stud. 79 (2003).

Craig, Paul, What Constitution does Europe Need? The Federal Trust Online Paper 26/03, at 8, available at www.fedtrust.co.uk/uploads/constitution/26_03.pdf.

Cremona, Marise, The Draft Constitutional Treaty: External Relations and External Action, 40 C.M.L.R. 1347 (2003).

Curtin, Deirdre, The Constitutional Structure of the Union: A Europe of Bits and Pieces, 30 C.M.L.R. 17 (1993).

Davies, Gareth, Subsidiarity: The Wrong Idea, in the Wrong Place, at the Wrong Time, 43 C.M.L.R. 63 (2006).

De Búrca, Gráinne, The Constitutional Challenge of New Governance in the European Union, 28 Eur. L. Rev. 814 (2003).

De Búrca, Gráinne, & Jo Beatrix Aschenbrenner, European Constitutionalism and the EU Charter of Fundamental Human Rights, 9 Colum. J. Eur. L. 355 (2003).

De la Rochère, Jacqueline Dutheil, The EU and the Individual: Fundamental Rights in the Draft Constitutional Treaty, 41 C.M.L.R. 345 (2004).

De Witte, Bruno, The Process of Ratification and the Crisis Options: A Legal Perspective, in The EU Constitution: The Best Way Forward? (Deirdre Curtin, Alfred E. Kellermann & Steven Blockmans, eds., 2005).

De Zwaan, Jaap W., European Citizenship: Origin, Contents and Perspectives, in The EU Constitution: The Best Way Forward? (Deirdre Curtin, Alfred E. Kellermann & Steven Blockmans, eds., 2005).

De Zwaan, Jaap W., The Legal Personality of the European Communities and the European Union, in Vol. XXX Netherlands Yearbook of International Law 75 (1999).

Devuyst, Youri, The European Union's Constitutional Order? Between Community Method and Ad Hoc Compromise, 18 Berkeley J. Int'l L. 1 (2000).

Di Fabio, Udo, A European Charter: Towards a Constitution for the Union, 7 Colum. J. Eur. L. 159 (2001).

Donnelly, Brendan, & Hoffmann, Lars, All change or no change? Convention, constitution and national sovereignty, The Federal Trust Policy Brief No. 1, at 3 (November 2003), available at www.fedtrust.co.uk/admin/uploads/PolicyBrief1.pdf.

Dougan, Michael, The Convention's Constitutional Treaty: A "Tidying-Up Exercise" that Needs Some Tidying-up of Its Own, The Federal Trust Online Paper 27/03, available at www.fedtrust.co.uk/uploads/constitution/27_03.pdf.

Dougan, Michael, The Convention's Draft Constitutional Treaty: Bringing Europe Closer to its Lawyers, 28 Eur. L. Rev. 763 (2003).

Douglas-Scott, Sionaidh, The Charter of Fundamental Rights as a Constitutional Document, 2004 Eur. Hum. Rts. L. Rev. 37 (2004).

Duina, Francesco, & Oliver, Michael J., National Parliaments in the European Union: Are There Any Benefits to Integration?, 11 Eur. L.J. 173 (2005).

Editorial, A Constitution Whose Bottle is Definitely Half-Full and Not Half-Empty, 28 Eur. L. Rev. 449 (2003).

Editorial, The Failure to Reach Agreement on the EU Constitution – Hard Questions, 41 C.M.L.R. 1 (2004).

Editorial Comments, A Constitution for Europe, 41 C.M.L.R. 899 (2004).

Eleftheriadis, Pavlos, The European Constitution and Cosmopolitan Ideals, 7 Colum. J. Eur. L. 21 (2001).

Emmanouilidis, Janis A., Historically Unique, Unfinished in Detail – An Evaluation of the Constitution, Centre for Applied Policy Research, 2004/3 EU Reform.

Emmanouilidis Janis A., & Giering, Claus, Light and Shade – An Evaluation of the Convention's Proposals, in Centre for Applied Policy Research, EU Reform, Convention Spotlight 1 (August 2003).

Estella, Antonio, Constitutional Legitimacy and Credible Commitments in the European Union, 11 Eur. L.J. 22 (2005).

European Policy Center, The Draft Constitutional Treaty – An Assessment at 30, Issue No. 5 (July 3, 2003).

Føllesdal, Andreas, Achieving Stability? Forms and Areas of Institutional and National Balances in the Draft Constitutional Treaty, The Federal Trust Online Paper 06/04, available at www.fedtrust.co.uk/uploads/constitution/06_04.pdf.

Føllesdal, Andreas, Citizenship and Political Rights in the European Union: Consensus and Questions, Inst. for Advanced Stud., 1, available at www.ihs.ac.at/public_rel/kbericht/ak1/fo.html.

Freil, Raymond J., Providing a Constitutional Framework for Withdrawal from the EU: Article 59 of the Draft European Constitution, 53 Int'l & Comp. L.Q. 407 (2004).

Friel, Raymond J., The Draft Constitution: Issues and Analyses: Secession from the European Union: Checking out of the Proverbial "Cockroach Motel," 27 U. Fordham Int'l L.J. 590 (2004).

Geelhoed, Ad, The Expanding Jurisdiction of the EU Court of Justice, in The EU Constitution: The Best Way Forward? (Deirdre Curtin, Alfred E. Kellermann & Steven Blockmans, eds., 2005).

Gibbs, Nathan, Examining the Aesthetic Dimensions of the Constitutional Treaty, 11 Eur. L.J. 326 (2005).

Goebel, Roger J., European Economic and Monetary Union: Will the EMU Ever Fly?, 4 Colum. J. Eur. L. 249 (1998).

Goebel, Roger J., The European Union in Transition: The Treaty of Nice in Effect; Enlargement in Sight; A Constitution in Doubt, 27 Fordham Int'l L. J. 455 (2004).

Grimm, Dieter, Does Europe Need a Constitution?, 1 Eur. L.J. 282 (1995).

Guild, Elspeth, Crime and the EU's Constitutional Future in an Area of Freedom, Security, and Justice, 10 Eur. L. J 218 (2004).

Habermas, Jürgen, Why Europe Needs a Constitution, 11 New Left Rev. 5 (2001).

Hautala, Heidi, The Role of Parliaments in the EU Constitutional Framework: A Partnership or Rivalry? in The EU Constitution: The Best Way Forward? (Deirdre Curtin, Alfred E. Kellermann & Steven Blockmans, eds., 2005).

Hoffmann, Lars, & Shaw, Jo, Constitutionalism and Federalism in the "Future of Europe" debate: The German Dimension, The Federal Trust Online Paper 03/04, at 7, available at www.fedtrust.co.uk/uploads/constitution/0304.pdf.

Hosli, Madeleine O., Coalitions and Power: Effects of Qualified Majority Voting in the Council of the European Union, 34 J. Common Mkt. Stud. 255 (1996).

Hughes, Kirsty, A Dynamic and Democratic EU or Muddling Through Again?, The Federal Trust Online Paper 3 (August 2003), available at www.fedtrust.co.uk/uploads/constitution/25_03.pdf.

Kokott, Juliane, & Rüth, Alexandra, The European Convention and its Draft Treaty Establishing a Constitution for Europe: Appropriate Answers to the Laeken Questions?, 40 C.M.L.R. 1315 (2003).

Kuijper, Pieter Jan, The Evolution of the Third Pillar from Maastricht to the European Constitution: Institutional Aspects, 41 C.M.L.R. 609 (2004).

Kumm, Mattias, The Jurisprudence of Constitutional Conflict: Constitutional Supremacy in Europe before and after the Constitutional Treaty, 11 Eur. L.J. 262 (2005).

Lang, John Temple, The Commission: The Key to the Constitutional Treaty for Europe, 26 Fordham Int'l L. J. 1598 (2003).

Lindahl, Hans, Finding a Place for Freedom, Security and Justice: The European Union's Claim to Territorial Unity, 29 Eur. L. Rev. 461 (2004).

Lindseth, Peter, Democratic Legitimacy and the Administrative Character of Supranationalism: The Example of the European Community, 99 Colum. L. Rev. 628 (1999).

Lord, Christopher, Assessing Democracy in a Contested Polity, 39 J. Common Mkt. Stud. 641 (2001).

MacCormick, Neil, Democracy, Subsidiarity, and Citizenship in the "European Commonwealth", 16 Law & Phil. 331 (1997).

Majone, Giandomenico, Europe's "Democratic Deficit": The Question of Standards, 4 Eur. L.J. 5 (1998).

Melossi, Dario, Security, Social Control, Democracy and Migration within the "Constitution" of the EU, 11 Eur. L.J. 5 (2005).

Mény, Yves, De la democratie en Europe: Old Concepts and New Challenges, 41 J. Common Mkt. Stud. 1 (2002).

Mény, Yves, The Achievements of the Convention, 14 J. Democracy 57 (2003).

Miliband, David, Perspectives on European Integration: A British View (Max Planck Inst. for the Study of Societies, Working Paper No. 02/02, 2002), available at www.mpi-fg-koeln.mpg.de/pu/workpap/wp02-2/wp02-2.html.

Moravcsik, Andrew, Conservative Idealism and International Institutions, 1 Chi. J. Int'l L. 291, 309 (2000).

Moravcsik, Andrew, In Defence of the "Democratic Deficit": Reassessing Legitimacy in the European Union, 40 J. Common Mkt. Stud. 603 (2002).

Mueller, Dennis C., Rights and Citizenship in the European Union, in A Constitution for the European Union (Charles B. Blankart & Dennis C. Mueller, eds., 2004).

Muller, Jan, Constitutionalism and the Founding of Constitutions: Carl Schmitt and the Constitution of Europe, 21 Cardozo L. Rev. 1777 (2000).

Müller-Bandeck-Bocquet, Gisela, The New CFSP and ESDP Decision-Making system of the European Union, 7 European Foreign Affairs Review 257 (2002).

Müller-Graff, Peter-Christian, The Process and Impact of EU Constitution-making: "Voice and Exit," in The EU Constitution: The Best Way Forward? (Deirdre Curtin, Alfred E. Kellermann & Steven Blockmans, eds., 2005).

Nicolaidis, Kalypso, The New Constitution as European Demoi-cracy?, The Federal Trust Online Paper 38/03, available at www.fedtrust.co.uk/uploads/constitution/38_03.pdf.

Passos, Ricardo, The Expanding Role of the European Parliament, in The EU Constitution: The Best Way Forward? (Deirdre Curtin, Alfred E. Kellermann & Steven Blockmans, eds., 2005).

Pernice, Ingolf, Integrating the Charter of Fundamental Rights into the Constitution of the European Union: Practical and Theoretical Propositions, 10 Colum. J. Eur. L. 5 (2004).

Petite, Michel, and Ladenburger, Clemens, The Evolution in the Role and Powers of the European Commission, in The EU Constitution: The Best Way Forward? (Deirdre Curtin, Alfred E. Kellermann & Steven Blockmans, eds., 2005).

Pinelli, Cesare, Conditionality and Enlargement in Light of EU Constitutional Developments, 10 Eur. L. J. 354 (2004).

Priban, Jiří, European Union Constitution-Making, Political Identity and Central European Reflections, 11 Eur. L.J. 135 (2005).

Puder, Markus G., Constitutionalizing the European Union – More Than a Sense of Direction From the Convention on the Future of Europe, 26 Fordham Int'l L.J. 1562 (2003).

Rabkin, Jeremy, Is EU Policy Eroding the Sovereignty of Non-Member States?, 1 Chi. J. Int'l L. 273 (2000).

Richardson, Keith, & Cox, Robert, Salvaging the Wreckage of Europe's Constitution, 2004 Friends of Eur. 3.

Röben, Volker, Constitutionalism of the European Union After the Draft Constitutional Treaty: How Much Hierarchy, 10 Colum. J. Eur. L. 339 (2004).

Sacerdoti, Giorgio, The European Charter of Fundamental Rights: From a Nation-State Europe to a Citizens' Europe, 8 Colum. J. Eur. L. 37 (2002).

Schwarze, Jürgen, The Convention's Draft Treaty Establishing a Constitution for Europe, 40 C.M.L.R. 1037 (2003).

Senelle, Robert, Federal Belgium, in Federalism and Regionalism in Europe 27 (Antonio D'Atena ed., 1998).

Sieberson, Stephen C., The Proposed European Union Constitution—Will it Eliminate the EU's Democratic Deficit?, 10 Colum. J. Eur. L. 173 (2004).

Sieberson, Stephen C., Did Symbolism Sink the Constitution? Reflections on the European Union's State-Like Attributes, 14 U.C. Davis J. of Int'l Law & Policy 1 (2008).

Skach, Cindy, We, the Peoples? Constitutionalizing the European Union, 43 J. Common Mkt. Stud. 149 (2005).

Snyder, Francis, Editorial: Enhancing EU Democracy, Constituting the European Union, 11 Eur. L.J. 131 (2005).

Spaventa, Eleanor, From Gebhard to Carpenter: Towards a (non-)economic European Constitution, 41 C.M.L.R. 743 (2004).

Stanbury, W.T., Accountability to Citizens in the Westminster Model of Government: More Myth Than Reality, Fraser Inst. Digital Publication (Feb. 2003) available at www.fraserinstitute.ca/admin/books/files/westminster.pdf.

Stein, Eric, International Integration and Democracy: No Love at First Sight, 95 Am. J. Int'l L. 489 (2001).

Sunstein, Cass, Constitutionalism and Secession, 58 U. Chi. L. Rev. 633 (1991).

Trubek, David M., & Trubek, Louise G., Hard and Soft Law in the Construction of Social Europe: the Role of the Open Method of Co-ordination, 11 Eur. L.J. 343 (2005).

Tsakatika, Myrto, The Open Method of Co-ordination in the European Convention: An Opportunity Lost?, in Political Theory and the European Constitution (Lynn Dobson & Andreas Føllesdal, eds., 2004).

Von Bogdandy, Armin, The European Union as a Supranational Federation: A Conceptual Attempt in the Light of the Amsterdam Treaty, 6 Colum. J. Eur. L. 27 (2000).

Walker, Neil, Constitutionalising Enlargement, Enlarging Constitutionalism, 9 Eur. L.J. 365 (2003).

Walker, Neil, Europe's Constitutional Passion Play, 28 Eur. L. Rev. 905 (2003).

Walker, Neil, The Charter of Fundamental Rights of the EU: Legal, Symbolic and Constitutional Implications, in The Post-Nice Process: Towards a European Constitution (Peter A. Zervakis & Peter J. Cullen, eds., 2002).

Ward, Ian, Identity and Difference: The European Union and Postmodernism, in New Legal Dynamics of European Union 15 (Jo Shaw & Gillian More, eds., 1995).

Weiler, Joseph H.H., Does Europe Need a Constitution? Demos, Telos and the German Maastricht Decision, 1 Eur. L.J. 219 (1995).

Weiler, Joseph H.H., Human rights, constitutionalism and integration, in Developing a Constitution for Europe (Erik Oddvar Eriksen, et al., eds., 2004).

Weiler, Joseph H.H., On the Power of the Word: Europe's Constitutional Iconography, in The EU Constitution: The Best Way Forward? (Deirdre Curtin, Alfred E. Kellermann & Steven Blockmans, eds., 2005).

Werts, Jan, The Unstoppable Advance of the European Council, in The EU Constitution: The Best Way Forward? (Deirdre Curtin, Alfred E. Kellermann & Steven Blockmans, eds., 2005).

Wouters, Jan, Drawing the Threads together from Parts I and III of the EU Constitution, in The EU Constitution: The Best Way Forward? (Deirdre Curtin, Alfred E. Kellermann & Steven Blockmans, eds., 2005).

Zamora, Stephen, Voting in International Economic Organizations, 74 Am. J. Int'l L. 566 (1980).

Articles in Magazines, Newspapers and Other Media

A draft EU constitution that is far from satisfactory, Times London, May 27, 2003, at 17.

Barroso calls for EU to move beyond constitution debacle, Guardian Online, http:// www.guardian.co.uk/print/0,,329602512-106710,00.html.

Bennhold, Katrin, EU cuts expansion from its to-do list, Int'l Herald Trib., June 14, 2005.

Bonello, Jesmond, Draft EU Constitution: MLP Sees Voluntary Withdrawal Clause as "Interesting," Times Malta, May 28, 2003, at www.timesofmalta.com/core/article.php?id=127081.

Bowley, Graham, EU Teeters on Edge of a Broader Crisis, Int'l Herald Trib., June 3, 2005.

Bowley, Graham, Luxembourg Approves EU charter, Int'l Herald Trib., July 11, 2005.

Charlemagne, Europe's Forgotten President: Why It Matters Who Runs the European Parliament, Economist, January 12, 2002, at 49.

Chronology–EU Common Agricultural Policy, Reuters, June 26, 2003, available at www.forbes.com/business/newswire/2003/06/26/rtr1011815.html.

Dickey, Christopher, & Michael Meyer, Is Europe Broken?, Newsweek, August 12, 2002, at 14.

Dombey, Daniel, & George Parker, Dual Ambitions, Fin. Times, May 24, 2002, at 13.

Duff, Andrew, Plan B: How to Rescue the European Constitution, Notre Europe, available at www.unizar.es/euroconstitucion/library/working%20papers/Duff% 202006.pdf.

EurActiv.com, Austria's Haider affair gave the EU an "emergency brake," 7 August, 2006, www.euractiv.com/en/agenda2004/austria-haider-affair-gave-eu-emergency-brake/article-151443.

Europa Website, The Schengen acquis and its integration into the Union, http://europa.eu.int/scadplus/leg/en/lvb/l33020.htm.

Europe's Convention: The Tortoise is Thinking of Moving, Economist, July 20, 2002, at 41.

Fuller, Thomas, Split on voting rights sinks the EU constitution, Int'l Herald Trib., December 15, 2004.

Funk, Lothar, A Legally Binding EU Charter of Fundamental Rights?, 37 Intereconomics 253 (2002).

Giovannini, Nicola, The Draft European Constitution and its antisecular article 51, 42 Am. Atheist Mag. 39 (Mar. 22, 2004).

Grevi, Giovanni, Light and shade of a quasi-Constitution – An Assessment, EPC Issue Paper No. 14 (June 23, 2004), available at www.theepc.net.

Head-to-Head: Is EU Blueprint Democratic?, BBC News, June 20, 2003, at http://news.bbc.co.uk/2/hi/europe/3006156.stm.

Heffer, Simon, & Amory, Edward Heathcoat, Blueprint for Tyranny, Daily Mail (London), May 8, 2003, at 12.

How Special Interests Infiltrate the European Union Constitution, Economist, May 22, 2004.

Kaletsky, Anatole, EU Blueprint Spells the Demise of Democracy, Times London, October 31, 2002, at 24.

Kaube, Jürgen, Espresso and Croissants, Frankfurter Allgemeine Zeitung, June 27, 2001, available at www.faz.com/IN/INtemplates/eFAZ/archive.asp?rub={B1311FFE-FBFB-11D2-B228-00105A9CAF88}&doc= {7E646849-6AE3-11D5-A3B5-009027BA22E4.

Kranenburg, Mark, The political branch of the polder model, NRC Handelsblad (July 1, 1999) available at www.nrc.nl/W2/Lab/Profiel/Netherlands/politics.html.

Kubusova, Lucia, Finland seeks better climate for revised EU constitution, Euobserver.com (June 30, 2006), http://euobserver.com/9/21995.

Lamy, Pascal, & Pisani-Ferry, Jean, Europe's Future and the Centre-left, Fin. Times (London), March 8, 2002, at 19.

Lobo-Fernandes, Luís, Por um sistema bicamarário na UE, Expresso (Lisbon), June 7, 2003, at 30 (Luís Lobo-Fernandes trans.).

Ludlow, Peter, The Thessaloniki European Council, EuroComment Briefing Note, No. 2.3, July 3, 2003.

Merkel's Constitution hopes on ice, Euractiv.com, www.euractiv.com/en/constitution/merkel-constitution-hopes-ice/article-159355.

Moravcsik, Andrew, If It Ain't Broke, Don't Fix It, Newsweek Int'l, March 4, 2002, at 15, available at 2002 WL 8965081.

Moravcsik, Andrew, The EU Ain't Broke, Prospect, March 2003, at 40, available at www.prospect-magazine.co.uk.

Nicolas Sarkozy's European Plans, Economist, May 10, 2007 available at www.economist.com/world/europe/displaystory.cfm?story_id=9149133.

Parker, George, Political Leaders Are Starting to Take Seriously Discussions on a New Constitution for an Enlarged Union, Fin. Times, December 31, 2002, at 13.

Peel, Quentin, Europe's constitution misses its moment, Fin. Times, June 17, 2003, at 23.

Rocard, Michel, Europe's Secular Mission, Taipei Times, May 28, 2003, at 9, available at www.taipeitimes.com/News/edit/archives/2003/05/28/2003053028.

Siedentop, Larry, We the People Do Not Understand, Fin. Times, June 5, 2003, at 21.

Straw, Jack, Special Report: A Constitution for Europe, The Economist, October 12, 2002, at 55.

Unconventional Wisdom, Times London, May 14, 2003, at 23.

Vinocur, John, An EU Constitution? No Big Deal, Int'l Herald Trib., June 25, 2003, at 1.

Will, George, EU Should Really Study America's Constitution, Register Guard (Eugene, OR), Jul. 29, 2003.

Working Papers

Armstrong, Kenneth, Civil Society and the White Paper: Bridging or Jumping the Gap? (Harvard Jean Monnet, Working Paper No.6/01, 2001), available at www.jeanmonnetprogram. org/papers/01/011601.html.

Dehousse, Franklin, Coussens, Wouter & Grevi, Giovanni, Integrating Europe: Multiple Speeds – One direction? (Eur. Pol'y Centre, Working Paper No. 9, 2004), available at www.theepc.net/en/default.asp?TYP=CE &LV=177&see=y&PG=TEWN/EN/detail&AI= 353&l=.

Hofmann, Herwig C.H., A Critical Analysis of the New Typology of Acts in the Draft Treaty Establishing a Constitution for Europe (Eur. Integration Online Papers, Working Paper No. 9, 2003), available at http://eiop.or.at/eiop/pdf/2003-009.pdf.

Miliband, David, Perspectives on European Integration: A British View (Max Planck Inst. for the Study of Societies, Working Paper No. 02/02, 2002), available at www.mpi-fg-koeln. mpg.de/pu/workpap/wp02-2/wp02-2.html.

Plechanovová, Bela, Draft Constitution and the Decision-Making Rule for the Council of Ministers of the EU – Looking for an Alternative Solution (Eur. Integration Online Papers, Working Paper No. 12, 2004).

Schneider, Heinrich, The Constitution Debate (Eur. Integration Online Papers, Working Paper No. 4, 2003).

C. MISCELLANEOUS

Catechism of the Catholic Church, United States Conference of Catholic Bishops, art. 1, ¶ 1883, available at www.usccb.org/catechism/text/pt3sect1chpt2.htm.

Letter from the Benelux countries to Valery Giscard d'Estaing, Chairman of the European Convention (Apr. 25, 2003) (on file with the Netherlands Ministry of Foreign Affairs), available at www.minbuza.nl/default.asp?CMS_ITEM=64E844AE637C4B2E89B3957CE202 8F89X88X67360X33.

INDEX

A. TREATY OF LISBON

Articles 3–7:

B. TREATY ON EUROPEAN UNION (TEU)

C. TREATY ESTABLISHING THE EUROPEAN ECONOMIC COMMUNITY (EC TREATY)

D. TREATY ESTABLISHING A CONSTITUTION FOR EUROPE

AUTHOR INDEX

General Index

Moldova, 122
Monopolies, 57
Morality, 57, 84
Multiannual financial framework, 39, 43, 50, 53, 67, 98, 133, 205, 268

NAFTA, 88
National Action Plans, 154
National central banks, 56
National courts, 12, 146, 184, 247
National parliaments, 10, 22, 41, 46, 47, 55, 57, 66, 68, 104, 107, 117, 119, 121, 131, 141, 142, 143, 144, 153, 156, 157, 162, 165, 205, 217, 223, 248, 249, 260
National security, 93, 145
NATO, 59, 65, 68, 127, 241
Negative opinion, 176, 267
Netherlands, Dutch, 12, 24, 25, 26, 28, 29, 30, 35, 44, 113, 121, 122, 126, 127, 236
Nice Declaration, 21, 22, 44, 148, 238
Nice, Treaty of, 1, 21, 25, 28, 32, 35, 36, 40, 43, 125, 135, 163, 172, 173, 191
Non-confessional organisations, 120
Non-discrimination, 39, 42, 49, 74, 226
Non-legislative acts, 171, 173, 186
Non-majoritarian, 114, 115
Norway, 122, 127

Objectives (see Union objectives)
Ombudsman, 38, 94, 103, 162
Open meetings (openness) (also see Transparency), 27, 38, 46, 49, 54, 66, 71, 101, 102, 116, 117, 118, 119, 173, 174, 175, 207, 246, 250
Open Method of Co-ordination (OMC), 154, 155, 156
Operating expenditures, 34, 53, 98, 163, 183, 259
Operational cooperation, 217, 223, 224, 263
Opinion, as legal instrument, 185
Opt-out, opt out, 54, 58, 127, 128, 196, 248
Ordinary legislative procedure, 50, 132, 133, 163, 182, 186, 187, 190, 191, 197, 205, 206, 208, 215, 246, 260, 269
Ordinary revision procedure, 131
Overseas countries and territories, 34, 39, 42, 50, 78, 122, 226, 236, 266, 269
Own resources, 35, 53, 97, 98, 99, 199, 268

Pacta sunt servanda, 123
Passerelle, 48, 62, 134, 205, 221, 239, 251, 259, 262, 269
Peer review programmes, 113, 154
Peoples, people, 12, 14, 15, 32, 52, 73, 75, 76, 79, 81, 93, 94, 109, 111, 138, 139, 252
Period of reflection, 26, 27
Permanent structured cooperation, 47, 59, 68, 127, 210, 241, 259
Personal data protection (data privacy), 38, 42, 49, 117, 119
Pioneer groups, 128
Poland, 26, 85, 121, 126, 172, 173, 175
Polder model, 113
Police and judicial cooperation, 16, 20, 36, 39, 166, 186, 190, 215, 216
Police cooperation, 39, 48, 57, 68, 203, 217, 223, 224
Political parties, EU level, 46, 110, 116, 117, 162
Political union, 10, 11, 29, 128
Portugal, 121, 126
Poverty, 79
Praesidium, 24
Presidency (see European Council Presidency, Council Presidency)
Presidency Conclusions, European Council, 26, 27, 144
Primacy, 2, 3, 30, 37, 45, 55, 59, 62, 87, 144, 145, 146, 147, 157, 209
Privileges and immunities, 53, 88, 90
Professional licensing, 49, 200, 229, 247
Property, ownership of, 53, 90, 145, 192
Proportionality, 45, 54, 55, 66, 92, 101, 103, 104, 139, 140, 141, 142, 143, 144, 146, 156, 188, 196, 228
Protocol on the application of the principles of subsidiarity and proportionality (Protocol on Subsidiarity), 66, 140, 141, 142, 144, 152, 156, 183
Protocol on the enlargement of the European Union, 92, 121, 163, 176, 178, 258
Protocol on the role of Member States' national parliaments, 66, 141, 142
Public health, 39, 42, 49, 57, 63, 64, 148, 150, 187, 208, 209, 211, 233, 265
Public initiative (see Citizen initiative)
Public Prosecutor, 64, 222, 262